J/

The University of Michigan
Center for Chinese Studies

Michigan Monographs in Chinese Studies
Volume 53

Educational Reform in Early Twentieth-Century China

by Marianne Bastid

translated by Paul J. Bailey

Ann Arbor

Center for Chinese Studies
The University of Michigan

1988

Originally published as *Aspects de la réforme de l'enseignement en Chine au début du 20ᵉ siècle, d'après des écrits de Zhang Jian.*
© 1971 Mouton Publishers, Division of Walter de Gruyter & Co.

English language edition © 1988 by Center for Chinese Studies, The University of Michigan.

Library of Congress Cataloging in Publication Data:

Bastid, Marianne.
    Educational reform in early twentieth-century China.

    (Michigan monographs in Chinese studies; no. 53)
    Includes bibliographical references.
    Translation of: Aspects de la réforme de l'enseignement en Chine au début du 20e siècle.
    Based on the writings of Zhang Jian.
    Bibliography: p. 269.
    1. Education-China-History- 20th century. 2. Education-China-Aims and objectives.
    I. Chang, Chien, 1853-1926. II. Title. III. Series: Michigan monographs in Chinese studies; no. 53.

LA1131.B3313   1986   370'.951   85-15201
ISBN 0-89264-061-8
ISBN 0-89264-062-6 (pbk.)

Printed in the United States of America

Cover by Catherine Doran

6 5 4 3 2 1

CONTENTS

PART III. APPENDICES

PART IV. NOTES AND BIBLIOGRAPHY

TRANSLATOR'S INTRODUCTION

Paul Bailey

During the early years of the twentieth century, the Manchu Qing dynasty, which had ruled China since 1644, attempted to implement a series of reforms in order to stave off internal and external threats to the established order. Such threats had been evident in 1900 during the Boxer uprising which, at various stages, was an attack on the dynasty itself as well as on the foreign presence in China. The subsequent allied occupation of Beijing and the imposition of a large indemnity and other severe penalties (e.g., the temporary suspension of the civil service examinations in some areas around Beijing) on the Qing court by the foreign powers further eroded the authority of the dynasty, which had been weakened throughout the nineteenth century as a result of internal rebellions and defeat in wars against foreign powers. As each power carved out its own sphere of economic influence in China, many Chinese of the time were convinced that China was about to be partitioned. They often referred to the fate of Poland in urging the court to implement wide-scale reforms in order to strengthen the country.

In the mid-nineteenth century high officials like Zeng Guofan and Li Hongzhang had begun such a reform movement, building arsenals to produce modern weapons and establishing military training schools. Students were sent abroad, principally to Europe, to study military techniques and navigation. Some Chinese scholars, however, thought that this "self-strengthening movement" did not go far enough, and after China's disastrous defeat at the hands of Japan in 1895 called for more thoroughgoing reforms, particularly in the political and institutional spheres. In 1898 the Guangxu Emperor, influenced by a group of reformers which included the scholar Kang Youwei, issued a series of edicts calling for the abolition of sinecure posts, the setting up of an advisory council to discuss institutional reform, and increased emphasis on the study of scientific and technical subjects. The edicts aroused the opposition of the Empress Dowager Cixi and a number of high conservative officials. The brief "reform" period, known as the Hundred Days Reform, was brought to an end in the same year when Cixi took over sole control, imprisoned Guangxu, and executed some of the reformers. Kang Youwei and Liang Qichao, Kang's disciple, were forced to flee to Japan with prices on their heads.

The Boxer uprising in 1900 and the allied occupation of Beijing, during which the court was forced to take refuge in Xi'an in West China, finally convinced the Empress Dowager that reforms were indeed necessary, both to preserve the life of the dynasty and to strengthen the country. Ironically, the series of reforms called for after 1901 in many ways resembled those put forward in 1898, including proposals to create a national army, establish provincial assemblies, and organize a national parliament. Education was a key aspect of the Manchu reform effort. In 1904 the court issued edicts concerning the establishment of a national school system, and in 1905 it abolished the traditional civil service examinations.

Traditionally, education had been primarily associated with the civil service examinations, the channel through which government officials were recruited. These examinations involved a thorough knowledge of the Confucian classics, and very few people could afford the time needed to gain such knowledge. Although there were official schools (guanxue) and academies (shuyuan) where scholars could study, the government was content to leave most education in the hands of local communities. A recent study has shown how the village (shexue) and charitable schools (yixue) often maintained by local gentry provided basic literacy training.[1]

After 1904, however, the court decreed that a national school system was to be established, comprising a hierarchy of primary, secondary, and higher level schools, and culminating in the Imperial University at Beijing, which had been established in 1898 and remained in existence after the conservative coup. The curriculum was to include "new" subjects such as science, mathematics, and physical education, and after the abolition of the civil service examinations in 1905 it was decreed that anyone wanting to enter government service had to be a graduate of these modern schools. Japan and Germany were frequently cited as countries in which the prevailing system of universal education had contributed to their strength and unity.

The Qing rulers believed that a widespread system of education would create a patriotic, loyal, and hard-working citizenry. This was evident in the "educational aims" issued by the newly established Board of Education in 1906, which ordered that modern schools inculcate the principles of honoring the monarch, Confucius, and the public good; develop a martial spirit; and encourage practical study.[2] In a more general sense, however, Manchu educational reform during the early twentieth century represented part of a wider change in attitudes towards education. It was during this period that specialist journals on education appeared, such as *Jiaoyu shijie* [The world of education] and *Jiaoyu zazhi* [Educational review]. The latter, established in 1909, continued publication throughout the 1920s and 1930s.[3] Contributors to these journals included well-known scholars and educational officials such as Luo Zhenyu as well as primary and secondary school teachers, many of whom came from traditional gentry backgrounds and had studied in Japan. In addition to discussing educational developments within China, these journals discussed pedagogical practice in other countries; published translations of educational laws and regulations in such countries as Japan, France, England, Germany, and the United States; and translated excerpts of the writings of foreign educators such as John Dewey and the German, Georg Kerschensteiner. Chinese educational journals regularly published reports of investigations carried out by Chinese educators abroad, particularly in Japan. Kerschensteiner's educational philosophy in particular, with its stress on practical work and patriotic training, was often discussed.[4]

Many new views on education appeared in the specialized journals and in official memorials at the beginning of the twentieth century. For example, in contrast to the traditional view, which associated education mainly with an official career, Chinese officials and educators began to emphasize the importance of vocational education. Education was frequently described as the means to "train people to earn a livelihood," and many people felt that it was essential for schools to promote the importance of economic activity, particularly in the industrial sphere. These ideas were applied during the early years of the Republic, when the Ministry of Education ordered that the models in moral training textbooks include entrepreneurs and industrialists as well as statesmen and military heroes. A related idea was that manual work be made more respectable in the schools. Handicrafts, for example, were introduced into the primary school curriculum during the last years of the dynasty.

Another issue raised was the need for professional educators, fully trained in the principles of pedagogy. This emphasis on specialization contrasted with the traditional ideal of the Confucian generalist, whose influence derived from moral example rather than acquaintance with practical techniques. After 1907 normal schools began to be established, designed to train students specifically for a career in education both in the schools and in administration. By 1913, for example, 20 of the 61 heads of provincial education offices and their departments were normal school graduates.[5]

Another topic frequently discussed by Chinese officials, scholars, and educators during the last years of the Qing was the importance of physical education. Traditional literary education was criticized for its neglect of physical training, which was increasingly considered as important as intellectual training in the development of a strong nation. The importance of physical training had been stressed before, notably by the seventeenth-century scholar Yan Yuan, and was already assumed by many Chinese writers and educators. It is therefore misleading of Stuart Schram to cite Mao Zedong's 1917 essay on physical education as an example of his "modern and nonconformist thinking" in this respect.[6]

Like the Qing rulers, many Chinese officials and educators in the early part of the twentieth century stressed the importance of schools in inculcating the ideals of patriotism and concern for the public good. However, whereas the Qing government was primarily concerned with using the new schools as a means to instill loyalty to the dynasty, many later Chinese educators stressed the importance of schools in inculcating the notion of the *patrie* per se. They also hoped the modern schools would train a disciplined and hard-working people. Although it is frequently noted that early twentieth-century Chinese scholars and writers condemned the selfishness of the people, concerned solely with private and family interests rather than those of the nation, it has been overlooked that they were equally critical when they compared the "lazy and indolent" Chinese people to the more energetic peoples of Japan and the West. Japan was the principal model to which the Chinese referred as illustrating that education could produce a patriotic, disciplined, and hard-working citizenry, but Western practice was also frequently cited. For example, Chinese writers often discussed the inculcation of patriotic ideals in American schools from an early age, noting the display of George Washington's portrait in all American schools. Many Chinese advocated that all Chinese schools should do likewise with the portrait of Confucius. They wanted to use Confucius as a *patriotic* symbol to cement national unity rather than think of him, as in the past, as a cultural "sage."

Educational reform, like other Manchu reforms, failed to stem the tide of unrest and opposition. Indeed, as Professor Bastid points out, the Manchu reforms ultimately hastened the downfall of the dynasty in 1911. However, this period is an important one within the context of Chinese educational history. Strangely enough, it has received little attention from Western sinologists. After the revolution of 1911 and into the 1920s and 1930s a number of English-language works on recent Chinese education appeared, many of them written by Chinese who had studied in Europe and the United States.[7] Most of them were not particularly profound, their approaches ranging from a denunciation of Chinese educational development after 1905 because of its "nationalistic excesses"[8] to praise of modern China's educational system, which had inherited the "democratic" approach of traditional China.[9] Chinese-language works on Chinese education written in the 1920s and 1930s were equally simplistic. Many simply summarized the school regulations of 1904 and 1912, supplementing them with some statistics.[10]

In recent years English-language works on educational reform in this period have tended to concentrate on modern schools established at the end of the nineteenth century by officials like Li Hongzhang and Zhang Zhidong who advocated "self-strengthening,"[11] or on the abolition of the civil service examinations in 1905.[12] Although there have been a number of studies on the last years of the Qing dynasty and early years of the Republic, educational reform is only briefly discussed in the context of increasing gentry control over local organs of government and of heavier tax burdens for the people.[13] The only exception has been a number of Japanese articles on educational reform, which focus on developments during the last years of the dynasty.[14] Professor Bastid's pioneering study is the only comprehensive work on late Qing educational reform now available. It is an invaluable contribution to our understanding of China during the last years of the Qing dynasty, covering the political, economic, social, and intellectual aspects of educational reform. In this book, she focuses on an analysis of the practice and results of educational reform from 1901 to 1912 by examining the activities and thought of Zhang Jian, a member of the group defined as "modern gentry" (men who held traditional degrees but were involved in modern industry or commerce). She discusses the initial collaboration of government and modern gentry in the establishment of modern schools and their later

conflict as the modern gentry began to perceive educational reform
as part of a wider program of "local autonomy," which would give
them, rather than the bureaucracy, control over local administration.
The Qing rulers hoped that educational reform, like the establishment of the provincial assemblies in 1909 and the national assembly
in 1910, would ensure their control over the elite. To this end they
established the Quanxueso (Office to Encourage Education) and
education associations, in which gentry participated under the strict
supervision of the district magistrate. However, such reforms simply
highlighted and widened the divergence of interests between the
government and modern gentry, and the latter, suspicious of the
dynasty's real intentions, clamored for greater authority over
provincial and local affairs. Professor Bastid describes other tensions
that arose as a result of educational reform. The gentry founders of
modern schools hoped to use them to fashion political and economic
development according to their vision, but students exposed to new
ideas of liberty and equality often turned them against their gentry
mentors. Modern schools were also the focus of popular discontent
rooted in such problems as increased tax burdens and anger due to
the housing of schools in temples, and was often stirred up by
conservative gentry or Buddhist monks. Sometimes even natural
catastrophes were blamed on the presence of modern schools.

Professor Bastid's book also shows the importance of Japanese
influence on educational reform in China and the ways in which it
occurred. Complete translations of Japanese school regulations and
laws were published in Chinese journals and well-known scholars
and minor officials like Luo Zhenyu and Wang Guowei visited
Japanese educational institutions. It was people like these, from
whom Zhang Jian himself sought advice, who advised high officials
such as Liu Kunyi and Zhang Zhidong on educational reform. New
ideas often reached students through Japanese translations of Western works. Japanese influence was also evident in the large number
of Japanese teachers employed in China. The reforming gentry
began to fear the "denationalization" of Chinese education and a reaction set in against reliance on foreign teachers and use of textbooks
which were translations of foreign material. They called for increased emphasis on the study of "national knowledge" *(guoxue)*,
which would comprise Chinese language, culture, and history.

Finally, Professor Bastid has translated nine texts written by
Zhang Jian which provide a concrete view of the practice of
educational reform. Text 1, for example, shows the importance of
Japanese influence on the establishment of Zhang Jian's normal

school in 1902, while texts 2 and 9 discuss the economic bases for the new schools, and the cost of modern education. The political and legal struggle between the reforming gentry and the government over the financial and administrative control of modern schools is well illustrated in texts 3, 4, and 5. The texts also illustrate the significant changes in attitudes towards education that I discussed above. In text 7 Zhang discusses the importance of education designed to train people for industry or commerce rather than government service; in texts 1 and 6, the emphasis given to physical education; in text 1, the necessity of training professional teachers; and in text 8, the stress on using schools to train a disciplined and orderly citizenry.

Since Professor Bastid's book was published, a five-volume collection of documents on Chinese education (covering the period from 1905 to the People's Republic) has appeared, edited and introduced by Japan's foremost historian of Chinese education, Taga Akigorō.[15] Together with the four-volume and three-volume collections of documents edited by Shu Xincheng, they are indispensable research materials for the study of twentieth-century Chinese education.

Postscript

Since I wrote this introduction, a new book has been published on early twentieth-century Chinese education: S. Borthwick's *Education and Social Change in China* (Stanford: Hoover Institution Press, 1983). It is a measure of the thoroughness of Bastid's work that this new book adds very little to what she has already discussed. In fact, a far more detailed and satisfactory analysis of several key issues such as Japanese influence on Chinese educational reform and the gentry's role in the foundation of modern schools is to be found in Bastid's book. Nevertheless, Borthwick's work is a welcome addition to an important aspect of early twentieth-century China too long neglected by Western sinologists. It is particularly effective in its use of personal memoirs to illustrate aspects of educational change during the last years of the Qing dynasty.[16]

Paul Bailey
Durham, 1985

PREFACE

Marianne Bastid

During the early years of the twentieth century education occupied, in practice and theory, a central role in one of China's most important endeavors: modernization. The aim was to transform the country into an industrial society capable of resisting encroachment by foreign powers. The culture transmitted by the traditional system of education, linked as it was to the hopes and needs of the political and social *ancien regime*, constituted one of the principal obstacles to change. However, in education, as in other domains, the opposition between tradition and modernity was further complicated by the conflict between nationalism and foreign influence. Didn't traditional culture contribute to giving China its national identity? If it were abandoned in order to adopt Western culture, would not China's subservience be even more extreme? These complex contradictions gave rise to a long-lasting cultural revolution which did not end in 1966, and during which a new China slowly emerged.

The first signs of this revolution date from the nineteenth century. Faced with the bombardment of Western gunboats, a number of Chinese began the search to discover the secret of Western superiority and began to cast doubts on their own culture. China's defeat by Japan in 1895 resulted in a burst of reforming zeal, quickly stifled by a conservative policy that still retained the support of most of the elite, who were convinced that China's difficulties could be overcome by a few minor changes. When, in 1900, forces of the Western powers sacked Beijing with the same ruthlessness as in 1860, the shock brutally dispelled any further illusions. The court resigned itself to a policy of reform. For the next few years those who proposed practical solutions to the problems of modernization were given a hearing. Some obstacles were removed and new institutions established. In the sphere of education the change was profound. Although the new approach adopted by the government did not prevent the fall of the dynasty, it did allow for more extensive efforts in an endeavor which ultimately contributed to the launching of a large-scale cultural revolution.

This endeavor was supported and inspired by a number of individuals, each of whom stamped the process with the imprint of his own personality and the social milieu to which he belonged. Zhang Jian was one such individual. He is especially known for his role in the economic development and political life of China, but his educational activities, doubtless not as original, were equally important. It is precisely because his educational activities were not exceptional that they are significant.

Educational reform has been the subject of a copious literature, especially in Chinese. However, such literature is limited in most cases to a summary of the laws and regulations. It seems worthwhile to go further, attempting to grasp the historical significance of this reform and trace its relationship to general change in China. The field is vast, the more so since there are still very few substantial works which examine in detail the economic and social aspects of the period 1900-12 and on which one can rely to deal with a specific question.[1] It was therefore safer to start from an individual case. At the same time, the very nature of the work undertaken — this study was presented as a doctoral thesis[2] — demanded the precise examination of a relatively narrow subject, based on the translation of documents.

Zhang Jian's writings present plentiful research material with which to examine his educational activities. The texts translated here reveal the different stages of Zhang's activities and also help in analyzing his personality. They give the reader a concrete view of the theoretical and practical difficulties encountered in educational reform. Through them, the reader gains a vivid picture of the essential problems involved in the change of institutions that began in the middle of the nineteenth century and which quickly accelerated at the turn of the century.

Certainly all examples are unique, and this work might be criticized for constantly shifting from a district to the whole of China. However, it was deliberately not restricted to the scope of a monograph. It seemed necessary and possible to outline a number of general hypotheses in the introduction as well as specific details of the activities of which the translated documents are a part. These general remarks are not based solely on the situation in Nantong, but on wider research, the details of which unfortunately cannot be given here due to the limits of space imposed by publication.

The years covered by this study, from 1901 to 1912, mark stages in the development of both the case being studied and general questions of educational reform. In 1901 the dynasty, under attack, undertook a fresh policy of reform. This was also the year in which Zhang Jian became involved with his first educational venture, the Nantong Normal School. The overthrow of the monarchy in 1912 altered the meaning of the attempts hitherto undertaken to gradually enlarge the bases of political power. The advent of the Republic gave rise to new problems.

Marianne Bastid
Paris, October 1968

MAP 1
Distribution of Modern Schools in the Department of Tongzhou
and Sub-Prefecture of Haimen

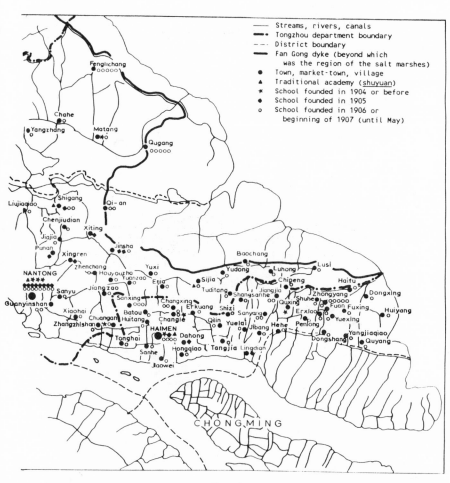

Based on the report of the education inspector
at the end of 1907: Xuebu Guanbao, nos. 82–87.

Marianne Bastid

MAP 2 Jiangsu

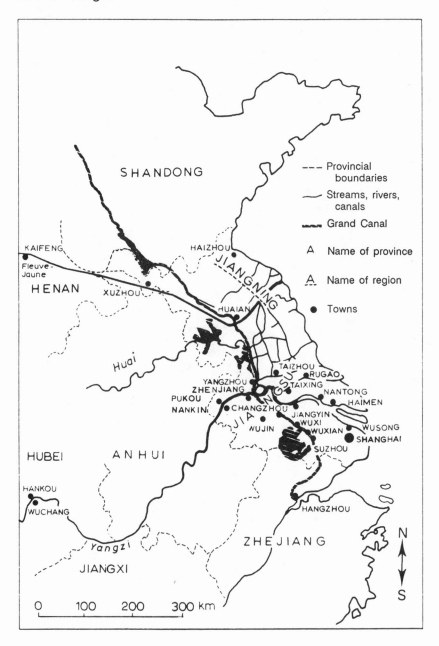

PART I
GENERAL INTRODUCTION

CHAPTER I

The New Imperial Policy

The Dynasty, Monarchy, and Empire under Attack, 1900-01

"The country is in danger and its future is uncertain; I, alone, am responsible for this. . . . I am the master of the empire but I have been unable to protect the people from misfortune."[1] Such was the confession that the Emperor Guangxu was forced to make upon the arrival of foreign troops in his capital in August 1900. A few months later he announced, in his name and that of the Empress Dowager Cixi, that since his arrival on the throne abuses had increased: "We have overlooked the foundations of Western knowledge and have only studied the surface, and even at that we have not excelled . . . the laws have not been reformed and obsolete customs have not been abolished. In order to rejuvenate [the country], as is our desire, it is necessary that ideas on reform be more widely circulated."[2] The emperor therefore requested his subjects to submit, as soon as possible, proposals concerning institutional reform and promised that he would implement them faithfully and without delay. What had caused this sudden display of humility and conversion to reform?

The danger facing the country, to which the edicts referred, had never been more serious. The international expeditionary force was occupying Beijing. The court, which had retreated to Xi'an, had capitulated once again to foreign powers. The treaty terms being negotiated stipulated that China pay an indemnity of 450 million *taels*, payable in gold. Furthermore, China's territorial integrity was being threatened. Russia had occupied Manchuria, taken possession of the Shanhaiguan-Beijing railway, and was claiming to include Zhili in its zone of influence. Germany was preparing to take possession of Yantai in order to expand its influence in Shandong; at Nanjing and Shanghai its gunboats were stationed in readiness to open up the Yangzi valley. England had come to an agreement with the governors-general of Liangjiang and Huguang to increase its privileges in these areas. At the same time, in order to gain the dominant position in the south of the country, England negotiated with Li Hongzhang the possibility of his establishing an independent power base in Liangguang. Japan coveted Fujian, where her troops had disembarked in August 1900. France wanted to establish her influence in Yunnan. The United States wanted to "lease" some ports in the Gulf of Zhili and at the mouth of the Yangzi.

The conflicting ambitions of the powers could have prevented them from proceeding to partition the empire, but the Boxer revolt had also demonstrated the risks that excessive demands entailed. Von Waldersee admitted that "neither Europe, nor America, nor Japan had sufficient moral and military force to dominate one-quarter of humanity." The disturbances had caused so much havoc in the north and the administration was so disorganized that dismemberment of the empire would have brought the powers more problems than advantages.

However, if China's misery, weakness, and internal disarray tempered the greed of the powers, they had also shaken the authority of the emperor. In attempting to find a cure for these ills the emperor wished to restore the strength of the monarchy as much as that of the country. Whether deliberately or not, the throne exploited the ambiguity of certain terms and the traditional confusion surrounding certain concepts: *guo* could refer to the country or the dynasty. The Boxer revolt, in fact, had clearly shown the dangers that the dynasty faced. Before being enrolled as official forces against the foreigners, the Boxers had openly declared their opposition to the Manchus; even afterwards they retained a mistrust and hostility towards them, while some of the rebels remained openly antidynastic.[3] In the northern provinces the latent animosity of Chinese officials and gentry toward Manchu domination was strengthened by the demagogic policy of the court. In the south, the governors-general of Liangjiang, Huguang, and Liangguang, Liu Kunyi, Zhang Zhidong, and Li Hongzhang, broke away from the central government in order to arrange for the mutual defense of the southeast (*dongnan hubao*). They openly regarded all decrees issued by the Empress Dowager after the declaration of war against the powers on 21 June as "false edicts."[4]

In the south it was not only Manchu supremacy, but the very form of government itself, absolute monarchy, that was placed in danger. During the spring and summer of 1900, the followers of Kang Youwei and Liang Qichao had organized an armed force at

Zhennanguan in Guangxi. They joined with secret societies from Guangdong in order to gain control over these two provinces and then to march on to Hunan and Hubei. In July Tang Caichang, who had links with the reformers, Sun Yat-sen, and secret societies, proposed to establish a "national Chinese assembly" at Shanghai and declared that he "no longer recognized a government characterized by false edicts and banditry." Tang organized an "independence society" (*zilihui*) and an "independence army" (*zilijun*) which had as their aim the overthrow of the Empress Dowager. The uprisings that he launched in August and September 1900 in Anhui, Hunan, and Hubei were suppressed by the authorities, but not without first receiving moral support from many young intellectuals, certain elements in the army, some important overseas Chinese groups, and even certain Shanghai merchants.[5]

In Guangdong, in the first few days of September, Sun Yat-sen and his friends of the Xingzhonghui organized a revolt at Huizhou. In two weeks they gathered the support of more than twenty thousand followers and were able to march on Amoy. Their aim was political revolution, and they were depending on material support from Japan. Japan had decided to support them in the hope of gaining an advantageous position in Fujian but abandoned them when it became evident that the other powers would not allow Japan to realize her ambitions. However, this uprising did not remain unnoticed. Sun Yat-sen wrote in his autobiography: "After my first failure in 1895, the whole country regarded me as a bandit and rebel, a man without principles, guilty of high treason. . . . But after my failure in 1900, people not only stopped slandering me, but progressive elements truly sympathized with me in my misfortune."[6]

In these uprisings in the south, the essential question was how to modernize China. The conservative politics of the court had failed and the country was defeated. The revolutionaries wanted to substitute a new order based on the Western model.

The differences and lack of coordination among the various groups that constituted the Boxers, the very fact that they were rebels, the secession of the southeast, and the uprisings in the provinces all presented another grave menace for the dynasty: the empire was in danger of falling apart. The most immediate danger was the enormous power that had accrued to the governors-general as a result of the disturbances. Yuan Shikai had been appointed governor of Shandong in December 1899 and he arrived at his post with the modern army he had just created. He enlarged it by twenty battalions while reorganizing the troops already stationed in his province. Yuan thereupon controlled the best-equipped military force in the empire, with which he pacified Shandong by driving out the Boxers. Yet, when he received the order on 15 June 1900 to transfer his army to Beijing, he did nothing. No doubt he concluded that his troops would be attacked by both Boxers and foreigners. Yuan had thus openly defied imperial orders without the court being able to impose the slightest sanction upon him. A similar situation arose with the southern governors-general. Li Hongzhang, Liu Kunyi, and Zhang Zhidong had all simply ignored the declaration of war. They had arranged for the defense of their own provinces and negotiated with the foreign powers independently of central government control. They controlled the army and finances of the richest area of the empire; with a network of followers among civil and military officials and the confidence placed in them by merchants and foreigners (whose interests they protected), the governors-general had considerable authority. The court was forced to accept this situation and to depend on their influence in order to save itself. On 11 August 1900 Li Hongzhang was appointed plenipotentiary to negotiate peace with the powers. Shortly afterwards, he was appointed governor-general of Zhili and superintendent of the northern ports, and ordered to suppress the Boxers. On his death in December 1901, Li was succeeded in these posts by Yuan Shikai, who was now in a position to exert direct pressure on the court. Elsewhere, in Sichuan, Zhejiang, and Yunnan, the independence of high officials was perhaps less flagrant, although they all strove to prevent their domains from being involved in the conflict. The general tendency since the middle of the nineteenth century, for governors to expand their powers at the expense of the central government, clearly had been strengthened as a result of the Boxer disturbances.[7]

The court thus saw its authority disintegrating under pressure exerted by liberal ideas from the West, by nationalism, and by localism. Both traditional and modern forces conspired to deny such an authority. It was essential that the court regain its control over the country. To achieve this, hostility to the regime had to be overcome, the elite had to be won over by conveying the impression that its opinions were being heard, and the country had to be reunited. In sum, it was necessary that the concept of the nation be centered henceforth on the person of the emperor. It was with this aim in mind that the court announced a policy of concessions in January 1901.

Imperial Concessions and Reform Ideas:
The Ambiguous and Contentious Domain of Education

What were these concessions? The edict of 29 January took up the favorite ideas and expressions of reformers at the end of the nineteenth century. The aim of the concessions was to "enrich and strengthen the country" (*fuqiang*). The means were to be a change in the laws, taking inspiration from the West. Until that time, the Chinese had limited themselves to the study of languages and the manufacture of machines "which are simply the superficial aspects of Western technology and not the basic principles of Western knowledge. . . . It is necessary to compare Chinese and foreign political systems in order to decide what has to be abolished, retained, or reformed concerning past laws on state institutions, the official system, the economy, the schools, the civil-service examinations, the army, and the finances."

These were ideas that Xue Fucheng had expressed since 1879, and they amounted to a criticism of the "Western affairs" policy (*yangwu*). Between 1885 and 1898 they were developed and expanded upon by a number of thinkers who were connected with political and business circles, including Chen Chi, Tang Shouqian, Zheng Guanying, He Qi, and Hu Liyuan. They influenced enlightened high officials like Weng Tonghe, Sun Jia'nai, and Zhang Zhidong.[8] In certain of their writings Kang Youwei and Tan Sitong adopted the same language, as did Sun Yat-sen, at least until 1895.[9] Nevertheless, the promises outlined in the 29 January 1901 edict did not go far enough to satisfy most of the 1898 reformers, much less the revolutionaries.

After 1885, the setbacks of the *yangwu* policy caused some to ponder the concept of "Western knowledge." Ma Jianzhong, Xue Fucheng, Zheng Guanying, Chen Chi, and Tang Shouqian explained that the concept of "Western knowledge" referred not only to techniques (*xiyi*) but also to political institutions, and that it was the latter which particularly explained the power and wealth of foreign nations. With China's 1894 defeat by Japan, a constitutional monarchy, this idea became more widespread, and even gained influence among court circles. In clearly distinguishing between *bianshi* (a change of things) and *bianfa* (a change of methods) as two opposing principles, Kang Youwei underlined the difference between advocates of "Western affairs" and reformers.[10] The former emphasized techniques and the latter emphasized the political system.

For Kang Youwei and Tan Sitong, who represented the most radical reform tendency at that time, a change of methods meant the complete renewal of the political structure and the adoption of Western institutions based on a renovated Confucianism. However, their contemporaries rarely made the distinction between a "change of things" and a "change of methods" so clear. In 1898 Liang Qichao and Yan Fu held to both principles, looking first to one and then to the other as a political objective. The concept of "political institutions" should have permitted a distinction between the two options; a "change of methods" necessarily depended on a "change in political institutions" (*bianzheng*). However, the use of the term *zheng*, whether in the expression "political institutions" or in "Western political institutions" (*xizheng*) varied from one thinker to the other, and sometimes in the same text. In its wider meaning *zheng* could refer to anything not connected with material technology. Generally the term referred to anything involved with politics and the organization of state and society: the form of government, the political regime, the laws, or the administrative system. An informed thinker like Kang Youwei knew quite well that the term "Western political institutions" covered a broad area. However, he considered its basic definition to be representative constitutional government and a body of laws uniformly applied throughout the country. His contemporaries were in agreement with him on this point, but Kang was alone in concluding that the form of government was the *sine qua non* of everything else.

In fact, there existed many shades of opinion between the concept of "Western affairs" which involved adopting only Western technology, and the radical reformism of Kang Youwei which assigned priority to the adoption of Western political institutions, permitting the subsequent reform of all other aspects of the country's life. Zhang Zhidong, for example, was well aware of the political foundations of Western superiority and deduced that China had to implement political reform in order to prosper. However, this did not mean in any way that this political reform should involve the adoption of the Western governmental system. On the contrary, Zhang would only adopt those elements of Western institutions that would allow the survival and strengthening of Chinese tradition. The essential aspect for Zhang was a body of laws that neither the monarch nor the people could violate.[11] His proposals aimed at establishing a "state of law" compatible with many types of political systems, from an authoritarian monarchy to a democracy.

The edict of January 1901 was influenced by such an attitude. As such, it did not have the scope of the Hundred Days Reform, in which its leader, Kang Youwei, saw the transformation of political power as the most essential task. The measures that the emperor envisaged would leave political power intact. The court accepted a "change of things" but not a "change of methods" as Kang Youwei understood it. The modification of "state institutions" (*guozheng*) might have had greater significance, but its scope should not be overestimated since the edict specified that ancestral principles and Confucian relationships should not be destroyed. Yet in the realm of a "change of things" the edict went beyond a program of "Western affairs" limited to material techniques. The court, in fact, promised as much, if not more, than it had during the 1898 reform period: all aspects of the country's life were to be affected.

Education occupied an important place in this program of practical reform. The edict of 20 August 1900 had already foreshadowed this preoccupation, which afterwards became a constant feature in official texts. What explained this enthusiasm for education? There were several reasons. First of all, it was educational reform that the reformers had insisted upon most strongly and for the longest period of time. The problem in this area comprised two closely related aspects: the schools and the civil-service examinations. Under the Qing the state had increasingly abandoned its responsibility over education *per se*, which took place in private institutions. There was official cooperation after a certain level without it ever becoming a government monopoly. On the other hand, absolute official control was exercised over the civil-service examinations, which were designed to recruit officials. The imperial government did, on occasion, sanction and fund education for its subjects, but it did not pay much attention to actually establishing education for them. The situation reached the point at which the requirements of the examinations determined, in large measure, the content of education, rather than the reverse. In the nineteenth century the content of these examinations was purely literary and it involved above all else the Confucian doctrine based on Zhu Xi's interpretation of the Confucian classics. One of the tests, the eight-legged essay (*bagu*), was an exercise in style involving rigid rules which were only mastered after long and time-wasting effort. The candidates were therefore not encouraged to occupy themselves with original ideas or knowledge.

Since the founding of the dynasty a number of scholars had advocated the reform of the examination system by introducing new subject-matter and abolishing the eight-legged essay. At the same time they proposed that school programs be enlarged. Some of them had even suggested the complete abolition of the examinations.[12] In criticizing the examination system these scholars were continuing a tradition established by independent thinkers during the Song, Yuan, and Ming dynasties. In proposing a new content for education, however, they were breaking new ground; they wished to destroy the dominant influence of Song and Ming scholastic philosophy (*lixue*) which diverted scholars from more practical matters. The inspiration of these thinkers was seen in many texts at the end of the nineteenth century, although from the Opium War onwards educational reform proposals became increasingly linked to, and conditioned by, current political demands.

The civil-service examinations assured the state's control over the population and the survival of a specific political, economic, and social regime. The educated elite, raised and steeped in Confucianism, served as a model for the people; it was thus theoretically in its interest to perpetuate a system which brought wealth and prestige. However, during the course of the nineteenth century the advantages offered by the examinations tended to decrease. It became less certain that degree-holders would obtain lucrative positions. In order to reward local districts for funds they had contributed, especially during the suppression of the Taiping rebellion, the government had increased degree quotas.[13] In addition, it sold degree-titles. Since the number of official posts generally remained fixed, the percentage of unemployed degree-holders rapidly increased. Furthermore, the egalitarianism that was supposed to characterize the examination system was becoming less of a reality. In the absence of public schools, education was the responsibility of the family. Although examination fraud was perhaps no more rampant than in previous centuries, there was a general tendency to favor the offspring of high officials. In addition to the sale of degree-titles, the sale of offices was also common,[14] and the amount of money needed to obtain an official post, even through the regular examination channel, rose to an enormous sum. Thus, the rich were in a privileged position. Instead of promoting social mobility, the examinations limited opportunity to a caste.

In accord with the wishes of the Qing government, the examination system was linked to the authoritarian tendencies of the state which originated in the Ming and remained under the Manchus. The system served to "domesticate" the elite and prevent it from forming any opposition. The preparation required for the examinations imposed a uniform intellectual outlook on the gentry, giving them neither the time nor the inclination to criticize the government. Yet with the increasing problems China had to face during the nineteenth century, this rigid literary education for officials and elite resulted in serious disadvantages. For this reason it was strongly criticized by progressive thinkers. Xue Fucheng, for example, wrote that the system "led hundreds of thousands, even millions, of scholars to exhaust their physical and mental energies over formal literary exercises without ever studying the art of governing or the lessons of history."[15]

Several strategies were proposed to remedy the situation. The advocates of "Western affairs" wanted to establish special schools in order to fill immediately the gap caused by lack of "technicians," especially in the army and diplomatic service. Such was the strategy adopted by Li Hongzhang and Zeng Guofan who, between 1860 and 1885, succeeded in establishing several military and foreign-language schools[16] and in sending military students abroad. Under the influence of Ying Gui, Shen Baozhen, and Zeng Guoquan, an attempt was made to eliminate abuses from the examination system and to emphasize concrete application of the classics to contemporary problems.[17] However, these efforts were not coordinated in practice or theory. The civil-service examinations and modern schools were kept separate.

Even before the Sino-French War, but especially afterwards, the idea developed that a broader, more modern education was required. In foreign countries, science, industrial, and agricultural techniques, law, and politics all had to be studied. In China it was essential that these subjects not only be taught in the schools but also that they be introduced into the examination system in the form of a special category which would offer the same degree-titles as those given by the traditional examinations. In 1860, Feng Guifen proposed more study of the physical sciences.[18] In his "Words on Change" in 1872, Zheng Guanying added agricultural, industrial, and commercial techniques. His "Warnings to a Prosperous Age" in 1892 further proposed the study of law and politics.[19] Between 1880 and 1890 similar ideas were expressed by Guo Songdao,[20] Wang Tao,[21] and Ma Jianzhong.[22] Zheng and Ma, however, were the first to propose the introduction of modern subjects to both schools and examinations through a coordination of the two and the reintroduction of several examination categories practiced during the Tang and early Song dynasties. These proposals were more advanced than the ideas of Li

Hongzhang,[23] but would still have left the traditional system more or less intact. Modern education was regarded as a mere addition.

It is in the memorials of Kang Youwei in 1895 that one discovers the first known attempt to envisage a true system of modern education which would subordinate examinations to the schools, and in which a large part of the school curriculum would be devoted to the teaching of sciences, technological skills, arts, and Western law.[24] This concept was developed by Li Duanfen in an 1896 memorial, probably inspired by Liang Qichao. Li emphasized that as long as the civil-service examinations remained the only way to gain a degree modern schools would never be able to develop. He suggested a plan more practical than Kang's which would integrate degree-holders and examinations into an educational system for which reformed academies (shuyuan) would serve as the base.[25] Liang Qichao expressed a similar idea in an essay entitled "On the Examination System" which appeared in the same year.[26]

Between 1895 and 1898 memorials concerning education increased in number (twenty-five are reproduced in Donghua Xulu), but none were as radical as those of Kang and Li. Zhang Zhidong, for example, in his "Exhortation to Study" of 1898 envisaged a hierarchical system of modern schools and a modification of the examination program without linking the two directly. Nevertheless, he did conceive of the educational system as a whole according to a unified plan. This is an important point and it was to characterize all reform proposals after 1895, whether moderate or radical. For everyone, in fact, it was no longer a question of simply modifying one sector of the state, but of reorganizing the state in order for it to survive. Since everyone involved in the debate had had a Confucian education, they all considered education as the architect of whatever form the state might take. Those whose ideals triumphed in education would triumph in politics. Hence concepts of education were directly influenced by political leanings.

For radicals like Kang Youwei and Tan Sitong a complete change in the educational system would accompany political reform. They gave priority to the latter, although they also considered education to be a political enterprise; to reform it was certainly a "change of methods" and not a "change of things." Educational reform would depend on political reform, which would shape and guide it. On the other hand, educational reform would form a new people and society without the support of which political reform could never be consolidated. For moderates like Zhang Zhidong and Liu Kunyi traditional political power had to be preserved. They acknowledged that internal and external circumstances threatened the bases of traditional political power. Their efforts were thus aimed at strengthening the traditional supports of the empire while adapting them to the modern age. Education also had an absolute priority in their reform proposals as the best tool to "unite the people's minds" in loyalty towards the monarchy and to "train men of talent equipped to deal with current affairs."[27]

Educational reform would serve to consolidate the authority of moderates in the state. It was not meant to raise questions concerning the form of government. Among more progressive thinkers there was no clear distinction in terms of priority between political and educational reform. Kang and Tan, who adopted the most radical analysis, subordinated one to the other, but nevertheless considered educational reform as a "change of methods" practically on the same level as the reform of political institutions. For both moderates and radicals, therefore, education was considered an essential conquest, the achievement of which assumed the control of political power rather than its immediate overthrow.

It is this fact that also explains why the emperor announced a plan for educational reforms. Without diminishing his authority, he hoped not only to gather additional support for the future, but also to regain the loyalty of those elements whose tendency to remove themselves from court control had been demonstrated by events in the south during the Boxer rebellion.

The Beneficiaries of the Reforms:
Enlightened Officials and Modern Gentry

Who was the court addressing when it announced its reforms? The reforms were not aimed at rallying the support of "bandits like Kang Youwei or Tang Caichang whose reforms resulted in sowing disorder,"[28] but were designed to convince the established elite, who were concerned about the national situation and beginning to sympathize with the rebels, of its good will. The elite comprised several different groups and it was the government's attempt to appeal to all of them at the same time that caused contradictions in its announcements and policy.

The court no doubt wished to reassure conservative officials and gentry by promising a vague and gradual program of reform and reaffirming the inviolability of the Confucian foundation of the empire. It promised that the "new administration" (*xinzheng*) and the "reforms" would lead to "good government" (*zhi*) and not "chaos" (*luan*) as had those of Kang Youwei. In upholding the traditional order, the court thus showed no desire to abandon its dependence on the traditional elite.

In addition, the court hoped to reconcile more liberal elements with its concessions. Since 1898 these elements had comprised three groups: in Japan, Kang Youwei, Liang Qichao, and their followers; in China, a certain number of officials on the one hand, and on the other, certain sections of the gentry. The first group was exiled. The court thus addressed itself to the other two groups, especially the high officials: governors-general like Liu Kunyi, Zhang Zhidong, and Yuan Shikai who controlled threatening power; and such enlightened officials, without whose competence the emperor could not govern, as Zhou Fu, Zhang Baixi, Tao Mo, and Sun Jia'nai.

As Chinese, these officials were suspicious of the imperial clan's influence and jealous of the privileges accorded to the Manchus. Their liberal tendencies were partially a reaction to the traditional and conservative thought of the Manchu princes and to domination by a "barbaric" race. They had had contact with the foreigners and had been obliged to negotiate with them. Their management of the provinces had made them aware of China's inferior position. They sincerely wanted to strengthen the country, not only by military means, but also by developing the economy and reorganizing the administration with Western methods. There were naturally differences of personality and ideas among them: Yuan Shikai stressed military and bureaucratic control, while Liu Kunyi and Zhang Zhidong were more sensitive to the economy and favored private initiative in this sphere. In their dealings with the foreign powers, Zhang and Liu were more firm than Yuan.

During the last years of the nineteenth century the failure of external policies and problems within China had aroused in these high officials a desire for reform that was based on nationalism. In general, however, this did not lead them to approve of the Hundred Days Reform. Their reasons for opposing the 1898 reformers varied in degree and nature, including personal animosity towards the reform leaders, political rivalries, and differences of conviction.[29] In addition, the advantages they gained from their ties to the *ancien regime* made all of them extremely fearful of the consequences of Kang Youwei's radical measures. In 1898 their ideas had been summarized in Zhang Zhidong's formula "Chinese learning as the substance, Western learning as the usage." Chinese learning was, in fact, the traditional political and social structure and the philosophy that underpinned it presented in ideal terms. At this time they still considered the maintenance of the monarchical system to be the best guarantor of their own authority as officials.

During the next few years their outlook changed. The "break-up of China" in 1899 and the humiliation suffered at the hands of the powers in 1900 were new blows to their nationalism. Although they remained loyal to the monarchy, they concluded that arbitrary imperial power had to be limited; no longer should a situation arise, as it had during the Boxer rebellion, in which the state would be led to ruin because the monarchy was under the control of "evil counsellors." At the same time, they no longer regarded monarchical absolutism as indispensable in legitimizing their own authority. In fact, the period during the Boxer crisis had been a very significant one for these high officials. Although not in an actual state of rebellion, they had been able to govern for several months without imperial sanction. In the southern provinces, the attempt had seemed successful; they had maintained order and kept the foreigners at arm's length. This success made them bolder, while their nationalism made them more sensitive to China's problems. The court was aware of this and attempted to reconcile them. However, the court's appeal was not limited to these enlightened officials; through them the court was addressing the very elements of the population who had supported their administrations during the crisis of 1900.

Under the Qing, political power depended on the social authority possessed by the gentry (shenshi). The traditional gentry were those who had obtained, either by knowledge or money, at least the lowest degree in the official examinations, the shengyuan. The laws, the government, and the people recognized two groups: the shen, the "official gentry," who were active, retired, or dismissed officials (including those who had purchased their titles or posts); and the shi or jin, the "scholar gentry," who were simply holders of degree and academic titles.[30]

The government, which had only a small number of officials and a relatively small army at its disposal, could not implement its orders without gentry cooperation, since the gentry, by virtue of family ties, moral example, and economic position, had influence over the local population. The magistrate's authority depended on gentry help, but also needed imperial approval to guarantee that the magistrate's acts conformed to the collective interests of the empire. However, during the "mutual defense of the southeast" in 1900 this guarantee had not been given by the emperor but by a certain section of the gentry that can be defined as "modern gentry," in contrast to the traditional gentry described above. It is undeniable that the success of the "mutual defense of the southeast" was due in great measure to the support offered by England.[31] However, as far as Chinese institutions were concerned, it had also clearly shown that the "modern gentry" had been able to substitute for the emperor in interpreting and protecting the interests of the state.

Who were these "modern gentry?" They were a heterogeneous and scattered group. Although they were only just beginning to emerge as a distinct section of the elite and were not as yet identifiable by a particular name, they were nearly always involved when contemporary documents referred to *shenshang*. *Shenshang* occasionally referred to official and scholar gentry on the one hand (*shen*) and merchants on the other (*shang*) as two different groups, distinct from both people (*min*) and serving officials (*chen* or *guan*). In general, however, when the term was applied to a group *shenshang* referred to official and scholar gentry who undertook commercial activities, merchants who had a literary or official title, or gentry and merchants who had ties with the first two. If the term was applied to an individual it referred only to the first two categories.[32] I propose to translate it as "commercial gentry" since their distinctive characteristic was economic activity. However, the word "commercial" must be understood in a wide sense, referring to involvement in banking, trade, industry, or enterprises having a capitalist character or at least a certain size. There were many individual differences. Shen Zipei, for example, one of the principal inspirers of the "mutual defense of the southeast," was a *jinshi*, had occupied official government posts and received his most obvious income from bureaucratic sinecures, scholarly works, and landed property, and yet he invested in banks and had interests in railway construction.[33] On the other hand, Ye Chengzhong and his sons, who owed their influence to numerous enterprises spread over a wide area, concentrated their efforts on acquiring official titles.[34]

Commercial gentry formed the majority of the modern gentry and constituted its most energetic and influential group. However, the two categories are not always synonymous. There were merchants, for example the bankers of Shanxi, who, despite the size of their enterprises, remained very traditional even in their economic outlook.[35] In addition, one must include among the modern gentry all those supporters of reform, a certain number of whom, whether old-style literati (*shidafu*) who made use of the traditional privileges of their position or urban-based intellectuals (*zhishifenzi*) depending solely on their brushes for a livelihood, had no immediate links with the world of commerce.[36] Did this group constitute a bourgeoisie? It certainly had some bourgeois elements, but traditional economic and social patterns still retained too strong an influence for it to be defined as a bourgeoisie. Furthermore, the bourgeois sections of the group cannot be separated from more traditional ones since they were often interwoven and interdependent. Although it is less precise and satisfying to speak of the action of the "modern gentry" rather than the "bourgeoisie," for 1900 at least the former comes closer to reality.

This elite was not large in number and was dispersed among provincial cities. The provinces where they were the most numerous were Zhili, Zhejiang, Jiangsu, Hubei, Hunan, and Guangdong. The activity of the new gentry was most evident in the treaty ports, but could also be seen in more remote areas. Nevertheless, with the exception of a few personal ties, their activities were never coordinated. Officials were easily able to play on their mutual rivalries and contradictions.

In fact, due to the variety of ways they entered the elite and the ambiguity of the positions they occupied, the modern gentry were a social group with conflicting interests among themselves. Some had interests in bureaucratic enterprises, of which several depended on foreign aid; others were compradores attached to businesses organized by international capital in China; still others were "national capitalists" who gained their revenue from enterprises created by private Chinese capital and managed by merchants. In individual cases, however, these categories were never quite so distinct. It was often the case that compradores established national enterprises with the profits earned from foreign firms while, conversely, national capitalists borrowed from foreigners or sold them their factories. Furthermore, bureaucratic enterprises functioned with merchant capital. When an official with funds invested in them, it was not always evident that he did so in the capacity of an official, while if he placed his funds in a merchant enterprise he could even be considered a private capitalist. Also, bureaucrats did not always clearly distinguish between state wealth and their own private fortunes. Everything depended on the success of the enterprise. If profits were distributed, officials claimed them as their personal income on the justification that they had invested their own money; if the enterprise suffered a failure, the state was expected to make up the deficit.

Bureaucratic capitalism did not necessarily depend on foreigners. On the contrary, it could often retard for a certain time the development of foreign enterprises in a particular sector. The debate among Chinese historians shows how difficult it is to determine the nature of enterprises at this time, and to distinguish clearly between compradore, bureaucratic, and national capital.

For modern gentry, land rent and moneylending remained an important, and sometimes essential, source of revenue. In general, however, their economic position did not automatically determine their political attitude, a fact which tended to increase contradictions among them. A compradore like Zheng Guanying, for example, was more extreme in his hostility to foreign imperialism and bureaucratic control than many "national capitalists." The nationalism of the modern gentry was not characterized by a hatred of foreigners. On the contrary, it made them more receptive to Western culture, which they admired and desired to emulate. This characteristic, which they shared with the revolutionary elite, illustrates the gulf separating both groups from the violent xenophobia of the masses. It is essential to remember also that this social group was composed of individuals, each entangled in a network of family, personal, and professional relationships in which, depending on the circumstances and temperament of the individual concerned, traditional principles existed side by side with those of the modern age. They desired to be listened to by the government and to have a larger participation in the management of public affairs. They were beginning to possess wealth, and they wanted their influence legally confirmed. Nevertheless, in 1901 their political ambitions actually remained quite limited for two reasons.

First of all, despite their dissatisfaction, they already belonged to the upper classes, from both an economic and social point of view. The ties that linked them with the bureaucracy and traditional elite were more numerous and stronger than the conflict of interest that was beginning to emerge between them. Secondly, with the exception of a minority, the modern gentry did not aspire to national prominence. They had nationalist reactions, but a national conscience had hardly developed among them. Their preoccupations were practical, concrete, and limited to the district or, at the most, provincial levels. It was in this sphere above all else that they desired to procure the political power of decision-making.

These gentry could exercise pressure on officials and officials could, in turn, use them to oppose central authority. The court could use the modern gentry to limit the power of the bureaucracy, while the modern gentry could make use of the central government to increase their local power. The relationships between the different groups were imprecise and many-faceted. In any event, in 1901 the imperial government had need of the modern gentry to reestablish its authority over the population and bureaucracy. It appealed to them in official organs, requesting them to draft reform proposals and then to help the government implement them.

The Attitude of Zhang Jian in 1901

The career of Zhang Jian illustrates the role and evolution of this social group during the last years of the Manchu dynasty. A sketch of his life up to 1901 will provide a clearer definition of the general characteristics noted above, and show under what conditions he tackled the problem of education, which was then the focus of reform proposals.[37]

Zhang Jian began his career as a brilliant young traditional scholar, with the merit of having begun life in poverty. This "poverty," however, was relative. He was born in 1853 in the market-town of Changle, in the subprefecture of Haimen, Jiangsu. Shortly after his birth, his parents returned to the village of Xiting (in the north of Nantong district) where his paternal ancestors originated. His father, Zhang Pengnian, owned nearly fifty *mu* of land (about three hectares) which he cultivated himself with the aid of a servant. In this region, where the average size of the individual landholding did not exceed twenty *mu*,[38] he was regarded as a "rich peasant." For as long as anyone could remember, Zhang Jian's father was the first of the family to have attended school, although (and this was rare for a woman) his mother also knew how to read.[39] Zhang Jian began his studies with the help of his parents. When he was five years old, he and his brothers had a private tutor. Afterwards he attended a private school. Since he showed a remarkable aptitude for study, his father decided to encourage him at all costs in the hope that he would finally become an official. At fifteen years of age, Zhang Jian was ready to take the district examinations.[40] For three generations no one in his family had succeeded in or even attempted this examination. Such being the case, the regulations stipulated that the candidate had to obtain a personal guarantee from a scholar of his own clan (*renbao*) and the collective guarantee of the *linsheng* of his district (*paibao*). Since, inevitably, all this had to be paid for, Zhang Jian's father, on the advice of a teacher, had his son adopted under a borrowed name by a member of the Rugao district gentry. The latter, in complicity with local magistrates, blackmailed Zhang Pengnian over the affair and Zhang was forced to sell a part of his land. Zhang Jian's brothers were thereupon so hostile to him that he was obliged to leave the home. However, the threat that the literary title Zhang had obtained at Rugao might be invalidated still remained. The situation was only rectified several years later due to the support of the Nantong subprefect, Sun Yunjin, who recognized Zhang's merits. Zhang Jian was finally registered among the *shengyuan* of Nantong under his own name. This episode is a good illustration of the practice of the traditional examination system under the Qing and shows the aristocratic nature of the system. Zhang Jian retained a painful memory of the humiliation he had suffered, and this could not but influence his ideas on education.[41]

Zhang Jian continued after this with the preparation for the next level of examinations, steeping himself in Song Neo-Confucianism and the style of the Tongcheng school.[42] In 1871 he entered the Shishan Academy in Haimen. In 1874 he left for Nanjing as the personal secretary of Sun Yunjin who had been appointed magistrate there. Due to Sun's generosity, Zhang was also able to pursue his studies and attend the Xiyin Academy. It was there he studied the reformers of the past, Lu Zhi, Wang Anshi, and Gu Yanwu, began a study of practical problems, and established ties with officials.[43] In 1876 Wu Changqing, the commander of the garrison at Pukou (opposite Nanjing on the Yangzi), offered Zhang a post in his service. Zhang remained there until 1884. It was in the service of Wu Changqing that he met some young people who were later to become famous: Yuan Shikai, Xue Fucheng, He Sikun, and Ma Jianzhong. He was also introduced to the great officials of the time, Li Hongzhang, Zeng Guoquan, Zhang Zhidong, and Weng Tonghe, who all took a liking to him. Weng Tonghe was especially impressed and offered Zhang a position in his personal secretariat. Zhang declined, no doubt concluding that his service with Wu left him more time to prepare for the examinations, gave him more practical duties to perform, and exposed him less to the uncertainties and trivialities inherent in official life.

Most of the friends and contacts Zhang had made up until this time belonged to the Qingliu, the "pure party." This group, which claimed to represent orthodoxy, was opposed to the advocates of "Western affairs," whom they accused of destroying the country with their false policy of self-strengthening (*ziqiang*). In line with traditional ideas, the group advocated resistance to the foreigner, stressing not only the renovation of the army but also economic development in general. The "pure party" played an important role between 1875 and 1884 when the Empress Dowager Cixi made use of it to counterbalance the influence of the powerful leaders of the rival faction, Li Hongzhang and Prince Gong. The Qingliu lost prestige during the Sino-French War and after 1885 its members split up. Some, like Xu Tong, ranged themselves with the conservatives; others, like Zhang Zhidong, turned, more or less, to self-strengthening but with a broader outlook; finally, others went further and were attracted to reformism.[44] Zhang Jian was an example of the last category.

The influence of the Qingliu on Zhang Jian is evident in the first texts in which he expressed a political opinion-two memorials, written in 1879, concerning the Treaty of Livadia with Russia.[45] He protested against the ineffectiveness of "self-strengthening," demanded resistance to foreign invasion, and underlined the necessity of moral strengthening: "It is necessary to gather men of talent . . . and to strengthen and unite the people's will."[46] The Korean crisis of 1882-83 allowed Zhang to put his ideas into practice. The efficient rapidity with which he organized the Chinese expeditionary force increased his renown. It was well known that he had wished to resist Japan and preserve the good will of the Korean government. Zhang's plans for the protection of Korea received total approval from the Qingliu. He wanted China to annex the northern region of Korea, impose internal reform on the country, and protect it by stationing Chinese troops in the country or by helping to modernize its army.[47] Zhang Jian was using both modern methods and the opportunities offered by the traditional tribute system to guarantee the integrity of national territory. In rejecting Zhang Jian's ideas and proposals on Korea, Li Hongzhang perhaps hastened the hour when Zhang realized that the enlightened aims of the "pure party" were insufficient.

With the death of Wu Changqing in 1884 and the dispersal of the Qingliu, Zhang Jian left official life. The disaster of the Sino-French War in 1885 shocked Zhang greatly, both as a Chinese and as an intellectual. That same year, in Beijing, he came in a brilliant second in the *juren* examinations, but failed the *jinshi* examination in 1886. Was it from this moment that Zhang decided to devote himself completely to the industrial development of his country?[48] The years 1885-86 certainly marked a decisive stage for him, as they did for his most enlightened contemporaries, but it appears that Zhang's desire to become a man of business developed only gradually. It is difficult to retrace exactly the progress of his thought in the years that follow, since his diary is rarely explicit on this matter and there exist very few of his writings dating from this period which, from the perspective of Chinese history in general, remains largely unexplored. An attempt will simply be made to outline the landmarks.

In 1886 Zhang attempted to establish a small sericulture business at Haimen which failed because of a lack of capital. In 1887, accepting the invitation of his former protector, Sun Yunjin, he accompanied Sun to the prefecture of Kaifeng where the governor of Henan appointed him to direct hydraulic works on the Yellow River. However, he resigned from his post a few months later, having given up hope that his projects would be accepted. Henceforth he was to refuse all official posts. He led the life of a traditional scholar, teaching in several well-known academies and dividing his time between his native district and Beijing where he had frequent meetings with Weng Tonghe. In 1889 he became acquainted with Tang Shouqian. While among this group of people, Zhang became familiar with current reform ideas and discovered that "the highest talent of China did not go beyond the eight-legged essay" (text 7). His practical and concrete turn of mind, however, made him wary of theoretical ideas. Moreover, he had few original ideas of his own at this time. The ideas Zhang imbibed were a mixture of those of Zeng Guofan and Tang Shouqian. He read the legalists, the works of Feng Guifen and Hu Linyi, and introduced himself to Western learning.[49] If he criticized the "Western affairs" policy on practical grounds, he was unaware of its essential difference with the reform thought that was emerging at this time: the question of political institutions. It is certain that industrial development was his main preoccupation.

He also considered the purpose of education to be training people for concrete tasks rather than adorning the mind, and urged that the examination program be changed.[50] Nevertheless, in his view, economic expansion had clear priority over educational reform.[51]

In 1894 Zhang Jian ranked first in the *jinshi* examinations. At forty-one he had reached the top of the traditional literary ladder. Yet instead of aiming for the highest official posts of the state, he accepted a proposition from Zhang Zhidong, in November 1895, to take charge of a bureau of commerce and establish a cotton mill in Nantong. Why had Zhang Jian broken with tradition? There are several reasons, among which it is difficult to ascertain the most important. First, he had become disgusted with examinations and official life.[52] Second, the death of his father, in October 1894, had obliged him to return to Nantong to observe the customary mourning period and prevented him in any case from taking up an official position. This chance happening was perhaps decisive, especially as Zhang had to pay off his father's debts.[53] However, since he accepted Zhang's invitation only after much thought, there were doubtless more general considerations taken into account.

Is it true, as Zhang wrote later, that "after 1894 [he] changed his ideas and became resolved to develop both industry and education, which mutually complement each other"[54] because "the strength of a country depends on education, but in order to develop education one has to first of all develop industry?" (text 7). As with all the enlightened elite, Zhang was dismayed by the defeat inflicted on China by Japan. In 1895 the national humiliation caused much intellectual and political agitation which precipitated a torrent of associations, pamphlets, and newspapers. Zhang joined the Qiangxuehui, the Society for the Study of Self-Strengthening, when a branch was established in Jiangsu under Zhang Zhidong's patronage.[55] He belonged to several reform societies and drafted many memorials calling for the development of agriculture and commerce.[56] Zhang's knowledge of Western material civilization expanded and deepened through his contact with these circles. He was also aware of the immediate economic danger posed by the Treaty of Shimonoseki because it had permitted the establishment of foreign manufacturing enterprises in the treaty ports. Zhang's ideas were always conditioned by concrete observation. In 1895 the handicraft weaving industry, which was one of the principal resources of Nantong district, had been seriously affected by the irregular supply of Japanese cotton thread resulting from the war. Zhang was suddenly made aware of the danger of depending on foreign supplies. With his characteristic realism, he decided "to do something" and "to devote all his attention to developing industry."[57]

Until 1901 there is no reference in his writings or diary to a scheme of thought according to which "the power and wealth of a country will have education for the father and industry for the mother." In his autobiography, the entry of April 1896 where he developed this theme was written much later. The idea was imposed on his actions after the fact. It served as a reply to conservatives who accused him of having offended scholarly morality, of "only having his own selfish interests in mind" (text 7). Furthermore, ideas such as this developed in a systematic way only in response to specific obstacles, caused by archaic Chinese structures and arrangements, with which the Dasheng cotton mill was faced during the course of its development. However, already in 1897, Zhang was writing: "The foundation of the state is not the army; its essential foundation is not commerce, but rather industry and agriculture, of which agriculture is the most important. Without agricultural production, industry cannot function, and, in this case, commerce has nothing to trade."[58] As for the cotton mill, it had been established "with the prosperity of the inhabitants of Tongzhou and the interests of China in mind" and "to promote local development and protect national interests."[59]

This line of thought was shared by other important scholars of the period. Zhang Jian's "conversion" was not unique. Lu Runxiang, who ranked first in the *jinshi* examinations in 1864, established the Sujing silk factory and Sulun spinning-mill at Suzhou in 1897. Sun Jia'nai, who had come first in the *jinshi* examinations in 1859, established the Guangyi spinning-mill at Anyang in 1906. However, both of them limited their economic activity in order to pursue parallel official careers. Zhang Jian, on the other hand, devoted all his time to developing his enterprises. He became an "entrepreneur," in the definition offered by Schumpeter, and thus a capitalist.

It was on this point that Zhang was different. What caused this difference? Is one to suppose that Western ideas were more influential with Zhang than with his contemporaries? Not at all. If foreign influence encouraged Zhang to enter the world of industry it was only in the sense that Zhang was aware of its political and economic threat to China. At this time he had only a fragmentary knowledge of Western ideas and their influence was indirect. The impulse for his action came more from Lu Zhi, Wang Anshi, and Gu Yanwu than Adam Smith.[60] If he had recourse to Chinese reformers, it was to help him "achieve his aim with a resolute energy." This aim consisted of "saving the country" (text 7). His natural tenacity, fortified by the tribulations of his youth; his liking for the practical and concrete; his desire to change things, inherited from his peasant background; his familiarity with the enlightened thinkers of the past; his patriotic enthusiasm in the face of foreign aggression; all these factors combined and contributed to leading him towards national capitalism. Other traditional scholars had entered industry with similar reasons, but one characteristic made Zhang unique: his social origins. This was perhaps the decisive factor which led Zhang, already a "new man" in scholarly circles, further along the new path than his contemporaries.

There is no need to go into details on the establishment of the Dasheng cotton-mill, Zhang Jian's first enterprise, since he describes the creation of the enterprise himself (text 7). The experience considerably enlarged his social horizons since he was obliged to "visit the rich" (i.e., the merchants) and learn to understand their interests, which he was soon to share. According to the historian Zhang Kaiyuan, "Zhang Jian's initial capital was his title of *jinshi*."[61] While it aroused at first some suspicion among merchants, it won him the confidence of the authorities. Ultimately, because the traditional mentality still retained a dominant influence, it served as a link between the two groups.

Zhang's enterprise was not controlled by officials (*guanban qiye*) such as those created by the *yangwu* advocates during the years 1860-70, neither was it managed by merchants under bureaucratic control (*guandu shangban*) such as those patronized by Sheng Xuanhuai. According to Zhang's own definition, it functioned with "capital subscribed by merchants, gentry management, and official help (*shanggu, shenban, guanzhu*)." The gentry of whom Zhang Jian spoke were those who, like himself, had had a traditional literary education. He assigned to them the role of intermediary between the bureaucracy and merchants, on the basis of common economic interests.[62] This was an important development in the evolution of Chinese society; it demonstrated the emergence of a new social class born of these three groups, united by a new activity-the development of capitalist enterprises. It was this connection with both the merchants and the bureaucracy that was to influence Zhang's political ideas after 1898.

During the years of Dasheng's development, Zhang Jian was mainly preoccupied with "changing things," and the specific task he set himself was to develop the economy. From May to July 1898 he was in Beijing. His reaction to the reform attempts of that year was one of skepticism and anxiety. He took a dislike to Kang Youwei, considering him arrogant and a hothead; he was also envious of the favor Kang had received from Weng Tonghe. Zhang commented: "Kang wants to change the institutions, but he does not know with what to replace them." Yet Zhang's stay in Beijing was a time of gathering new ideas and experiences. He had plenty of opportunity to engage in discussions with reform leaders and even foreigners like Timothy Richard. He read translations of political and technical works, and drafted Weng Tonghe's memorials.[63] Ultimately, he regretted the failure of the Hundred Days Reform, believing its leaders to have been the victims of deception and bad faith. He wrote to Liang Qichao: "You continually walk a dangerous path, and continually stir up danger. But danger does not lead anywhere."[64]

When Zhang returned to Nantong, on 15 July 1898, Dasheng was in considerable difficulty. The mill began to produce in 1899 but it needed protection against foreign competition and faced internal obstacles caused by the persistence of traditional structures. During the Boxer uprising Zhang's attitude was dictated by this necessity. He supported the "mutual defense of the southeast" as the only way to limit the damage of war and foreign invasion, but he was well aware that this policy had done little to reduce the national humiliation for which the court had been responsible. He therefore came increasingly to the conclusion that a complete set of reforms was necessary. Even so, his ideas on reform were far less radical than those of Kang and Liang. What is significant about his ideas is that they were based on concrete experience and were an attempt to express the views of a particular social group.

Zhang presented his ideas only after the promulgation of the 29 January edict calling for reform proposals. In fifteen days he wrote a pamphlet of twenty thousand characters which he entitled "A Reasoned Discussion On Reform" [Bianfa pingyi].[65] The title itself was significant; Zhang was posing as an arbiter. As at the Dasheng mill, Zhang, in his capacity as scholar, was the intermediary and link. The opinions he expressed in his pamphlet were none other than those of his merchant and bureaucratic associates at the mill. He was thereupon using his scholarly credentials to present himself as the representative of the modern gentry.

In his introduction and conclusion, Zhang criticized both the "new party" and the "old party" and rejected "hasty," "wholesale" reform as well as the "immobility" of the status quo. In effect, he was more in line with the "new party" but considered the Hundred Days Reform to have been excessive. He desired to convince the Manchus to abandon their dominant position and gradually establish a new regime. He envisaged four stages of reform, all of which were arranged under the six traditional boards; the structure of government was thus to remain intact. Of the forty-two proposals Zhang suggested, the majority concerned a "change of things"; there were only two which signified a "change of methods." One involved the establishment of a Council of Institutions (Yizhengyuan) which would recast old laws and draft new ones based on foreign models, and which would serve as intermediary between the government and institutions like Kang Youwei's Office of Coordination (Zhiduju), but without the latter's representative character. The other proposal concerned the creation of "prefectural and district councils." However, this was to be affected during the third stage and hence some time in the future. These councils would comprise only five members, chosen from among wealthy and influential gentry, and their role was purely consultative. The monarchic principle was not to be questioned in any way, while Sino-Manchu hostility was to be alleviated by cooperation. Zhang did not even specifically mention the establishment of a constitution.

In fact, Zhang considered the time inappropriate for a constitution. Even the application of his own reform proposals would meet with difficulty due to the lack of competent officials. "Reform needs men of talent that only the schools can provide."[66] He thus concluded that educational reform was the precondition for political reform.[67] Zhang took up the idea previously expressed by Li Duanfen and emphasized that the examinations were an obstacle to the development of the schools. He proposed to abolish the practice of official recruitment through the examinations and to have potential officials trained in the schools. The examinations, completely modified, would merely be the conclusion of studies already completed in the schools. A complete school system would be established, beginning at the primary level and ending with the university, with technical and professional schools occupying an important place. Zhang stressed the necessity of educating people who would be useful to all aspects of the country's development.[68]

In his "Reasoned Discussion on Reform" it seemed that proposals for educational reform, which were the most complete and far-reaching, were a substitute for the proposals concerning total political reform that Zhang did not make openly, perhaps for reasons of prudence but especially because he considered political reform premature. For Zhang, it was a question of first establishing order in the state; reorganizing and simplifying administration to make it more efficient and, at the same time, offering opportunities for gentry initiative. These strategies, Zhang hoped, would contribute to the foundations of a new regime. Zhang's program was less radical than that of Kang Youwei in 1898, but the radical reformers had themselves revised their position in 1901. Liang Qichao, for example, estimated that at least twenty years preparation was required before the establishment of a constitutional regime.[69] The pragmatic nature of Zhang's reforms represented the wishes of merchants and businessmen who, at this time, were beset with concrete difficulties: the anarchy of the fiscal system and the system of weights and measures, the incoherence of the laws, and official ignorance of economic problems. The proposals, through their moderate character, revealed the continued ascendancy of traditional thought, not only over Zhang Jian, but also over the social milieu that Zhang claimed to represent. They showed Zhang's desire to rally the support of the bureaucracy, and not to break with the government.

Zhang's pamphlet quickly gained prominence.[70] He sent it to Liu Kunyi, who submitted it to the court. The memorials written by Liu and Zhang Zhidong showed traces of its influence, as did the imperial measures adopted during the first years of the century. The ideas expressed in the pamphlet also became the basis of the constitutional movement, of which Zhang was to be one of the leaders.

In 1901 Zhang Jian's traditional education and official contacts gave him considerable prestige, but he nevertheless turned his attention towards more modern activities. These activities provided him with important financial resources, but they also led to new demands on his part. For Zhang, at this time, the most important one was that calling for the development of modern education. In the face of government promises, what would his attitude be, and how would he be able to reconcile the traditional aims of the gentry, the needs of the new social group he represented, and the wishes of the court?

CHAPTER II

Cooperation between Gentry and Government, 1901-06

From 1901 to 1906, Zhang Jian responded enthusiastically to the new imperial policy. He undertook to develop education at Nantong, in close and compliant cooperation with the authorities.

Traditional Education: Nantong in 1901

At the beginning of the twentieth century education in the region of Nantong was still very traditional. The district was situated on the north bank of the Yangzi near the river mouth and contained a population of more than one million inhabitants in an area of 1,860 square kilometers. It was one of the most densely populated areas in Jiangsu; in order to earn a livelihood, part of its population was forced to emigrate to Shanghai where they led destitute lives.[1] Along the bank of the river, wide stretches of alluvium and marsh were the domain of salt-makers. More than one-third of the surface area of the district was uncultivated. The population was concentrated in scattered villages surrounding the city of Nantong, which had a population of about 250,000. Besides wheat and soybean, whose yields were small, cotton was the major crop. It was of an excellent quality (text 7) and had given birth to a famous weaving handicraft industry several centuries old, which partly made up for the low agricultural yields. The region was cut off from the principal channels of the provincial economy since it had neither a good port on the Yangzi nor on the coast. The cloth trade used canals, the traditional mode of transport, without bringing the region the modernity that was beginning to transform the larger, neighboring towns.

Foreign missionaries had only a limited presence in the district. A few dozen Christians lived near a church established by the Jesuits in the eastern suburb of Nantong.[2] In 1895 the Foreign Christian Missionary Society had opened a chapel and lecture-hall on the main street of the town. This had met with violent opposition from officials and gentry. Missionary activities only started to increase after 1909 when a hospital was established in the wake of the modernization projects then being undertaken by Zhang Jian.[3]

The inhabitants of Tongzhou retained traditional ways of thinking. For example, when the Dasheng mill was being constructed, more than three hundred gentry banded together to prevent its completion and cloth-makers attempted to put fire to the building.[4] Old beliefs still held sway over the population.[5]

The education that was offered in the district did not change this state of affairs. In order to obtain an idea of educational conditions in Nantong in 1901, one is obliged to refer to the local gazetteer of 1875. It reveals that the district had one "official school" (guanxue or ruxue), three academies (shuyuan), twelve "village schools" (shexue) and four "charitable schools" (yixue).[6] The official school assembled the shengyuan from time to time for conferences and ceremonies, and distributed scholarships to the best of them. It was under the control of the magistrate and the director of studies (xuezheng). The academies were places where those taking the examinations could further their knowledge and prepare for the approaching examination under the direction of instructors, whose quality depended on the wealth of the academy (text 3). Only one of Nantong's academies, the Wenzhang shuyuan, was of a reasonably high standard. The village schools (shexue) were designed, in principle, for children twelve to twenty years of age who already knew how to read. The teacher was a shengyuan and the expenses were met by the local community. The magistrate exercised some control since these schools were inevitably meant to propagate Confucian morality in order to strengthen popular loyalty.[7] The charitable schools (yixue) were maintained with donations from wealthy gentry. They were free, and were meant for children younger than those who attended the shexue.[8]

Unfortunately, the Nantong gazetteer makes no mention of the sishu (private schools). Yet they were the most numerous and important. An idea of them can be obtained from Zhang's autobiography and other contemporary reports. There were several kinds of private schools. A clan or a guild could employ a teacher to instruct the children of its members. Sometimes a scholar opened a school in his residence, or two or three families might get together to pay for a teacher. Finally, the rich employed private tutors who lived in their homes and taught their children.[9]

In these establishments, as in the charitable schools, the curriculum was virtually the same from one end of the country to the other, since the purpose was to prepare for the examinations. A student first learned characters with pieces of wood or paper models. Afterwards he read the *Three-Character Classic* [Sanzijing], *Classic of One Hundred Names* [Baijiaxing], and *Thousand Character Classic* [Qianziwen], which were rhyming works of no great interest except that they allowed the student to learn basic vocabulary and some principles of Confucian morality. The student was also taught to calculate on the abacus. After this the student was introduced to the classics proper: the *Classic of Filial Piety,* the *Analects, Mencius,* and the *Doctrine of the Mean.* Explanations were given only of individual characters and the student's sole task was to learn the words by heart. Later the texts were read again with other classics, and some explanation of their general meaning was given. At the same time, there were exercises in writing the compositions required for the examinations. These tasks occupied the student until he was fifteen, after which he studied histories and literary anthologies to improve his style.[10] Teaching methods relied solely on rote memory and repetition. Students had to know all the classics by heart and be able to write fluently, using parallel phrases and rhyming sentences. The teacher did not supervise all the students at the same time. He gave them instructions and then made them recite individually. The classroom often did not have a table, seats, or blackboard. Discipline was severe. Students were in school from eight in the morning until six in the evening, with an annual holiday of from fifteen days to six weeks.[11] As Guo Moruo remarked with bitterness in his "Memories of Childhood," traditional education trained "premature adults" (*xiao daren*).

Despite an apparent uniformity, standards varied. In certain villages some guild schools could offer a more practical education, teaching more arithmetic or even providing the kind of professional training given to apprentices. One factor which helps explain the great differences among schools was the ability of the teacher, which depended very often on the salary he was given. Hu Shi recalled how his teacher explained the classics carefully to him because his mother had given the teacher six dollars, while this same teacher simply made the other students read and recite because he had only received two dollars from them.[12] Some teachers were not even *shengyuan,* while others were *juren*. Not all teachers encouraged their students, as Zhang Jian's teacher had done, so that they could take the *shengyuan* examinations at fifteen years of age.

It is impossible to evaluate the availability of education in Nantong from existing documents. A similar problem arises for China as a whole. Moreover, taking into consideration the difficulty of the Chinese language and the fact that the classical style predominated in all writings of the period, at what point could one say that a person knew how to read? Even the poorest peasants were able to recognize a few characters, but access to the written culture and its privileges was reserved for an elite which probably did not exceed 6 or 7 percent of the population.[13] Yet the immediate costs of education were not excessively burdensome. The majority of teachers at the elementary level earned five Mexican dollars a year, in addition to a modest income in kind for their food ration.[14] Although education was completely out of reach for agricultural laborers and small farmers, in good years rich peasants and artisans could think of sending their children to school. The problem was that the education they received seemed to have no immediate value and they did not have sufficient resources to allow their children to continue for the long time required to become an official.[15] Despite the importance the Chinese attached to the acquisition of knowledge, many of them were reluctant to send their children to school.

This phenomenon seemed to become more widespread in the second half of the nineteenth century due to increasing economic difficulties, which explains the decrease in the number of examination candidates who were not from scholar families. At Nantong, one of the few localities where a complete list of examination candidates exists, this tendency was clear; the proportion of "new men" among *shengyuan*, which was about 50 percent during the years 1880-90, fell to about 40 percent during the years 1890-1902.[16] Yet, due to the increases during the Taiping rebellion (text 2), the degree quota enjoyed by that district for the civil and military examinations, 36 and 27 respectively, made Nantong one of the most privileged localities in the country.[17] However, as Zhang Jian wrote, "this had not benefitted the peasants, artisans, or tradesmen." In fact, they were in danger of receiving less benefit since, even if they succeeded in becoming *shengyuan* in their district, the general increase in the *shengyuan* quota made it virtually impossible to become a *juren* afterwards (and hence obtain an office) because of the fierce competition involved.[18] In fact, Nantong did not have a reputation for scholarly brilliance. No great official had come from Nantong, while

Zhang Jian was the first person from the district since remote times to rank first in the *jinshi* examinations. From 1882 to 1900 there were at least 483 *juren* from Jiangsu, of whom 11 came from Tongzhou (i.e., one-forty-fourth of the total while the district comprised one-twentieth of the provincial population).[19] Since, according to the gazetteer, the whole of the department (i.e., the districts of Nantong, Taixing, and Rugao, and the subprefecture of Haimen) provided one-tenth of the *juren* candidates for the entire province, the results were meager.[20] There were relatively more successes at the *jinshi* level, but since the candidates prepared elsewhere for the examination this fact does not have relevance for the quality of education in the district.

Education in Nantong was perhaps no different from that in the average Chinese district, but in the province of Jiangsu, where education was more developed, it appeared below average.

Nevertheless, in the last years of the nineteenth century something brought change to this calm district lulled by the routine of traditional life. At first the mill established by Zhang Jian aroused the fierce hostility of the gentry; three hundred of them signed petitions and attempted with all the means at their disposal to sabotage the enterprise. However, from the beginning Zhang found collaborators among his countrymen: Shen Xiejun, Sha Yuanbing, Wu Qilu, Liu Yishan, and Chen Chutao.[21] When it became known that the enterprise was working successfully, skepticism gradually gave way to interest, while opposition was forced to become less open. Zhang's position was not always easy, but his literary titles, his contacts with the official world, and his economic success gave him an authority that was difficult to dispute openly. Besides, the increasing links Nantong was beginning to establish with Shanghai through the mill directed the gentry's attention towards new activities and ideas, while at the same time the "new administration" (*xinzheng*) set in progress by the court opened up legal channels for this development.

The Achievements of Zhang Jian within Official Policy

As with the establishment of his first enterprise, Zhang Jian waited for official encouragement before creating schools. Citing the administration's incapacity to assume "the complete responsibility for educational development" (text 1), he took the initiative in establishing a normal school.

During the first years of the reform, the impetus seemed to come primarily from important enlightened officials. In 1903, 67 percent of the modern schools were established by officials; in 1904 the percentage was 85. The proportion was reversed only in 1905 with official schools representing not more than 35 percent of the total.[22] The new schools were concentrated in the provinces of Shandong, Zhili, Shanxi, Henan, Jiangsu, Jiangxi, Hunan, Hubei, and Zhejiang. These were the domains of reforming high officials, whose memorials filled the official publications of the time-Yuan Shikai, Zhang Zhidong, Liu Kunyi, Xi Liang, Cen Chunxuan, and Nie Qigui. This fact has led some historians to conclude that the Manchu government was "sincere in its desire for reform"[23] or, moreover, that "in the vast program of modernization that was implemented throughout the empire" from 1901 to 1906 the "most important initiatives continued to come from the provincial governors."[24] In sum, the reforms were propagated and implemented due to the action of the government and a certain number of officials. In contrast to this view, other historians have defined the court's program as "false reforms," of which few were effectively implemented.[25] The role that Zhang Jian played in collaboration with high officials in Jiangsu and neighboring provinces shows that the reality was much more complex than that presented by either of the hypotheses described above.

After the promulgation of the edict of 29 January 1901, Zhang discussed educational reform with the governor-general of Liangguang, Liu Kunyi, and the governor-general of Huguang, Zhang Zhidong. In between, he discussed plans with a number of well-known people in the province-Shen Zipei, Luo Zhenyu, Zheng Xiaoxu, and Miao Quancun (all of whom were also consulted by the governors-general). Zhang also had meetings with such Nantong gentry as Sha Yuanbing, Li Shenzhi, and Fan Dangshi.[26] His plan apparently was to have the administration implement projects suggested by the gentry. In effect, the memorials of Zhang Zhidong and Liu Kunyi in 1901 and 1902 contained the suggestions, practically word for word, put forward by Zhang Jian and his friends.[27] Zhang's concrete plans were to establish immediately a large number of primary schools as well as normal schools to train the teachers; Nantong was evidently going to have one such normal school. Nothing definite was achieved for a year. In the interval, the government only issued general directives: the edict of 16 November 1901 concerning the conversion of academies into schools; the decree of 25 November 1901 ordering the new schools to follow the regulations established by Yuan Shikai in Shandong (text 1); and the statutes concerning the University of Beijing. In the other provinces modern schools began to appear with the encouragement of the gentry and officials.[28] In Jiangsu, the governor-general, Liu Kunyi, shared Zhang Jian's views but dared not adopt any energetic measures, complaining that he "had neither men nor money." Finally, at an audience with officials where the project of the normal school at Nantong was to be discussed, the opposition from the provincial treasurer, salt intendent, and circuit intendent was such that Zhang had to give up any hopes for official aid. "China," they remarked, "is different in all respects from other countries. She has no need to copy the foreigner in order to learn. Zhang Jian is committing an error, he is far too pro-Japanese."[29] Secretly disappointed and angry, Zhang persisted in his plan which he considered useful and proper. He decided to establish the normal school himself, using the funds he received from Dasheng and from individual contributions. "Posterity," he wrote on that day, "will know that the creation of the first Chinese normal school resulted from the desire to combat the stupidity of three officials."[30]

Text 1 describes its establishment. The original plan was respected. The school's originality was to be found, first, in the fact that it was established specifically for the training of teachers. This proved that Zhang's reformism was not superficial. He concerned himself with the basic problems involved in a general plan for the development of modern education, taking into account China's special conditions. Although the normal school only concerned Nantong, Zhang hoped that the lack of official schools would make it a model for the whole country. A second feature of the normal school's originality was that its regulations exactly foreshadowed those of 1902 and 1904 concerning schools in the empire. This explains why the Nantong schools were easily integrated into the general system of education that was instituted a little later.

On 15 August 1902, the emperor sanctioned the regulations on schools proposed by Zhang Baixi, the director of Beijing University.[31] Until this time the schools had developed in a disorganized way. Some modern schools dated from before 1900;[32] there were some which had disappeared and then reappeared, completely transformed, like the University of Beijing. Finally, there were others that had just been established. With the exception of schools in Shandong and Zhili where Yuan Shikai had laid down a number of rules, these schools were part of no coordinated hierarchy. Furthermore, no administrative organ had been established to manage them, the result being that they had a tendency to slip away from official control.[33]

The Board of Rites, which was in charge of the civil-service examinations, was unable to deal with the schools. In nominating Zhang Baixi as "director of studies" (*guanxue dachen*) at the University of Beijing on 10 January 1902, the emperor also assigned him the duty of drafting regulations on the education system and of coordinating and administering the schools.[34]

Zhang Baixi's regulations provided for three levels of education, the details and curricula of which are given in tables 1 and 2 (see pages 38-41). The first seven years of primary education were to be compulsory. After secondary school students could enter a higher-level school (*gaodeng xuetang*) or, in Beijing, a university preparatory course (*daxue yubei ke*) which was to be divided into political and technical sections. After three years students would enter the university (*daxuetang*) which would comprise seven faculties: politics, literature, science, agriculture, technology, commerce, and medicine. The total period of study required twenty years. The Institute for Higher Studies (Daxueyuan) was primarily a research institution and the number of years to be spent there was not specified. Besides general education, provision was also made for a system of technical and normal schools.

These regulations were promulgated throughout the empire but little concrete action resulted except that the "universities" which had been established in several provinces were "demoted" to the rank of higher-level schools.[35] In fact, the regulations were incomplete. Educational administration and education itself remained intertwined; secondary schools, for example, did not limit themselves to accepting primary school graduates but also actually managed the primary schools. There was no provision for a shorter period of professional education for children whose parents could not afford to pay for the twenty years involved. The reclassification of literary degrees was considered, but the link between the schools and examinations was not specified.

On the other hand, Zhang Baixi in his new post exerted more and more influence. Sincerely dedicated to the idea of reform (as shown by the few hours devoted to the classics in his school curricula),[36] he strove to gather the support of progressive elements by appointing the most capable. He succeeded sufficiently for conservative Manchus and Mongols at the court to distrust his authority and the privileges he accorded to Han Chinese. In February 1903 Rong Qing, a Mongol, was appointed Zhang's assistant to deal with education. His sole aim was to reestablish the traditional system, which certainly did nothing to allay the increasing agitation in the schools.[37] Meanwhile, in May 1903, Zhang Zhidong returned to Beijing and the court appealed to him to put an end to the awkward situation. On 29 May, the court charged him, as well as Zhang Baixi and Rong Qing, with completely revising the regulations for the University of Beijing and the schools.

The new regulations were promulgated on 13 January 1904. With the exception of a few modifications and additions, they remained the basis of the new education until 1912. The large text, in sixteen volumes, was widely distributed. Tables 1 and 2 show the essential school system and curricula.[38] What were the differences with the 1902 regulations? Kindergartens (optional) replaced elementary schools. Compulsory education was reduced to five years. In total, the period of study was to last twenty-five years, although the number of hours of attendance was reduced, with provision being made for one rest day per week instead of every twelve days. There were specific regulations on normal and technical schools as well as on the internal administration of schools. Some provision was made to offer children from low-income families the possibility of a short professional education. In order to encourage attendance at the modern schools, the quotas for the traditional examinations were reduced and the official degree titles of *jinshi, juren,* and *gongsheng* were to be awarded to the graduates of the modern schools. This encouraged an increase in the number of schools in 1904-05; nevertheless, it was still easier to acquire a degree through the traditional channel. This competition was not eliminated until the complete abolition of the examinations on 2 September 1905. It was only after this date, as W. Franke has stressed, that general progress in modern education took place.[39]

It was within this government-designed framework that Zhang Jian developed education in Nantong and the surrounding areas. He added specialized departments to the normal school, and established a normal school for girls, some primary schools, an apprentice school, and a secondary school. His plans followed the official regulations (text 2). At Wusong, Yangzhou, and Wuxian, Zhang participated in the establishment of technical and general schools. In Shanghai, he also assisted Aurore College, which had broken away from the Jesuits.[40]

The regulations remained imprecise concerning one fundamental aspect: the financing of the schools. Zhang described the way in which he dealt with this problem: "Not daring to hope for any

TABLE 1: SUBJECTS TAUGHT AS A PERCENTAGE OF TOTAL HOURS

	Lower Primary School			Higher Primary School	
	Elementary School 1902	Primary School 1902	1904	1902	1904
Moral training	16.6	16.6	6.7	5.5	5.6
Chinese	33.3	16.6	13.3	16.1–13.9[a]	22.2
Classics	16.6		40.0	16.6	33.3
Arithmetic		5.5–11.1	20.0	11.1	8.3
Chinese history	8.3	16.6	3.3	13.9	5.5
Chinese geography	8.3	11.1–5.5	3.3	11.1–8.3	5.5
Natural sciences			3.3	6.9–13.9	5.5
Physical education	16.6	16.6	10.0	8.3–5.5	8.3
Drawing			optional	8.3–11.1[b]	5.5
Handicrafts			optional		optional
Total hours	72/12 days	72/12 days	30/week	72/12 days	36/week

TABLE 1 (continued)

| | | Secondary School | | | |
| | | Japan | | | |
	1902	1st, 2nd, 3rd Years 1904	4th, 5th Years	1st, 2nd, 3rd Years 1904	4th, 5th Years 1904
Moral training	5.2	3.5	3.3	2.7	2.7
Drawing	5.2	7.0	0–3.3	2.7	0–2.7
Physical education	5.2	10.7	10.0	5.5	5.5
Classics	7.9			2.5	2.5
Mathematics	15.7	14.2	13.3	11.1	11.1
Chinese and foreign history	7.9	} 10.7	} 10.7	5.5	5.5
Geography	7.9			8.3	0–5.5
Chinese literature	7.9	28.5	20.0	11.1	8.3
Foreign languages	23.6	21.4	23.3	22.2	16.6
Physical and natural sciences	13.1	7.1	13.3–16.6	5.5	16.6
Political science			6.6		8.3
Total hours per week	38.0	28.0	30.0	36.0	36.0

[a]Schools had the choice of reducing the number of hours for Chinese and adding 5.5 percent of time for foreign languages.
[b]Courses in industrial, commercial, and agricultural vocational training could replace drawing.

Sources: Shu Xincheng, *Ziliao*, vol. 2; *Education in Japan*, vol. 4, 1–10.

TABLE 2: SCHOOL SYSTEMS

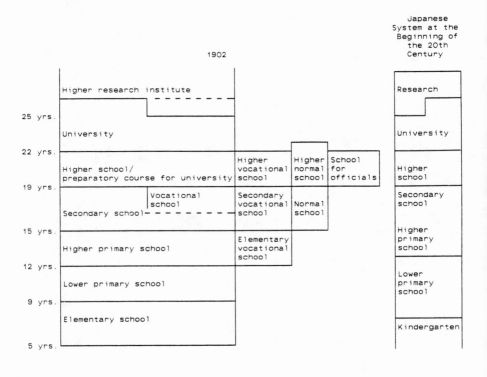

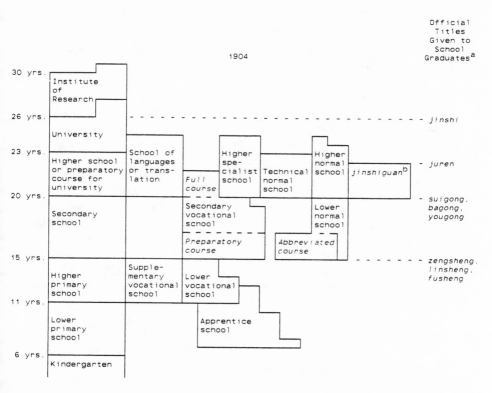

Official
Titles
Given to
School
Graduates[a]

1904

30 yrs.
Institute
of
Research

26 yrs. — *jinshi*

University

23 yrs.
Higher school | School of | Higher | Higher
or preparatory | languages | spe- | normal
course for | or trans- | cialist | Technical | school | *jinshiguan*[b] — *juren*
university | lation | *Full* | school | normal
course | school

20 yrs. — *suigong,*
bagong,
yougong
Secondary | Secondary | Lower
school | vocational | normal
school | school

Preparatory | Abbreviated
course | course

15 yrs. — — — — — — — *zengsheng,*
linsheng,
Higher | Supple- | *fusheng*
primary | mentary | Lower
school | vocational | vocational
school | school

11 yrs.
Lower | Apprentice
primary | school
school

6 yrs. Kindergarten

[a] *Jiangli.*

[b] *Jinshiguan* (school for *jinshi*) aimed at retraining the holders of traditional *jinshi* before
they entered administration.

government funds, we are obliged to rely on ourselves" (texts 1 and 2, also the commentary). The bulk of the funds was drawn from his personal wealth and the profits of the Dasheng mill which, from 1902 to 1906, contributed 85,260 *taels* to the normal school.[41] Zhang was anxious not to encroach on the public domain or to depend on official help. In 1905 and 1906 this was a general tendency, since the majority of new schools were financed by the gentry. Japan's victory over Russia had aroused an enthusiasm for reform, which contained a taste for speculation because students rushing to the schools were ready to pay much for an education, the quality of which they did not know how to evaluate.

Even if the state was incapable of assuming completely the new functions of education, the management of the schools and the implementation of the regulations nevertheless required some kind of administrative control. A new organization was gradually created. At the end of January 1904, following the proposal put forward by Zhang Zhidong, Zhang Baixi, and Rong Qing, the post of "director of studies" (occupied by Zhang Baixi) was abolished and replaced by that of a superintendent of education (*zongli xuewu dachen*) to which Sun Jia'nai was appointed.[42] The superintendent was assisted by an inspector-general of education, the first one being Zhang Xiangjia. They controlled six offices which dealt with different aspects of educational administration. This was the beginning of a ministry, although it lacked organization in the provinces. An edict of 12 May 1904 ordered provisional examiners to oversee examinations in the schools; on 22 September the control over provincial examiners was transferred from the Board of Rites to the superintendent of education. The regulations of 1904 provided for the establishment of "education offices" (*xuewuchu*) in each province. Some were, in fact, created in Zhili, Hubei, and Jiangsu.[43]

On 31 January 1905 Zhang Jian requested that a bureau of education (*xuewu gongsuo*) be established for Tongzhou and its dependencies. His request was granted and the bureau opened on 3 June.[44] It comprised gentry who acted in concert with the local magistrate and the education office in Nanjing over such matters as the distribution of public funds destined for education, school inspection, coordination of teaching methods and curricula, and propagating the cause of modern education (text 2). Thus, from the administrative point of view, district education was attached to the general system while at the same time leaving sufficient initiative to its local promoter. The need to supplement a deficient administration and to create a coordinating institution to deal with problems at the provincial level was one of the factors which led to the organization of the Jiangsu Education Society at the beginning of October 1905 (text 4). Through these institutions, Zhang Jian and the gentry collaborated with officials in new ways to put into practice the new program of modern education that had just been promulgated.

However, this administrative arrangement was too flexible and loose to satisfy the government and to accord with official needs. With the abolition of traditional examinations in September 1905, the new schools suddenly acquired new prestige.[45] In one year the number of new schools doubled,[46] making the problem acute. Within a few months a complete administrative system was suddenly created. An edict of 6 December 1905 established a Ministry of Education and details of its internal organization were issued on 13 May 1906.[47] On the same day the provincial examiners were replaced by commissioners of education; their duties were outlined in more detail shortly afterwards. The "offices of education" became "education bureaus" (xuewu gongsuo). Besides having an administrative function, they had a certain legislative role; they could propose regulations on provincial education. These education bureaus were not only staffed by officials; the education commissioner was to be assisted by a council comprising gentry and people involved in education. "Offices to encourage education" (quanxuesuo) were established in which gentry were under the control of the local magistrate. A similar arrangement took place with the regulations on education associations promulgated on 28 July 1906, ordering their increase but under strict official supervision (texts 3 and 4).

Officials had taken up their positions by the summer of 1906. The education associations and offices to encourage education took longer to organize. However, in Jiangsu, due to early development in preceding years, the new administrative structure was already functioning by the end of 1906. The rapid growth in the number of students and schools apparently testified to the efficacy of the new measures (see table 3, page 44). Judging from the case of Zhang Jian, it appeared that gentry and officials were working closely together and that private and official action was complementary. What was the cause of this cooperation?

TABLE 3: NUMBER OF MODERN SCHOOLS

	1902	1903	1904	1905	1906
Jiangsu	67	140	228	564	1,182
Nantong		2	6	23	53

Sources: The figures for Jiangsu are calculated from *Jiaoyu tongji tubiao,* 1907, *gesheng,* 27. The figures for Nantong are calculated from *"Jingwai xuewu baogao"* [Report on education in the provinces], *Xuebu guanbao* 3, no. 82 (XT1/1 February): 147–61. Zhang Jian, *Jiaoyu,* II/18a-20a, and text 2.

The Sources of Inspiration

Officials and gentry shared a common admiration for Japan. Japan was the only Asian country that had successfully resisted the West. It had been able to modernize without abandoning its traditions, and was culturally close to China. On reading Zhang Jian's writings from 1902 to 1904 and government regulations in the same period, one is constantly reminded of this source of common inspiration. There are abundant examples showing its effect. Japan's influence was seen in the arrangement of the schools, as is shown in tables 1 and 2. It influenced the administrative system that was created: the Ministry of Education with its specialized branches, the creation of a hierarchical system of councils and education associations working with officials in charge of the routine business of education, and the network of educational regions (*xuequ*) established in each district under the supervision of the Office to Encourage Education (*Quanxuesuo*) to ensure the equitable distribution of schools. Details on school administration were drawn directly from Japanese laws; for example, those concerning the size of the buildings, the directors, censors, supervisors responsible for discipline, and the distinction among official, public, and private schools.[48] Finally, at once the cause and effect of the attraction towards Japan, the majority of foreign teachers employed in the new schools were Japanese.

There are no complete statistics on foreign teachers, and one is therefore limited to gathering fragmentary information to evaluate Japanese influence. In any event, out of the thirty-thousand or so teachers in the new schools in 1906 the proportion of foreigners was small and foreign teachers generally did not occupy the highest positions. Nevertheless, in some strategic areas, the Japanese occupied key positions. In 1903 all military schools and police schools had at least one Japanese instructor; sometimes, as in Hangzhou, all the instructors were Japanese.[49] A Japanese missionary in 1904, quoting from official figures, referred to 174 Japanese teachers employed in China.[50] This number may not have included those who were recruited by private institutions. At the Nantong Normal School, for example, three out of the fourteen teachers were Japanese. In the best secondary schools and higher schools of Hunan, in 1906, 20 percent of the teachers were Japanese.[51] In Shanxi, the higher school of agriculture and the police school in Taiyuan each had two Japanese teachers.[52] In Zhili, there were Japanese teaching at the Baoding Normal School, agricultural school, and military school, and at the Tianjin technical school and medical school.[53] In 1906, in the provincial capital of Fujian, the military school, the normal school, and higher school each had from three to seven Japanese teachers.[54] The Japanese had not yet established any schools in China for Chinese students, but there were several Japanese establishments in China that trained "experts in cultural cooperation." The principal organization was, since 1901, the Tōa Dōbunkai (Society for a Common Language) which was patronized by Prince Konoe. It had established facilities in Shantou and Shanghai where Japanese could learn Chinese with the aim of eventually being employed by the Chinese or Japanese governments.[55] The Society was also involved in translation and publishing and it owned bookshops in Shanghai and Hankou.[56] This aspect of its work was so successful that in the several schools with Japanese teachers, sometimes even Japanese-language textbooks were used.[57] The specially-compiled texts in use at the Nantong Normal School followed a Japanese outline.[58]

At this time, Westerners protested loudly against the "Japanization of China."[59] Later on, the evolution of Japanese foreign policy caused both Chinese and foreigners, for different reasons, to minimize the influence Japan had exercised on the beginnings of modern education in China. Nevertheless, Japanese influence left a lasting impression on Chinese nationalism. Although some writers have referred to the results of this influence,[60] they have not specified exactly the channels through which it passed from the sphere of ideas to that of reality. The roles played by translations of Japanese works,[61] by Chinese students returning from Japan,[62] and by Japanese in China have all been described, but the concrete results in specific cases have not been examined.

Certain aspects of the problem can perhaps be clarified by focusing on the example of Zhang Jian. Until 1903, most of what Zhang knew of Japan was gained from his friend Luo Zhenyu. Because Luo ended his days as a minister in the Japanese puppet regime of Manchukuo, he became a *persona non grata*, but this does not detract from the fact that he played a very important role in official and scholarly circles at the beginning of the twentieth century. In the spring of 1897, he founded in Shanghai the Agricultural Society (Nonghui) whose members included Zhang Jian, Wang Kangnian, Liang Qichao, Tan Sitong, Tang Shouqian, Sha Yuanbing, Ma Liang, and other enlightened personalities originating from all the provinces. In the following five years, under Luo's direction, a small group among them, often referred to as the Agronomy Society (Nongxueshe), translated, mainly from the Japanese, more than one hundred works on agriculture. They were published in a journal entitled *Journal of Agronomy* [*Nongxue bao*] as well as in other publications.[63] The translations were a source of guidance for Zhang Jian when he embarked on enterprises involving the clearing and cultivation of land. He also possessed a number of them, which he later deposited in the library at Nantong.[64] After 1898 the society gained the patronage of Liu Kunyi and two years later Luo Zhenyu was appointed director of the Bureau of Agriculture (Nongwuju) that Zhang Zhidong had created in Wuchang. Luo thus associated with both officials and gentry; Japanese ideas propagated by his writings therefore found a convenient sphere for their implementation. Luo also founded the Society for the Study of Asian Culture (Dongwen xueshe) in order to train the translators he needed.[65] Taking advantage of the enthusiasm for reform, at the beginning of 1901 he created the Education Society (Jiaoyushe) which edited a fortnightly journal *The World of Education* [*Jiaoyu shijie*] and a series of translations entitled *A Collection of Writings on Education* [*Jiaoyu congshu*]. It was in these publications that there appeared, from 1901 to 1903, all the regulations on Japanese education and a hundred or so works and articles on education translated from the Japanese. Zhang Jian read and used these texts (text 1, commentary; text 8, n. 2).

Luo Zhenyu was assisted by several young scholars. Among them was Wang Guowei who, after failing the *juren* examinations, tried his luck in journalism and studied Japanese with the Society for the Study of Asian Culture. He succeeded Luo Zhenyu as director of the Agronomy Society. Zhang Jian met Wang quite often and it was through Wang that Zhang recruited the Japanese teachers for Nantong.[66] The regular translators for *The World of Education*, Chen Yi, Gao Fengqian, and Shen Hong had all studied in Japan. In 1901, Luo sent Wang there to familiarize himself with the sciences. Luo joined him in the winter while on an official journey ordered by Zhang Zhidong to study educational conditions in Japan.[67] Both Luo and Wang returned to Shanghai at the beginning of 1902. Equally influential in the society were the Japanese recruited by Luo Zhenyu, Taoka Reiun (1867-1912), and, especially, Fujita Toyohachi (1870-1929), a distinguished sinologist. Fujita taught Japanese for the Society for the Study of Asian Culture, advised Luo Zhenyu and, in November 1905, was appointed director of studies at the normal school in Suzhou where Luo became principal.[68] Zhang Jian was influenced by Fujita when he drafted the school regulations that he submitted to Liu Kunyi and Zhang Zhidong and used afterwards for the normal school.[69]

The influential gentry for whom Zhang served as an intermediary with high officials, Shen Zipei, Miao Quancun, Zheng Xiaoxu, and Tang Shouqian, were all acquainted with Luo and shared his ideas. Thus, in addition to Luo's personal influence while holding semi-official posts under Zhang Zhidong from 1901 to 1906, important gentry also exerted pressure concerning the same ideas. It is known that in reality Zhang Baixi and Rong Qing did not have a hand in the 1904 regulations and that Zhang Zhidong was primarily responsible. Apart from the general guidelines for education that reflected Zhang's personal ideas, the overall Japanese influence on the regulations was certainly due to the small group from Jiangsu which was influenced by Luo Zhenyu. Moreover, Wang Guowei wrote an article in January 1906 in which he mentioned that the regulations had been drafted by Chen Yi,[70] the latter being the very person who had translated the Japanese regulations for *The World of Education*. At the beginning of 1906, Luo Zhenyu was given a post in the Ministry of Education where he met up again with several of his friends from Shanghai, all of whom, like Luo, were admirers of Japan.[71]

The role, at once theoretical and practical, that Luo Zhenyu played was not an isolated case. One can also refer to the example of

Wu Rulun, who was influential in the compilation of the regulations of 1902. Wu, a scholar and protegé of Li Hongzhang, had concerned himself with educational reform since 1889; he had gathered around him such brilliant scholars as Fan Dangshi, the compatriot and friend of Zhang Jian. Zhang Baixi appointed him director of studies at the University of Beijing in 1902 and they had collaborated on the drafting of the school regulations. From July to October 1902 Wu conducted an investigation of education in Japan and then wrote a report of his trip which was well received among enlightened circles. On his return Wu stopped over in Shanghai. This was the time that Zhang Jian was organizing the normal school and having constant meetings with high officials concerning educational development. He had a long discussion with Wu on this matter.[72]

After his own trip to Japan from 21 May to 27 July 1903, Zhang became a direct agent for Japanese influence. Invited by the Japanese consul in Shanghai to visit the industrial exhibition in Osaka, Zhang remained ten weeks in Japan, visiting more than thirty enterprises and thirty-five educational establishments. He also met Japanese businessmen and intellectuals. He was accompanied on his trip by two of Luo Zhenyu's collaborators, Jiang Bofu and Zhang Lianyuan.[73] Zhang returned more convinced than ever of the excellence of the Japanese model, but with a deeper understanding of it, as will be noted later. Zhang's experience made it worthwhile for high officials to consult him with even greater frequency. Besides an account of his trip to Japan and a book on the Japanese constitution, on his return Zhang also drafted a constitutional plan for the benefit of the governors-general Zhang Zhidong and Wei Guangdao.[74] They used it in their memorials to the throne, especially the passages where Zhang showed how education served to strengthen the state.

The Japanese character of educational reform in China until 1906 thus owed much to people like Luo Zhenyu, Zhang Jian, Zheng Xiaoxu, Wu Rulun, and those mentioned above. Behind the two or three officials whose names are mentioned in the edicts, they made suggestions and participated in their implementation. Although not professional officials or pure traditional scholars they were able to influence opinion and begin supplanting the regular bureaucracy. Their principal concern was to strengthen the power of the state. In stressing this aspect of Japanese concepts of education, they gained official confidence.

Was Japan the sole source of inspiration for officials and gentry involved in reforming education? Western works were translated, but their number was relatively few and most of them were translated from the Japanese.[75] A large number of books and articles on the West did appear, but the information in these also generally came from the Japanese. Among missionary publications, religious works constituted the majority. The important Western philosophical and political works had indeed been translated and they held a certain fascination for youth[76] and progressive scholars like Cai Yuanpei. Among gentry like Zhang Jian these works aroused an intellectual curiosity which varied according to temperament. However, it was not from these works that the required ideas on practical reform were sought. Neither were they sought from the missionaries or other foreigners residing in China.

Zhang never even considered emulating the missionary schools which were numerous enough in Jiangsu. He completely ignored them and displayed only indifference towards missionaries. When Aurore College split in 1906 he became a patron of the new Chinese establishment without expressing the slightest appreciation of the Jesuits. Except in a case where public order was disturbed by the assassination of a priest, the limited world of the missionary did not interfere with Zhang's own world or that of the gentry and officials with whom Zhang had contact. Proud of their status as scholars, they were not willing to be treated scornfully as heathen. They were suspicious of the missionaries' political motives and considered, justifiably, that the majority of missionary schools were not worthwhile from an intellectual point of view and, since China was seeking the development of material culture, that it was better to look elsewhere. Finally, the missionaries stressed the importance of the individual and not one's duties towards the state: this went against both the gentry's Confucian sensibilities and their ideas of current national needs. One must not be deceived by the treaty port newspapers, which are always cited because they are the most accessible; by the missionary pamphlets; or by biased historiography. An examination of Chinese texts of the time written by those involved in policy-making, shows that missionary influence on educational reform was minimal, at least until 1912.[77] To say that educational reform was implemented as part of a deliberate anti-missionary strategy is perhaps to exaggerate the missionaries' importance among the preoccupations of contemporary Chinese. However, one can cite the grievance expressed by certain American missionaries to their legation: "The reform of education," they remarked, "is blocking the route to our influence."[78] In fact, modern science could henceforth be studied in the Chinese schools.

The West inspired the reformers, but there were several models: that of Anglo-Saxon or French democracy, or that of Russian and German monarchy. Within each model there were several currents; each Chinese thinker learned what he wanted to know, in his own way, from each Western thinker.[79] As a contemporary observer noted, the general tendency of Chinese works published between 1900 and 1905 was to "present what was American, German, or Japanese as the same thing in order to give the Chinese the impression of *Western ideas* as a whole."[80] As for Zhang Jian, he hardly concerned himself with differences of principle among Western nations. He had a general idea of the differences, but his theoretical model remained that of Japan, which had been able to adapt the secret of Western strength to the special conditions of an Asian country. He only sought from the West very specific improvements, that is to say the purchase of machines or the employment of engineers. Western influence on education came entirely via Japan. The normal school at Nantong no doubt had American and French influences, but these were relayed through the Japanese.[81] Occupied by innumerable tasks, Zhang Jian sought efficient results above all else, and it was only when these did not materialize that he looked again to principles. It was thus only at such times that he showed concern for authenticity (text 6). This attitude was often shared among those gentry with whom Zhang had contact. Some were more aware of the theoretical aspects and referred more often to the West.[82] Nevertheless, the model they proposed to adopt remained that of the Japanese monarchy.

In the reform of education the emulation of Japan was therefore the common ground on which gentry and enlightened officials agreed. Due to this common source of inspiration the two groups were able to cooperate. However, behind this apparent harmony there began to appear antagonisms, since the Japanese model did not have the same significance for everyone.

The Aims of the Reformers

The objectives of all the reformers appeared similar because they used the same words, borrowed from a common source. The imperial edicts and the memorials of the high officials stated: "It is necessary to train men of talent since they are indispensable for good administration, and without schools one cannot train men of talent."[83] Zhang Jian entirely agreed with this opinion and he admired "the imperial aim of reforming laws and seeking talent" (text 1). These were also the aims of reformers after 1885. By 1905 the official view had gone beyond this stage: "The establishment of schools is not only to recruit men of talent; the essential aim is to enlarge the people's intelligence by allowing all to have access to a general education and to have the opportunity of acquiring general knowledge and skills."[84] It was necessary "to increase greatly the intelligence of the people."[85] Zhang Jian repeated this idea: "The principal task of the school is to expand the intelligence of the majority of people" (text 2). He thus agreed with the authorities in making education an instrument of national policy. Education fulfilled this role in Japan. Such an idea also existed in the Confucian tradition. However, what was novel was the emphasis on the importance of education proper, which the state had neglected for several centuries. Henceforth, what was considered important was general education for the nation, and not the selection of the most talented individuals.

The content and meaning of the new education were Japanese-inspired and modern. It was a question of creating a "nation" (*guomin*). This term could be found in official edicts[86] as well as in the writings of Zhang Jian or Liang Qichao. What did this term comprise and how was it defined? Opinions differed.

According to the official view, "in the schools loyalty and filial piety must be the foundation of the doctrines that are taught, the traditional rites must form the source of all customs inculcated, and a technical education must be a practical tool to train people to earn a livelihood."[87] In April 1906, in response to several memorials and suggestions put forward in the press, an edict was issued which defined the general aims of education. Education was to train people to "be loyal towards the monarch, to honor Confucius, to cultivate a public spirit, military spirit, and practical spirit."[88] For the authorities, the main ingredient of the nationalism inspired by the schools was a complete loyalty to the monarch, a loyalty that would be useful because of the opportunity for subjects to acquire at the same time certain military, industrial, commercial, and agricultural skills. The idea of the nation gained prominence among officials in relation to the internal dangers of disunity and as a reaction against various forces that represented new ideas, individualism, and a localism that supported a still-primitive, compartmentalized economy. The aim was to restore the traditional unity centered on the emperor and to consolidate it so that all obstacles would be overcome. This loyalty towards the monarch was based entirely on precepts of traditional morality rather than any new idea of the *patrie* or the state. However, it would allow the monarch to avail himself of modern developments such as the consolidation of military power and of the economy. As in Japan, "the people and the monarch would form one body"[89] but the strength of this unity would profit only the monarch. Such was the idea of the nation that was to be produced in the new schools. As far as the government was concerned, educational reform was therefore an instrument of political stability.

In the minds of gentry like Zhang Jian, the idea of the nation was developed above all else in relation to external dangers:

> Today, we Chinese, descendants of the glorious Yellow Emperor, of Yao and Shun, have become backward and lethargic; we are in a humiliating position and we have almost reached the stage where we are considered as slaves. Should we not be ashamed of this? Without seeking knowledge we will have nothing with which to wash away this shame. Without offering a national education, we will have no one to seek for knowledge.[90]

In developing education, Zhang Jian hoped to make the nation more capable of resisting foreign invaders with the tenacity and courage of the Filipinos.[91] This awareness of the threat of imperialism was very acute among reform followers in the opening years of the twentieth century, even more acute than among revolutionaries, who had fewer material interests to defend.[92] In China, someone like Luo Zhenyu could write that "by developing education, thirty years from now China will be the strongest country in Asia." She would thus escape the fate that had befallen India, Poland, and the Jews.[93] Exiled in Japan, Liang Qichao expressed the same fears with regard to the foreign menace and he placed his confidence in education, "the instrument with which to form the nation."[94] The nation that the reformers called for would be united around the monarch, but its strength would come from the people who, after reaching a certain cultural level, would understand the needs of the nation and would be capable of meeting them. The government and officials would no longer be the only ones to decide on and manage public affairs. For Zhang Jian and the enlightened gentry, therefore, educational reform was an instrument of political change.

Did Zhang Jian have any original ideas on this subject? From 1900 to 1906 Kang Youwei and, especially, Liang Qichao were very active in Japan. They gathered around them a large number of young Chinese who had come there to study, and rallied to their cause a number of overseas Chinese. Liang outlined his program in *Qingyibao* [China discussion] until December 1901 and then, from February 1902, in *Xinmin congbao* [New people's miscellany]. These publications were secretly distributed within China where they found a certain audience. Later, when Liang had become an authority, he spread, or had others spread, the theory that his publications had played a determining role in the reformist movement within China. In any event, it does not seem that Zhang Jian had ever read them.[95] It is also interesting to note that *Qingyibao* only devoted articles to education in its last issues, and that the main points on education developed in this journal and *Xinmin congbao* had already been expressed in *Jiaoyu shijie* edited by Luo Zhenyu. Sometimes one even has the impression that it was simply plagiarism.[96] It is true that similarities could have arisen from the use of common Japanese sources; yet several articles in Liang's journals criticized opinions expressed by the Japanese. It is also a fact, moreover, that Liang Qichao showed this renewed interest in education exactly at the time when Luo Zhenyu made his trip to Japan. This coincidence merits emphasis since it is very likely that Luo, who had been well acquainted with Liang between 1895 and 1898, saw Liang again on the occasion of his visit.[97] Under these circumstances, far from receiving their inspiration from Liang Qichao, the reformers within China served as Liang's mentors. More involved in public affairs and more informed on concrete problems, they had been, in any case, the first to state precisely the conditions in which education was to serve the policy of political change.

According to Zhang Jian, educational reform was above all closely linked with the idea of local autonomy (*difang zizhi*). "As the state is going to widely extend the benefits of education in the country, the gentry hope for local autonomy" (text 2). What Zhang meant by local autonomy was the right of the gentry to participate in the administration of their district. In practice, "local autonomy" had existed in China for a long time. However, it had only gained substance as a political doctrine immediately following the Boxer rebellion, drawing its content from Japanese theory and practice, and to a lesser degree from those of Europe and America. It was a question, then, of legally restricting the power of the bureaucracy. The idea was raised in the *Yong shu* of Chen Chi in 1893; it was taken up again in the memorials of Kang Youwei in 1898; the term itself (*difang zizhi*) only appeared, it seems, after the Hundred Days Reform.[98] Zhang Jian started to use it in 1901.

Until 1903, local autonomy seemed to Zhang the most appropriate way to guarantee the expansion of his enterprises under bureaucratic protection, and gradually to reform the state while awaiting a constitution sometime in the distant future. For Zhang, industry and education were the bases of local autonomy. The schools had a special importance: they were to train the future leaders of local autonomy. Their management was henceforth to be taken out of the hands of the magistrate (texts 2 and 3). During these years Zhang was more preoccupied with education than with industry, to which he had already given considerable encouragement. However, during his trip to Japan in 1903 he discovered that the political reform of the state by means of a constitution was the necessary precondition for local autonomy.

After 1904 the establishment of a constitution became Zhang's principal concern. He contrasted Japan's progress with the backwardness of China: "In China," he remarked, "people have their heads in the sand. It is not that the Chinese are any different, but that China is a despotism while Japan is a constitutional state. It is the political situation in China that is wrong. Yet no one says this to the emperor."[99] From this time on the significance of local autonomy underwent a change; it would no longer be a political strategy, a preparation for a constitutional regime, but rather an advanced social and economic system which would be established as a result of the transformation of the political structure. Zhang Jian's commitment to constitutionalism did not prevent him from continuing to argue for local autonomy and to increase the number of his enterprises, schools, and charitable institutions (texts 2 and 7). He knew that local autonomy could not fully expand without a constitution, but hoped to hasten its arrival.

For Zhang Jian, local autonomy took the place that democracy held among radical thinkers as the objective that had to be achieved by political evolution. As an ideal, it was inferior to that of democracy since it did not assume political equality. The gentry would be the sole holders of power. Yet in a sense this local autonomy went further than the purely political democracy dreamed of by the majority of liberals before 1906. It depended on economic progress and a certain social development which would, with the sanction of law, designate the new beneficiaries of political rights. In Zhang's conception, the masters of the state would be neither the people nor the traditional elite, but the modern elite, which had proved itself by contributing to the material prosperity of the country. Zhang protested against those men of talent who still dreamed of an official career. "It is no longer necessary to be an official" he declared in front of his friends, "it is in industry and education that one must make a career."[100] Such a statement indicated the beginnings of a capitalist philosophy.

With this new plan, politics, economic enterprises, and education had, theoretically, equal importance. Zhang Jian occupied himself more with politics after 1904-05 because there was everything to do in this domain: he became one of the leaders of the constitutional movement. Education was on the same level as industry. By "raising the level of the people" Zhang hoped to overcome the opposition of conservatives to a constitutional regime, to provide technicians for industry, and hence to speed up the advent of local autonomy.[101] Education would therefore be not only an instrument of political evolution but also of economic and social evolution.

Zhang's position was different from that of other reform followers. Up to the beginning of 1907 the latter retained the point of view that Zhang had abandoned in 1904, namely that it was necessary to develop education in order to create local autonomy before a constitution could be established. After 1907 they adopted the same attitude as Zhang Jian: a constitution was to be the priority.[102] After this time their idea of local autonomy became more liberal. They were concerned with political equality but less attentive to economic and social problems than Zhang Jian. As a result, education, for the majority of them, was restricted to the role of an accelerator of political evolution. This difference had to do with the entrepreneurial activities and realistic temperament of Zhang Jian. It was reflected in certain peculiarities in the Nantong schools, as will be seen later on.

In any event, as far as education was concerned the views of the government and those of the reformers were, in reality, contradictory; education was an instrument of stability for the former and an instrument of change for the latter. This contradiction produced little antagonism until 1906, since the gentry were still enthusiastic about their success, full of hope, and afraid of the revolutionaries.[103]

The question of the school curriculum might have caused dispute, but it was settled without too much fuss. Zhang Baixi's plan had been too "Western" for either camp, and they agreed on increasing the proportion of "Chinese knowledge" in the curriculum.

Yet one must be careful in interpreting this fact. For the conservatives, "Chinese knowledge" meant indoctrination in the Confucian classics which would preserve traditional ideology and the moral foundations of absolutism. Officials would continue to be trained according to traditional norms. For enlightened officials like Zhang Zhidong, the "restoration" or the "preservation of the past" (*fugu, cungu*) also meant upholding traditional morals and policy, but he also added a certain nationalist concern for preserving Chinese authenticity. This concern was even more evident among the reforming gentry. Many of them were very fearful of the "denationalizing" effects of modern education: through force of circumstance, China was obliged to employ foreign teachers; many of the courses were not given in Chinese; textbooks were translations of foreign materials; some students returning from abroad were incapable of reading or writing their own language; and the educational subject-matter itself was a series of implicit criticisms of "backward" China. These fears for the future of the national identity[104] were acompanied by the fear that China would lose her "educational rights" (*jiaoyu zhiquan*):

> The Americans say that Chinese finances are in the hands of the English, Chinese military affairs are in the hands of the Germans, and that they, the Americans, do not want to let education escape from them. They are secretly carrying out their plot of pillage; if we do not destroy this plot, they will fill their sack and take it away. If we tolerate this situation, they will unfurl their wings and fly away and China will never recover the men of talent that are trained in the schools.[105]

This is the problem of the "brain drain," familiar to all countries in the process of development.[106] The text is prophetic.

In order to combat these dangers, the reformers suggested the propagation of what they called "national knowledge"[107] (*guoxue*) which comprised three aspects: ideology,[108] language, and history. It would be destined to "preserve the national essence (*guocui*) and to develop patriotism," and was advocated in opposition to the "classical knowledge" (*jingxue*) extolled by Zhang Zhidong and many high officials in the government.[109] This "classical knowledge," according to its detractors, was merely the passive cult of a Confucianism distorted by commentators for the sake of unscrupulous monarchs and would be incapable of awakening the national conscience.

The reforming gentry were therefore not fooled as to the real intentions of the government when, in 1904, it increased the amount of time in the curriculum devoted to the classics. However, as far as possible, they used this ruling to their own advantage (text 3). At the Nantong Normal School, the time spent on the classics was devoted to a study of the original texts and to the most revolutionary commentators such as Gu Yanwu, Wang Fuzhi, and Huang Zongxi. Neo-Confucianism was ignored. Study of the classics was not to be a question of recitation or scholarship but rather of reflection.[110] At the primary school Zhang ordered the teaching of moral training but not the classics. Zhang also attached importance to the written language (*guowen*) because at this time it remained the most suitable method of communication throughout the country and because it would uphold the "national essence."[111] The Confucian past represented for Zhang Jian and his friends what the Roman republic had represented for the Jacobins. Neither was thinking of a return to slavery; they were simply searching for a pure and authentic ideal.[112] This explains the use of quotations from the classics with which Zhang adorned his writings. Certainly, this was the common hallmark of a scholar, but Zhang only drew from "authentic" texts. The enlightened gentry therefore accommodated themselves to the ruling on the classics as laid down in the 1906 curriculum. If they had cause to regret that the teaching of political subjects had been much reduced, they could at least be satisfied with the introduction of technical subjects and the development of a system of technical schools.

Yet from 1905 onwards, especially, clashes between the authorities and the gentry became more frequent. The gentry had the impression that despite its fine words the government was not fully supporting their efforts to reform education. They therefore decided to form organizations of their own: thus in October 1905 the Jiangsu Education Association was founded (texts 3 and 4). The establishment of a new organ specializing in education was the occasion of heated dispute (text 3). With the beginnings of the constitutional movement, collaboration between the reformers and the court ceased to be harmonious. The aims of both sides became increasingly divergent. The government attempted to recapture the prerogatives that the gentry had arrogated to themselves in practice, while the gentry attempted to extend them and to have them legalized. They made use of education as a base of opposition.

Nevertheless, this opposition still remained an "opposition faithful to the emperor." It was limited to "warning" and "imploring" and did not rule out a certain collaboration; it was not subversive. But would the gentry's action run the risk of being overtaken by other, more dangerous, antagonisms that were caused by educational reform?

CHAPTER III

Opposition, 1907-12

Educational reform, in the first years, had been accomplished by the joint effort of government, officials, and gentry. It had seemed to be a source of unity. However, between 1907 and 1912 educational reform became a source of division among the different groups, within each group, and between these groups and the rest of the population. Aspects of this development are shown in the disputes between Zhang Jian and the authorities, the students, and other elements of the provincial elite.

Education, the Arm of the Moderate Opposition

In the hands of the enlightened gentry, modern education became an instrument of opposition which was at once ideological and practical. In the domain of ideas, the pursuit of educational reform was now subordinated to the question of political reform. However, the subject continued to be raised frequently in the memorials addressed to the throne by the supporters of a constitution. In fact, after 1906 the constitutional movement developed rapidly. Economic progress increased the number of its adherents and its material strength. The number of industrial enterprises increased from 15,500 in 1907 to 20,749 in 1912; that of commercial companies from 620 to 977 (1,171 if branch companies are included).[1] From 1905 to 1911, the capital invested in national industry nearly trebled.[2] The holders of this new wealth appeared more and more like a bourgeoisie. In Jiangsu, this rapid growth was particularly noticeable: in the cotton industry the number of factories increased from nine in 1896 to twenty-three in 1911 and totalled 997,238 spindles, that is to say 74 percent of the national total.[3] All

59

kinds of enterprises were created which had effects that went beyond
district and provincial boundaries. Zhang Jian played an important
role in this economic expansion. In 1907 he founded a second cotton
mill, Dasheng No. 2. With the establishment of this mill, Zhang
owned 5 percent of the spindles in the country. He developed a complete economic system (text 7) which, in 1911, grouped twenty
enterprises under the name of the Industrial Company of Nantong.[4]
It included metallurgical, transport, chemical, foodstuff, and
agricultural enterprises. The businesses in which Zhang was
involved represented a capital of nearly six million *taels*.[5] Their
economic influence extended as far as Shanghai, Xuzhou, Haizhou,
and Suzhou, bringing Zhang into close contact with men of varied
business interests like Li Houyou and with the most active
entrepreneurs at the provincial level like Xu Dinglin and Sha
Yuanbing. Zhang also tapped the capital of his scholar friends for his
modern enterprises; thus Tang Shouqian, Shen Zipei, Zhao
Fengchang, and Zheng Xiaoxu all contributed money to Zhang's
enterprises, as well as to other business interests.[6] This, moreover,
was a general tendency after 1906. All those gentry who had been
supporters of reform since 1895 now had industrial interests.
Besides those referred to above, among Zhang's acquaintances, Ma
Liang had invested in a flour-mill and a silk-manufacturing
enterprise, Xiong Xiling in the production of porcelain, and Zhang
Yuanji, Lei Fen, and Chen Sanli in railways, in which all the others
had an interest as well.[7]

On two occasions Zhang was tempted to enlarge his interests
even further by relying on Western capital.[8] The attempts did not
materialize, partly because of circumstances at the time, but also
because Zhang hesitated at the prospect of committing a "betrayal."
In fact, concerned with protecting their new economic interests, the
modern gentry were becoming increasingly sensitive to foreign
competition. An economic nationalism was added to their political
nationalism and influenced their constitutional demands; at the same
time their material strength was becoming evident to the government.

The boycott of 1905 gave the new gentry a new awareness of
themselves. During a period of several months, merchants, gentry,
students, and dock workers united to boycott American goods in
reprisal against the anti-Chinese nature of American immigration
laws and the mistreatment suffered by the Chinese in the United
States. The demonstrators also lodged their protests with the
Chinese authorities and the American government.[9] The movement

was led by the recently created chambers of commerce and by the gentry. Its leaders were, like Zhang Jian, individuals who had links with both the traditional elite and with commercial circles.[10] Although coming from different backgrounds, these people became aware of their common interests and their collective strength. The merchants, perceiving the external threat, now took into account the need for economic development accompanied by a political will. From this time on they supported the constitutional demands already formulated by the gentry. The gentry themselves showed a more active concern with economic problems. In education, a pre-occupation with professional training was a manifestation of this development: two social groups-an already distinct merchant bourgeoisie and a gentry bourgeoisie that was gradually emerging from among the traditional elite-coming together with the tendency to form one class, united at first by material interests.

The 1905 boycott therefore swelled the ranks of the constitutionalists and proved that they were capable of successfully opposing the foreigner. They did not neglect to use this advantage in their opposition to court policy up until 1911, while Japan and the other powers quarrelled over the annexation of Manchuria and the financial monopoly of the railways.

Economic strength and an aggressive nationalism were not the only elements that reinforced the position of the constitutionalists vis-à-vis the government. The main element during the last years of the monarchy was without doubt the fact that the constitutional movement presented itself as an alternative to revolution (end of text 4). On 20 August 1905, Sun Yat-sen established in Tokyo a new party, the Tongmenghui (Alliance league), uniting several societies and revolutionary groups that up until then had acted independently. Through its organ *Minbao* [People's report], the Tongmenghui had defined a program, the "three principles of the people," which called for the overthrow of the Manchus, the establishment of a democratic government, and a policy of nationalization. From 1905 to 1906 *Minbao* conducted a fierce polemic against the constitutional ideas expressed by Liang Qichao in *Xinmin congbao*, thus clarifying the doctrinal positions of the two groups, which were still frequently thought of as one united bloc by the government and public. The constitutionalists lost some support among the young but gained increasing credit with the government as the danger of revolution became more serious. From 1906 to 1908, the Tongmenghui organized or supported seven attempts at armed uprising in Hunan, Guangdong, Guangxi, Yunnan, and Anhui,[11] while individual revolutionaries indulged in acts of terrorism.[12]

The government was forced to make concessions. In January 1906 two missions were sent to fourteen countries in order to study foreign political, economic, and social institutions.[13] On their return, an edict of 1 September announced the preparation of a constitution.[14] Immediately afterwards, the Public Association to Prepare for the Establishment of a Constitution was founded in Shanghai. On 16 December 1906, Zhang Jian and Tang Shouqian were elected vice-presidents, while their friend Zheng Xiaoxu became president. The association included among its members all the important figures of Shanghai commerce and the provincial elite.[15] Associations of this kind mushroomed everywhere under different names: the Public Association for a Constitutional Government (Xianzheng gonghui) in Hunan, and the Association for Local Autonomy in Guangdong.[16] They even appeared in prefectures of secondary importance, such as Huai'an.[17]

These groups harassed magistrates with their memorials. In order to channel their activities, the government became converted to the idea of local autonomy. It was implemented first in Fengtian and Zhili under bureaucratic supervision.[18] In October 1907, the government announced the creation of provincial assemblies (ziyiju) which did not actually meet until 1909. In December 1908, in accordance with the nine-year preparation program for a constitution, regulations on city, town, and village (xiang) assemblies were promulgated. One year later regulations were issued on prefectural, subprefectural, and district assemblies.[19] The local councils thus instituted had legislative power concerning education. Theoretically, this was an important victory for the gentry, who now became the principal beneficiaries of the new system.

However, in practice, the authorities attempted to regain what they had conceded in principle. Already, in 1906, the regulations on education associations stipulated that they were established in order "to assist administration." When the local councils were created it was clearly specified that their decisions on education could not contravene those of the minister of education without the latter's consent, and that they were to be limited to local affairs. Furthermore, finances remained under the control of the magistrate and the elected representatives could only make suggestions. As a result of the administrative system then in force, the magistrate's management of finances was more closely supervised by the central government. In practice, by agreeing to legalize the participation of gentry in public affairs the court had increased the centralization of power, whereby it hoped to restore its authority. The gentry councils served as a counterweight to provincial officials, whose independence had alarmed the monarchy. The differences that would inevitably arise in the course of a now obligatory collaboration were to be settled, to its advantage, by the central government. The risk of collusion between bureaucrats and gentry was averted by a rapid turnover in the appointment of officials.[20]

The enlightened gentry were not fooled by this scheme. Educational reform had served as a theoretical justification to obtain local autonomy. They made use of it in a practical way to enlarge their field of action.

The education associations were the organs through which the gentry were able to exert their influence. Texts 4 and 5 describe certain aspects of the organization and role of the Jiangsu Education Association. Not all associations were as powerful as the Jiangsu one, but many of its features can be considered representative. These associations appeared at different times.[21] There were 506 education associations in 1908 comprising 37,118 members, and 723 in 1909 with 48,432 members. In 1909 Jiangsu had 55 with 8,593 members; three years later it had 115.[22] The former study societies (xuehui)[23] often formed the foundation of the education associations, thereby determining their social composition, which official regulations later ratified. Thus, the recruitment of members for the education associations had greater social and political significance than recruitment for the chambers of commerce that the former somewhat resembled. In fact, enlistment was not related to professional qualifications. Teachers even formed a minority among association members. What was represented was a certain social group, ranging from scholar-officials to merchants. Members were noted for their learning and wealth, their abilities as administrators, and the collective responsibilities which they undertook. The group was an aristocracy of wealth and ability determined to compel the bureaucracy to implement reforms. The Jiangsu Education Association and the Association to Prepare for the Establishment of a Constitution, over which Zhang Jian presided, comprised the same people: Ma Liang, Lei Fen, Meng Sen, Tang Shouqian, Meng Zhaochang, and Huang Yanpei; there were others who were also members of the Shanghai Chamber of Commerce: Xu Dinglin, Sha Yuanbing, and Shen Xiejun.[24]

The finances for the education associations came from official subsidies and, above all, from members' subscriptions and contributions.[25] The associations conducted a legal struggle against bureaucratic tyranny (text 5)[26] and developed certain aspects of education which the authorities either ignored or considered dangerous, such as the study of law,[27] short-term teacher training, and workers' education. In Jiangsu, the education association had its own inspectors who toured the schools. The association published their reports and organized conferences to discuss ways of improving education.[28] It was the Jiangsu Education Association that prepared proposals on educational laws and budgets for the provincial assembly, proposals which were the source of epic struggles between the assembly and the governor-general after 1909.[29] It directly approached the ministry to have the assembly's powers expanded. A similar situation arose in many other provinces where the members of education associations and provincial assemblies were often the same people, concerned with thoroughly exploiting the powers over education accorded to the assemblies.[30] The severity of the disputes depended on the personalities of the officials. In Jiangsu, the relationship between officials and provincial assemblies and associations, which had been friendly enough under the aegis of the competent and sufficiently liberal Duan Fang, became increasingly acrimonious under Duan's successors. The social importance of the education associations was recognized by the authorities: thus Yuan Shikai entrusted the Tianjin Education Association with the duty of choosing half of the members of the district consultative council in 1907.[31]

Due to fear or hostility, the majority of officials attempted to limit the political influence of the associations, but this did not prevent them from becoming increasingly bolder. In March 1910 the Jiangsu Education Association proposed to the other provincial associations that a joint delegation be sent to Beijing in order to support the petitioners from provincial assemblies who were demanding the immediate convocation of a parliament.[32] The delegation collected numerous signatures for a petition that was later submitted to the throne. In May 1911 the Jiangsu association organized a "national conference of education associations" at Shanghai to arrange for common action. Eleven provinces responded to the appeal and they established a new organ, the National Federation of Education Associations, which was to meet once every year.[33] The resolutions adopted at the conference were conveyed to local educators; those which involved general principles were submitted to the Ministry of Education. They are interesting because they define the attitudes and objectives of the education associations on the eve of the revolution. The resolutions called for: (1) the promulgation of the principle of a national military education (*junguomin jiaoyu zhuyi*), which meant having military drill and weapons training in all schools, including private ones; (2) the teaching of a uniform "national language" from primary school onwards, involving the simplification of characters and the introduction of a phonetic script;[34] (3) the abolition of official degree-titles awarded to school graduates; (4) the reform of primary education: compulsory manual activities, the complete elimination of the classics, coeducation until the age of ten, and more short-term schools for the education of children from poor families and of adults; and (5) the reform of higher education. It was noted that higher education was relatively overdeveloped, given the lack of secondary schools and the lack of opportunities for graduates. It was proposed to reduce the literary departments by combining the departments of classics and literature, and those of commerce and law; science departments were to remain as before. It was also proposed that the status of university be lowered to that of a higher-level school, thereby shortening the study period.

The outstanding feature of these propositions was the desire they represented for national unity and social and economic development.

The Ministry of Education responded by convening in Beijing, from 15 July to 3 August 1911, a central committee of education composed of officials and people especially appointed by the administration.[35] Despite bureaucratic pressure, the committee sided with the positions adopted at Shanghai. An eyewitness reported that during the debates two parties were opposed to one another, "those of the court and those outside the court" (*chao ye*).[36] Those outside the court (i.e., those not connected with officialdom) had to accept the rejection of weapons training in the schools and to give up any hopes for higher education reform. Although they carried the day with the resolution on coeducation, the Ministry of Education chose to ignore it. On the other hand, the ministry was obliged to agree to the reduction of time devoted to the classics and the abolition of official degree titles that officials had defended so energetically "to preserve sinecures for their children." The ministry also had to recognize the principle of compulsory education financed by state resources, which would henceforth be subject to the control of the gentry in their capacity as members of the parliament and provincial assemblies.[37] Objectively, the gentry had therefore gained some important victories; the struggle they had so patiently conducted over each concrete problem at the local level concluded with a victory on their propositions at the national level. However, they were convinced that more coordinated action would have won them even greater concessions. Thus, after the end of the committee meetings, Zhang Jian, Zhang Yuanji, and other progressive individuals took the initiative in immediately creating unofficial organs to ensure long-term coordination of policy: the National Federation of Normal Schools and the Chinese Society of Education.[38] The latter, whose membership was open to all, survived the 1911 Revolution and played an important role under the Republic. This clearly showed that it was established both to resist absolutism and to ensure liberal gentry domination over the new education at the national level.

At once the cause and result of this manipulation of education as a weapon of opposition, the number of schools increased considerably from 1907 to 1911. This growth is shown in table 4 (see pages 68-69). For Nantong and Jiangsu as a whole, the 1912 figures are drawn from the provincial report on education; they most certainly include the 30 to 35 percent of the traditional primary schools that the Jiangsu Education Association intended to modernize. (See the figures given by Zhang Jian for Nantong in 1911, text 7.) This large increase in comparison to the 1909 figures was not due solely to the building of new schools. The fall in the national total during the same period is explained by the closure or destruction of many schools during the revolution. On the other hand, those schools that survived were able to expand.

These figures are not meant to give a completely accurate picture, since the nature of the sources does not permit this. However, they do indicate the extent of the increase. The role of the gentry is particularly noticeable; the development of schools depended on their initiative and resources. In Nantong all the schools were dependent on them and the more advanced position of Jiangsu in relation to other provinces was due to gentry initiative. It should also be noted that in the area of primary education Nantong allowed itself to be overtaken by wealthier districts. By 1912 Nantong was no higher than eleventh place as far as the number of primary schools was concerned. However, for secondary and vocational education Nantong district was in third place, surpassed only by Shanghai and Wuxi-the two large industrial centers of the province.[39] This was brought about by the efforts of Zhang Jian, who established and personally directed the eight secondary and vocational schools in Nantong (text 9).

In order to have a clearer understanding of the significance of modern educational development during the last years of the monarchy, it would be necessary to evaluate the financial effort that sustained it. The gross national product and the revenue of each province and district would have to be calculated, after which the amount invested in education, and in what form, would have to be determined. The sources available do not permit this. One can, however, focus on some aspects of the problem. Text 3 gives some indication of the educational budget for Nantong during the first years of the reform. They are of particular interest since there exist few statistics on educational budgets for the rest of the country during this period. For subsequent years the figures can be completed with the aid of yearly official estimates which are, unfortunately, sporadic.

Table 5 shows the continuous growth in educational expenditures (see page 70). The amount spent in Nantong was, at the beginning, the highest in the province in proportion to its population, but tended to become more proportional later on. However, the distribution of funds according to the different levels of education favored secondary and specialized education. This explains the characteristic of Nantong schools noted earlier: nothing exceptional at the primary level, but an advanced position at higher levels.

In the country as a whole, including Nantong, investment in education exceeded that in industry, as shown in table 6 (see page 71). Did traditional influences make the gentry more attracted to education, or did they consider education a more profitable long-term enterprise? Both explanations are valid, but the latter more for political than economic reasons. Educational investment was not high in absolute terms, but it has to be remembered that in the subsistence economy which still prevailed the Chinese people had barely enough to maintain a livelihood; the excess funds available were limited, despite the size of the country.[40]

How, then, are the percentages given in table 7 (page 71) to be interpreted? They show that at the provincial level funds could not be mobilized without the aid of government. It should also be noted that 1907 and 1908 were famine years which adversely affected private wealth. Nevertheless, the percentage of public funds in the financing of education remained lower in the richer, more industrialized regions such as Suzhou than in a predominantly agricultural region like Jiangning. Public investment in 1909 is low for several reasons. Although the amount of public funds invested in education did in fact increase, with the end of the agricultural crisis

TABLE 4: PERCENTAGE OF PRIVATELY FUNDED SCHOOLS

		Nantong District		Jiangsu Province		National Total	
		Total	Privately Funded (%)	Total	Privately Funded (%)	Total	Privately Funded (%)
1907	Schools	56	100	1,615	72	35,787	67
	Pupils	1,732	100	55,779		1,006,743	
1908	Schools	64	100	1,870	79	42,424	70
	Pupils	2,203	100	66,215		1,278,242	
1909	Schools	74	100	2,135	80	101,382	72
	Pupils	3,058	100	82,166		1,573,740	
1912	Schools	194	20	5,343	18	87,272	
	Pupils	7,892	19	236,351	18	2,933,387	

Note: Until 1912 the government distinguished between officials schools, managed and maintained by the state (from provincial and central government funds); public schools, managed and maintained by local communities; and private schools, managed and maintained by individuals. The last two categories of schools could receive government subsidies. In fact, public schools, which for the most part were district schools, often functioned with the aid of government revenues (i.e., a proportion of the funds designed for the provincial or central government treasury, a proportion of district government funds, or locally imposed special taxes). Nevertheless, public and private schools essentially depended on local notables. They have been classed as one category in order to measure the ground gained by local notables vis-à-vis the government bureaucracy. The 1912 figures adopted the new classification instituted by the law of 6 November: public schools, established by people in public positions, and private schools, established by private individuals. Only this second category was included, to the exclusion of the former public schools. This explains the apparent reduction in the percentage of establishments controlled by local notables. In fact, the proportion increased since in the first year of the Republic the notables often filled the gap left by a near bankrupt administration.

Sources: *Jiaoyu tongji tubiao*, 1907, 1908, 1909, 1915; *Jiangsu sheng jiaoyu xingzheng baogaoshu*, I, 251–66; "*Jingwai xuewu baogao*," *Xuebu guanbao* 3, no. 82 (XT1/1 February): 147–61.

TABLE 5: EXPENDITURES FOR MODERN EDUCATION

	Wholesale Price Index (1913=100)	National Total			Jiangsu			Nantong		
		Expenditures Mexican $	Actual Fluctuation (1913 $)[b]	Index	Expenditures Mexican $	Actual Fluctuation (1913 $)[b]	Index	Expenditures Mexican $	Actual Fluctuation (1913 $)[b]	Index
1907	104	24,079,374[c]	23,116,199	82	26,585,588[c]	2,553,244	86	145,327[c]	139,513	100.4
1908	110	29,182,208[d]	27,263,987	97	2,845,555[d]	2,560,999	86	134,127[d]	120,714	94
1909	111	36,910,906[e]	33,219,816	119.1	4,651,629[e]	4,186,466	141.4			
1912	106	29,667,803[f]	27,887,734	100	3,148,288	2,959,390	100	147,802[g]	138,903	100

[a] R. Cheng, *The Financing of Public Education in China*, 48.

[b] Based on the value of the 1913 dollar given by R. Cheng for each year shown (op. cit., 48).

[c] *Jiaoyu tongji tubiao*, 1907.

[d] Ibid., 1908.

[e] Ibid., 1909.

[f] Ibid., 1915, I/100, II/184.

[g] *Jiangsu sheng jiaoyu xingzheng baogaoshu*, I/259–65.

TABLE 6: COMPARISON OF EDUCATIONAL INVESTMENT,
INDUSTRIAL INVESTMENT, AND NATIONAL BUDGET (IN 1913 $)

	National Expenditures on Education (Public and Private)	Annual Capital Investment in Mines and Industry (by the State and Private Individuals)[a]	Estimated State Revenue (in Millions)[b]
1907	23,116,199	13,990,121	360 − 430
1908	27,263,987	20,274,604	360 − 430
1909	33,219,816	8,952,528	360 − 430

[a]Based on Yan Zhongping, *Tongji ziliao*, 93.
[b]Based on *China Mission Yearbook*, 1913, 307-8.

TABLE 7: EDUCATIONAL EXPENDITURES AS A
PERCENTAGE OF GOVERNMENT REVENUE

	Jiangsu Province	Region of Suzhou[a]	Region of Nanking[b]	Nantong
1907	50	39	61	10
1908	50	45	61	21
1909	28	19	37	23

[a]Also called Jiangsu.
[b]Also called Jiangning.

Source: *Jiaoyu tongji tubiao*, 1907, 1908, 1909 (Jiangsu, Jiangning).

private investment regained its dominant position. Another reason is that in the enthusiasm of the constitutional movement, the gentry made extra efforts to invest in education in order to weaken the bureaucratic control that accompanied public investment in their schools. Unfortunately, a lack of sources prevents us from observing whether this tendency persisted until 1911. It is likely that with the establishment of provincial assemblies, which gave the gentry a certain control over the bureaucracy, the proportion of public funds in the financing of education increased rather than decreased.[41] In any event, this is what happened in Nantong by means of the district council which was functioning from 1908, even before the promulgation of the official regulations. Skillfully managed by Zhang Jian, this council was able to claim public funds without an increase in official control. During this period, the meaning of the financial link which connected many public and private schools to the state changed. In the beginning, this link signified dependence; later it was the expression of gentry strength vis-à-vis the bureaucracy. Nevertheless, it continued to oblige the gentry to adopt a certain caution; this fact partly explains the double game played by the moderate local elite-on the one hand, they harassed the government, but on the other they cooperated with liberal-minded officials in order to impose upon the people a share of the financial burden for the reforms of which they were the principal beneficiaries.

Could it have been otherwise? Table 8 shows that more than half of the educational funds for Nantong came from industry and commerce.[42] A similar situation existed in other economically advanced districts. Yet neither industry nor commerce was sufficiently developed to meet all the financial needs of education. The resources that Zhang could take from his enterprises for education had reached their limit.[43] Extra funds had to be raised from agriculture, which meant that the peasants had to contribute in some way to the expenses without receiving any tangible returns. This development constituted a danger. Was there not a risk that educational reform, which the gentry had exploited with success to secure power, would be turned against them?

TABLE 8: FUNDING OF EDUCATION IN NANTONG, 1907

Industrial profits	46%	Most to the normal school and attached primary school
Agricultural profits	2	
Commercial profits	1.5	From rental income and merchants' contributions
	2.5	From officially imposed commercial taxes, especially the *lijin*
Undetermined	48	Included are contributions from unknown benefactors, tuition fees, and surcharges added to unspecified taxes

Source: Based on the investigations of each school in "*Jingwai xuewu baogao*" [Report on education in the provinces], *Xuebu guanbao* 3, no. 82: 147–61.

Educational Reform, a Source of Division

Educational development itself bred the intellectual and social origins of a many-faceted opposition.

In many places, the creation of modern schools aroused the anger of the people. In certain cases the reasons were due to religious or superstitious feelings; for example, if a school was opened in a temple the peasants, angered by this sacrilege, would invade the premises, destroying school equipment and assaulting or killing the teacher as well as the pupils. Although not always the case, the protesters were often led by monks who claimed that their temples had been pillaged, or by reactionary gentry.[44] Many rural gentry were hostile to the modern features of the schools. Normally, they resorted to obstruction or passive resistance, but when the occasion presented itself, they did not hesitate to exploit popular discontent.[45] This discontent exploded into violence with each subsistence crisis. Although it could have a religious motif, in general this discontent focused on the schools simply because new taxes had been levied in order to maintain them. These taxes assumed various forms: a special school tax (xuejuan); increases of the lijin or of the collection charges for the land tax and grain tribute. In times of scarcity the peasants attributed the blame for the high cost of food to these extra charges. The waves of school destruction coincided precisely with periods of famine: 1906 in Jiangsu, 1907 in Zhejiang, and 1910 in both of these provinces.[46] In 1910 the schools suffered the greatest damage because the famine of that year coincided with a new census that made a credulous population fear the worst.[47] Violence extended throughout the entire country. In Jiangsu the violence was such that the education association requested that the governor-general use soldiers to protect the schools. The request was granted.[48] Order was reestablished, despite some acts of arson in the spring of 1911. However, the schools once again became a target of peasant hostility during the revolution,[49] when the authorities again had cause to resort to military protection.

By itself, modern education did not provide the means for the general populace to improve its livelihood. The numerical increase of schools noted earlier did not signify an increase in the number of educated people.

During the course of the nineteenth century, in the wake of population growth, internal rebellions, and general impoverishment, the cultural level of the countryside declined.[50] It is very likely that during the initial period of educational reform this decline continued.[51] Traditional schools were closed and tuition fees in the new schools were beyond the financial reach of many families accustomed to having their children educated (text 9). In Nantong, in 1907, there were only five or six free schools, and they could only accept about one hundred pupils. Elsewhere, tuition fees for elementary schools amounted to two to six dollars per year in addition to a minimum of ten dollars for midday meals. This was approximately double the cost of traditional education.[52] In the schools established by Zhang Jian fees were even higher, as text 9 demonstrates.[53] Destruction and student strikes often obliged the new schools to close temporarily. Finally, the educational subject-matter clashed with traditional practices and was even less relevant than before to the needs of the rural population (text 6). One is tempted to consider what happened in China to be the same phenomenon that had occurred in Japan and India during the introduction of Western-style education. In Japan the decrease in the literacy rate only lasted a few years, during which time the temple schools (terakoya), the mainstay of traditional education, were poorly integrated into the new system.[54] In India, the quantitative decline lasted much longer; the literacy rate was, from the beginning, lower than in Japan, and India became a colony. School attendance only reached the level it had attained at the beginning of the nineteenth century after 1919, when the responsibility for education was "transferred" to elected provincial councils.[55] The introduction of Western-style education was accomplished by completely abandoning the traditional system of native schools. Such a process had greatly hindered progress in India. In China, also, there was little continuity; despite some efforts (text 3) the academies only served as buildings. The new primary schools drained resources that could have been used to maintain traditional schools. For a poor and heavily populated country, this extravagance was disastrous. Previously, in the clan schools children from families of modest means were able to acquire the rudiments of arithmetic and writing, as well as general knowledge useful for local life. If they showed ability it was possible for them to advance even further. From the time when the rich families who had subsidized the clan schools sent their children to a modern public school, for which privilege they had to pay a large sum, they no longer concerned themselves with supporting the clan school. Poor peasants therefore no longer had access to education, and the distance between elite and masses was increased further.

The creation of modern schools underlined the contrast between the powerful and the weak. It also opened up divisions within the ruling class itself. Behind the new education there was a social group, different from the traditional elite, which was involved in both politics and business. It sought to perpetuate itself as a class by educating its children and the academically superior children from the lower classes. In 1907 Zhang Jian contrasted the West, where government and society were united in close collaboration, with China: "Under the despotic regime that China has had up until now, society (*shehui*) and government were separate. China has had a government but no society. . . . Now that the court has announced the establishment of a constitutional regime in nine years, society and government will be united; the government will have to depend on a social body."[56] Zhang concluded that it was essential to develop and educate this social body so that it could assume its responsibilities. An analysis of the writings of Zhang Jian and his friends in the constitutional movement and education associations shows that their aim was to fashion a new society with its own hierarchy, norms, and principles, to be established within the "cultural lordships" they were in the process of creating (texts 4, 7, 9).

Until 1912 there was neither the time nor means for this recasting of society to affect anybody other than the elite. In what way was the elite "renewed"?

The first students of the modern schools were *juren, gongsheng, jiansheng,* and *shengyuan;* these traditional scholars obtained a different outlook in the schools.[57] As administrative reform required many experts in "Western knowledge," a large number of them turned towards official careers after graduation. The teaching profession also attracted a good many because the salaries were relatively high. Some of them suceeded in obtaining positions in commercial or industrial enterprises: Jiang Daomin, Jiang Qian, and Liu Housheng, who worked in Zhang Jian's enterprises, belonged to this category.

Lack of documentation makes it difficult to determine the social origins of the new generations that entered modern schools.[58] A 1909 list of graduates from the No. 1 Higher Primary School of Nantong shows that nineteen of the thirty-nine pupils had not come from scholar families.[59] The proportion was thus little higher than it had been before among degree-holders. An examination of the family origins of important individuals like Mao Zedong, Zhu De, and others who were in school at this time, reveals that the social base for the recruitment of pupils had expanded slightly. More of the sons of well-to-do peasants, artisans, and, especially, merchants were able to pursue their studies to a higher level than before. This expansion of the elite did not mitigate the decline in popular cultural levels, a process referred to earlier. On the contrary, it tended to accentuate the imbalance. Due to the type of career they embraced, many modern students at first came to swell the ranks of the opposition formed by the gentry. Out of 974 graduates of the Nantong Normal School between 1903 and 1922, 825 continued to be involved in education.[60] It is true that Zhang Jian did his best to discourage school graduates from entering official careers; this did not happen everywhere.

However, even if the graduates of the new schools became officials, the education they had received gave them, in general, a different mentality; they had more demands to make of the government. If they obtained a position in an enterprise, personal experience made them more ready to denounce the restraints of the *ancien regime*. They therefore supported gentry action; proof of this can be seen in a petition of August 1906 signed by ninety thousand teachers and students of modern schools in Zhili, demanding a constitution and a parliament.[61] Among the young men who collaborated with Zhang Jian, such as members of the provincial assemblies, education associations, and constitutional groups, there were many who were products of the new education. The most striking example of this is that of the pupils of the Nantong schools who in 1911 came out in orderly ranks behind the director of the normal school to welcome the detachment of revolutionary troops with which the local gentry had come to an agreement some time before.[62] Yet was this not above all the result of rigorous discipline imposed by Zhang Jian upon the students (text 8)?

Due to the nature and content of what was taught, the development of modern education created an opposition force which, although undermining absolutism, also turned against the enlightened gentry. The completely novel experiences the new schools brought future intellectuals during their childhoods cannot be overemphasized: classes in common, the imposition of discipline, and the encouragement of collective work. Their fathers had become somewhat acquainted with these aspects of education in the academies, but at a more advanced age and, despite everything, in a teaching environment that was much more individualist. However, this does not mean that modern schools at first succeeded in impressing upon the students the virtues of working as a group. On the contrary, the schools had considerable difficulty in making the turbulent students respect the most elementary rules of group life.[63] Teachers who had been trained according to traditional ways were unable to use Western methods. The young teachers trained in Japan and China lacked practical experience and, in many cases, a grasp of theoretical knowledge as well. Foreign teachers, who were often of mediocre standard, were inconvenienced by the necessity of having to teach through an interpreter. Throughout this period the shortage of teachers was acute; there was a lack of competent teachers and, among the minority who were of superior quality, many, deliberately or not, encouraged their students to "rebel." [64]

In fact, the new political ideals of "liberty" and "equality" stimulated the students. Physical education, which was now regarded with favor, increased their energy. They were more unmanageable than the examination candidates of former times with their "greying hair and pale faces," as Zhang Jian described them. The immediate consequence of this common class education, for better or worse, was that youth became aware of their strength and the power of group action; they immediately used this power by launching numerous student strikes (text 3).[65]

What was taught to the students inevitably bred demands that could not be met. The curricula were too advanced in relation to the level of China's economic and social development and hence divorced from reality (text 6). The teachers were often unaware of this, or else they remained too "scholarly" to be able to make the abstract knowledge they taught more relevant in a practical way.[66] The most serious problem concerned those who had received a mediocre education; the majority of students, in fact, belonged to this category. Their knowledge could not be put to use in the institutions which existed. Industry, still in its infancy, could not afford to employ people of below average ability. The number of personnel positions in the bureaucracy was limited. The profession of education did not accept everyone. Finally, prejudice often closed the doors of traditional enterprises to graduates of modern schools (text 7).

The traditional system of education had also given rise to unemployed degree-holders, but the majority were eventually able to find some task among local activities which enabled them to maintain a livelihood. Also, the moral principles in which they had been inculcated and the economic and social system in which they were rooted inhibited them from making excessive demands. Furthermore, the principle of provincial quotas in the examinations introduced a certain equality which, although doubtless superficial, conveniently soothed provincial sensibilities. The new system bred a generation of frustrated intellectuals. "Classical knowledge" and moral principles with which the schools attempted to indoctrinate the students were brought into question by everything they read and learned elsewhere.[67] Teachers who could make of their students "loyal samurai" were rare. The differences among provinces increased and embittered relations between local elites. The regions of Beijing and the lower Yangzi monopolized cultural development; their intellectuals occupied the best positions, although not all of them were able to find a position. Due to their lack of ability, intellectuals from poorer regions not only lacked outlets in their own regions, but were denied opportunities elsewhere. National military education (junguomin jiaoyu) made youth more aggressive, but this aggressiveness was not accompanied by the increased loyalty to the emperor which, in Japan, had assured the stability of the state.[68] Rather, it was channelled into a militant nationalism, the political content of which was sometimes social revolution or, more often, simply revolution. Due to its mentality and urban way of life, the new intelligentsia became increasingly cut off from the masses; the injustices it felt were in regard to itself rather than to the ordinary people. This was sufficient to threaten the gentry insofar as it was the gentry who held effective power and represented the established order; it did not mean that the new intelligentsia would establish a more truly democratic regime. On the contrary, these divisions augured conflict and political instability.

Thus, while developing as a useful weapon against absolutism, modern education heightened the antagonisms between the elite and the masses and between revolutionaries and moderates. Rather than promoting the evolution of the country, had not modern education hastened the prospect of revolution and difficult times ahead?

Educational Reform and the Advent of the Republic

The moderates who directed educational reform perceived its flaws. In order to remedy the situation, they endeavored to implement a strategy which had three aspects: the development of popular education, vocational training, and the introduction of civic training.

The necessity of making elementary education free and compulsory was frequently mentioned in the constitutional press from 1906 onwards in conjunction with political problems.[69] It was not a question of being content with enunciating the principle, as had been done in the 1904 regulations, but rather of seeking practical ways to put it into practice. In 1909 new regulations limited the duration of elementary school to four years and reduced its curriculum (text 6).[70] In 1905 well-meaning gentry had begun to establish short-term literacy schools (*jianyi zhizi xuetang*), which were sanctioned by official regulations in 1909.[71] These schools were free, and classes were held in the evening so that working people could attend. Graduates could, if they wished, enter the third year of a regular lower primary school. More original perhaps were the half-day schools (*banri xuetang*) which were at first established by employers for their apprentices but which were later created for peasants and merchants.[72] They also received official sanction in 1906. Under the supervision of Meng Zhaochang, the Jiangsu Education Association devoted much effort to organizing public lectures and evening courses, training rural teachers, and modernizing existing private traditional schools. The last activity had been started by a scholar from Shanghai in July 1904. He had established a society which inspected the schools, offered advice for their improvement, and distributed awards to the successful ones.[73] This strategy, which involved little expense, encouraged emulation since there was a sudden increase in the number of reformed schools. The results of such an approach proved beneficial and represented one of the rare attempts to use intelligently the heritage of the past to build, more rapidly and at less expense, an education for the future. The Jiangsu Education Association absorbed the original society in 1908. Similar initiatives were taken elsewhere, notably in Hubei and Beijing.[74]

In order to guarantee job openings for students, especially those from average-income families, to make education more responsive to economic needs, to solve the unemployment problem, and to avert the risks of an excessively abstract education, educators made a concrete effort to develop vocational instruction.[75] They insisted on the necessity of practical instruction[76] and added to the schools fields and workshops where students underwent regular training.

Finally, in order to neutralize the harmful effects of modern education on youth the enlightened gentry paid considerable attention to the inculcation of civic virtues. This moral preoccupation was manifested in various ways. The development of female education, for example, was considered relevant in certain aspects to the spreading of civic virtue. "Women form half the nation; if education is not extended to them, this means that half the nation is uneducated. This will have bad consequences for the male half of the population, since mothers will not raise their sons correctly."[77] The first school for girls directed by Chinese had opened on 1 June 1898; it was obliged to close down one year later.[78] The campaign for female education resumed in 1901, supported by merchants, gentry, and some officials. At the beginning of 1907 Shanghai had twelve schools for girls, supported and controlled by Chinese, and comprising more than eight hundred students. Also in 1907 the Ministry of Education finally promulgated regulations on female education,[79] not provided for in either the 1902 or 1904 regulations. Primary and normal schools were to be established for girls, but no concessions were made concerning secondary education. For many of its ardent supporters, like Zhang Jian, female education was not designed to grant women equality with men. They were too steeped in traditional attitudes to consider such a question. However, from a practical point of view, they considered it necessary for women's condition to be improved so they would be able to fulfill specific tasks and assist the men. Giving women the opportunity to acquire skills in agriculture and industry was to enable them to perform certain duties and not for management. On the other hand, the woman's role in education was considered extremely important; suitably prepared, women would be capable of implanting civic virtues in the minds of their children, the future citizens of the country.[80]

The same concern to prevent the corruption of youth prompted a reduction in the number of foreign teachers allowed to teach in Chinese schools and the attempt to sinicize education. Japan's victory in 1905 had increased her prestige, but it was not long before her expansionist aims aroused apprehension. Among the political and business circles in which Zhang moved, the wholehearted admiration and slavish imitation of Japan came to an end.[81] The recruitment of foreign teachers became stricter and their employment was limited to the teaching of technical subjects.[82] "The foreign yoke is felt with increasing impatience each year" wrote an American and, concerning external cultural aid, he commented: "The Chinese are suspicious of charity; they see in it political designs."[83] By 1911 only 545 foreign teachers remained in Chinese schools.[84]

At the same time, "national knowledge" gained popularity.[85] This was shown by the stress on patriotism in history textbooks, which glorified the prosperous periods of the Tang and Song dynasties as well as national resistance to the foreigner in the recent past. These texts emphasized the positive effects that could result from unity, discipline, and loyalty towards a leader like Lin Zexu during the Opium War.[86] Attempts were made to inculcate "public virtue" and the concept of the state (texts 6 and 7). The gentry, who hoped soon to control government, were anxious to "make the people understand the justice of the principles of taxation and military service." However, when the principles were applied to them personally, they protested that "to demand of the people that they ruin their personal interests in order to serve the collectivity is not a just policy" (text 4). Yet it would not be fair to view the gentry's efforts only in this light.[87] Besides loyalty, self-sacrifice, and an *esprit de corps*, educators like Zhang Jian preached the virtues of self-will and energy (text 8) to enable China to resist the foreigner and "maintain its position in international competition."[88]

The results of these efforts to mitigate the shortcomings of educational reform were very uneven. In Nantong they were successful insofar as one of their aims had been to check the danger of revolution and to strengthen the obedience of the masses and not to establish a base for democracy. In fact, despite all the schemes Zhang Jian proposed to increase the number of primary schools (texts 1, 2, 6), the rate of school attendance in 1912 reached only 5.09 percent for boys and 2 percent for girls of school age.[89] These figures were clearly higher than the national average of 1 percent, but lower than other districts in Jiangsu. If there was no destruction of schools in Nantong, with the exception of two village schools that were burnt down in 1905,[90] it was not because peasants were able to send their sons to these schools. Due to the contributions from the Dasheng mills, peasants suffered less of a financial burden from school taxes, and the local militia was well organized. Finally, a sufficiently numerous elite kept careful watch over these establishments, from which they derived much benefit.

The strength of the new education in Nantong lay in its ability to combine the gradual raising of scientific levels with adaptation to local needs. The people principally responsible for this development were Zhang Jian, his brother Zhang Cha, and some of their friends, Shen Xiejun, Xu Dinglin, Wu Qilu, and Sha Yuanbing. They proved themselves capable of laying the intellectual foundations for regional economic development. No unemployment problem arose for graduates from Nantong schools; positions were found for them almost immediately in the district.[91] Education was constantly improved and expanded to meet new demands from industry and agriculture (texts 7 and 8). As a whole, education was organized according to the concept of local autonomy as understood by Zhang Jian, namely a system of economic and social development. In 1912 nearly 25 percent of the pupils in Nantong were receiving vocational training, as opposed to 2 percent in the rest of the country.[92]

The enthusiastic stress on vocational aspects that was a feature of the Nantong schools had consequences for female education. Girls represented 14 percent of the student population, in contrast to only 5 percent for China as a whole.[93] Too little time had elapsed to judge whether the earnest and strict education they received had the desired influence in their households, but in any event there appeared no trace of a movement for revolutionary emancipation that broke out elsewhere; emancipation took place in a gradual and peaceful way.

The moral discipline that held sway in the Nantong schools ultimately stifled student demands. There were certainly individual cases of disobedience at the beginning, but until 1912 there were no student strikes. During the revolution students loyally followed the instructions of their teachers. It seemed that the civic training inculcated by Zhang Jian had borne fruit. Due to the lack of contemporary reports on the atmosphere in Nantong schools, it is difficult to add much more in this respect.[94] Elsewhere, civic training did indeed increase patriotism among youth; its ethical content probably left deeper traces on the students than is generally believed. Is it not possible that the "public virtue" and "collective interest" to which political leaders in the last forty years have so often appealed are the recollections of what was taught them by their schoolteachers? This does not mean that they practiced such virtues at the time. In the short-term, this moral training, rarely taught with so much vigilance as in Nantong, did not achieve its aim: to rally the students to the support of the empire. Measures taken by the gentry to remedy the shortcomings of educational reform had mitigated divisions within the elite to a certain extent. It had not, however, diminished the risk of revolution.

The moderate gentry broke with the Qing very late. No doubt the question of the railways in the summer of 1911 was the decisive factor.[95] However, experiences in several areas had already prepared them for the rupture. Education was one in which the moderate gentry had proved to themselves that they were capable of implementing and directing a new policy. Their attempts at cooperation with the bureaucracy showed them that it was a permanent obstacle to all far-reaching reforms. Therefore in the last years of the dynasty they strove to monopolize power for themselves. As a result, they noticed that the management of public affairs proceeded more smoothly. They gave themselves all the credit for this and desired even more strongly the establishment of a constitutional regime. Gradually, the modern gentry detached itself from the monarchy, since the only thing that mattered was its own participation in government. It is strange to observe how, among the moral principles Zhang Jian propagated so frequently from 1907 onwards, there was never any mention of loyalty towards the monarch. Preoccupied solely with the content and reality of politics, Zhang acted as if he had become indifferent to the external form of the regime.[96] He was at first hostile to the revolution because he feared disorder and violence; he welcomed it when, with his friends, he felt strong enough to limit and use it for his own ends.

Students trained in the schools felt even less attachment to the Manchu dynasty. Their impatience, demands, and revolutionary activities forced the constitutionalists to adopt a more radical stance until the court, which "relied on limited measures to deal with the situation" (text 7), was incapable of satisfying their aspirations.

As with other reforms launched as a result of the new imperial policy, educational reform had proved unable to rally enlightened opinion to the support of the dynasty. On the contrary, it had led to the modern gentry's disenchantment with the monarchy. The modern schools had greatly contributed to the development of a nationalism which was not focused on the person of the emperor and which comprised too many conflicting influences for it to crystallize around a political regime. This was one of the dramatic facts faced by the Chinese on the morrow of the imperial abdication.

In 1912 progressive elements in the new government attempted to establish a republican system of education. Cai Yuanpei, the minister of education, took the lead in this attempt.[97] He mobilized public opinion to support the return of students to the schools they had deserted during the revolution.[98] In order to reorganize educational finances, Cai sought to increase the proportion of the national budget devoted to education. Finally, he defined new objectives for education and submitted the draft of a revised school system to a "provisional education conference" convened in Beijing from 10 July to 10 August 1912.[99] This conference originated with the National Federation of Education Associations which had been organized the preceding year in Shanghai. It was composed of specialists rather than bureaucrats, and the amendments and additions it made to Cai's program represented a continuity with the efforts undertaken by the education associations during the Qing as well as with the resolutions adopted in May 1911.

Some changes in vocabulary were introduced to emphasize the break with the *ancien regime*.[100] However, in conformity with the wishes expressed in 1911, the schooling period was reduced to eighteen years; the abolition of official degree titles and the principles of compulsory education, coeducation in elementary school, and equality of education for boys and girls were reconfirmed; and the classics were eliminated from the curriculum, to be replaced by handicraft training. For secondary education, the distinction between the arts and science sections, which had not succeeded in attracting students to a science career, was abolished and a unified curriculum was adopted in which science subjects occupied more teaching time. On announcing the revision of textbooks, the conference insisted that the same books be used throughout the country.

Cai Yuanpei proposed five educational aims involving national military education, practical training, the inculcation of civic morality, the teaching of a universal point of view (i.e., independent of political, religious, or philosophical prejudices), and aesthetic education.[101] The conference deleted the fourth aim and diluted the third and fifth. A decree of 2 September ratified its decision; the aims of education would be "to insist upon a moral education, supplementing it with practical training and national military education, and completing it with aesthetic education."[102] The new educational laws promulgated a few days afterwards bequeathed a system that was, in substance, identical to that of the former regime.[103] The Ministry of Education also ordered the strict observance of Confucius' birthday on 7 October.[104]

Cai resigned on 14 July, feeling that he had been neither supported nor understood. Civic morality for him had meant the "liberty, equality, and fraternity proclaimed by the French Revolution." He had tried in vain to emphasize the similarity of these ideals to the Confucian virtues of righteousness, reciprocity, and benevolence. They were too foreign and too radical for Cai's audience to approve them.[105] The "specialists" invited to Beijing were private individuals recruited from among the gentry who had played an important role in education. They may have been enlightened gentry but they remained gentry nevertheless. Concerned with detaching education from the traditional control of political power, Cai no doubt had failed to take into account the nature and strength of social control over education.

In education, more than any other area, the bourgeoisie, gentry, and former constitutionalists were best prepared to occupy the territory they had been unable to conquer under the monarchy and which the revolution had just opened up by overthrowing the Qing. This territory was the machinery of the state. Important members of the bourgeoisie and of the gentry succeeded in controlling it in

1912. Fan Yuanlian, who succeeded Cai Yuanpei as Minister of Education, was one such member; administrative posts in education came to be filled by contributors to *Jiaoyu zazhi* [The education review] and members of the education associations.[106] What were the objectives and attitudes of the social group for whom they acted? Those of Zhang Jian can serve as an example. He was not a democrat, but rather an aristocrat in the strict (i.e., literal) sense of the word. He accepted the establishment of a republic insofar as it left leadership in the hands of the most deserving, that is to say those who were the most experienced and most competent, whose abilities had been confirmed by their material success.[107] Zhang applied himself to exploiting and consolidating this newly-gained power. He made use of the power of the state to sustain his schools (text 9) and developed a conservative ideology, namely, "the love of order and respect for public morality" (text 8). Such were the principles imposed by the laws of 1912.

Moral education took the place of republican education and it was inevitable that conflicts would arise over the interpretation of the morality to be taught and over the political implications of the new system. On the interpretation of morality, the bourgeoisie and modern gentry clashed with traditional forces, former bureaucrats, and the militarists from whom Yuan Shikai derived his support. The former were sincerely concerned with morality and sought to inculcate the modern concept of the state, a concept in which Confucianism would play a role as a system of thought to cement national unity in time and space and thus complement the scientific spirit which was as yet insufficiently developed to assume this role. The latter identified morality with Confucianism, paying attention only to its institutional value and stressing its religious, as much as its intellectual, aspects; they distrusted science, which appeared to them to have no moral value. The former wished to guide social evolution; the latter wished to halt it.

As far as the political implications of the educational system were concerned, moderates and traditionalists confronted more radical elements. Democratic ideas gained ground among students and young teachers, as demonstrated by the strikes of 1912 (text 8). Despite all Zhang Jian's efforts, the enthusiasm generated by May Fourth affected all the schools in Nantong and his normal school was one of the first establishments in which the Chinese Communist Party was able to organize a cell.[108]

These problems constitute a new period in the history of Chinese education. It was no longer a question of reforming a traditional regime but of constructing a new one. The revolution had allowed the strength of the social group to which Zhang Jian belonged to fully exert itself. Insofar as this social group now held power it became more vulnerable. It moved from the offence to the defense.

CONCLUSION

"Education is the area in which the new administration (*xinzheng*) has succeeded most" observed a Chinese educator in 1911.[1] In fact, within ten years the foundations for modern education had been laid. The examination system had been abolished and the awarding of government degree-titles had recently been discontinued. A coherent school system and a specialized administration had been established. Teaching methods had been improved. The curricula had been enlarged and youth had begun to be acquainted with the concepts of the *patrie* and the state. A start had been made in developing vocational and specialized education, while at the same time the number of primary schools was increased in the hope of being able to implement compulsory education. According to statistics, the growth was spectacular: from 1903 to 1909 the number of schools increased 73 times, while that of students in the modern schools increased 225 times.

The principal cause of this success was the enthusiasm that educational reform had aroused among the enlightened gentry. The initiatives taken by Zhang Jian and the role of the modern gentry in creating schools and improving education bear witness to this fact. These efforts were part of a general movement that attempted to emulate the Meiji Restoration's achievements in Japan: modernization of the state under the aegis of the monarch. Yet instead of strengthening the monarchy, the attempt contributed to its downfall. In the specific case of education, the documents presented here may clarify some aspects of the problem. They do not shed light on all aspects of Chinese educational reform. For example, there are no references to the problem of Chinese overseas students, missionary schools, or military schools. Furthermore, only contrast or allusion hint at the conflicts and revolutionary trends involved in educational reform. These texts are written by a member of the established order and therefore reflect it. However, it was precisely *within* the established order that the emulation of the Meiji model took place.

Even with their limitations, Zhang Jian's writings reveal the major features of this movement.

The example of Zhang Jian and the men who surrounded him shows that China had people capable of conceiving and applying innovations. They were able to assimilate lessons from abroad very quickly without any special preparation. Contrary to what is often claimed, Confucianism did not shut them off from modern trends. Just as the Italian merchant in the Middle Ages dealt with religion, the modern gentry were able to separate traditional ethics from their personal interests and only combined them when they reinforced each other. With Zhang Jian one is struck by the appearance of new attitudes which are exemplified in two sentences from text 2: "We live in a time when it is the exchange of knowledge that is valuable," and "everyone is the master of his own will; nothing in the world can limit the power of the will." These statements represent a desire to open up to the world, but with the aim of doing it oneself-the idea being that moral vigor would compensate for the lack of material development. This faith involved more than the simple desire to develop the country. It is tempting to detect in this faith a similarity with the "voluntarism" that characterized the Chinese revolutionary movement under Mao Zedong, and to regard it as a specific element in a certain kind of response to modernization, a response doubtless based on national rather than doctrinal grounds.

China in 1901 possessed as much of the material means for the accomplishment of reforms as Japan had in 1868. However, the budgets of the modern schools indicate that resources may have been wasted on costly and needless projects while traditional establishments, which could have been transformed into modern schools at no great expense, were neglected. This was not the only difference between China and Japan. In China, the collaboration between government and elite, an essential element in the success of the Meiji Restoration, was not based on firm foundations. Only a few officials sincerely desired reform, and their influence was frequently dissipated by factional disputes. The impulse for reform from above, therefore, lacked spontaneity and continuity. If reform was achieved it was due more to the action of the governed. Merchants and gentry were able to exploit thoroughly the possibilities that had been offered so grudgingly by the authorities. During this process, a feeling of national solidarity and an awareness of political problems had developed among them which were ultimately turned against the monarchy itself. The modern gentry discovered that public affairs proceeded in a more efficient way under their direction and that the bureaucracy obstructed the implementation of new measures, even if some officials were willing to support such measures.

What failed in 1912 was the idea that China could achieve a "Meiji Restoration" according to the specific Japanese model of a reforming monarchy. Yet insofar as the "Meiji model" signified for its Chinese supporters reform, as opposed to revolution, the formula itself did not appear to have been rejected. The bourgeoisie and gentry even intended to perpetuate the idea. Nevertheless, had it not been compromised in practice?

The moderates had the field of education to themselves until 1911. There were two reasons for this. In the first place, they had more experience in education than the revolutionaries. As scholars they were accustomed to accepting a role in education; as businessmen they had experience in practical management. On the other hand, the revolutionaries were preoccupied above all else with changing the political regime; they had no concrete policy on education and were little interested in the subject.[2] Yet a sudden change took place in 1912. Insofar as they controlled, with the exception of the military, the principal levers of state, the former constitutionalists found themselves in the same position occupied by the Qing in 1904: they had more to lose than gain by change. Why was this? They were not a "conquering bourgeoisie" but rather remained on the whole dependent on, or connected with, traditional social leaders. The latter's existence had never been threatened. This was no doubt one of the major causes for the failure of the new imperial policy; the survival of this traditional group also constituted a burden for the future.

In Japan, the success of the Meiji Restoration was based on the elimination of the leaders in traditional society. Such a process had opened the way for political and administrative reform. This did not mean that traditional society itself was destroyed; rather, by abolishing feudal privileges, an irreversible process of change was speeded up. In China the social framework was not affected by reform since it was an instrument of imperial power and not the base of an opposition manipulated by a *shogunate*. Even the importance attributed to educational reform in China revealed a difference. In China an attack was begun on the "superstructure" without dealing with the "basic structure." The capitalist bourgeoisie itself contributed more to preserving the traditional structure than to overthrowing it. In the schools, the new and foreign ideas introduced by the modern gentry overturned all traditional notions. Yet precisely because of their novelty and strangeness the ideas were more difficult to assimilate for those who did not belong to the elite. These "modern ideas" therefore contributed to widening the gap between the privileged and the masses. At the same time, hindered in its growth by foreign imperialism, the bourgeoisie rebelled against all that was foreign; it also saw turned against itself the very ideas that had been so indiscriminately imported from abroad. However, it had little intellectual material with which to forge its own ideology of resistance. A small and scattered group, its sole resource in facing up to the foreign menace was to seek support among the traditional elite, from which it had partly originated. In order to gather the support of conservative elements and to create national unity, the bourgeoisie and modern gentry strove to maintain continuity with the past, even at the risk of sliding towards reaction. They developed an ambiguous nationalism which, via the schools, left its divisive imprint on a whole generation. Here again appears the fundamental contradiction that undermined the Chinese bourgeoisie as well as the national modern economy from which it was born: the dependence on the foreigner which both stimulated and limited its development.

The problem was not unique to China. China's experiences were and are similar to those of other countries. The synthesis that the new Chinese elite attempted to establish in education during the last ten years of the monarchy had its counterpart elsewhere with different people and different results. Is there not an analogy between Zhang Jian's efforts and those of Chandra Nath Bose or Shibusawa Eiichi? Zhang's activities in Nantong show both what a Chinese "Meiji Restoration" might have been and why it failed. Nantong was sufficiently close to Shanghai to benefit from the advantages of modernity imported from the metropolis and, at the same time, sufficiently remote for it to escape the foreign control which existed in Shanghai. The changes that Zhang Jian introduced in his district were adapted to concrete conditions. By his very personality, Zhang Jian represented the transitional period between the traditional and modern worlds. However, in an immense country like China, such success bred localist and centrifrugal tendencies: the district withdrew into itself in order to escape the troubles of national life and attempted to monopolize provincial resources to develop its own enterprises. The birth of the myth of Nantong as a "model district" was at once the consummation of Zhang's "hegemonistic talent" (ba cai)[3] and the demonstration of its failure to play a role in the general political life of the country.

PART II
TEXTS

PRELIMINARY REMARKS*

Choice of Documents

The documents presented here are selected from the works of Zhang Jian published by his son, Zhang Xiaoruo, in 1931 and entitled *Zhang Jizi jiu lu* [The nine anthologies of Zhang Jian]. This collection is divided by topic and use has been made of the section dealing with education (*Jiaoyu lu*). Preference was shown for texts that described concrete situations, or projects that were put into practice. Ideas themselves seemed less important to me than what was actually done-the daily functioning of education and the part played in it by Zhang Jian. The more original and daring ideas, in any case, tended to be held by others. With this criterion in mind, I chose nine of the forty-five texts that date from this period from the *Jiaoyu lu*. They consist of memorials, letters, and speeches. Specialists who have had access to the originals do not doubt the authenticity of the texts. For those texts that appeared in previous publications I have been able to check that the version given by Zhang Xiaoruo does not differ in any way.

Dating of the Texts

The publisher did not specify the circumstances in which the texts were composed, and evidently did not include the letters of those to whom Zhang was writing or replying. The texts were simply given a heading where one was lacking, and a date. However, the date is often inaccurate, a fact that makes use of the collection difficult. Internal evidence and cross-checking with other sources, especially Zhang Jian's diary, has generally permitted the

----

*I have omitted remarks concerning the French translation of Chinese terms which are not relevant to the English reader. Translator

restoration of an accurate chronology. This has been done for all texts cited in the book. For the translated documents I have given, in parentheses, the date mentioned by the publisher and the final corrected date, preceeded by p.d. (proposed date). The evidence for the changed date is given in the commentary. The dates mentioned in the documents themselves are based on the lunar calender, which continued to be used officially in China until the end of 1911. Their equivalent in the Western calender has been included in brackets in the translation.

Problems of Translation

Two categories of terms present particular difficulties, those for administration and those pertaining to education.

For the former I have followed the rules and equivalents used by M. C. Bergère in *Une crise financière à Shanghai* [A financial crisis in Shanghai], since it is advisable that all French works on the last years of the Qing use the same translation of Chinese terms. For terms which do not appear in M. C. Bergère's work, I have followed the translations given by Brunnert and Hagelstrom in *Present Day Political Organization in China*.

For vocabulary concerning modern education, a literal translation accords well with Chinese reality, which often drew on foreign practice. I have tried, as far as possible, to follow changes in vocabulary, except for *xuetang* and *xuexiao*, which have both been translated as "school" without therefore suggesting the sense of a more traditional institution attached to the former term.

Transcription

I have used *pinyin*, the system officially in use in China. I have not used the transcription of the Shanghai dialect for the names of Zhang Jian's factories, which would have confused the reader and been at odds with the transcription of the Beijing dialect used throughout the work.

Problems Concerning Currency

Normally Zhang Jian calculated in silver currency, either Mexican dollars (*yangyuan*, *yinyuan*, or *yuan*) or Shanghai *taels* (*yinliang* or *liang*). However, because it was evident to him, Zhang often did not specify the money unit when he discussed prices. It is not so clear to the modern reader. The most well-known Chinese scholars have conflicting ideas on currency. With no explanation, some render the unit as dollars while others render it as *taels*. For the translated documents it seems, after cross-checking with other sources, that when a unit of money is not specified, Zhang is referring to *taels*. However, this observation cannot be regarded as absolutely valid in all cases.

Different Names for Nantong

The documents refer to the area that Zhang Jian brought to prominence under several different names, Tongzhou, Nantong, and Tong. "Tongzhou" refers to the town itself or to the district (*xian*) which was made up of the town and the surrounding rural townships (*xiang*). "Tongzhou" also refers to the department (*zhou*) made up of the actual Tongzhou district, and of Taixing and Rugao districts. "Nantong" and "Tong" referred to either the town or the district, but not the department. Although the variety of names can confuse the reader, the context generally leaves no doubt as to what area is being discussed.

TEXT 1

Zhang Jian, *Jiaoyu*, I/5b-8b

Memorial Requesting the Establishment of a Normal School for Nantong and Haimen (twenty-eighth year of the reign of Guangxu: 1902; p.d. 24 May 1902).

We have respectfully read the imperial edict of the fourth day of the eighth month of the twenty-seventh year of Guangxu's reign (16 September 1901).[1] It orders that all the academies[2] of provincial capitals be transformed into universities, those of prefectures and departments into secondary schools, those of subprefectures and districts into primary schools, and that, besides this, many elementary schools should be established.[3] We have also read the imperial edicts of the fifteenth and twenty-fifth days of the tenth month (25 November and 15 December 1901) and that of the third day of the second month of the twenty-eighth year (12 March 1902) which urge the hastening of preparations for the opening of schools.[4] We gaze with admiration upon the wisdom and clear-sightedness of the emperor, upon all his plans to honor education and encourage study, his basic aims to reform laws and seek talents, his encouragement of officials, and his vigilant apprehension over any delay. Although our talents are minimal and we are living in retirement in Jianghai,[5] as subjects there are tasks we must all share with the emperor, and on the other hand, there are duties we personally must undertake in our locality. At this time, when thoughts are constrained and the resources of the people are meager, if one lays the entire responsibility for the development of education on the administration, if one ignores reality and instead has empty illusions, when will success be achieved? Our shame will be even more profound.

Three types of schools appear in all other countries: official, public, and private. Those established with the aid of state taxes are defined as official schools; those established with the aid of local taxes are defined as public schools; and those established with the aid of the private resources of individuals are defined as private schools.[6] The official schools are called "model schools," that is to say they offer the people a model of the official system decreed by the Ministry of Culture.[7] Private schools are called "substitute schools," that is to say the people establish them but the officials exercise control over regulations and curricula. If they do not contravene the regulations of the Ministry of Culture, they are recognized as substitutes for official schools.[8] Students from these substitute schools are considerably encouraged because their graduation diplomas and the benefits they can receive from the state are on an equal basis with those of students from official schools. The expenses involved in establishing education are in this way diminished, while the benefits are increased. We are ignorant and do not overestimate our abilities; nevertheless, we would like to contribute our personal funds, request the assistance of our parents and friends and, in the footsteps of the local official schools, emulate the example of foreign private schools.[9] Little by little we will therefore offer our imperfect assistance to educational development.

Let us now explain the curriculum and teaching methods. In the administrative system of the state, the magistrate of an independent department is equivalent to a prefect.[10] It is therefore appropriate that the department of Nantong has both secondary and primary schools. The local magistrates have already made provision for their establishment. Yet if there is no normal school, all administrative and teaching plans will be illusion. Having no normal school will be like waiting for people without offering assistance when they want to cross a river with no bridge.[11] Although the provincial capital has plans to establish a normal school with two sections, higher and lower,[12] this will not be sufficient to meet personnel needs in administration and teaching for the three or four official primary and secondary schools in the departments and districts of just one prefecture. This will be true even if the departments and districts of a prefecture only enroll a few students and this contingent enters the lower section of the normal school in order to finish the course quickly. How can development be anticipated? In other countries, after students finish their studies at a higher primary school, they enter a lower normal school and after that they undertake the duties of teaching. It is also necessary that a primary school be established within the lower normal school to serve as a place where normal school students can gain teaching experience. In the primary school and normal school, theory and practice will be mutually complementary. This is why if a normal school is established it is also necessary to establish a primary school comprising higher and lower courses.[13] Such is a general view of the lower normal school and primary school, having higher and lower courses, that we propose to establish.

A normal school involves specialized training; those who specialize in a field must first have completed a general education. However, to insist absolutely on this now is tantamount to searching for delicacies in order to mitigate a famine or waiting three years for a remedy to cure an illness. To insist on such a qualification would certainly be the better approach, but a delay cannot be allowed. For the time being, therefore, we propose to choose students for the normal school from among those *juren, gongsheng, shengyuan,* and *jiansheng*[14] of the department, subprefecture, and districts who have succeeded well in their studies and whose character and behavior are blameless, and to offer them additional courses. As teachers for the normal school, I propose to recruit Chinese with general knowledge and Japanese versed in school administration and pedagogy. Provision will be made for regular, short-term, and introductory courses, the classes of which will be differentiated according to the age, abilities, and wishes of the students.[15] Those who are older and from poor families who wish to enter the introductory course will form a class lasting one year. Those who are older, whether from poor families or not, who wish to enter the short-term course, will form a class lasting two years. Younger students, whether from well-off families or not, who wish to enter the regular course, will form a class lasting four years. Eight months after the establishment of the normal school, a primary school will be added to offer the students in the introductory course the opportunity of practical training. The following year, graduation certificates will be awarded to the students of the introductory course, after which they will teach in lower primary schools in the townships. The attached primary school will also provide practical training for the students of the short-term course, who will receive a graduation certificate after two years and then teach in the lower primary schools in the townships. The attached primary school will also serve as a place of practical training for students in the regular course. At the end of three years, the number of students in the introductory and short-term courses will be reduced, and the number of students in the regular course will be increased. At the end of four years, a higher primary school will be established. Such is a general view of the stages in the creation of the lower normal school and primary school, comprising higher and lower sections, that we propose to establish.

Students from the department, subprefecture, districts, and townships will total seventy to eighty at the maximum, fifty to sixty at the minimum. The number of teachers, administrators, and servants will amount to a little over ten. To accommodate teaching methods to the education of mind and body extolled by foreign educators[16] it is absolutely necessary to plan carefully for the location and construction of the school. If the normal school is located with undue haste in a building in town where the atmosphere is noisy and unwholesome, it will present problems. If a new building is constructed, the budget required for the construction of a library, laboratory, gymnasium, and ceremonial hall will also present problems. Beyond the ditches of Nantong, to the southeast, is situated the Temple of the One Thousand Buddhas, which was built during the reign of Wanli of the Ming dynasty.[17] It is surrounded by water on three sides and occupies an area of several tens of *jian*.[18] It has not been maintained for a long time and the main building was recently burnt down. Also, it does not have a land endowment and the temple only keeps one monk. Beside the temple there is a certain amount of empty land and some old trees. The location is truly splendid; it is uninhabited and tranquil and, what is more, such a location would be a secure base. According to rough calculations, more than 10,000 dollars will be needed for repair work and new construction; this is economical in comparison with the expenses incurred in buying a piece of land and constructing an entirely new building. Nevertheless, even with sufficient funds, materials, and labor, the project could not be completed within a year. As this neither meets the desire of the court to see daily progress in new projects nor satisfies the impatience and expectation of our compatriots, we propose that while undertaking work at the Temple of the One Thousand Buddhas, we temporarily rent the common building of Jingjiang, in the western part of town, so that courses can begin.[19] We estimate that in two or three months time we will have purchased the books, scientific apparatus, and furniture, hired the teachers, selected the students, and assigned duties according to abilities. Such is the general plan we propose in order to implement the short- and long-term projects for the normal and primary schools.

In the twenty-fourth year of the reign of Guangxu (1898) an edict ordered that Buddhist and Taoist temples in the empire be transformed into schools.[20] This has been done in all the provinces, departments, and districts. It is even more fitting that in the case of an abandoned monastery in a remote area, we are exempted from all suspicion of encroaching upon property. It will, however, be inevitable that, to flatter the Buddha and honor the demons, as is the custom, people will say such an action is dishonest and villainous. All common people will have this point of view, but the sage scorns all slander.[21] Yet we cannot refrain from feeling somewhat anxious about this. We therefore propose that the local authorities be ordered to publish a proclamation allowing us to apply all our abilities sincerely to the task. We have given a clear and detailed account, including the advantages and drawbacks, of the private schools we propose to establish-the normal school and the higher and lower primary schools-as well as the successive methods to be used in the short and long terms. If we receive authorization, we humbly request that we be given instructions for the registration of the schools. We shall respectfully await the publication of official regulations and list of school textbooks. If this has not been done by the time the schools open, we shall resubmit our detailed proposals for official sanction. While lodging this request, we impatiently desire to receive orders on this matter.

Appendix: Regulations for the Opening of the School

(1) The regulations on foreign private schools have been consulted in the establishment of local primary schools in our department, subprefecture, and districts. In creating the lower normal school, an attempt will be made to ensure that pedagogy, school management, moral training, history, geography, arithmetic, Chinese language, physics, chemistry, drawing, and gymnastics become the basis of education. However, students who already possess Chinese knowledge will devote themselves first to the specialized subjects necessary for the public interest.

(2) It is appropriate to establish a primary school within the normal school to serve as a place for the normal school students to acquire experience and practice. We therefore propose that eight months after the opening of the normal school a primary school, comprising higher and lower sections, be attached to the normal school.

(3) The associates shall address a memorial to the governor-general concerning this enterprise so that the governor-general can give his sanction and instruct the local authorities to register the school. The associates will mobilize funds for launching the enterprise through subscriptions.

(4) We propose to employ four professors for the normal school: one Japanese to teach pedagogy, school administration, and Japanese; and three Chinese who will share duties in the teaching of moral training, arithmetic, drawing, gymnastics, Chinese language, history, geography, physics, and chemistry. There will be one administrative head, one principal, one accountant, one librarian, and thirteen servants.

(5) The number of students sent to the normal school by the department, subprefecture, and districts will depend on participation in the financing of the school. For Tongzhou there will be approximately twenty students; for Taixing and Rugao about sixteen students each; and for Jinghai and Haimen about ten students each.[22] If, lacking resources for the time being, an area desires to send students at a later date, and as the number of students are fixed according to the participation of each area in the school's financing, the school will keep places open until such time those students can be sent.

(6) We shall select students for the normal school from among *juren, gongsheng, shengyuan,* and *jiansheng* who have upright characters, a sincere bearing, and a cultivated literary style. When they apply they will have to provide a letter of recommendation from a prestigious individual.[23] An admission list will be published after the inquiries and school entrance examinations have been completed.

(7) We have proposed to borrow the public building of Jingjiang so that the school can provisionally be opened there. However, as the dormitories there possess numerous disadvantages, provision will afterwards be made to repair and enlarge the Temple of the One Thousand Buddhas. Calculating the economic costs of a ceremonial hall, a lecture hall, premises for a library and laboratory, a sportsfield, a refectory, dormitories, a president's office, classrooms, an accountant's office, reception room, and the provision of books, apparatus, and educational materials, the sum will come to over 20,000 dollars. (We had at first calculated 15,000 dollars, but we have added 5,000 to 6,000 dollars since none of the original buildings will be appropriate as they now exist.)

(8) We anticipate the spending of about 3,400 dollars annually for the salaries and upkeep of the professors and the supervisors [and] general expenses incurred by the school principal, and the wages for the bursar; 220 dollars for the servants' wages; 1,200 dollars for food; and 160 dollars for lamp-oil, paper, and miscellaneous articles. Adding 300 dollars for books and scientific apparatus and for the maintenance of the premises, the total comes

to 5,280 dollars. The remuneration of the president is not included in the budget.

(9) Normal school students from Tongzhou, Taixing, Rugao, Jinghai, and Haimen will not have to pay tuition fees but only annual boarding fees. Estimating these to be 4 dollars a month (hot water and lamp-oil included), the fees will amount to 40 dollars for ten months, to be paid on the first and seventh months. On first entering the school, the student will pay for six months in advance.

(10) If a local benefactor contributes more than 500 dollars to the school's ordinary budget (contributions of land or books will be equivalent to cash contributions),[24] one of his children shall be exempt from the payment of boarding fees while attending the school, and the benefactor himself will have the right to inspect the school.

(11) *Juren, gongsheng, shengyuan,* and *jiansheng* residing in our department, subprefecture, and districts, but who are originally from another prefecture or province, and who desire to gain admittance to our school, must pay tuition fees in addition to boarding fees. At 2 dollars a month the fees will amount to 20 dollars for ten months. If people in another area contribute a subsidy of 300 dollars, one student who is originally from that area will be exempt from tuition fees during his course of study. Item 10 of the regulations comes into effect with a contribution of 500 dollars. Tuition and boarding fees for those who come from another prefecture or province will be in line with those for residents. Exemptions from boarding and tuition fees will be in proportion to cash contributions, as cited in the cases listed above.

(12) Curriculum, school regulations, and administrative statutes will be published before the opening of the school.

Commentary

In his diary Zhang Jian mentioned that he wrote this memorial on 24 May 1902.[1] It was addressed to the governor-general of Liangguang, Liu Kunyi, to request that he officially authorize the opening of a normal school in Nantong and convey his decision to the local magistrate. According to Chinese administrative custom, Zhang Jian had already spoken with Liu Kunyi on this subject during the course of personal discussions on 7 and 12 April.[2] The written request was purely a formality, but it allowed Zhang to give more details on the proposal.

Zhang's original idea was to establish a normal school controlled and financed by the province. Liu Kunyi had at first consented to the idea but, in the face of opposition from some of the most powerful provincial officials, he withdrew his support. Zhang thereupon decided to create the school with his own resources while also appealing to other private benefactors. He did not give up hope that the authorities might change their minds again and offer funds for the project. These initial disappointments accounted for Zhang's skepticism with regard to imperial regulations, expressed at the end of the first paragraph and beginning of the fourth. He had much more faith in the efficacy of local gentry initiative than in the authority of the administration.

The plan that Zhang proposed to implement had been conceived with the help of such reputable scholars as Shen Zipei, Miao Quancun, Luo Zhenyu, and Tang Shouqian, and such wealthy Tongzhou gentry as Sha Yuanbing, Fan Dangshi, and Li Shenzhi.[3] They had contributed to giving the project two principal features: the imitation of Japan and a concern with adapting the school to Chinese conditions. From July to September 1901, Luo Zhenyu published in his journal, *The World of Education*, a complete translation of all the regulations for normal schools in Japan.[4] Zhang referred frequently to this translation, as did those with whom he spoke. Zhang also made use of a work on modern education written by Luo's Japanese collaborator, Fujita Toyohachi.[5] Thus, emulating Japanese practice, the normal school was arranged in a three-level school hierarchy: lower primary, higher primary, and secondary. The normal school was specifically designed to train teachers rather than officials, and to equip them with initial practical experience, something quite unknown to Chinese education of former times. With the exception of Chinese, the proposed subjects were more like those contained in the curricula for Japanese schools of the same category than those in the curriculum of traditional Chinese schools. A Japanese teacher was to teach the more "foreign" subjects in the curriculum-pedagogy, school administration, and Japanese. Finally, the arrangements concerning the personnel and the location of the school conformed with the practice of modern schools in Japan. Despite the references to "all other countries," Japan was the country to be emulated.

However, the normal school was not seen as an isolated creation entirely imported from without. The school was an integral part of a specific plan for local and provincial educational development largely inspired by Luo Zhenyu.[6] Such a plan also met the concerns of Zhang

Jian and the entreaties of his friends in Nantong. Zhang was anxious to harmonize his initiatives with those of the authorities, to balance the recruitment of teachers with the opening of primary schools in the districts, and to coordinate the various levels of education. In order to achieve these aims, an attempt was made to adapt the normal school project to potential difficulties rather than to overcome them. The recruitment of students would draw on traditional degree holders within the department, who would be equivalent in number to the quota for the traditional examinations; courses would be adapted to the situation and needs of the students, with the regular system being implemented gradually over time. A similar concern for economy governed the other provisions: a restricted number of students, and a site chosen with the least expense. For a modern school, the budget was moderate; the level of salaries was a little higher than that in local academies. Zhang Jian did not seek sources of finance other than those which had sustained traditional schools: contributions and endowments from gentry. He also ensured that the expenses would not exceed the 20,000 dollars already in hand.[7]

Despite its modern objective, the plan was therefore characterized by a realistic and cautious approach. It provided the means to implement a concrete measure within the limits of local possibilities, taking into account any potential dissatisfaction and providing for gradual change over a period of time.

TEXT 2

Zhang Jian, *Jiaoyu*, II/15b-17b

Memorial Requesting that a Portion of Certain Taxes Be Used to Subsidize a Secondary School in Tongzhou (thirty-first year of the reign of Guangxu: 1905; p.d. 25 March to 12 April 1906).

We think that after the abolition of the examinations it is urgent to develop education.[1] We have received on several occasions edicts ordering that the creation of schools everywhere be encouraged and that the number of lower primary and half-day primary schools be increased. We admire the concern with which the emperor governs. The governor-general has published the edicts, sent circulars to all the prefectures, departments, and districts, and personally received the gentry to admonish them repeatedly that they devote their attention to the development of education. It can be said, therefore, that he has not ceased giving written or oral instructions. We admire the efficacy of His Excellency in the exercise of his duties. It seems to us that the principal aim of the examination system was to cultivate individual talent, while the principal duty of the school is to expand the intelligence of the majority of the people.[2] Since the scope of each is different, the measures involved must also be different. Provision has been made to create a large number of primary schools. It is therefore necessary that steps be taken early in order to expand the system by establishing higher primary schools and secondary schools. Speaking just of the local situation in Tongzhou, there are already two higher primary schools, one with 240 pupils, and the other, attached to the normal school, with 60 pupils.[3] The surface area of the three townships of the east, west, and north is comparatively large.[4] We propose that two schools be built in the eastern township, as well as two other schools, one to be situated in the northwest area and the other to be situated in the northeast area, that is to say four schools in all, comprising 120 pupils each. This will make in total 780 pupils in the six schools.

Of the lower primary schools to be constructed in stages by the townships within the next three to five years, forty-seven have been completed and it is recorded that work on ten more will proceed during this coming year. Within five years there will be approximately 100 lower primary schools. Assuming an average of 60 pupils per school, this will mean a total enrollment of 6,000 pupils. In the future there will be 1,200 graduates each year. Calculating that 200 will enter the six higher primary schools, which do not now have the facilities to accept all of them, in four years there will be 800 higher primary school graduates. If 80 enter the secondary school after this, there will be 320 secondary school students in four years.

According to the current plan, the secondary school for the five administrative divisions in the department of Tongzhou will accept a total of 480 pupils. As Nantong assumes four-tenths of the expenses for its establishment, four-tenths of the enrollment will be composed of its students, that is to say, 190 pupils in four years, making only 48 pupils per year.[5] This total amounts to only six-tenths of the minimum number (i.e., 80) of pupils who should enter the secondary school each year. Where will the remaining four-tenths go? The current project for a secondary school of 480 pupils is insufficient to meet this need. Therefore, it is necessary to make additional provision for the future: such provision would involve preparing for the annual admission of 60 extra students in four or five years time. Four years after these extra pupils are admitted, the total number, added to the previous figure (i.e., 480), would come to 720 pupils. At present, a building of only four rooms at the most is being constructed, that is to say, an area of a dozen *jian* in all.[6] In the future it will also be necessary to build dormitories for 240 people near the school. The costs of actual construction and purchase of adjacent land; the transfer of administrative offices and the granary; the arrangement of their new premises; the construction of school buildings comprising an area of 300 *jian;* and the provision of furniture, books, and equipment have amounted to 161,500 dollars from last winter to the first month of this year, despite several restrictions imposed on the original cost estimates. The reason for this is that the bricks, tiles, wood, and stone are 30 to 40 percent more expensive than five years ago, and the price of labor has also risen because there are not enough people to meet the increasing offers of local employment.[7] The project has been revised four times but nothing can be done. It has been decided to invite all the magistrates and gentry of the department of Nantong, the districts of Taixing and Rugao, the township of Jinghai, and the subprefecture of Haimen for a conference on the twentieth of this month.[8] The five districts are sharing the financial burden, but Tongzhou is assuming the greatest share. In the last five years, Tongzhou has established an apprentice-school, a training center for sericulture and the dyeing and weaving of silk, a public museum, and an orphanage.[9] The gentry, officials, and myself have obtained 160,000 to 170,000 dollars for the higher primary school and forty-seven lower primary schools for which we are responsible. Private sources are again exhausted. During successive years we have received 50,000 dollars from a tax on brokerage licenses[10] and 5,000 dollars from registration fees;[11] the prisoners' training center has given 14,000 to 15,000 dollars;[12] the governor-general has enjoined the province ceaselessly to provide funds, and contributions have come to 70,000 dollars. However, these funds have been exhausted. At present, it is calculated that expenses for the establishment of the secondary school will amount to 161,500 dollars. If one divides this sum into ten equal parts, four-tenths will be the responsibility of Tongzhou, two-tenths each will be the responsibility of Taixing and Rugao, and one-tenth each will be the responsibility of Jinghai township and the subprefecture of Haimen. The four-tenths that Tongzhou must assume will come to 64,000 dollars. As Jinghai has inhabitants but no area of jurisdiction, Tongzhou is responsible for its affairs and has jurisdiction over educational matters. This practice has been established since the beginning of the dynasty.[13] Tongzhou must therefore assume Jinghai's one-tenth of the financial burden, making five-tenths altogether, that is to say 80,750 dollars. Apart from the 28,000 dollars that we have supplied, the recovery of the old granary and the sale of bricks, tiles, wood, and stone of the neighboring buildings have brought a total of 12,000 dollars.[14] The prefect of the department has generously offered 1,000 dollars. We have personally offered 6,000 dollars. More than 30,000 dollars is therefore still lacking: it is obviously necessary that we reevaluate the portions of the financial burden in order to meet the costs. However, we know that the arrow of such a policy will not succeed in piercing the gauze; to pick up soil by handfuls will not suffice to lift a mountain. The court has decreed the implementation of compulsory education, but if it involves difficulties I fear that educational development will be impeded. The Ministry of Education has been ordered to subsidize education from government funds. However, not daring to hope for government funds, we are obliged to rely on ourselves.

According to the general rule adopted by other countries, at first it is necessary that all schools be established by the state so that they can serve as models. In the districts of Nanjing and Suzhou official schools are in the majority, but Tongzhou has only public and private schools.[15] We think that when the imperial family is encountering financial difficulties, the people also have a responsibility to face them. We do not wish to incur shame by forever begging and inconveniencing the governor-general. Referring to the example of foreign countries where education is developed with the aid of local taxes, from the reigns of Xianfeng and Tongzhi[16] until now Tongzhou has remitted more than ten million dollars each year in taxes and special contributions. The sole benefit to Tongzhou is that it has been assured a certain quota for the examinations. This has surely not affected the peasants, artisans, and merchants.[17] As the state is going to spread the benefits of education throughout the country, the gentry hope that local autonomy will be implemented. As far as the secondary school is concerned, the gentry have been the only ones to exhaust all their financial means.

The tax on the transfer of goods has come about by changing the name of the previous tax on river defense.[18] The original tax was created at a time when the bandits of Guangxi and Guangdong[19] were powerful in Jiangnan and travellers found themselves at risk; officials therefore imposed a tax on merchants in order to equip the boats and assure protection. When the rebellion was put down the name of the tax was changed to "tax on the transfer of goods" and officials continued to collect it without questioning its validity. The "two-tenths repair tax" for Nanjing and Yangzhou was established for the reorganization and reconstruction of these two places after the rebellions, Nanjing being the major city of the province and Yangzhou a neighboring prefecture.[20] It has lasted fifty years without any time limit being imposed. The tax on the transfer of goods, which has still not been abolished, has already brought in several millions of dollars. In the twenty-first year of the reign of Guangxu (1895) I addressed a memorial to former Governor-general Zhang Zhidong to create a local militia for Nantong and Haimen.[21] There were no means for borrowing the money and so we were granted half of the receipts from the "two-tenths repair tax" for Nanjing and Yangzhou and three-tenths of the receipts from the tax on the transfer of goods. The granting of these concessions is recorded in the archives.

A time of war is different from a time of peace. However, the principles of good government require that national education take priority over military policy, and our concrete situation demands that the difficulties of the people take second place to the question of education.[22] We have unanimously decided to ask the governor-general, by virtue of the precedent set by the former governor-general in the twenty-first year of the reign of Guangxu whereby he granted us one-half of the receipts from the "two-tenths repair tax" and three-tenths of the receipts from the tax on the transfer of goods, if he can grant us these receipts now for one year. Moreover, the governor-general had previously granted that one-tenth of the receipts from the combined tax on the sale of cloth raised in the department and districts of Nantong should go towards our local school budget.[23] Previously, the public treasury of Tongzhou hardly remitted more than 10,000 *taels* annually.[24] The total amount remitted by the other public treasuries dependent on Nanjing did not exceed several thousands of *taels*. The gentry and merchants, not knowing exactly how much the public treasuries in fact received, venture to calculate the figure only as approximately 40,000 *taels*. Afterwards, the combined tax was reformed by fixing it at 50 percent. The governor-general considered that this rate reduced the financial burden of the merchants; however, since the receipts from the tax turned out to be too meager, the governor-general abolished the 10 percent concession for our school budget. Now, based on the figure of more than 50,000 *taels* already obtained since the eighth month of last year to the present, we can foresee that receipts will total 70,000 to 80,000 *taels* by the end of the remaining five months. Thus, during the coming year when cloth is in abundance, the state will receive four or five times more than this, which has never happened before.

When the people render service to their superiors they rejoice in the opportunity to give genuine proof of their loyalty. When superiors exhort the people, they must also be content to distribute benefits. We resubmit our request, asking the governor-general to inform the central treasury of Nanjing that one-tenth of the amount it collects be remitted to the treasury of Tongzhou so that this sum can be deposited with the Tongzhou office of education[25] under the title of financial assistance. We would otherwise request that henceforth, when the annual receipts of this tax exceed 40,000 *taels*, one-tenth will be granted to supply the ordinary annual budget of the secondary school. Such a measure will meet with everlasting gratitude. All the projects for the secondary school are facing financial difficulties. We ask that, by virtue of the precedent set concerning the transfer of tax receipts, one-tenth of the receipts from the tax on the sale of cloth be set aside according to the request we have expressed. The reasons for such a measure have been carefully stated. We join together in beseeching that, in the general interest, the necessary funds be granted after due consideration.

Commentary

According to the allusions in the first and third paragraphs, this memorial was written after the edict of 2 September 1905 abolishing the examinations. It was drafted during the days preceding a meeting of magistrates and gentry from Tongzhou concerning the secondary school. Zhang Jian's diary mentions that this meeting took place on 13 April 1906,[1] and therefore the text must have been written between 25 March and 12 April 1906. The information on the date of the memorial given by Zhang Xiaoruo is inaccurate.

The memorial solicits from the governor-general of Liangjiang, Zhou Fu (1837-1921), official authorization to establish a public secondary school serving the department of Tongzhou and the subprefecture of Haimen. It also requests the granting of a temporary subsidy from *lijin* receipts and the permanent concession of 10 percent of the receipts from the cloth tax when receipts exceed 40,000 *taels*.

In Jiangnan, Tongzhou was, along with Nanjing, the most advanced area in matters of education.[2] This text shows that in three years Tongzhou invested 310,000 dollars in education, to which must be added the contribution for the normal school, 60,400 dollars contributed by the Dasheng mill, and approximately 80,000 dollars of private donations, making a total, therefore, of more than 450,000 dollars-a considerable sum in view of the scarcity of cash and resources in Tongzhou, where financial receipts hardly exceeded 400,000 dollars annually.[3] There is no precise information on educational investment for other areas during this period. The scattered information in the reports of *Dongfang zazhi* and the *North China Herald* indicates nevertheless that considerable sums were invested in a similar way in many other provinces. In Nantong the impetus by Zhang Jian and the wealth created by his enterprises accelerated educational development. It appears that in many other places, even in those remote from centers of commerce and industry, the gentry spontaneously contributed funds to education, a striking amount when one considers the difficulty in mobilizing capital experienced by Chinese factories. It was more often the case that in small areas gentry provided 10,000 dollars or more in order to establish schools. Motives included the desire to compete with other regions and, sometimes, speculation: educational investment was more attractive than industrial investment. However, after 1906 many schools that were insufficiently endowed were unable to balance their budgets; in order to hasten the founding of new schools the gentry sought public funds to make up the difference.

Such was the case in Nantong where, moreover, there were also economic difficulties due to general poverty. The situation was particularly delicate in Jiangning because of the obstruction of all expenditures on modern establishments posed by the new provincial treasurer, Enming:[4] hence the insistence and the minute attention to detail with which Zhang Jian stated the precedents. However, contrary to the usual practice with this kind of document, the memorial was not limited to a request for a palliative. It presented a rational plan to develop and finance education in a whole department. Zhang Jian wished to construct a hierarchy of schools in such a way that, from the primary to secondary levels, Nantong would have a coherent system. He wanted to ensure that the gentry had real power over education and, through the financing of the schools, to reserve for them the management of part of the public funds. The permanent allocation of a percentage of tax receipts gave the gentry means to exercise more control over the local magistrate's financial administration than the award of a fixed subsidy would have done.

For his plan Zhang Jian invoked the foreign model as guarantee of its efficacy. He drew his information on this from the press and from facts gathered during his trip to Japan. He had at that time focused his attention with interest on the way local communities assumed the financial responsibility for education, which was combined with a right of control.[5] The idea of the people's duties and rights is referred to several times in Zhang's text in order to justify his proposals. As in the articles appearing in *Dongfang zazhi* and *Jiaoyu shijie*, where it was frequently expressed at the time, the idea was used for political ends and the references to Confucian morality as justification for the idea assumed minor importance.

Despite its aim and modern inspiration, the project remained conservative in its methods of implementation. Zhang Jian objected to the examination system as being too oligarchic, but he still favored restricting education to an elite. Assuming that a graduate from the secondary school would be equivalent to a *shengyuan*, Zhang Jian's plan, calling for 80 graduates a year, would have tripled Nantong's traditional quota of *shengyuan* (72 every three years, not counting special examinations). Yet by fixing the annual number of primary school graduates at 1,200, he had barely expanded education for a school-age population approaching 90,000.[6] Although swelling the numbers of the elite, Zhang would continue to recruit its members from among a minority. From the point of view of administrative techniques, Zhang would retain traditional procedures for guaranteeing the financial base of the school, even though the precedent to which he referred concerned an exceptional grant from the receipts of a special tax and even though he requested, for an unlimited period, a percentage from the receipts of an ordinary tax. The principal resource for the school would continue to come from voluntary and random contributions.

Because of these limitations, Zhang's proposal fell short of the aims of some revolutionaries who wished to "smash the monopoly over culture possessed by the scholars."[7] In comparison to the reformers demanding free and compulsory education in order to facilitate the establishment of a constitutional regime,[8] Zhang's Malthusianism was perhaps more apparent than real. Since 1904 Zhang Jian had been convinced that political reform was the prerequisite for the universalization of education.[9] For the time being, he simply sought to strengthen the elite capable of helping him accomplish this political reform. Most of the reformers only adopted this idea a few months later, after the official announcement concerning the preparation program for a constitutional regime. They then advocated concrete and practical schemes,[10] of which this text is in some way a prototype.

TEXT 3

Zhang Jian, *Jiaoyu*, III/4a-5b

Letter to the Governor-general, Governor, and Commissioners of Education, Suggesting that the Nanqing Higher School Be Converted into a Higher Literary School[1] (first year of the reign of Xuantong: 1909; p.d. 20 December 1906 to 13 January 1907).

The Nanqing Higher School of Jiangyin was previously the Nanqing Academy.[2] The academy was the joint creation of the former provincial examiner, Vice-president Huang Tifang[3] and former Governor-general Zuo Zongtang.[4] The academy was well run and had a considerable reputation, bringing together the intellectual elite from both shores of the Yangzi. It was easy in those times for the provincial examiner residing in Jiangyin to keep an eye on the students in the academy.[5] Following an imperial edict, the academy was converted into a school.[6] By replacing the provincial examiners this year with commissioners of education, the province of Jiangsu has been divided into two areas, the capitals of which are Nanjing and Suzhou.[7] As a result of the two commissioners of education being moved to these two capitals, growing disturbances have taken place at the Nanqing school in Jiangyin.[8]

I read in the *Beijing Gazette* that the minister had learned of the suggestion that a university comprising several faculties be established in the southern provinces.[9] At a meeting of the Jiangsu Provincial Education Association in the ninth month at Shanghai,[10] members noted that the characteristics of Nanqing are similar to those of a faculty of letters. If in the future Chinese studies are not given a solid basis in the curriculum, the expansion of modern studies will have no support. If we sit and do nothing, I fear that in ten years teachers of Chinese studies will become as rare as stars in the morning.[11] Since it is feared that Chinese culture is approaching oblivion,[12] it would be best to convert Nanqing into a higher literary

117

school. Its departments of industry, agriculture, medicine, law, and sciences can be transferred to Nanjing, Suzhou, and Shanghai. The teaching staff will be selected and distributed according to local needs. However, the financing of such a measure is very difficult and, above all, there is a lack of competent teachers. The outlines of the plan are being discussed and we are doing the best we can to help solve practical problems. Moreover, we are awaiting the arrival of the two education commissioners, who will be able to take charge and tackle the problem on a regular and long-term basis.

When I returned to Shanghai at the beginning of this month, Cai Junyong[13] and other advisers from our association told me that there have been frequent disturbances at Nanqing. Among the students from Suzhou, more than forty have taken leaves of absence.[14] The province is split between northerners and southerners. Cai Junyong and the others are all former students of the school. They have received a joint letter from more than sixty students from the Suzhou region which they cannot allow themselves to ignore. They have taken the opportunity to request an interview with the two education commissioners in order to discuss the implementation of the plan to transform Nanqing into a higher literary school. The expenditures for Nanqing are considerable; with the proposed change, the budget will be reduced by one-half and efficiency will be doubled. They also propose that Miao Quansun[15] assume control over the college, and that Ma Liang[16] assist in the teaching duties; the school will receive much benefit from their services. Cai has handed me the students' letter, and the grievances expressed therein are only what has been told me by others.

The head of the school, Jin Shi, obtained the highest literary distinctions when the examination system existed,[17] but there is a great difference between the head of a school today and the director of an academy in former times. While having genuine love for people,[18] I truly fear that their talents are not being used properly.

According to the regulations, the students have to pay certain charges; the annual expenses for oil and candles have reached the exorbitant amount of more than 5,000 strings of cash and the expenses for food are the same.[19] The criticism of this practice cannot be refuted. Also, students are often enrolled too easily, therefore people continue to complain about the Nanqing school. We think, moreover, that once the education commissioners have moved to the capitals, this letter's criticisms of the school will be considered justified.

When the lute and zither are not in harmony, one adjusts their strings:[20] this is what has to be done today. We propose that the education commissioners of Nanjing and Suzhou be sent to Jiangyin at the end of the year in order to jointly hold an examination for all the students of the school. They would then grant a diploma or school certificate to those who attain the required standard; those who are completely below the required standard would be sent elsewhere. They will also be able to establish the higher literary school. A doctor cares for the sick; when a finger is cankerous it is better to amputate the finger than to let the infection spread to the arm. If the doctor does not amputate a finger because the patient wants to keep it, the infection will spread to the arm and then the whole body will be affected without the doctor being able to check the infection. It is not just today that I have heard criticisms of the school, and the problem did not begin with Director Jin. Without destroying a malignancy, one cannot grow and become healthy. If one wants to enlarge the new, it is first of all necessary to eliminate the old; all other solutions are merely temporary. If one only cuts off a piece of flesh in order to cure an ulcer, the flesh will rot before the ulcer has healed; this is not what I mean. Director Jin and myself are old friends. I believe sincerely that it is because I love Nanqing that I love Director Jin.

I am only considering of the truth and have no desire to offer unjust and random criticisms. I hope you will consider the matter and decide what is best.

Commentary

According to the first paragraph, this letter was written in 1906, the same year in which the post of education commissioner was created. It was written after the Jiangsu Education Association meeting in the ninth month. Zhang Jian states that he returned from Shanghai at the beginning of the month in which he wrote the letter. According to his diary, Zhang remained in Nantong during the tenth month, and was in Shanghai through the following month.[1] The letter can therefore be dated as written during the eleventh month of the thirty-second year of the reign of Guangxu, that is to say between 20 December 1906 and 13 January 1907. The date given by Zhang Xiaoruo is incorrect.

Zhang Jian wrote this letter to the highest provincial education authorities in his capacity as chairman of the Provincial Education Association. He requested, for financial, intellectual, and political reasons, that the Nanqing Higher School in Jiangyin have only a literary department.

Like the previous text, this letter illustrates the economic difficulties experienced by modern education after 1906, but the example given in this letter is particularly significant since it involves a traditional educational establishment which had been converted into a modern school. Although standards varied, many academies (*shuyuan*) were active intellectual centers in the nineteenth century,[2] and some of them played an important role in the introduction of Western science to China. It was in the academies, rather than in the Tongwenguan or missionary schools, that the first successful efforts were made, without foreign help, to acquaint China with modern knowledge.[3]

The 1898 reformers were aware of this when they used the academies as the foundation of a new education system. Their opponents also recognized this fact when, on restoring the traditional system, they declared in November 1898 that apart from the name the academies were no different from the schools. Despite the edict of September 1901 ordering once again the conversion of academies into schools, these establishments did not, on the whole, play the decisive role that was expected of them. There were several reasons for this, as is shown by the example of Nanqing. The first was that the quality of each academy did not depend on its geographical location. The edict established such a strict equivalence between the administrative level of each locality in which the academy was situated and the level of education that the academy would henceforth offer, that an excellent district academy like Nanqing had to be converted into a primary school while a mediocre academy in a provincial capital could become a higher school. If Nanqing was promoted to the level of a higher school, it was only due to the vigorous intercession of the provincial examiner; this did not happen everywhere.[4] In fact, possessing 50,000 *mu* and several thousand *taels* deposited in banks or with usurers,[5] Nanqing constituted a convenient source of income that the provincial examiner shared with the gentry; if Nanqing had been converted into a primary school, the provincial examiner would no longer have had control over it.

However, and this is another reason for the decline of the academies, the funds which had been ample to support students and offer financial benefits to gentry and officials in charge of the academies were not sufficient to maintain a school. The additions and changes that had to be made to the buildings, in addition to the salaries for a larger staff, increased the budget. It seems, moreover, that the gentry responsible for collecting the endowment revenues took advantage of the confusion resulting from the reorganization of the academy to keep a larger part of the funds than usual for themselves.[6] Under these conditions, there was a tendency to economize on the employment of teaching staff, and the quality of education therefore suffered.[7]

The necessity for reform was felt by both authorities and gentry. The Ministry of Education had wanted to convert Nanqing into a higher normal school. According to the 1904 regulations, higher normal schools were to be under close government control and, in principle, free. Official control would thus have been maintained and strengthened, and the increased expenditures would have compelled gentry to abandon their appropriation of the revenues. Moreover, graduates from a higher normal school were not permitted to enter Beijing University and hence gain access to high official posts.[8] On this point localism presented a stumbling block; the inhabitants of southern Jiangsu were afraid of losing their special position, whereas for some time official policy had favored the development of Jiangning. Zhang Jian skillfully took into account local sensitivities and flattered local pride by proposing to restore Nanqing's fame.

However, the idea of reviving "Chinese studies" was not meant to be just a contingency measure. Zhang Jian was personally convinced that Chinese culture had priority in education, with foreign culture of secondary importance.[9] This Chinese culture was not to comprise a slavish veneration of the classics, but rather a familiarity with China's past and characteristics. It was to be a guarantee of national integrity. The text was contemporaneous with the reaction following the excessive imitation of foreign models during the early years of educational reform, and reflected the gentry's concern to make education more Chinese.[10] The letter was written on the eve of the boycott against the United States, which was itself a further manifestation of nationalism.

In the eyes of the gentry, honoring Chinese culture was also a way to maintain order and unity. The student strikes no doubt alarmed them. These strikes were part of the violent agitation in student circles, especially those in Jiangsu and Zhejiang, that had begun with the student strike of November 1902 at Nanyang College in Shanghai. Student revolts broke out for a variety of reasons, ranging from protests against the government to dissatisfaction with the cooks; nevertheless, they were all symptoms of a deep political uneasiness.[11] In 1905 and 1906 Jiangyin was the scene of several incidents; the science sections of the college were precisely the most restless because of the actions of a professor of physics and chemistry, Zhong Xianchang, who distributed revolutionary propaganda in secret.[12] The grievances to which the letter refers certainly met with the sympathy of some gentry and this is why Zhang Jian treated the subject with caution. However, it is clear that Zhang, like the education association, wanted to prevent any further outbreak of disturbances and to discipline the students by steeping them more in the morality of the classics.

In the conflict between local interests and the authorities, the education association acted as a mediator in its capacity as the mouthpiece of the gentry. Perhaps more important, the education association was also an organ through which gentry opinion could unite and take shape at the provincial level rather than just at the local level. Due to meetings and discussions, gentry could agree on a common program; they could act as an effective pressure group and gain acceptance of their ideas.[13]

This letter therefore illustrates some of the important problems faced by higher education: how to reform prestigious traditional establishments, maintain the quality of education, rally the support of youth, and offer equal opportunities to all regions of the country when the memory of examination quotas was still fresh in people's minds. These aims had to be achieved with moderate finances and inadequate administrative structures. The letter also shows how the gentry strove to gain control over modern education in order to fashion it to their aims.

TEXT 4

Zhang Jian, *Jiaoyu*, III/11a-12b

Explanation of the Reasons for Zhang's Renunciation of the Chairmanship of the Jiangsu Provincial Education Association (third year of the reign of Xuantong: 1911; p.d. 15 to 30 October 1907).

I have been unduly honored with the chairmanship of the Jiangsu Provincial Education Association for the two years since its establishment.[1] I have been unable to contribute to the spread of education desired by the emperor and the court. I have been equally unable to follow the wishes of my compatriots and enlarge the bases for local autonomy in this province. My intelligence is insufficient and my resolution is weak. My shame cannot be expressed. Even if during normal times I have managed by chance to settle one or two problems arising from the management of education in the departments and districts, I have had more cause to rely on the advisers and members of the education office in order to deliberate and act collectively. I deeply regret the inadequacy of my collaboration.

This is now the third general meeting of our association. You who belong to scholarly circles from the departments and districts of the entire province, have come far and wide to this meeting to bring me your advice. I am very grateful for this. At last year's meeting my resignation was refused;[2] one year has gone by and I am compelled to explain in detail how concrete obstacles are jeopardizing the general interest and my own peace of mind, hoping that you will allow me to resign this time.

Originally, Jiangsu was a single province. Yet now the governor-general and the governor reside separately in Nanjing and Suzhou, as do the two education commissioners. The result is that the province has been divided into two, something that does not exist in the other twenty-one provinces. Under these conditions, it was

123

insisted that the education association be based in Shanghai in order
to preserve unity, while offices were established separately in
Nanjing and Suzhou to serve as administrative organs under the
education commissioner.[3] At that time I proposed that individuals
from Nanjing and Suzhou assume in rotation the chairmanship and
vice-chairmanship of the education association since I feared that if
one depended too much on people from only one of these two places, a
breakdown in communication would result and misunderstandings
would arise. Such a result could only lead to suspicion. If suspicion
was to exist then the original purpose of preserving cohesion would
be threatened, and the very unity of the province broken. I am from
the Nanjing area.[4] I have already been chairman of the association
for two years, and according to my original suggestion, it would now
be appropriate to nominate someone from the Suzhou area. In the
original regulations concerning the duration of appointments it is
stated that they are held for one year and are renewable.
Appointments can be renewed indefinitely but in practice this cannot
apply to the post of chairman as it can to other posts. It seems more
suitable to replace the chairman once every two years. This is the
first point I want to make. (Some people will say that Nanjing and
Suzhou do not have the same dialect, but it is for this very reason
that haste must be made to unite them.)[5]

The region of Tongzhou, where I am occupied with my
enterprises and with educational affairs, is in a remote location and I
cannot put up with the exhaustion of traveling 200 *li* in a hurry
every week.[6] In these last few years I have been coming to Shanghai
regularly: these frantic journeys are extremely troublesome.
Between my first and last trips of last year, I spent only thirty-nine
days at my home. My personal expenditures amount to nearly
10,000 *taels*. It is not only my mind that cannot concentrate on the
job, but even my eyes and ears. If the situation is like this each year
would I be able to endure it? Not stopping to talk and write; while
traveling, not stopping to think; while sleeping, not stopping to worry
over things; to see and hear confusion on the outside, while inside the
mind is stretched to the limit: very few people are capable of
enduring all this. Although I have benefitted in these two years from
the support of advisers and executive officers who have prevented
me from collapsing with exhaustion, I do not have a peaceful mind. I
have usurped a hollow title with what benefits for the collectivity?
Nevertheless, to insist that people ruin their personal interests in
order to serve the collectivity is not an equitable approach. This is
my second point.

These two points reveal the sincere reasons for my resignation. Perhaps certain people will say that because I have recently been accused of heading a political "party," I am resigning in order to avoid trouble.[7] This has nothing to do with it. When I was twenty-one I read about the life of Fan Pang in the *History of the Later Han dynasty*. When Fan Pang was arrested, he said to his son: "I would like to tell you to avenge me, but one must not do wrong. I would like to tell you to be good, even though I have done no wrong."[8] This passage made me cry and I was unable to lift my head; the tears I shed dampened several wads of paper. The crow of a cock in a storm, such must be, I believe, the personal endeavor of the scholar.[9] Besides, what is the name given to my party? The education association is not a party. If this charge means that I was one of the first to propose the establishment of a constitution, it should be noted that in reality this constitution was granted by an imperial edict. If this charge means that I am a revolutionary, it should be noted that when one sanctions revolution one does not talk of establishing a constitution. If people want to treat me like Fan Pang, I shall willingly agree but I do not think I am worthy of such an honor. How do people know that I am in an awkward predicament? These words show that people do not know me. My resignation really has to do with preserving cohesion and unity. It is necessary that the tasks of the country be clearly distributed and then cohesion will follow.

I have been advised to send a letter of resignation saying that enough time as chairman has elapsed and requesting to step down from the post, thereby avoiding having to come to the meeting. However, I recall that for two years you have generously offered your goodwill: there is nothing, therefore, that we cannot discuss together. I feel guilty for adopting such irregular behavior. Please consider this.

Commentary

The date given by Zhang Xiaoruo for the text is inaccurate. Zhang Jian mentions that he had been chairman for two years and that the meeting was the third for the association. The education association was founded in October 1905 and Zhang Jian was elected chairman at that time. He was renominated as chairman in 1906. The third meeting was therefore held in 1907. One detail confirms

this: Zhang said that he had only spent 39 days at home during the
preceding year; this statement can be found in Zhang's diary for the
last day of the thirty-second year of the reign of Guangxu (1906).
The diary mentions a journey to Shanghai from 15 to 30 October
1907, with no other information. It was doubtless during this time
that Zhang Jian took part in the annual meeting of the association,
usually held in the autumn, and made his resignation speech-a
speech which had no effect since he still held the post of chairman the
following year.[1]

In this speech Zhang made known his desire, in the interests of
cohesion and efficiency, to be relieved of his duties as chairman of the
Jiangsu Education Association in favor of someone from Suzhou.
Zhang also referred to concern over his health and his enterprises.
He refuted those who accused him of being involved in factious
activities and defined his political attitudes.

The text gives information on the organization and functioning
of the Jiangsu Education Association, which was discussed in the
previous text. It was one of the first institutions in which local
gentry could participate on the basis of a legal and permanent repre-
sentation in the administration. With the political reforms that
followed the Boxer uprising a variety of groups and associations were
created. Sidestepping the ban on the formation of "parties" (dang),
they sheltered under the name of "study societies" (xuehui) in order
to carry out activities that were more or less political in nature.
Some of them were openly revolutionary, like the Chinese Education
Association (Zhongguo jiaoyu hui), while others were more moderate,
preoccupied above all else with encouraging modernization.[2]

The Jiangsu Study Society (Jiangsu xuehui), from which arose
the Provincial Education Association, was formed in Shanghai at the
beginning of October 1905 by thirty gentry, on the initiative of Yun
Zuqi, a native of Yanghu, and Wang Qingmu, a native of
Chongming. The founders of the society, which included Ma Liang
and Zhang Jian, came from all regions of the province, and their
reputation and influence generally extended beyond their own
districts. Some of them were concerned exclusively with education
and literary pursuits, while others were simply enlightened
businessmen who were patrons of the arts but who generally lacked
an official examination degree-title.[3] They regarded it their duty to
"promote education without interfering in matters outside this
domain, to develop above all normal schools and technical education,
to promote the respectability of a military spirit, and to prepare for
local autonomy . . . while giving courses in law to train judges and

police officials."[4] They wished to forge links between provincial intellectual circles in order to organize investigations of education abroad, to inspect the schools on a regular basis, and to invite public speakers to give talks on relevant topics. The internal organization was very detailed, based on that of education societies in Japan. Some members were the representatives of different localities and were chosen by the founding members and gentry of the particular locality, from among those responsible for education, chairmen of study societies, administrators of local public works,[5] and persons of note in the area. Others were eligible for membership on a personal basis on the condition that they were "scholars having links with education, or willing to finance education development, or having industrial or commercial success to their credit." In all cases potential members had to be at least twenty-five years of age, which excluded all potentially troublesome students. Provision was made for one annual general meeting and extraordinary sessions to deal with urgent business. The secretariat comprised one chairman and two vice-chairmen (whose appointments could be renewed annually), a group of advisers (the number of whom was proportional to the number of subprefectures and districts in each prefecture), one full-time member for each district, and twenty executive members divided into four commissions and elected once every two years. The chairman had the power to call together the secretariat and to hold special meetings, in addition to proposing ideas and executing decisions made by the society (in conjunction with full-time members when such decisions involved questions of local finance). The vice-chairmen assisted the chairman and substituted for him when he was not available. In order to be implemented, proposals from advisers had to be presented by at least two of them, accepted unanimously by all advisers, and finally receive the approval of two-thirds of the full assembly. The full-time members were elected by the districts and approved by the chairman and advisers, and were responsible for implementing assembly decisions at the local level. Finally, executive members were charged with preparing reports for the assembly, examining the accounts, managing the schools, assessing textbooks, and establishing ties with the authorities.

After the adoption of the regulations the founding members drafted a memorial in order to inform the governor-general and the Ministry of Education of the creation of the society and to request official support. Imperial sanction was given at the beginning of the summer of 1906, whereupon the society changed its name to the

Provincial Association for Education Affairs (Jiangsu xuewu zonghui). It finally became the Provincial Education Association after the promulgation of official regulations on education associations on 28 July 1906. These regulations integrated the Jiangsu association into the new administration created for education without in any way altering its composition.

What is especially significant about the association regulations was the concern to establish equality between the districts. Zhang Jian stressed in his speech that this was the prerequisite for provincial unity. Such a concern represented a new and important phenomenon-the desire to go beyond, and even eliminate, localism and to carry out concerted activities. The choice of Shanghai, the modern city of Jiangsu, as the headquarters of the association was symbolic. Doubtless this preoccupation with unity had partly to do with the recently revived jealously between the southern and northern regions of the province, but various reports from elsewhere in China also testify to this concern.[6] The creation of chambers of commerce throughout the country was also a response to the need felt for unity. A short time before, Liang Qichao had insisted on the need to transform China from an existing "aggregate of clans" into a unified "nation."[7] The influence of this idea was reinforced by the effects of economic and social change.

Because of its prior establishment and the skill and influence of its members, the Jiangsu Education Association partially escaped from the official control that was established by the 1906 regulations. Nevertheless, the latter part of the text shows the limits of this independence. These limits were due not only to legal threats that accompanied the slightest political deviation by the associations but also, more importantly, to the social ties and mentality of association members. In the conclusion of his speech, Zhang Jian was perfectly sincere and a reading of his diary confirms this. He gave in his concluding remarks the clearest definition of his outlook: calculated selfishness, confidence in individual action rather than in an organized collective movement, constitutionalism under a monarchy, and hostility to revolution. His individualism had helped Zhang succeed in his enterprises, but it should not be forgotten that he was also inspired in part by the traditional scholar ideal. He wanted to see improvements made to the established order, but did not wish to overthrow it because it guaranteed his social authority. These contradictions were typical of the social group from which education association members were recruited, and they explain the limited results of the attempt at organizing a legal opposition.

TEXT 5

Zhang Jian, *Jiaoyu*, III/6a-6b

A Reply to Mao, Education Commissioner of Jiangsu[1] (second year of the reign of Xuantong: 1910; p.d. 3 March to 5 April 1908).

I thank you for your letter of the first moon of the new year, as well as your note which was enclosed with it.[2] Your far-reaching plans arouse a widespread respect and everlasting gratitude.

The reform of Nanqing began in the winter of 1906.[3] It was proposed to first close the school for one year in order to prepare everything. The schedules for repair work, the time for announcing the holding of entrance examinations, the organization of academic departments, and the planning of the budget were all in the preparation plans.

I learn by the letter that you wrote at the end of the year to Zhang Jizhi, a compiler of the second class,[4] inviting him to visit the south, that plans had again been made to repair school buildings this spring. Such timing does not correspond with the anticipated date, but is clearly prompted by the concern to proceed with matters in a cautious way. Before receiving your letter there was no way of knowing your views on the plan and this is why the education association has repeatedly requested your guidance on this matter.

I am tied to my enterprises in Nantong and Haimen,[5] and I am only able to go to Shanghai once a month or once every several months. Yet each organization mistakenly nominates me as director or deputy-director and when urgent and important matters arise, I always have to take part in the discussions. The Provincial Education Association was established two years ago; its internal organization is now more or less complete.[6] Each month there are ordinary meetings for executive members and advisers. When the chairman of the association is absent from Shanghai, he designates a temporary substitute chairman. When resolutions are passed, the

129

most important are sent by post to the chairman so that he can
countersign them and only then are they implemented. You say that
when members have dealt regularly with a matter in general
meetings it is not necessary to discuss it with the chairman, but this
is not the case. Even when I take part in discussions in Shanghai
and must comply with the vote of the majority, the chairman still
has the deciding vote. This is the case with the majority of debate
procedures adopted by organizations. However, in dealing with
matters of interest to the society it should not be that one or two
individuals act on their own authority or that they assume sole
responsibility. In the regulations promulgated by the Ministry of
Education on offices of education, provision is made for the posts of
head adviser and adviser but clauses concerning debate procedures
and how decisions are made have yet to be issued.[7] These can be provided for according to the level of each province. In some of the
provinces, the chambers of commerce and study societies have
already acquainted themselves with such procedures, which constitute, in fact, the starting point for local autonomy.

You are well versed in Chinese and foreign history: if the law is
supreme, all organizations from their beginnings possess an
unchangeable nature which is independent of any change in
personnel. If men have supremacy,[8] even if they have the reputation
for being enlightened, there is no continuity; the example of Xiao who
legislated and Cao who carried out the laws is an exception in ancient
history.[9] An individual's policy ends with his death; this is one of the
principal reasons for the weakness of our country during the last several thousand years.

Impressed by the diligent concern shown in your letter, I have
thus given you a brief account concerning the situation of our society.
When the matter of the Nanqing school has been debated by the
Provincial Education Association, I shall inform you of the results.

Commentary

This text cannot have been written in the second year of
Xuantong (10 February 1910 to 29 January 1911) since the only
education commissioner for Jiangsu with the name of Mao, Mao
Qingfan, occupied the post from 27 May 1907 to 29 August 1908.
Furthermore, Zhang mentions that the Jiangsu Education
Association had existed for two complete years; the association had

been established at the end of 1905. Mao's letter was sent during the first moon, that is to say between 2 February and 2 March 1908. Zhang Jian's reply was not sent during the same month, but was certainly sent before his visit to Nanjing in April 1908, during which he called upon the local branch of the association.[1] The letter can therefore be dated between 3 March and the beginning of April 1908.

In his letter Zhang indicated that he had received news of the modifications Mao had made to the plan for the reform of Nanqing, and gave Mao specific details concerning the customary internal procedures of associations and groups in the province.

The text illustrates an episode in the legal struggle waged by the gentry against the bureaucracy in the field of education. What did such a struggle in fact involve? Since Mao's letter cannot be located, the main points have to be reconstituted from Zhang's reply. The new commissioner of education, on his own authority, had apparently modified a reform plan which should have been within the Provincial Education Association's sphere of competence. Mao no doubt made it known that it was more efficient for a small number of individuals to deal with matters on their own. Since the rules of the education association deprived Zhang of all real decision-making power, Mao preferred to consult him in his capacity as head adviser of the office of education. In short, Mao surreptitiously attempted to perpetuate traditional methods of governing. Practical necessity prompted Mao to reinforce his authority by gaining gentry consent, but he intended to achieve this on a personal, rather than legal, basis. He appealed to Zhang as an influential individual among provincial circles, and disputed the validity of Zhang's legal title of chairman of the education association-a title that theoretically enabled Zhang to serve as an intermediary between rulers and ruled. Mao therefore upheld the notion that attributed a discretionary power to the bureaucracy.

Zhang Jian replied by demonstrating that his personal influence derived from the positions he had been given by his fellow citizens. While conferring upon Zhang a genuine power of decision making, this trust also imposed upon him the duty of respecting legal procedures which were the very guarantee of his own authority. These legal procedures included regular consultation with a representative body of the organization. If Zhang Jian acknowledged that persons responsible for executing decisions could hold a special sanctioning power, he nevertheless defended the idea of a government limited by the legally expressed opinion of concerned citizens. It was this practice that Zhang wanted to see implemented in newly created administrative organs like the offices of education. He contrasted the arbitrary power of officials appointed by a despotic central government with local autonomy, which seemed to him a politically progressive arrangement suitable for dealing with modern problems. In this respect, his use of the expresssion "level (*chengdu*) of the province" and his idea that new habits were being formed are interesting because they show how an intellectual like Zhang, with a traditional education, could assimilate foreign ideas of progress and development. Even more significant is Zhang's use of the new expression, *shehui* (society): up until this time Zhang had conceived of the population as a whole only in relation to the monarch or the authorities. Thus he had referred to the population as *xia* (inferiors), in contrast to *shang* (superiors), or *min* (the ordinary people), in contrast to *chen* or *guan* (officials). He thought of the population only as "subjects." Now, however, he specifically referred to the "society" as an independent reality with its own demands to which the structures of the state had to adapt. For Zhang the state should become an instrument of the social collectivity rather than the latter simply existing in relation to the state.

The example in the text of the legal struggle between gentry and bureaucracy is not unique. Numerous cases of this kind can be found in the relations between the chambers of commerce, education associations, and authorities.[2] This legal struggle was particularly acute in the field of education because it represented a new administrative sphere in which there were fewer traditions to deal with and in which it was easier to establish new structures. Furthermore, the control of education assured a lasting control over the state.

This text reveals the mentality of the gentry on the eve of the revolution and describes the forms of their resistance to the Qing government. It is interesting to compare the passage in which Zhang referred to the legalists with the phrase written by Albert Dicey in 1885 which defined the principal idea that had allowed the expansion of English power: "the rule of law." The phrase that Dicey created, without having read Han Fei, is the best equivalent of the Chinese expression *yi fa zhi*. While harking back to slogans in Chinese tradition, Zhang was advocating the establishment of an *état de droit*, necessary for the development of capitalism.

TEXT 6

Zhang Jian, *Jiaoyu*, III/2a-3a

Some Reasons Why It Is Necessary to Reform Education in Lower Primary Schools (thirty-fourth year of the reign of Guangxu: 1908; p.d. beginning of April to beginning of May 1909).

Why is education necessary to a state? It is, quite simply, because education is expected to acquaint people with the very existence of the state and with the fact that the state can only sufficiently fulfill its role if everyone pays taxes and performs military service without the majority complaining about such duties.

The Duke of Zhou, in order to establish the monarchy, created a complete system of local officialdom; his laws were detailed.[1] Shang Yang had ambitions of hegemony and attributed importance to agriculture and war; his laws were brief.[2] When laws are detailed, their application is tortuous and complicated; it is necessary to guide the people through education to obtain the desired results. When laws are brief, their application is coercive and strict: it is not necessary to have recourse to education since the laws can be put into effect immediately. Generally, if the effectiveness of the law is slow to come about, the dangers are at the beginning; if the results of implementing the laws are immediate, the dangers are at the end.

The government has now acquired the habit of stressing education. The arrangements concerning education for the coming nine years anticipate the establishment of one primary school for every two hundred households.[3] However, no concern has been shown for providing funds with which to construct schools, methods for recruiting teachers, and ways to coordinate and carry out the plans. Such matters have been completely ignored. The laws have been given a fine appearance to deceive the emperor, and the regulations are a trick meant to lead the people astray. Everyone surely realizes that even if the emperor can be deceived, the people cannot be led astray.

In 1901 the government began to speak of the importance of education.[4] After reflecting on the Boxer catastrophe of 1900, the government concluded that adhesion to heterodox beliefs among the people almost led to disaster for the land of our ancestors. Since no one was directly responsible for this, the catastrophe was attributed to people's foolishness. Study is necessary to cure ignorance and it was therefore inevitable that the government would make use of education. At this time Beijing University was suddenly established.[5] I proposed that normal schools be established first,[6] however, numerous detractors and opponents frustrated me beyond imagination. Without considering the cost, I donated my meager personal resources to implement my scheme in the department. A little over a year later there were official normal schools in Jiangchu [Jiangsu and Hubei].[7] I thought results would gradually be achieved over a ten year period. Time has gone by now, and eight years have quickly elapsed. The number of students who are reasonably competent in Chinese studies, as they were in former times, is daily diminishing on the enrollment registers. Previously, some private primary schools were established in the townships, but the initiative was not followed up. According to the ministry regulations, Tongzhou, with a surface area of 8,000 square *li* and 150,892 households, should now have 758 lower primary schools.[8] It is imperative that the number of trained teachers for primary schools be increased. The normal school that now exists in Tongzhou can accept fifty students annually for the next five years. Despite the fact that during the annual enrollment the required number of eligible students is never attained, and that even if every effort were made to ensure the acceptance of the full quota, one or two out of ten would drop out, the maximum number of students per year is still only fifty. Fifteen years are therefore needed before the demand for primary school teachers can be met.

We might very well ask where the fifty students who are supposed to enter the school each year will come from. It is imperative that a larger number of lower primary schools be established; these schools will serve as a gradual preparation for higher primary school. However, one faces again the difficulty of a lack of teachers. Is there an escape from this vicious circle? Even if the existing funds and personnel are brought together now, the schools still will not fulfill even six- or seven-tenths of the envisaged plan. Thus, as far as the spread of education in just the single department of Tongzhou is concerned, even if development is planned for a period of twenty instead of fifteen years, the results are uncertain. The general application of these conclusions provides an overview of the situation as a whole for the 1,400 departments, subprefectures, and districts. At a time when the national situation is critical, when it is urgent that people be made to understand the righteousness of paying taxes and performing military service, and when the difficulty of advancing education is so apparent, people still make no haste to find ways to deal with the situation. Instead, they proceed in a slow and faltering way, deceiving the emperor and leading the people astray. This is like digging a well to satisfy thirst, or indulging in formal greetings while coming to help extinguish a fire. How can success be the result?

I also implemented the ministry regulations on curricula for lower primary schools in the department. Six or seven years have passed since then, and there have been more than three graduating classes. In Chinese language the graduates can only recognize characters and give the most simple explanation of their meaning; they cannot read newspapers. In arithmetic they only know how to deal with figures on paper and are incapable of applying their knowledge to practical problems. In gymnastics they can just move their arms and legs and they are incapable of developing their courage. In moral training they only know how to recite anecdotes and principles and are ignorant of propriety. These students cannot read newspapers, cannot solve practical problems, do not have courage, and are ignorant of propriety. How can we expect that they will accept the payment of taxes and the performance of military service without protest? The Ministry of Education in its confusion has evidently been unable to enlighten the people. Our nation has yet to be awakened; we are in the throes of a long and deep night. How can we escape from this critical situation?

During the course of eight years I have acquired a certain level of experience, and feel that development in the future will become increasingly restricted. I know that my collaborators also have this fear. This is why I have asked my student Jiang[9] to draft a summary of the viewpoints expressed in our previous debates. I await the enlightened opinions of those in the empire who do not want education to harm the people. I would be grateful if they would have the goodwill to instruct me on this matter.

Commentary

The decree of 27 August 1908 anticipated nine years of preparation for the establishment of a constitutional regime. It outlined the main points of the program in each field, with each relevant ministry responsible for proposing concrete measures.[1] The duty of the Ministry of Education was "to open up the minds of the people by universalizing education." Consequently, at the end of March 1909, the ministry informed the provinces that compulsory education would be implemented. Each district had to conduct a census of the population in order to establish a sufficient number of schools for a ratio of one school for every two hundred households. This ratio was in accordance with the regulations of 1904: Zhang refers to them in the third paragraph of the text.[2] The nine-year program for education was promulgated on 16 April 1909. The plan aroused such criticism that the ministry immediately requested those responsible for education in the provinces to suggest ways of improving the 1904 regulations.[3]

In May the Jiangsu Provincial Education Association presented a memorial on the subject; the ideas it contained, identical to those of Zhang Jian, were incorporated (along with the same terms) into the new regulations on lower primary schools on 15 May 1909.[4] The text, therefore, was certainly not written in the thirty-fourth year of the reign of Guangxu. Moreover, Zhang states that he had been involved with education for eight years; his interest in education had begun in 1901. He also says that he had implemented the Ministry of Education regulations six or seven years previously; he was referring to the opening, in 1903, of the primary school attached to the Nantong Normal School. The text is no doubt a record of a speech Zhang gave to a meeting of the education association between the beginning of April and the beginning of May 1909, before the promulgation of new regulations on primary schools. It can also be assumed that the "summary of viewpoints," the drafting of which was Jiang Qian's responsibility, represented either the very text or the initial draft of the Jiangsu Education Association's memorial on primary education.

Zhang pointed out that education had failed in its duty to strengthen the state, reproached the Ministry of Education with promulgating incoherent and over-ambitious regulations, and demanded concrete measures to develop lower primary schools.

The text gives an indication of the results obtained by modern education eight years after it had been put into force. Zhang painted a gloomy picture, and for once forgot to praise the success of Nantong or give the new schools their due: he criticized the schools on both quantitative and qualitative grounds. His comments thus coincided with the criticisms frequently expressed at the time by Chinese as well as by foreigners.[5] It is true that the creation of new schools, already insufficient vis-à-vis the needs of the country, had a tendency to slow down after 1907. This slowdown varied among the regions. It was more apparent in provinces where development had begun earlier-a situation with which Zhang was familiar. Yet elsewhere, in provinces where development had begun later, the enthusiasm for creating schools was still at a peak, the result being that statistically the decrease in the number of schools is much less evident.[6] Also, Zhang's opinion on the standards of education should not be considered completely valid for all areas. Inspection reports, investigations, and contemporary eye-witness accounts show that standards varied greatly, not only from one region to another but also among schools in the same locality. In 1910, at the model primary school in Tianjin, "all classes were directed by teachers who not only had an understanding of modern pedagogical methods but who were also capable of applying them," wrote H. E. King. "I found there," he continued, "the best run primary school that I ever saw in China. The pupils were well disciplined, attentive and keen, and they revealed by their reading out loud in class a good control of the subject-matter; I have never seen better results in American schools." These remarks did not prevent him from remarking later on: "the progress made in most of the primary schools I visited, although a little better than that in traditional schools, was very much inferior to what one would call progress in the United States."[7]

One is struck by the way Zhang reproached the Ministry of Education with the failure of modern education. His tone is more virulent than in any of the preceding texts. The document obviously was not intended for the administration, but it should not be forgotten that this was the very period when memorials demanding the opening of a parliament were being drafted. The gentry, conscious of their strength and tired of waiting for government action, were no longer as hesitant as they had been to denounce the negligence and duplicity of the government.[8] While criticizing the performance of the Ministry of Education, Zhang defined the objective that education had to achieve. This objective was the same as that suggested by Liang Qichao and Luo Zhenyu eight years before: to create a "nation" (*guomin*).[9] Zhang Jian, however, stressed state control, the duties of the people, and obedience to the state; he made no mention of the political rights to which people could have access as a result of education. For Zhang national education was a guarantee of order: there would be no further "catastrophes" like the Boxer uprising. Official documents, which Zhang criticized for their lack of concrete results, expressed very much the same idea: "The most important aims of national education are to make everyone perform their duties and to preserve order";[10] "the three great misfortunes from which China suffers are localism, weakness, and an impractical spirit. In order to eradicate these misfortunes and improve the situation, it is essential to cultivate a public spirit, a military spirit, and a practical spirit."[11] The constitutional plan of 1908 envisaged that "Chinese subjects, in accordance with the laws, would have the duties of paying taxes and performing military service."[12] The antagonism between Zhang Jian and the government was therefore far from absolute. The text thus gives a good example of the change in attitudes and political situation of the moderate reformers during the last years of the monarchy. The growth of the revolutionary movement, in fact, drove them towards the right. For the moderate reformers, it was much more a question of compelling the government to implement a policy that would safeguard their interests than fundamentally reforming all the institutions of the state. Although conscious of the external threat to the country, they were no less aware of the danger that could befall them as a result of internal disorder.

TEXT 7

Zhang Jian, *Jiaoyu*, III/19b-22b

Speech at the Commercial School of Beijing[1] (second year of the Republic: 1913; p.d. 20 June 1911).

I had proposed that we meet yesterday at three o'clock. Due to an incident at the last moment, I was obliged to change the date. I am extremely sorry for the inconvenience caused. This is why I put aside my affairs for today in order to come and meet you here. I have a keen desire to visit all kinds of schools during my trip to the north.[2] I also wish to offer my knowledge to those who have the same aims I do in the fields of education and industry. The reason for this is that we are living at a time when the exchange of knowledge is valuable and not at a time when each person keeps his knowledge secret. How can people today persist in behaving selfishly?

I was brought up on the traditional examination system; I received the *jinshi* in 1894. I have seen the state become more endangered daily, while in Beijing and at the court high officials relied on limited ideas to deal with the situation.[3] It has frequently been said that in aspects of material civilization, such as the manufacture of guns and cannon, China had yielded superiority to the West, but in intellectual culture, China's claim to eminence, there was absolutely nothing that China need borrow from the foreigner. After having studied the question carefully, I believe that "China's claim to eminence" does not go beyond the eight-legged essay.[4] There are some sciences in which we have excelled, and others in which we have not.[5] It is no exaggeration to say that there was not a single person who knew anything about educational organization and pedagogy. Gradually, the idea of establishing schools was broached. However, it was necessary to begin the undertaking from the ground up; to establish universities before primary schools can be considered a failure to establish the foundations.[6] For primary schools the essential requirement is to have teachers: normal schools are therefore of the utmost importance. I decided to create a normal school, and soon began to go to work on the project. In order to create a normal school funds were needed. I was a poor scholar; how was I to obtain the necessary funds? At that time I had succeeded in attaining official rank, but I thought that an official should not think of enriching himself. The ancients remarked that when a person is poor he becomes an official, but this proverb only applies to the guards of the city gates.[7] From the lowest to the highest rank, an official should not openly seek to enrich himself. From the point of view of justice and fairness, it is only in industry that people can openly seek to enrich themselves. It was this fact that induced me to create industrial enterprises.

On what economic base did these enterprises get started? I am a native of Tongzhou and I knew that cotton was its most profitable product.[8] With the exception of that in the United States, this cotton has no equal in the world. It was for this reason that I established a spinning-mill. However, since the funds from one individual were insufficent to start the enterprise, I was forced to make an appeal for outside capital. The time was just after the bankruptcy of the textile mills in Shanghai.[9] I am of an honest disposition; in my leisure hours I had not assiduously frequented rich people and I therefore did not have friends among them. However, in these circumstances I wanted them to contribute funds in the form of share capital. Since enterprises in the same economic sector had gone bankrupt, it was evident that this was not an easy thing to achieve. I made haste to get things moving and resolutely faced the difficulties. After forty-four months the arrangements were practically settled. The complications of the intervening months cannot be described in a few words. It was originally predicted that 500,000 *taels* would be invested; in fact, funds did not even amount to 200,000 *taels* and only a few people invested money. At first, several tens of thousands of *taels* were invested. Just when the construction of the mill had been completed, it was announced all the funds were exhausted.[10] A few more tens of thousands of *taels* were collected, not enough to buy the necessary supplies of raw cotton, and it was announced the funds were again exhausted. I sought money wherever I could. I was in a perpetual financial squeeze, and on top of that I had to endure the obstructions placed in my path by petty-minded people. There was also external opposition.[11] No one has ever experienced such difficulties and, considering my past, I myself have rarely known such difficulties. Yet I was not in the least discouraged. If I had at that time been discouraged and abandoned the enterprise, not only would the mill have been incomplete but the shareholders' investment would have lost all value. You can imagine how few people would have still been willing to advance me credit if I had done this. This is why I had no fear of sacrificing my immediate interests and was intent on facing the difficulties. Moreover, I have always been a calm person, gazing with the same eye upon foul or fair weather. While I am on the subject, I would very much like to draw your attention to the fact that this enterprise was established in forty-four months, that the total administrative costs were less than 10,000 *taels*, and that I have not received any salary owed to me.

I have observed businessmen of today: by the time they have assembled capital the foundations of an enterprise have barely been established. These so-called industrialists, with their horses and carriages, occupy their time in entertaining and amusing themselves in society. Within five to six years, or three to four years, their businesses go bankrupt and the shareholders' capital and interest go down the drain. Whenever this happens, once people have lost confidence in them, it is the end even for seemingly prosperous businessmen. By noting this fact, I have realized that effort, frugality, and forebearance are the prime virtues and constitute the sole path to success. After 1900, among those who came to Beijing, some said that if I had abandoned public office in order to manage enterprises it must have been because industry was more profitable than officialdom. Others said that I had obtained a profit of several tens of thousands of *taels* and wondered why I was continuing to appeal for capital. At that time people believed that I was merely thinking of my own fortune. If I had considered only my personal interests, the establishment of the mill would have been impossible. With the collective interest in mind was anything impossible?

Since the mill needed supplies of raw cotton and since cotton cultivation necessarily depended on agriculture, I established a land reclamation company.[12] Then, as cottonseed contains oil, I established an oil-works as a subsidiary industry.[13] After this, in order to expand the market and facilitate communications, I established a steamship company.[14] You have to realize that the reason for my unceasing activity was my concern to sustain the cotton mill. I want above all to use this occasion to prove to you the sincerity of my motives. The circumstances were such that if I had only my personal fortune in mind, even if I had amassed millions of *taels* this would have brought no benefits.

When the financial foundations of the mill were secure I proposed to create a normal school in order to fulfill a lifelong ambition. At that time the atmosphere was still not receptive to new ideas, especially in the field of education. I donated the entire salary owed to me by the mill over several years, as well as the interest it had produced, in order to finance the school. The following year, the normal schools of Lianghu and Liangjiang were established.[15] At present there are in Tongzhou a normal school, a commercial secondary school, an agricultural secondary school, and a girls' normal school. In that year I proposed to convert the commercial secondary school into a commercial primary school. The 87 primary schools are supported by the normal school. I am proposing that in five years their number should reach 280.[16] The material success I have achieved over the last several years has entirely financed the two normal schools. A poor scholar, I have obtained concrete results through a firm will and arduous effort. The scholars of the empire could do even more. Even though, in my case, it cannot be said that support was completely absent, people should remember the example of Wu Xun, a native of Shandong, who is famous throughout the empire.[17] Wu spent his time begging, with the sky for his roof and the ground for his mattress. He was bereft of everything and had absolutely no support, yet he devoted himself to the development of education. By daily accumulating the alms he received, he was able to muster considerable funds and to create several private schools. This should make scholars and high officials blush. For man, the worst thing is to have no will or to be unable to pursue one's goal with resolute energy. The significance of the result depends on individual ability and other conditions, but if the goal is pursued with resolute energy the importance of the result does not matter. It is impossible, in any case, that there will be no result.[18] Everyone is the master of his own will and nothing in the world can limit this power.

By undertaking land reclamation in the three northeastern provinces, I am going to pursue my goals.[19] When our contemporaries are faced with something to do, they at first have the idea, even before implementation, that it will not succeed: this is a troublesome phenomenon. It will not do to be anxious about it if the foreigners have extensive demands. If they want to take something that I do not want to give, the two sides should face up to each other; each side has an equal chance to gain the advantage. If they want to take something and I do not dare to withhold it, I have admitted defeat in advance without resistance. At the end of the Ming, under the reigns of Tianqi and Chongzhen,[20] while the empire could have still continued to function, everyone thought that the dynasty was basically finished. People awaited death with their hands tied. After the establishment of the present dynasty some disturbances persisted in the south, but it was already too late. The history of China shows, therefore, that general security or danger depends on the safety or loss of the north. Today, in seeking a policy of national salvation can the example of the fall of the Ming be ignored? Moreover, if we want to safeguard the three northeastern provinces today, it is much easier to achieve this than during the time of the Ming. In fact, the establishment of industry in this area can bring about wealth, the strengthening of the frontier, the prosperity of the country, and the well-being of the people. During the last few years many people have proposed that land reclamation be undertaken in the three northeastern provinces. I myself submitted such a proposal to the Jiangsu Provincial Assembly and it was approved by a majority vote. There is no difficulty in simply talking about such a proposal, but several years have elapsed without anyone putting it into practice. Spurious excuses have been given, for example, that it is difficult to mobilize the capital, or that because the security of the three northeastern provinces remains questionable investments in this region would incur enormous risks. In my opinion, if a proposal which has been approved is not implemented, is it not because people believe that such a proposal cannot succeed? As for me, I took the initiative in proposing this project, and am ashamed of having spoken without knowing how to act.[21] This is why, rolling up my sleeves with resolute determination, I have decided to apply myself to this great task.

There is something else that I would like to speak to you about today. You are at present studying in a commercial school, but later on after your graduation what will you in fact do? Will you profit from your title,[22] discard what you have learned, and become officials? Or will you, making use of what you have learned, take up a career in commerce? If you choose the first alternative your studies will be of no use to you: your commercial studies will have as much value as the eight-legged essay. Yet I fear that you will not be capable of embarking on the career offered in the second alternative. I have observed the duties undertaken by apprentices in commercial firms: they offer cigarettes, pour tea, and obey the employer in every way. Could you do this? I fear the answer is no. In foreign commercial firms which employ graduates, the situation is completely different. However, it is extremely difficult to change

overnight traditional practices to which our country is accustomed.
This is why I sincerely hope that you will have endurance and
patience. There is nothing the other apprentices do of which you are
not capable, and you alone have the knowledge to surpass them. By
revealing your qualities vis-à-vis the shortcomings of the other
apprentices, you will succeed in your aims. Nevertheless, you should
realize that there is absolutely no reason why your personal
pleasures and enjoyment should exceed those of others. Since all
men are alike, why should your way of life be extravagant?
Formerly, at Nanjing, in addition to my ordinary duties I was in
charge of a commercial school.[23] I shall pass on to you now some
remarks I made which enlightened the students of that school. Our
personal pleasures must not exceed in the slightest way those
enjoyed by the most ordinary of our contemporaries, while the force
of our will must not in the slightest way be inferior to that
manifested by the most eminent of the ancients. Since you are being
trained in commerce, I hope that after graduation you will not
discard what you have learned and that you will be able to contribute
to society. Above all, you should not be deficient in the virtues of
endurance and patience.

   Time is running short today and I am obliged to end my talk
after having raised only a few points. I have more or less explained
my ideas and I hope you will correct them.

Commentary

   The text was composed before the fall of the Qing, since Zhang
Jian spoke of "the present dynasty." He also mentioned that the
normal school of Liangjiang was operating; it was closed down only
after the Wuchang uprising. Finally, Zhang indicated that he was on
his way to the three northeastern provinces; it was in July 1911 that
he undertook this journey, during his stay in Beijing. Moreover, his
diary mentions that the speech at the commercial school took place
on 20 June 1911.[1] The date given by Zhang Xiaoruo is therefore too
late.

   Addressing himself to an audience of students, Zhang retraced
the stages of his career and his successes in industry and education,
as well as specifying the moral principles that had guided him. He
pointed out the exemplary value of his experience for Chinese internal and foreign policy, and concluded by urging his audience to be
modest and hardworking.

This is one of the first texts in which Zhang began to create his own myth and that of Nantong: the model district managed by a model public figure. It is significant that he began this task in front of a young audience. Zhang in 1911 was a man who had attained first-rank prominence and who was influential at the national level. He was among the wealthiest in his province, the most prosperous area of China. He presided over the provincial assembly and directed numerous associations, and was one of the leaders of the constitutional movement. At Beijing the Prince Regent had received Zhang in a long audience and had offered him the chance of becoming the emperor's tutor. Among high officials he was treated as an equal. There is therefore nothing surprising in the fact that he wished to propagate his personal ideals.

The retrospective logic Zhang applied to the development of his career is striking. He began by critically reflecting upon the decline of his country. In order to overcome China's intellectual inferiority, he thought of developing education; in order to assure China of necessary resources, he created various industries. Each stage of his career was carefully planned. In order to spread education, there was a need for teachers; Zhang therefore began by establishing normal schools. Zhang based industry on the most convenient raw material and methodically developed the economic sectors connected with it to improve its chances of success. When he had sufficient funds he began to create schools and gradually organized a complete educational system. Zhang was anxious to show that moral principles were behind the process of this development: honesty had prevented him from seeking to enrich himself as an official, a concern for public well-being had led him to develop industry and education, and sincere concern for the public interest had encouraged him to donate his time and money to such matters. Even more than all this, he had been constantly supported by the strength of his will. Was all this true?

The facts that Zhang presented were true, but he neglected to mention that he had begun the construction of the Tongzhou mill at the request of Zhang Zhidong. It is true that, like many of his contemporaries, he could have refused or eventually given up in the face of difficulties. It is no less true that Zhang did not embark on a career in industry entirely on his own initiative. This must necessarily prompt caution when analyzing Zhang's statements concerning his intentions. The apparent inner logic of his projects Zhang emphasized occurred to him after the event, although he easily imagined that he had always had such long-term plans.[2]

However, the moral justification that he gave for his actions brings into question his modernism.

Zhang presented himself as having the aspirations and virtues of the sage. Numerous citations from the classics enhance the Confucian tone of Zhang's spiritual "biography." Yet three elements disturb the harmonious image of the Confucian gentleman: Zhang's purely intellectual way of thinking, which was the starting point for his activity; his voluntarism; and his stress on the independent development of industry. His rational outlook and his willpower were due to his temperament and common sense. Zhang cultivated these characteristics by following the precepts of enlightened eighteenth-century philosophers and they are confirmed in his biographies, as well as other texts.[3] Such personality traits indicate that Zhang's respect for Confucian orthodoxy did not limit his mental horizon. However, the most important aspect of Zhang's character concerns his attitude towards industry. In the text he gives away his real thoughts on the subject. Even if at the beginning Zhang thought of industry as a simple adjunct to education, this text shows that with the establishment of the first enterprise (the cotton mill), Zhang became involved with the establishment of a system of inter-dependent industries. Industry should no longer be surbordinated to education but rather was an end in itself; its importance tended to outweigh that of education more and more. With the emphasis on mechanization, accumulation of capital, and the facility of communications, this industry would be quite different from traditional ways of production. Zhang's concern for education (even modern education) can be strictly considered as representing continuity with the Confucian tradition, but his desire for the continuous production of wealth and the unlimited exploitation of raw materials reveals a new attitude, that of modern capitalism. With Zhang Jian modern attitudes and activities were grafted onto traditional ideas and practices; they gave life to one another. Confucianism, far from being the main obstacle to the introduction of capitalism, served to legitimize and even promote it.

Zhang cited political as well as moral justification for his actions: the growth of capitalism would guarantee national independence. Zhang mentioned territorial integrity and referred to the establishment of the Qing dynasty as a national catastrophe; he made no reference to his activities in the reform and constitutional movements. This shows how much Zhang's ideas had changed a few months before the revolution: the capitalism that he called for was no longer destined to support the dynasty. Zhang's capitalism was purely nationalistic, with no regard for the form of government. This attitude, which was not unique to Zhang Jian, explains why the overthrow of the monarchy encountered hardly any opposition from the gentry.

What preoccupied Zhang in his plans for the future was that those who possessed technical superiority through their education should make "a contribution to society," that is to say, that they devote all their efforts to the modernization of the country. However, Zhang knew that in order to achieve this the educated had to overcome all traditional obstacles by means of self-denial, endurance, patience, and frugality. In sum, this text shows Zhang Jian's view that modern education would serve to train the elite of a future capitalist society which would only come about through the practice of Confucian virtues.

TEXT 8

Zhang Jian, *Jiaoyu*, III/12b-13a

A Discussion of Discipline as a Guiding Idea in Education (first year of the Republic: 1912; p.d. September to December 1912).

No indiscipline in the army, no indiscipline in the schools: such is the general rule in all republics today. If the army is undisciplined, the general can no longer command; if there is no discipline in the school, the teacher can no longer teach. If the general cannot command, the army will be defeated; if the teacher cannot teach, the school will fail. For a country, there is no greater catastrophe. The *Xue ji* states: "In all forms of study the most difficult condition to fulfill is the strictness of the teacher. If the teacher is strict, the Way is respected; if the Way is respected, people will know how to study."[1] Schools in Europe and America, in addition to teaching methods and school administration, emphasize the importance of training and obedience. That Rousseau's theory of undisciplined education is not viable has already been recognized by educators throughout the world.[2] In China, as in other countries, pedagogy should emphasize discipline, without which there can be neither instruction nor study.

Recently, political reform has ushered in the Republic.[3] Some students who do not have a clear understanding of matters mistakenly think that indiscipline is a feature of the Republic. They consider order as old-fashioned,[4] and accuse strict teachers of being despots: I have heard such comments many times in private discussions. It is forgotten that in Europe and America republican citizens are brought up solely on respect for public morality and love of order. It is said that all offenses against public morality and violations of order are a danger to the Republic. I shall use an analogy: if you go south in order to get to a place in the north, the further you go the further you are from your goal.[5] Today, cries for a republic can be heard all over the country. Yet the educational level of the people is insufficient, and we are therefore increasingly traveling along a false path. I have often noticed this. All this is the heritage of the corruption of education in former times under the Qing. The evil effects have spread throughout the entire country. It is necessary today to begin purifying the stench and eliminating the poison. In his *Letter of Precepts to My Son*, Zhu Gezhongwu said: "Talent demands study; study demands calm. Without study one cannot develop talent; without calm one cannot achieve study."[6]

Finally, it is necessary that both teachers and pupils, showing concern for the future of the Republic, firmly adhere to the following principles: the rule for all instruction is strictness, and the rule for all study is calm. Those who disturb others should be expelled without hesitation. Because I sincerely believe in the importance of education and because I have a true affection for the pupils, I give this warning against what appears to me a danger.[7]

Commentary

Zhang Xiaoruo maintains that this text was written in 1912, which accords with the reference Zhang makes to the "recent" establishment of the Republic. The text was certainly written before the *Decree on Education* promulgated by Yuan Shikai on 22 January 1913,[1] and sometime at the end of 1912 after the wave of student strikes and disturbances that followed the revolution.

In this text Zhang Jian reminded his audience that discipline, as a guarantee for study, order, and morality, was essential in the training of republican citizens.

The author's scornful irony gives some indication of the atmosphere in Chinese schools during the first months of the Republic. Even in those schools where previously discipline and order had reigned, as in Nantong, the revolution aroused an extraordinary enthusiasm among the students. This enthusiasm reached a point at which all regulations and authority were considered an abuse against which it was necessary to rebel in the name of freedom and equality.[2] The students derived their ideas from their reading material, among which Rousseau was a favorite.[3] This explains why Zhang went to special pains to denigrate him. Moreover, during the first year of the Republic the established order was disputed without any one faction or group being able to impose a new order on the country. There was no official authority or social pressure capable of compelling students to respect their teachers and avoid involvement in politics, which had become so strong that the slightest student-teacher clash took on the appearance of a political conflict. In one year, the eleven provincial secondary schools of Zhejiang witnessed eight strikes; the eleven provincial secondary schools of Jiangsu witnessed five.[4] Politicization of students was more noticeable than during the student disturbances at the end of the monarchy and affected secondary as much as higher education. It was not simply a question of employing words like "despot" to insult teachers or of advocating misdirected slogans, as Zhang Jian would have his audience believe. A substantial change was occurring: the political consciousness of the students had been awoken and students showed themselves capable of organized action. They became, in fact, an autonomous force in public life. The phenomenon, as Zhang admitted, spread across the country and this is why he felt it necessary to give a solemn warning; under the Qing he had never specifically condemned student disturbances.[5] Zhang Xiaoruo mentions that as far as education in Nantong was concerned, his father "was always an advocate of discipline and not compromise," and that "from 1912 onwards he had a firm outlook from which he never wavered," an outlook revealed in the text (to which Zhang's son referred).[6] The text was probably not intended exclusively for schools in Nantong; in any event, it quickly became well-known.[7]

In the text Zhang Jian defined his view of the relationship among education, politics, and morality. He compared the school to an army. Such a comparison showed the influence of ideas on "national militarization" (junminzhuyi), "national military education" (junguomin jiaoyu), and a "militant citizenry" (junguomin), that had appeared in 1901 and now regained popularity as anarchy threatened the young Republic.[8] These ideas came from Japan and Germany. They comprised two aspects: military education, which Zhang advocated under the Qing but refrained from mentioning in the text; and the submission to a national discipline, the organization of society using the army as a model, with everyone strictly obeying orders, absolute equality within each level of the hierarchy, and a universally respected moral code. The revolutionaries advocated militarization so that the people could take power. The moderates had advocated militarization because they wanted to see the rebirth of a national spirit, and thus the restoration of national sovereignty. After the establishment of the Republic, the Tongmenghui, and then the Guomindang, also adopted this view. Cai Yuanpei had "national

military education" included among the official aims of education
promulgated in July 1912, in the hope that the military caste would
eventually disappear.[9] On the other hand, Zhang Jian and his
moderate friends henceforth emphasized discipline and military-like
obedience more than instruction in the use of firearms, which
appeared to them dangerous internally and useless externally.[10]
Zhang indicated that this discipline was a precept of traditional
Chinese morality. Behind this call for a return to the ways of
antiquity (a call that also contained elements of nationalism), is the
idea of the "national essence" which had been embraced with
enthusiasm by a number of reformist and revolutionary thinkers
during the last ten years of the dynasty.[11] However, in a new set of
circumstances its meaning had changed. Desiring to convince radical
youth of the necessity for discipline, Zhang contrived to prove that
discipline and obedience were the bases of Western democracies.
Towards this end, he omitted any reference to the political
significance of a republican regime and presented the state as an
absolute to which citizens were tied by a nonreciprocal moral
obligation. Zhang identified the established order with a moral order,
a typically conservative attitude. Under the monarchy, Zhang had
agreed that citizens had moral duties towards the state, but only on
the condition that the latter fulfilled certain obligations itself. Then,
when he had lost all hope that the government might be reformed, he
agreed that citizens had moral duties towards society, but with the
condition that they had the right to guide society. In contrast, this
text recalls the attitude of the Qing government and its tone reminds
the reader of the Sacred Edict and other Confucian exhortations in
imperial decrees.

The text suggests that the revolution had satisfied most of
Zhang Jian's desires by giving him the opportunity to participate
directly in government. He now wished to conserve his power and to
prevent any disorder that might threaten his interests. In
competition with, rather than in opposition to, the traditional elite
from which he had come and with which he shared a Confucian
education, it was natural that once Zhang had succeeded in attaining
a dominant position he would think of using moral props in order to
justify his authority. The form of the regime mattered little to him,
provided that it preserve the dominance of the social group that he
represented: thus Zhang preferred to support Yuan Shikai rather
than the Guomindang. If he considered that "the level of the people
was too low," he refrained from advocating that the people's political
level should be raised. Education could still be used to train obedient

and competent citizens, but not to train the political supporters of a republic.

The attitude that this text reveals was not transitory; as Zhang Xiaoruo noted, Zhang Jian maintained such an outlook until his death. It indicates the strength of the ties that linked the bourgeoisie with the *ancien regime*, ties that limited the bourgeoisie's political opportunities as well as its independent choice of action. By neglecting to educate youth in the ways of parliamentary democracy, did not the bourgeoisie risk quickly losing its control of power? Some people were aware of this danger: although the text soon became part of the conservatives' propaganda arsenal, it also became a target of condemnation by liberals.[12]

TEXT 9

Zhang Jian, *Jiaoyu*, III/13a-14b

Letter to Huang Renzhi on the Normal School and Primary Schools[1] (first year of the Republic: 1912; p.d. end of December 1912 to beginning of January 1913).

I have just returned from Shanghai, and am in the process of arranging some matters concerning education that have to be dealt with immediately. I have to discuss some of these matters thoroughly with you and request your assistance in accelerating progress in general and specialized education.[2] I shall discuss the items below one by one; my greatest hope is that you will be able to help me.

Lower Normal School

The school currently belongs to the category of substitute school.[3] Next year students' tuition and boarding fees will be paid by the province. We can therefore look forward to an increasing number of students. However, there remains some construction work which has been started but not yet completed. (a) It is necessary to enlarge the second covered sports ground. The cost involved in expanding to a width of thirty-six or forty feet, a length of one hundred feet and, at the same time, in making provision for a storage area of nine *jian* for the apparatus, will amount to three thousand dollars. (b) The cost involved in the construction of dormitories for the attached higher primary school (an area of twenty-three *jian* in all containing 120 students), in addition to the costs for the furniture, will amount to six thousand dollars. Altogether, the costs will amount to nine thousand dollars.

I calculate that ordinary expenditures and debts for the normal school will be approximately forty thousand dollars. The repayment of debts can be stretched out over a number of years, while awaiting the returns from land endowments.[4] If ordinary expenditures are fourteen or fifteen thousand dollars, to which would be added the annual financial aid for the orphanage and a part of the financial responsiblity for the girls' normal school (there are expenditures that my brother and I share between us), amounting to another five to six thousand dollars, my resources will not be sufficient. The two items of construction work for the normal school would thus not be undertaken and the school would ultimately suffer. I have previously observed that in the annual provincial education expenditures, fifty thousand dollars is given to substitute schools. I suggest that we first of all think of asking for twenty thousand dollars. After deducting eleven thousand dollars for student fellowships, we would then have nine thousand dollars of provincial funds: the two items of construction work noted above could thus be completed. If nine thousand dollars is not sufficient, it will only be a matter of about one to two thousand dollars more. I would do my best to make up for the rest. So much for the normal school.

Attached Lower and Higher Primary Schools[5]

As a rule, tuition fees for the lower primary school are four dollars per year and those for the higher primary school are eight dollars per year. Most of the pupils come from families who are able to support them; one-third find it difficult to pay the fees. There are often cases of hardship. Nevertheless, among the students accepted by the normal school each year, a great many have not reached the standard of those who enter the normal school after having graduated from the attached higher primary school. In order to plan for the development of the normal school, it would be appropriate to first make plans for the attached lower and higher primary schools. This is an example of vegetables and fruit you grow yourself tasting better than those you buy at the market. I therefore propose that from next year the lower primary school fees be reduced by three-quarters or abolished completely; this will cost over four hundred dollars. Higher primary school fees should be reduced by one-half; this will cost another four to five hundred dollars.

It is therefore necessary to anticipate an additional one thousand dollars in the financial assistance given to the normal school; such a sum would assure the satisfactory development of the normal school's base (i.e., the primary schools). So much for this matter.

Agricultural Schools in the Province

There are three established by the province: two are situated south of the Yangzi and one north of the Yangzi.[6] People say this is an unequal distribution. At the present moment the equipment for the Tongzhou Agricultural School is nearly all in place and the curriculum is practically all settled. This year, due to special construction work, expenditures have exceeded ten thousand dollars. I have undertaken responsibility for everything. If the province recognizes this school also as a substitute school, it will cost the province about six thousand dollars next year. Students will be divided into two groups, A and B, and will form six classes; each class will comprise thirty pupils. If the province subsidizes the costs by two-thirds (that is to say, four thousand dollars) or by one-half (that is to say, three thousand dollars), we shall be able to accept students from Yangzhou and Huaian.[7] The province's reputation will be enhanced by this and my own financial resources could then be used to increase the number of primary schools for the poor, among other areas in education. So much for this question.

Girls' Normal School[8]

I request that this school also be recognized as a substitute school. The final draft of the annual provincial budget is nearly completed. On my return to Tongzhou, I again made inquiries as to whether the district assembly intended to make the girls' normal school a district school.[9] The assembly members vie with each other in uttering empty words and that is all. In fact, they are incapable of assuming the costs. The district council suggested abandoning the idea and leaving the school, as before, under private management.[10] Even if the school is privately managed, it can still be recognized as a substitute school. My original request was that next year, apart from the little over five thousand dollars for students' boarding and tuition fees, fifteen thousand dollars should first of all be contributed so that we can construct centers for training women in sericulture, child care, and medical knowledge. Female education has to be vigorously encouraged. You should make an effort to help me implement this proposal. So much for this question.

The province originally calculated a sum of fifty thousand to cover costs for any establishment that was recognized as a substitute school. If the boys' and girls' normal schools were both recognized as substitute schools, costs would not exceed forty-two thousand dollars in all: eight thousand dollars could thus be saved. Approximately twenty-five thousand dollars for repair work and enlargement of buildings at the two normal schools would be needed for only one year. In 1914 the subsidy for the two normal schools will not exceed twenty thousand dollars at the most: nearly thirty thousand dollars will be saved. I will personally still have to contribute fifteen to twenty thousand dollars. You will gladly approve of this plan.

Regarding the original proposal to assist agricultural schools with a provincial annual subsidy, we are asking at the moment for four thousand dollars only, and later on six thousand dollars at the most. With this subsidy we will be able to reduce student fees by one-half which, for the 180 students of the two groups, amount to eight thousand dollars in all. This sum represents only one-half percent of the provincial budget of one million and fifty thousand dollars. Our motives for requesting such a subsidy are, moreover, justifiable and worthy.

To come to the subject of the Nantong Commercial School, I proposed that it offer two specialized fields-banking and taxation.[11] Due to a lack of funds, we have been restricted to just the specialized field of banking. I propose that industrial enterprises put aside two thousand dollars annually to serve as a contribution towards the commercial school: we will therefore be able to employ more teachers and the school will have the two sections on banking and taxation.

The commercial exhibition hall has now been transferred to the Guandi Temple (it used to be situated in the Lodge of the Kui Stars on the island in the middle of the water; the site was inconvenient for visitors, hence the change).[12] However, funds for the commercial exhibition hall are also exhausted. I request an annual subsidy of three thousand dollars. For the three items mentioned above, the total will be less than ten thousand dollars. If this sum can be granted I will await your reply before ordering the chamber of commerce and the agricultural school to draft a memorial. I am sure you will approve. I believe that the sum I am requesting for these six items is without doubt very moderate in comparison to what is being asked for in other districts. Yet I dare not expect too much from human goodwill. You will have to forgive me. I fervently hope that when you have received my letter you will reply to me point by point in order to dispel my worries.

Commentary

The financial requests that Zhang addressed to Huang Yanpei show that the latter was already the head of the Jiangsu Office of Education; he had been appointed to this post on 19 December 1912.[1] The communication concerns the budget of 1913, since Zhang says that the financial needs would be less exorbitant in 1914. Moreover, the normal school had just been recognized as a substitute school-an event that took place at the end of December 1912.[2] These details, which accord with the information given in *Jiaoyu zazhi*, show that the text was composed during the last days of December 1912, or the beginning of 1913 if Zhang considered "next year" as the lunar year (which is probable). *Jiaoyu zazhi*, in fact, mentions that on 10 January 1913, after having finally accepted the conversion of the normal school, Zhang Jian addressed a report to the *dudu* on the expenditures and anticipated number of students for the first six months of 1913.[3] The text, which is a letter, was a private document aimed at coming to an amicable agreement over certain matters with the official directly involved. This practice was quite common in Chinese administrative procedure, whereby each official measure had to have a prior unofficial agreement before it could be implemented. Such an unofficial agreement may not have necessarily always been subsequently honored, but it allowed the memorialist to save face.

Zhang gave specific details on the budget for his schools, and took advantage of his personal relationship with Huang Yanpei to ask him to set aside a subsidy of 50,000 dollars from the 1913 provincial budget.

Unlike other sources, this text gives information on the costs of education at Nantong. The upkeep of the two normal schools and the attached primary school amounted to a minimum of 35,000 dollars (that is to say, 20 dollars per student each year for the primary school, 100 dollars for the boys' normal school and 125 dollars for the girls' normal school, not including costs for food and repair work). The costs for the attached primary school had been reduced compared to those in 1907, when they were 30 dollars per student each year, but remained clearly higher than the provincial average of 14.1 dollars for schools of a similar level. Out of sixty districts, only in four were the average costs higher than 20 dollars per pupil; in ten districts the average costs were less than 10 dollars per pupil. The boys' normal school had reduced its costs, which were 150

dollars per student in 1907. However, due to new development, costs
for the girls' normal school had increased by one-quarter. Costs for
the two normal schools remained much more burdensome than
elsewhere in Jiangsu, where the average costs for schools of this
category amounted to 50 dollars per student each year. There were
only two districts where costs exceeded 100 dollars per student.[4]
This was because at Nantong the personnel were more numerous:
fourteen teachers and administrators for two hundred students at
the boys' normal school; nine teachers and eight administrators for
less than one hundred students at the girls' normal school; and
eleven teachers and two administrators for the attached primary
school. Elsewhere there was generally only one teacher for every
thirty pupils. Zhang did not spare any less expense on school
equipment, books, maps, and furniture, or on the upkeep of
buildings.

In meeting these expenses, the funds furnished by the land
endowment contributed little, that is to say hardly one-tenth of the
total. Private contributions furnished nearly one-half of the financial
resources. Public funds were donated in a haphazard fashion; Zhang
wanted to see the share of public funds increased and put on a
permanent basis, thus making the school's budget more secure.[5] It
was for this reason that he accepted the conversion of the normal
school into a substitute school. Despite this, however, school fees
remained an essential resource for these establishments. The fees
were high: thirty dollars per year for the boys' normal school,[6] fifteen
dollars per year for the girls' normal school, and from four to eight
dollars per year for the primary school. Such fees were generally
similar to those charged by good schools in Nanjing, Shanghai, and
Beijing.[7] In a poor region such as Nantong, these fees obviously
restricted the social circle in which recruitment of pupils took place, a
circle already limited enough elsewhere. Zhang's letter is one of the
rare documents of the period that gives some details on the problem.

Zhang remarked that one-third of the primary school pupils
"have difficulty in paying their fees," but this does not necessarily
mean that they came from poor families. To the tuition fees must be
added boarding fees since the practice was that students lived in;
these amounted to thirty to forty dollars per year. In order to
educate a child at the primary school, a family therefore needed to
spend thirty-five to fifty dollars per year. At this time workers in
Zhang Jian's enterprises earned fifty to one hundred dollars per
year, while an agricultural wage-laborer received twelve to fifteen
dollars per year in addition to food and lodging.[8] At Nantong, in

1912, thirty-five dollars represented the annual rent for eighteen *mu* of land of ordinary quality; such a sum was equivalent to approximately four-tenths of the land's produce. The surface area of the average landholding at that time was fourteen *mu*.[9] For the majority of tenants and landholding peasants, who comprised nine-tenths of the population, there was no question of sending their sons to the normal school or attached primary school. However, children from the richest families did not attend either; they were educated in their homes and then sent elsewhere because attendance at the normal school carried with it the obligation to teach in Nantong after graduation. Such a requirement made the school unattractive. It was therefore from among an intermediate social group that these schools recruited their pupils: sons of gentry and landowners involved in local commerce or sharing in the profits of district industries, sons of officials, teachers established in Nantong, merchants, or, finally, sons of rich peasants whose participation in weaving handicrafts, which flourished in the region, allowed them to earn a cash surplus.[10] Those who depended mainly on traditional revenues such as scholar gentry (who earned about one hundred dollars per year) were only just able to meet the costs required by modern education.[11]

Comparing this text with text 2 makes it clear that education in Tongzhou remained in a precarious financial situation. However, this time Zhang attempted to make the situation more stable by a procedure that was more modern in nature: he wanted to make the cost of education in Tongzhou a regular item of the provincial budget. The provincial budget had risen to approximately ten million, of which one million was reserved for education.[12] By requesting fifty thousand and then twenty thousand dollars for Tongzhou, Zhang would have secured one-twentieth or one-fortieth of the provincial educational budget, with as many as sixty districts in Jiangsu. However, the financial share was proportional to the demographic importance of Nantong for the province as a whole.

By accepting financial aid from the province, Zhang was apparently surrendering his undisputed control over education in Nantong. In fact, his aims were to extend free education and to enlarge the schools so that the middle classes could have increased access to them. He knew very well that with official support and the influence he possessed the system of official subsidies would not in any way remove the control that he exercised over education. This control, in 1912, represented what the Chinese called *xuefa,* a "cultural lordship," analogous to "military lordships" (*junfa*). In ten years the number of schools in Nantong had increased considerably. Due to his wealth and his duties as chairman of the local and provincial education associations, Zhang Jian had inspection rights over all of them, as well as over many others in the province. Above all, he personally managed all specialist schools and directed several others outside the district, in which graduates from his schools could receive a higher education. The ideology of this cultural sway is defined in the previous text. This text reveals its material foundations: the recruitment of students from among an intermediate class; the control of all the schools, in particular those that trained technicians; and the monopoly of public resources.

Zhang Jian's "cultural lordship" comprised social, economic, and political aspects. It corresponded to a general tendency in China that took shape after 1911: the preponderance of centrifrugal forces.[13] As with the warlords, Zhang's contemporaries, Zhang Jian sought to appropriate the authority of the state in order to benefit local interests. Although his methods were pacific, like the warlords he erected a personal stronghold.

PART III

APPENDICES

APPENDIX I

Friends and Collaborators of Zhang Jian during the Years 1901-12

There is no attempt here to give full biographies, especially in the case of important people like Wang Guowei. Only certain details useful in describing the political and social circles in which Zhang moved will be given.

Chen Chutao

A merchant from Haimen who had interests in several industrial and commercial enterprises in the region, Chen possessed a degree-title. He cooperated financially with Zhang Jian, notably to create Dasheng, and supported his actions in other fields.

Chen Sanli (1862-1937)

Chen was a native of Jiangxi who obtained the *jinshi* degree in 1886. He assisted his father, who was governor of Hunan in 1895, to launch a program of reform in the province. He established close ties with Liang Qichao and Tan Sitong, and was dismissed from official life after the Hundred Days Reform. In 1900 he collaborated with Zhang Jian in the organization of the "mutual defense of the southeast." This collaboration continued afterwards, particularly in railway enterprises. In 1907 Chen became chief administrator of the Nanchang-Jiujiang railway. He also shared literary interests with Zhang. Chen starved himself to death after the Japanese had occupied Beijing.

Fan Dangshi (1854-1904)

A *juren* degree holder who originally came from Nantong, Fan had studied with Zhang Jian. He enjoyed a considerable literary reputation and taught in several academies. He was a supporter of reforms and an admirer of Japan. Zhang consulted him often and benefitted from his prestige in Tongzhou.

Huang Yanpei (1879-1965)

See text 9, n. 1.

Jiang Daomin

Jiang was a pupil of Zhang Jian's at the Wenzheng Academy in Nanjing. After its closure, in 1898, he completed his studies at the military school. Zhang employed him afterwards to assist in his enterprises, especially those concerned with land clearance. He carried out map surveys of the district and took charge of urban works.

Jiang Qian

See text 6, n. 9.

Lei Fen (1879-?)

A native of Songjiang in Jiangsu, Lei graduated from Waseda University in Japan. Afterwards he worked as a journalist for *Shibao* [The times of Shanghai] and became a member of the Jiangsu Education Association and the Public Association to Prepare for the Establishment of a Constitution. Zhang Jian met with him frequently from 1906 onwards. Lei became a member of the parliament elected in 1910 and played an important role under Cheng Dequan during the 1911 Revolution. During the Republic he occupied the post of finance minister.

Li Houyou

Originally from Zhejiang, Li was president of the Shanghai Chamber of Commerce. He founded, with Zhang Jian, the Dada Wharf Company. He was interested in developing Manchuria and controlled banks, factories, and land-clearing companies from Fengtian to Fujian.

Li Shenzhi

Li, a close friend of Zhang's, was a scholar from Nantong. He collaborated with Zhang in the establishment of the normal school and the founding of Zhang's land-clearing companies.

Liu Yishan

A merchant from Nantong with an official degree-title, Liu was one of the first investors in Dasheng and a loyal supporter of Zhang Jian.

Luo Zhenyu (1866-1940)

Born in Huaian, Jiangsu, of a gentry family that originally came from Zhejiang, he was an accomplished scholar who was converted to the cause of reform after the Sino-French war. Luo's initial inspiration was the enlightened Chinese thinkers of the eighteenth century and then, later, Japan. In 1897 he founded an agricultural society, and then an Asian study society to publish translations. In 1901 he established the Society of Education, which published *The World of Education*. Zhang Zhidong and Liu Kunyi both appealed to him for assistance. Zhang Jian consulted with him frequently on matters dealing with schools, his land-clearing companies, and his political plans. In 1906 Luo was offered a post in the Ministry of Education and his relationship with Zhang Jian thereafter became less close. He lived in Beijing until 1911. After the revolution, he remained a fervent monarchist, partly because of his admiration for the Japanese model. He divided his time between Japan and the Japanese concessions in China, all the time refusing to cut off his queue. In 1921 he became an adviser to Puyi and remained in this post until his death. He played a key role in the arrangement concluded with the Japanese to place Puyi on the throne of Manchukuo. In the academic world Luo was known for his remarkable learning and his specialized knowledge of bronze and bone inscriptions, to which he devoted many of his considerable written works. In 1902 Luo was the first to decipher and date the Shang oracle bones discovered in Henan.

Ma Liang (1840-1939)

See text 3, n. 16.

Meng Sen (1867-1937)

Meng came from Wujin in Jiangsu. After classical studies in China, he studied law and political science in Japan. With Zhang Jian, he was very active in the constitutional movement as well as in the sphere of education. He took charge of the courses in politics and law organized by the Jiangsu Education Association. At the same time he was an important contributor to the *Dongfang zazhi*. Meng became a representative of the Jiangsu Provincial Assembly and, later on, a member of the national parliament. He ended his career as a professor of history at Beijing University.

Miao Quansun (1844-1919)

See text 3, n. 15.

Sha Yuanbing (1865-1927)

A native of Rugao, Sha was a *jinshi* (1894) and the recipient of many official honors. He was a friend and close collaborator of Zhang Jian and had interests in most of Zhang's enterprises. He himself established several factories and schools in Rugao, where he presided over the education association and the chamber of commerce. Sha was one of the most vigorous supporters of Zhang Jian at the local and provincial levels.

Shen Xiejun

A native of Haimen and the holder of the *shengyuan* degree, Shen was one of the investors in Dasheng, of which he became an administrator. He contributed funds to the normal school, supported Zhang Jian in all his enterprises, and played a role in Haimen similar to that of Sha Yuanbing in Rugao. Like Sha, Shen maintained business, literary, and political ties with Zhang.

Shen Zengzhi (Zipei) (1850-1922)

Originally from Jiaxing in Zhejiang, and a *jinshi* of 1880, Shen occupied several posts in Beijing. He came under the influence of Weng Tonghe and then Zhang Zhidong. He was active in government reform and, in the process, struck up a close friendship with Zhang Jian. They joined forces to bring about the "mutual defense of the southeast" and then afterwards to implement reforms, inspired by Japan, that Shen was promoting. Shen personally established a paper mill and, among the provincial duties that he undertook in 1911, worked to resist foreign control of mines and railways. He remained a monarchist and lived in retirement under the Republic, ending his days writing scholarly works on Mongol history.

Tang Shouqian (1857-1917)

A native of Zhejiang, Tang received the *jinshi* in 1892 and became well-known among reformist circles through his writings, which contained ideas foreshadowing, and at times more radical than, those of Kang Youwei. After 1900 he went into business with Zhang Jian while, at the same time, directing the constitutional movement. Tang even occupied the post of provincial education commissioner for Yunnan and Guangxi. He also had capital invested in land-clearing companies, navigation companies, the glass industry, and banks. In 1905 he became chief administrator of railways in Zhejiang. He was the first republican governor of Zhejiang.

Wang Guowei (1877-1927)

Wang came from Haining in Zhejiang. A *shengyuan,* Wang joined the Asian Study Society in Shanghai in 1898, where he studied Japanese with Fujita Toyohashi. His intellectual talents, which later brought him renown, were recognized by Luo Zhenyu, who appointed him as his personal secretary; Wang was therefore given the opportunity of perfecting his knowledge of Japan. Through his sponsor Wang established ties with Zhang Jian, especially in educational matters.

Wu Qilu (1873-1935)

Originally from Dantu in Jiangsu and holder of the *shengyuan* degree, Wang was an active and efficient supporter of Zhang Jian in matters dealing with Zhang's industrial enterprises and local activities.

Xu Dinglin (1857-1915)

Xu was a *juren* from Ganyu in Jiangsu who performed the same tasks in Haizhou and his native district as Sha Yuanbing and Shen Xiejun performed in theirs. His influence was stronger than theirs at the provincial level, partly due to his friendship with Zhang Jian. Xu was Chinese consul in Peru from 1893 to 1897 and had spent time with the Chinese legation in Washington. On his return he successfully filled a number of official posts aimed at promoting the economic development of Zhejiang and Jiangsu. At the same time he personally launched many private businesses and became vicechairman of the Jiangsu Education Association. He was elected chairman of the provincial council in 1912.

Zhang Cha (1851-1932)

Elder brother of Zhang Jian, and a *juren,* Zhang began his official career in a minor post. He ran into financial problems while in that post; thereupon Zhang Jian paid off his debts and offered him a position at Nantong. A capable and efficient administrator, Zhang was able to assist his younger brother in the running of his enterprises and local affairs.

Zhang Yuanji (1866-1959)

From Haiyan in Zhejiang, and a *jinshi* of 1892, Zhang occupied posts in the central administration and was an adviser to the emperor during the Hundred Days Reform. He founded the Commercial Press in 1902, directing its bureau of translation. Two years later he was one of the editors of *Dongfang zazhi.* Zhang Jian became acquainted with him in the service of Weng Tonghe and often consulted him on political, railway, and educational matters. Zhang was chairman of the Zhejiang Education Association and administrator of the Jiangsu-Zhejiang railway.

Zhao Fengchang (1856-?)

Zhao was from Wujin in Jiangsu. Having failed in the examinations, he worked in a *qianzhuang* (traditional bank); afterwards a benefactor purchased for him the post of magistrate's assistant for Canton district. There he was noticed by Zhang Zhidong, who gave him a position. While in the post Zhao amassed much wealth. He occupied a post in Shanghai, but was above all one of the leading administrators and profiteers of official industrial enterprises. This did not prevent him from also investing in private business. He joined with Zhang Jian politically in 1900 and during the constitutional movement. With Zhang, Zhao was one of the founders of the Public Association to Prepare for the Establishment of a Constitution in 1906 and of the Tongyidang (United Party) in 1912.

Zheng Xiaoxu (1860-1938)

Zheng was born in Suzhou, but his family originally came from Fujian. Zheng obtained the *juren* in 1882 and began his career in the service of Li Hongzhang. He was a diplomat in Japan from 1891 to 1894 after which he joined the staff of Zhang Zhidong. Zhang was able to benefit from Zheng's experience in Japan and his support in the reform effort. Zhang Jian visited him frequently from 1899 to 1903, while he was occupied with railways and technical schools at Lianghu, and from 1905 to 1908 when he was involved in a number of enterprises in Shanghai, such as the Commercial Press, the Shanghai Savings Bank, and Jiangnan Arsenal; and in constitutional

activities. Loyal to the monarchy, Zheng retired to Shanghai after
the 1911 Revolution until 1923, when he entered the service of Puyi
and eventually became prime minister of Manchukuo from 1932 to
1935.

APPENDIX II
General Glossary of Names and Terms

List of names and terms mentioned in the introduction, notes, and commentaries (except those appearing in the texts). For persons' names, the surnames or familiar names under which they are given in Zhang Jian's *Diary* have also been added to make subsequent research easier.

Anyang	安阳	*bushidō*	武士道
bacai	霸才	Cai Yuanpei	蔡元培
bagong	拔贡	Cen Chunxuan	岑春煊
bagu	八股	Changle	常乐
Baijiaxing	百家姓	Changsha	长沙
banri xuetang	半日学堂	Changzhou	常州
Baoding	保定	*chao ye*	朝野
bianfa	变法	*chen*	臣
Bianfa pingyi	变法平议	Chen Botao	陈伯陶
bianshi	变事	Chen Chi	陈炽
bianzheng	变政	Chen Chutao	陈楚涛

Chen Kuilong	陈夔龙	Feng Guifen	冯桂芬
Chen Sanli 陈三立　字：伯严，散原		Fudan gongxue	复旦公学
Chen Yi	陈毅	*fugu*	复古
Cixi	慈西	Fujita Toyohachi	藤田丰八
cungu	存古	*fuqiang*	富强
dachun	大纯	*fusheng*	附生
Dada neihe lunchuan gongsi 大达内河轮船公司		Gaodeng xuetang	高等学堂
dantu	丹徒	Gao Fengqian	高凤谦
Dasheng	大生	Gu Yanwu	顾炎武
Dasheng lunchuan gongsi 大生轮船公司		*guan*	官
		guanban qiye	官办起业
daxuetang	大学堂	*guandu shangban*	官督商办
daxueyuan	大学院	*guanxue*	官学
difang zizhi	地方自治	*guanxue dachen*	管学大臣
difang zongtong	地方总董	Guangsheng	广生
dongnan hubao	东南互保	Guangxu	光绪
Dongwen xueshe	东文学社	Guangyi	广益
Duan Fang 端方　字：午桥　号：陶斋		*guocui*	国粹
dudu	都督	*guojiao*	国教
Fan Dangshi	范当世　号：肯堂	*guomin*	国民
Fan Yuanlian	范源廉	Guomindang	国民党

guominzhuyi	国民主义	Hu Shi	胡适
Guo Moruo	郭沫若	Huasheng	华生
Guo Songdao	郭嵩焘	Huai'an	淮安
guowen	国文	Huang Xing	黄兴
guoxue	国学	Huang Yanpei 黄炎培　字：仁之	
Guoxue baocun hui 国学保存会		Huang Zongxi	黄宗羲
guoyu	国语	*jiansheng*	监生
guozheng	国政	Jianyi zhizi xuetang 简易知字学堂	
Guozijian	国子监	Jiang Bofu	蒋伯斧
Haimen	海门	Jiang Daomin	江导岷
Haizhou	海州	Jianghuai	江淮
Han	汉	Jiangning	江宁
Hankou	汉口	Jiang Qian	江谦
Hanyeping	汉冶萍	Jiangsu xuehui	江苏学会
Hangzhou	杭州	Jiangsu xuewu zonghui 江苏学务总会	
He Qi (He Kai)	何启	Jiang Weiqiao	蒋维乔
He Sikun 何嗣焜　号：眉孙		Jiaoyubu	教育部
Huguang	湖广	Jiaoyushe	教育社
Hu Liyuan	胡礼垣	*jiaoyu zhi quan*	教育之权
Hu Linyi	胡林翼	Jin	缙

jinshi	进士	Lin Zexu	林则徐
jingxue	经学	Liu Housheng	刘厚生
juren	举人	Liu Kunyi	刘坤一
junfa	军伐	Liu Yishan	刘一山
junguomin jiaoyu zhuyi 军国民教育主义		Lu Runxiang	陆润庠
		Lu Zhi	陆贽
junminzhuyi	军民主义	*luan*	乱
Kaifeng	开封	Luo Zhenyu	
Kang Youwei	康有为	罗振玉 字：叔蕴，叔言 号：雪堂	
Kongdao	孔道	Ma Jianzhong	
Kongjiao	孔教	马建忠 字：眉叔	
Lei Fen	雷奋 号：退翁	Ma Liang	
Li Duanfen	李端棻	马良 字：相伯	
Li Hongzhang	李鸿章	Mao Qingfan	毛庆蕃
Li Houyou	李厚祐	Mao Zedong	毛泽东
lijin	厘金	Meng Sen	
Li Shenzhi	李审之 号：盘硕	孟森 字：莼荪 笔名：心史	
lixue	理学	Meng Zhaochang	孟昭常
Liangjiang	两江	Miao Quansun	
Liang Qichao	梁启超 字：任公	缪荃孙 字：小山，筱珊 号：艺风堂	
linsheng	廪生	*min*	民
		Minbao	民报
		Nanhai	南海
		Nantong shiye gongsi 南通实业公司	
		Nanyang gongxue	南洋公学

Nie Qigui 聂缉椝

Nongwuju 农务局

Nongxueshe 农学社

paibao 派保

Pukou 浦口

Qian zi wen 千字文

Qiangxuehui 强学会

Qinding xuetang zhangcheng
钦定学堂章程

Qingliu 清流

Qingyibao 清议报

quanxueso 劝学所

renbao 认保

Rong Qing 荣庆

Rugao 如皋

ruxue 儒学

Sanjiang shifan xuetang
三江师范学堂

Sanzijing 三字经

Sha Yuanbing
沙元炳　字: 文明　号: 健庵

Shanhaiguan 山海关

Shanhouju 善后局

Shantou (Swatow) 汕头

shanggu shenban guanzhu
商股绅办官助

shehui 社会

shexue 社学

Shen Baozhen 沈葆楨

Shen Hong 沈纮

shenshang 绅商

shenshi 绅士

Shen Xiejun
沈燮均　字: 敬夫

Shen Zengzhi (Zipei)
沈曾植　字: 予培　号: 乙庵

Sheng Xuanhuai
盛宣怀　字: 杏荪　号: 愚斋

shengyuan 生员

Shibusawa Eiichi 渋泽荣一

shidafu 士大夫

Shishan shuyuan 师山书院

shiye jiaoyu 实业教育

shuyuan 书院

sishu 私塾

Sishu gailiang hui
私塾改良会

Sujing	苏经	Tongmenghui	同盟会
Sulun	苏纶	Tongshi zhibu	通师支部
Suzhou	苏州	Tongwenguan	同文馆
suigong	岁贡	Wang Anshi	王安石
Sun Jia'nai	孙家鼐	Wang Fuzhi	王夫之

Sun Yat-sen (Zhongshan)
孙逸仙

Wang Guowei
王国维　字：静安

Sun Yunjin	孙云锦	Wang Kangnian	汪康年
		Wang Qingmu	王清穆
Taiping	太平	Wang Tao	王韬
Taixing	泰兴	Wei Guangdao	魏光焘
Taiyuan	太原	Wenzheng shuyuan	文正书院
Tan Sitong	谭嗣同		

Weng Tonghe
翁同龢　字：松禅　号：虞山,虞阳,瓶庐

Tang Caichang	唐才常	Wuchang	武昌
Tang Eryong	唐尔镛	Wu Changqing	吴长庆

Tang Shouqian
唐寿潜,　名：震　字：翼仙　号：执先,蛰仙

Wujin　武进

Tao Mo	陶模	Wu Qilu	

吴寄鹿　别名：兆曾　字：缙云

Taoka Reiun	田冈岭云	Wu Rulun	吴汝纶
terakoya	寺子屋	Wusong	吴淞
tidu xuezheng	提督学政	Wuxi	无锡
Tōa Dōbunkai	東亜同文会館	Wuxian	吴县
Tongcheng	桐城	Xiliang	锡良

Xiting	西亭	*xuetang*	学堂
xixue	西学	*xuewuchu*	学务处
xiyi	西艺	Xuewugongsuo 学务公所	
Xiyin shuyuan	惜阴书院	*xuexiao*	学校
xizheng	西政	*xuexiaosi*	学校司
xian	县	*xuezheng*	学政
Xianzheng gonghui	宪政公会	Yan Fu	严复
xiang	乡	Yan Yuan	颜元
xiao daren	小大人	*yangwu*	洋务
xinzheng	新政	Yangzhou	杨州
Xingzhonghui	兴中会	Yao Nai	姚鼐
Xiong Xiling	熊希龄	*yixue*	义学
Xu Dinglin	许鼎霖 字：久香	Yizhengyuan	议政院
Xu Tong	徐桐	Ying Gui	英桂
Xuzhou	徐州	*yougong*	优贡
Xuebu	学部	Yubei lixian gonghui 预备立宪公会	
xuefa	学伐	Yujin	裕晋
Xue Fucheng	薛福成	Yuan Shikai	袁世凯
xuehui	学会	Yun Zuqi	恽祖祁
xuejuan	学捐	Zeng Guofan	曾国藩
xuequ	学区		

Zeng Guoquan	曾国荃			

zengsheng　　　　增生

Zhang Baixi　　　　张百熙

Zhang Binglin
　章炳麟　字：枚权　号：太炎

Zhang Cha　　　　张詧

Zhang Jian
　张謇　字：季直　季子　号：啬庵　啬翁

Zhang Liangyuan　　章亮元　字：静轩

Zhang Xiangjia　　　张享嘉

Zhang Yuanji
　张元济　字：小斋　号：菊生

Zhang Zhidong　　　张之洞　　南皮

Zhao Fengchang　　　赵凤昌

Zhendan xueyuan　　　震旦学院

Zhennanguan　　　　镇南关

zheng　　　　　　政

Zheng Guanying　　郑观应　号：陶斋

Zhenglun　　　　政论

Zhengwuchu　　　　政务处

Zheng Xiaoxu
　郑孝胥　字：苏戡，太夷　号：海藏

Zhiduju　　　　　制度局

zhiye jiaoyu　　　　职业教育

Zhongguo jiaoyuhui
　中国教育会

Zhongguo ziqiang ce
　中国自强策

Zhongxi xuetang　　　中西学堂

Zhong Xianchang　　　钟宪鬯

zhou　　　　　　　州

Zhou Fu　　　　　周馥

Zhou Shumo　　　　周树模

Zhu De　　　　　　朱德

Zhu Xi　　　　　　朱熹

Zilihui　　　　　　自立会

Zilijun　　　　　　自立军

ziqiang　　　　　自强

Ziyiju　　　　　　谘议局

zongli xuewu dachen
　总理学务大臣

APPENDIX III
Glossary of Terms Concerning Education

bagong	拔贡	imperial student by selection, chosen from among *shengyuan* who took a provincial examination once every twelve years. The title enables the holder to be eligible for an official post
bagu	八股	a long essay in eight sections
ban	班	class
banri xuetang	半日学堂	half-day school
baoming	报名	to register
benke	本科	regular course
biye	毕业	to graduate
biye pingdeng	毕业凭证	graduation certificate
buzhu	补助	to subsidize, subsidy
cehui	测绘	drawing

chengji	程级	stage of education
chudeng xiaoxuetang	初等小学堂	lower primary school
daiyong xuexiao	代用学校	substitute school
daxuetang	大学堂	university
daxueyuan	大学院	institute of higher learning
daxue yubei ke	大学预备科	university preparatory course
deyu, zhiyu, tiyu	德育，智育，体育	moral, intellectual, and physical education
e	额	quota, fixed number for examinations or a school
fengchao	风潮	agitation, unrest; e.g., among students
fenke daxue	分科大学	university comprising several faculties
fusheng	附生	supplementary *shengyuan; shengyuan* who had not yet passed, or come in last-the exams required of them for registration purposes
ganshiyuan	干事员	executive member; e.g., of an education association
gaodeng shifan xuetang	高等师范学堂	higher normal school
gaodeng xiaoxuetang	高等小学堂	higher primary school

gaodeng xuetang	高等学堂	higher school
gongli xuetang	公立学堂	public school
gongli xuexiao	公立学校	public school
gongsheng	贡生	imperial student; chosen by seniority or from among *shengyuan* who had done well in a special examination; the holder could aspire to an official post
guanli xuetang	官立学堂	official school
guanxue	官学	official district or prefectural school for *shengyuan*
guanxue dachen	管学大臣	director of studies, 1902-04
guowen	国文	written national language
guoyu	国语	national language
Guozijian	国子监	Imperial College; theoretically for the education of *gongsheng* and *jiansheng*. It provided above all else sinecure posts for the officials attached to it.
jiandu	监督	school supervisor

jiansheng	监生	student of the Imperial College; title obtained by purchase or imperial favor. The holder had the same privileges as a *shengyuan* and was permitted to take the *juren* examinations.
jianyi zhizi xuetang	简易知字学堂	literacy school for basic characters
jiangli	奖励	official title, borrowed from the term for the traditional examinations, which was given under certain conditions to school graduates, 1904-11
jiangxi ke	讲习科	introductory course
jiaoshi	教室	classroom
jiaoshou	教授	professor
jiaoshouxue	教授学	pedagogy
jiaoyu	教育	education
Jiaoyubu	教育部	Ministry of Education
jiaoyu zhi quan	教育之权	educational rights
jiaoyuan	教员	teacher
jinshi	进士	degree title for the highest level of examinations, which took place in the capital
jingxue	经学	classical knowledge

junguomin jiaoyu zhuyi	军国民教育主义	principle of national military education
juren	举人	degree title awarded in the provincial examinations
kaixue	开学	to begin a course
ke	科	subject, faculty, section of an administrative unit
kecheng	课程	curriculum
keju	科举	traditional examinations
lihua	理化	physics and chemistry
linsheng	廪生	*shengyuan* scholarship holder; holder of *shengyuan* degree who succeeded with merit in the exams *shengyuan* were required to take once every three years and who thus received a sum of money donated by his district
lunli	伦理	ethics
mengyang xuetang	蒙养学堂	elementary school
mofan xuexiao	模范学校	model school
nongye xuetang	农业学堂	agricultural school

paibao	派保	collective guarantee by the district *linsheng;* necessary to take the examinations if for three generations there had been no scholar in the candidate's family
pingyiyuan	评议员	adviser; e.g., to an education association
putong jiaoyu	普通教育	general education
quanxuesuo	劝学所	office for encouraging education in subprefectures and districts
renbao	认保	personal guarantee from a scholar member of the clan; necessary for the candidate who took the *shengyuan* examinations
ruxue	儒学	traditional official school for *shengyuan*
shanfei	膳费	boarding fees
shanzhang	山长	director of an academy-*shuyuan*
shangye xuetang	商业学堂	commercial school
shexue	社学	traditional village school
sheng	升	to be promoted from one class or school to a higher one

shengyuan	生员	successful candidate in the district examinations and student of official district or prefectural school
shifan xuexiao (xuetang)	师范学校	normal school
shiye jiaoyu	实业教育	vocational education
shuyuan	书院	academy
sili xuetang (xuexiao)	私立学堂	private school
sishu	私塾	private traditional school
sushe	宿舍	dormitory
suanshu	算术	arithmetic
suigong	岁贡	imperial student through seniority; chosen from among *linsheng;* the holder could aspire to an official post
ticao	体操	gymnastics
tixueshi	提学使	provincial commissioner of education-1906-11
tongsu jiaoyu	通俗教育	popular education
Wenbu	文部	Ministry of Culture Japan
wenke	文科	arts faculty
wenping	文凭	certificate
xixue	西学	Western knowledge

xiyi	西艺	Western techniques
xizheng	西政	Western political institutions and political science
xiaotong	校董	school director
xiaoxuetang	小学堂	primary school
xiushen	修身	moral training
Xuebu	学部	Ministry of Studies-1905-11
xuefa	学伐	cultural lordship
xuefei	学费	tuition fees
xuehui	学会	study society
xueji	学籍	administrative division pertaining to examinations in which an individual could legally register for the district examinations
xuejuan	学捐	special tax for the maintenance of schools
xueke	学科	subject, course, curriculum
xueqi	学期	school term
xuequ	学区	school district
xuetang	学堂	school
xuewuchu	学务处	office of education-1904
xuewugongsuo	学务公所	Bureau of Education

xuexiao	学校	school
xuexiaosi	学校司	office for schools; Zhili, 1902-06
xuezheng (tidu xuezheng)	学政（提督学政）	provincial examiner
xuezheng	学正	director of studies in a department
xuezhi	学制	school system
xunchang shifan xuetang	寻常师范学堂	lower normal school; equivalent to secondary education
xunchang xiaoxue	寻常小学	lower primary school
yishen	议绅	councillor-*xuewugongsuo*
yitu xuexiao	艺徒学校	apprentice school
yixue	义学	traditional charitable school
yiye	肄业	to study; e.g., in an academy
yizhang	议长	head councillor-*xuewugongso*
yougong	优贡	imperial student by merit; chosen once every three years from among *linsheng* and *zengsheng;* the holder was eligible for an official post
yuyingtang	育婴堂	orphanage

zengsheng	增生	additional *shengyuan;* i.e., *shengyuan* who were placed after *linsheng* in the registration examinations; the holder did not receive a scholarship
zhangcheng	章程	regulations, statutes
zhiye jiaoyu	职业教育	professional education
Zhongxue	中学	Chinese knowledge
zhongxuetang	中学堂	secondary school
zhuanke	专科	specialized subject, course
zhuanxisuo	传习所	apprenticeship center, training center
zongjiaoxi	总教习	director of studies
zongli xuewu dachen	总理学务大臣	superintendent of education; 1904-05
zuye	卒业	to finish one's studies without necessarily receiving a diploma

PART IV

NOTES AND BIBLIOGRAPHY

NOTES

Abbreviations Used in Notes

DFZZ   *Dongfang zazhi* [Eastern miscellany]
FEQ   *Far Eastern Quarterly*
GX   Guangxu reign
JAS   *Journal of Asian Studies*
JYZZ   *Jiaoyu zazhi* [Educational review]
MG   Republican period (*minguo*)
NCH   *North China Herald*
XT   Xuantong reign

Zhang Jian's Works

In references to *Zhang Jizi jiu lu* [The nine collections of Zhang Jian's writings], the romanized title of the particular collection is given. The nine titles are:

> *Zhengwen lu* [Politics]
> *Shiye lu* [Industry]
> *Jiaoyu lu* [Education]
> *Zizhi lu* [Local autonomy]
> *Cishan lu* [Charitable works]
> *Wen lu* [Essays]
> *Shi lu* [Poems]
> *Zhuan lu* [Special topics]
> *Wai lu* [Supplementary]

Zhang Jian's diary is cited under the title *Diary*. Since it is not paginated, only the date (according to the lunar calender which Zhang used) of the entry is given. For example, GX30/X/3 is the third day of the tenth month of the thirtieth year of the reign of Guangxu.

The autobiography is cited as *Nianpu*, with the pagination of the most accessible edition, that produced in Taibei in 1965. This is a photocopy of the 1930 edition and follows the biography written by Zhang Xiaoruo.

Titles of Chinese and Japanese articles are given in English. In order to prevent the notes from being unwieldy, the romanizations of the original titles are not given.

In the notes to the translated texts, the references to the classics are taken from the French edition of Séraphin Couvreur (Sien Hsien, 1828-1934).

[Dating for a number of the Chinese journals appearing in the notes presents several problems, particularly when the publishers began converting from the traditional lunar and reign period system to the Western one. When publishing information was provided exclusively in the traditional system, that method was employed here (e.g., *Xuebu guanbao*). In the case of *Dongfang zazhi*, which used both, dates are given here according to the lunar year. An attempt was made to find full citations for several journals and other early reference works not provided in original French text; in instances where the original work was not available, the interested reader can locate the original by reference to issue number.—Trans.]

Translator's Introduction

1. Evelyn Rawski, *Education and Popular Literacy in Ch'ing China* (Ann Arbor, Michigan, 1979).
2. This important document is published in *Jindai Zhongguo jiaoyushi ziliao*, comp. Shu Xincheng (Beijing, 1961), 1: 220-26. For an analysis of its significance, as well as the items discussed below, see my unpublished Ph.D. dissertation, "Popular Education in China 1904-1919: New Ideas and Developments" (Vancouver, British Columbia, 1982).
3. After the establishment of the Republic in 1912 a spate of journals devoted specifically to education appeared. The longest running included *Zhonghua jiaoyujie* [The world of Chinese education] and *Jingshi jiaoyubao* [Beijing educational review].
4. I have dealt with Kerschensteiner's influence on Chinese educators during the late Qing and early Republic in my Ph.D. dissertation, cited above.

5. *Jiaoyubu bianzuanqu yuekan* [Monthly journal of the Education Ministry's Compilation Bureau], no. 6 (1913): *fulu*, 1-6.

6. Mao Zedong, *Une Etude de l'Education Physique,* translated and introduced by S. Schram (Paris, 1962), 31-32. See also Schram's introduction to Li Jui, *The Early Revolutionary Activities of Comrade Mao Tse-tung* (New York, 1977), xxiii, xxvi.

7. See Professor Bastid's bibliography. Some not included are Chiling Yin, *Reconstruction of Modern Educational Organizations in China* (Shanghai, 1926); T. Y. Teng and T. T. Lew, *Education in China* (Beijing, 1922); and Tao Chih-hsing, *Education in China* (Beijing, 1925).

8. C. Peake, *Nationalism and Education in Modern China* (New York, 1932).

9. Kuo Ping-wen, *The Chinese System of Public Education* (New York, 1914).

10. A recent Chinese study of education from 1840 to 1919 is likewise rather superficial, although there is an interesting section on the educational thought of such pre-1911 Chinese revolutionaries as Cai Yuanpai, Chen Tianhua, and Zhang Binglin. See Chen Jingpan, *Zhongguo jindai jiaoyushi* [A history of modern Chinese education] (Beijing, 1979).

11. Knight Biggerstaff, *The Earliest Modern Government Schools in China* (Ithaca, New York, 1961); W. Ayers, *Chang Chih-tung and Educational Reform in China* (Cambridge, Massachusetts, 1971).

12. W. Franke, *The Reform and Abolition of the Traditional Chinese Examination System* (Cambridge, Massachusetts, 1960).

13. See, for example, Joseph Esherick, *Reform and Revolution: The 1911 Revolution in Hunan and Hubei* (Berkeley, California, 1976); and E. Rhoads, *China's Republican Revolution: The Case of Kwangtung 1895-1913* (Cambridge, Massachusetts, 1975).

14. Some are listed in Professor Bastid's bibliography. However, some of the most interesting are not. They include: Taga Akigorō, "Kindai Chūgoku ni okeru zokujuku no seikaku" [On the nature of clan schools in modern China] in *Kindai Chūgoku Kenkyū,* no. 4 (1960) which analyzes the evolution of clan schools after the establishment of the modern school system in 1904; Nakamura Tsune, "Shinmatsu gakudō setsuritsu o meguru kōsetsu nōson shakai no ichi danmen" [A look at rural society in Jiangsu and Zhejiang based on the establishment of schools at the end of the Qing], in *Rekishi Kyōiku* 10, no. 11

(1962), which focuses on the reasons for the people's opposition to modern schools; and Saitō Akio, "Chūgoku gakusei kaikaku no shisō to genjitsu" [Theory and practice in the reform of China's educational system], in *Senshū Jimbun Ronshū* (December 1969), which describes life in the modern schools based on personal accounts by Shu Xincheng, later to be a prominent educator and writer, and Xu Zhimo, the future poet.

15. Taga Akigorō, comp., *Kindai Chūgoku Kyōiku Shi Shiryō* [Materials on the history of education in modern China], 5 vols. (Tokyo, 1972). Other relevant Chinese-language works that have appeared since the publication of Professor Bastid's book include: Su Yunfeng, *Zhang Zhidong yu Hubei jiaoyu gaige* [Zhang Zhidong and educational reform in Hubei] (Taibei, 1976) (useful for showing the change of emphasis by reforming high officials from creating a limited number of specialist schools to establishing a wider network of general education); *Qingmo choubei lixian dang'an shiliao* [Archival materials on the preparation of a constitution at the end of the Qing], 2 vols. (Beijing, 1979) (contains a section on memorials from provincial officials concerning educational reform); Zhang Nan and Wang Renzhi, comp., *Xinhai geming qian shinianjian shibian xuanji* [A selection of articles from the ten years before the 1911 Revolution] (Beijing, 1977), vol. 3; Gao Pingshu, comp., *Cai Yuanpei jiaoyu wenxuan* [Selected essays of Cai Yuanpei on education] (Beijing, 1980); and Gu Mingyuan et al., *Lu Xun de jiaoyu sixiang yu shijian* [Lu Xun's educational thought and practice] (Beijing, 1981) (contains interesting sections on the great writer's educational thought before 1911 and his activities while working for the Ministry of Education during the early years of the Republic).

16. See, for example, the illuminating discussion (pp. 138-39) concerning the introduction of sports in modern schools. One problem with Borthwick's book is its scattered and rather simplistic references to educational developments in the West. Thus her statement (p. 14) that education in the West accompanied modern and industrial developments is not necessarily true and, in any case, touches on a far more complex issue than this bland statement would suggest. The example of England shows that despite being the most industrialized power throughout most of the nineteenth century, a national primary school system was not introduced there until the end of the nineteenth century. Conversely, France, as a recent study has shown,

despite its late industrialization (compared to Britain) possessed educational institutions during the first half of the nineteenth century that bore the characteristics normally attributed to those in industrial society. See M. Vaughan and M. Archer, *Social Conflict and Educational Change in England and France 1789-1848* (Cambridge University Press, 1971). A detailed and more rigorous comparison of Chinese educational developments in the early twentieth century with those in Western countries such as Britain, France, Germany, and the United States would be a useful addition to educational history in general as well as placing educational debates and practice in China in a wider context. I hope to do this in a revised version of my Ph.D. thesis.

Preface

1. The works of M. C. Bergère, *La Bourgeoisie chinoise et la révolution de 1911* (Paris, 1968) and *China in Revolution: The First Phase 1900-1913*, ed. M. C. Wright (New Haven, 1968) appeared too late to be used in this study.
2. The thesis was defended in February 1968 at the University of Paris.

Chapter I

1. *Shi'er chao donghua lu*, (Taibei, 1963), GX8: 4518-19 (20 August 1900).
2. Ibid. 4584 (29 January 1901).
3. V. Purcell, *The Boxer Uprising* (Cambridge, Massachusetts, 1963), 194-222.
4. Telegram from Li Hongzhang to Sheng Xuanhuai on 25 June 1900 (*Yihetuan* [Shanghai, 1951], 3: 334).
5. Jian Bozan, ed., *Zhongguo shi gangyao* (Beijing, 1964), 4: 103. For Tang Caichang's uprising, see also E. Smythe, "The Tzu-li Hui: Some Chinese and Their Rebellions," *Harvard Papers on China* 12 (1958): 51-68.
6. Sun Yat-sen, *Zhongshan quanshu*, I/22, cited in *Zhongguo jindai shi ziliao xuanji*, ed. Rong Mengyuan (Beijing, 1954), 548.
7. Shen Naizheng, "The Concentration of Power in the Hands of

the Governors-General and the Central Government, and the Joint Management of Administration at the End of the Qing," *Shehui kexue* 2, no. 2 (January 1937): 311-15.

8. On the thought of Xue Fucheng, see Liu Shihai, "The Economic and Social Thought of Xue Fucheng and His Economic and Social Background," *Xin jianshe*, no. 3 (1955): 52-59. On Chen Chi, Tang Shouqian, Zheng Guanying, He Qi, and Hu Liyuan, see L. Eastman, "Political Reformism in China before the Sino-Japanese War," JAS 27, no. 4 (August 1968): 695-710. The best study on Zheng Guanying is by Professor Shao Xunzheng: "On Zheng Guanying" (unpublished article, mimeographed by the Department of History of Beijing University, August 1964); Hsiao Kung-ch'uan, "Weng T'ung-ho and the Reform Movement of 1898," *Tsing-hua hsüeh-pao*, new series, 1, no. 2 (April 1957): 150-56, compares the ideas of Chen Chi, Tang Shouqian, Zhang Zhidong, and Weng Tonghe. Among the texts that contained, in thought and vocabulary, striking similarities with the edict of 1901, one can cite: Chen Chi, *Yong shu* 4, *shenji*, 45a-46b; Zhang Zhidong, *Exhortation à l'étude*, trans. J. Tobar (Shanghai, 1909), 120-28; Sun Jia'nai, "Memorial of August 1896 on the Opening of a University in Beijing," *Wuxu bianfa*, 4 vols. (Shanghai, 1953), 2: 426; Weng Tonghe, *Weng Wenkong riji* [Diary] (Shanghai, 1925), ce 36, 131a (GX23/XII/24).

9. In particular, the sixth memorial of Kang Youwei of 29 January 1898 (*Wuxu bianfa*, 2: 197-98); the letter of Tan Sitong translated in Ssu-yu Teng and J. K. Fairbank, *China's Response to the West: A Documentary Survey* (Cambridge, Massachusetts, 1954), 159; on the ideas of Sun Yat-sen before 1895, his letter to Li Hongzhang is very significant (Sun Yat-sen, *Sun Zhongshan xuanji* [Beijing, 1956], 7-18).

10. The idea was present in Kang's first memorial in 1888 (*Wuxu bianfa*, 2: 129), but the expression itself appeared in a text of 19 June 1898 (ibid., 216).

11. Zhang Zhidong, *Exhortation à l'étude*, 122, 128.

12. On the ideas of these various thinkers: W. Franke, *Reform and Abolition*, 16-27; Ren Shixian, *Zhongguo jiaoyu sixiang shi* (Shanghai, 1937), 255-98.

13. Chang Chung-li, *The Chinese Gentry*, 102.

14. Xu Daling, *Qingdai juanna zhidu* (Beijing, 1950), 76, 129-66.

15. Xue Fucheng, *Yong'an quanji* (Shanghai, 1897), I/1a.

16. These are the schools described by Knight Biggerstaff in *The Earliest Modern Government Schools in China,* in particular the

Tongwenguan (Office of Translation) in Beijing.

17. M. Wright, *The Last Stand of Chinese Conservatism*, 79-84.

18. Feng Guifen, "Cai xixue yi" [Proposal on the adoption of Western knowledge], *Jiao bin lu kangyi*, (N.p., 1898).

19. Zheng Guanying, *Yiyan* (N.p., 1880); sections on "Schools," "Western Knowledge," and "Examinations"; Zheng Guanying, *Shengshi weiyan* (reprint, Taibei, 1965), vol. 1. On the development of Zheng's thought: Shao Xunzheng, "On Zheng Guanying," 107-9.

20. See the texts cited by Teng and Fairbank, *China's Response to the West*, 100-101.

21. Wang Tao, *Tao yuan wenlu waibian* (reprint, Beijing, 1969), 34-35, 38-39, 372-75.

22. Ma Jianzhong, *Shike zhai jiyan* (reprint, Beijing, 1960), 31, 45-47.

23. In 1875 Li Hongzhang requested the establishment of an examination subject on "Western affairs," but this was for a restricted quota of military experts and Li did not make any provision for teaching the new subject. A similar situation arose with an edict of 1887 which allowed three candidates versed in mathematics to be granted a *shengyuan* degree over and above the normal quota, but only on condition that they succeeded in the regular tests.

24. W. Franke gives a long and penetrating analysis of Kang's plan which it is not possible to reproduce here (*Reform and Abolition*, 33-37). The memorials are in *Wuxu bianfa*, 2: 131-74.

25. *Wuxu bianfa*, 2: 292-97.

26. This is a section of *Bianfa tonglun* included in Liang Qichao, *Yin bing shi wenji*, First Collection (Shanghai, 1936), 2: 1-8b.

27. Zhang Zhidong, *Exhortation à l'étude*, 50, 130.

28. Edict of 29 January 1901, *Shi'er chao donghua lu* (Taibei, 1963), GX8: 4583.

29. Chen Qiao, "The Political Thought of the Opponents of Reform at the Time of the 1898 Political Reforms," *Yanjing xuebao*, no. 25 (1939): 60-80.

30. Ch'u T'ung-tsu, *Local Government in China*, 171-72.

31. Jian Bozan, *Yihetuan* (Shanghai, 1951), 3: 327-28, 336.

32. These observations are drawn from a study of official texts of 1900-01 (memorials, telegrams) and of the reports in DFZZ, 1904, 1905, and 1906. The list of references would be too long to give here.

33. *Dalu zazhi* 24, no. 6 (31 March 1962): 32.

34. *East of Asia,* June 1904, 24-26; *Zhongguo jindai gongyeshi ziliao,* ed. Wang Jingyu (Shanghai, 1957), 2: 954-56.
35. M. C. Bergère, *Une crise financière à Shanghai,* 3.
36. Zhou Gucheng proposes to keep the term *shidafu* to refer to intellectuals during the period before the introduction of industrial civilization in China, and to use the term *zhishifenzi,* which is a translation of "intelligentsia," for the period subsequent to the introduction of industrial civilization (*Zhongguo shehui zhi jiegou* [Shanghai, 1930], 236-37). The period around 1900 is one of change: for an analysis of individuals, the distinction is very useful. There were certainly more "intellectuals" among the ranks of the Tongmenghui than among the modern gentry.
37. See the detailed and well-documented study by S. Chu, *Reformer in Modern China: Chang Chien 1853-1926* (New York and London, 1965), for a complete account of Zhang Jian's life. Only certain aspects which are less developed in Chu's work will be mentioned here. The essential sources are Zhang's *Diary,* which Chu was unable to use, his autobiography (*Nianpu*), the works of Zhang Jian, and the contemporary accounts of Zhang Xiaoruo, Liu Housheng, and Song Xishang.
38. Qiao Qiming, *Jiangsu Kunshan Nantong, Anhui Suxian nongtian zhidu zhi bijiao yiji gailiang nongtian wenti zhi jianyi* (Nanjing, 1926), 14.
39. Zhang Xiaoruo, *Zhuanji,* 6, 9. Zhang Jian's father attended school until the age of fifteen (Zhang Jian, *Nianpu,* 1).
40. Ibid., 1-8; Zhang Xiaoruo, *Zhuanji,* 5-24.
41. Zhang often recalled these ordeals and wrote an account of them (*Zhuan,* III/1a-11b).
42. Zhang Jian, *Nianpu,* 10, 12. The Tongcheng school was a literary school that flourished in the eighteenth century. It was composed of scholars originating from the district of Tongcheng in Anhui under the leadership of Yao Nai. It glorified the teachings of Zhu Xi and the style of Neo-Confucian authors. Around 1870, the school enjoyed considerable prestige when Zeng Guofan and his followers and friends revived and honored its principles.
43. Zhang Jian, *Nianpu,* 13-16.
44. Contemporary Western sources completely ignored the "pure party" and included its members among the ranks of the "obdurate conservatives." The modern character of their patriotism was obviously irritating for the foreigners. This group is studied by Hao Yan-p'ing, "A Study of the Ch'ing-liu Tang,"

Harvard Papers on China 16: 40-65; L. Eastman, "Ch'ing-yi and Chinese Policy Formation," JAS 24, no. 4 (August 1965): 595-611; L. Eastman, *Throne and Mandarins*, 17-29 and passim; W. Ayers, *Chang Chih-tung*, 90-93, 101-4, 133; Li Shiyue offers a penetrating analysis in *Zhang Jian he lixianpai* (Beijing, 1962), 5-11. Li is the only one to use Zhang Jian's autobiography to clarify the difficult problem concerning the exact composition of the Qingliu.

45. Zhang Jian, *Zhengwen*, I/1a-5a, 5a-7a. The latter memorial is reproduced with an incorrect title and date; it concerned the conflict between China and Russia in 1879 and not that of the Sino-Japanese dispute of 1882. Internal evidence within the memorial testifies to this.

46. Zhang Jian, *Zhengwen*, I/3a.

47. Zhang Jian published several works on this issue. The three most important ones are lost, but one can reconstruct his attitude from those that remain (*Zhengwen*, I/9a-19a, III/35b-36b).

48. In the introduction to his "Diary of a Trip to Japan" Zhang wrote for 21 May 1903: "After my failure in the *jinshi* examination of 1886, I was persuaded that China had to develop industry and that the responsibility for this fell first of all to the scholars [*shidafu*]. As my father was busy with agriculture and sericulture, I myself spent eight years arguing with and resisting opposing forces in order, finally, to establish merely a silk mill in Haimen" (*Diary*, GX29/IV/25, reproduced in *Nianpu*, 54, and *Zhuan*, IV/1a). On the strength of this text, Zhang's biographers, who do not give its date, confirm that Zhang substantially had these ideas in 1886 (Chang Min, "More on Zhang Jian," *Jianghai xuekan* [February 1962]: 10-11; Li Shiyue, *Zhang Jian he lixianpai*, 14; Zhang Xiaoruo, *Zhuanji*, 68; *Nantong Zhang Jian xiansheng shishi sishi zhounian jinian ji*, 23-24). Without overlooking the scandalous effect that such ideas might have caused at the time, it appears strange that someone with Zhang Jian's courageous and verbose nature should have waited seventeen years before expressing them.

49. Zhang Jian, *Nianpu*, 29-37; *Diary*, GX17/VII/27.

50. Zhang Jian, *Wai*, I/20a-b.

51. The most significant text is a memorial composed in 1895 in the name of Zhang Zhidong (*Zhengwen*, I/13a-23a).

52. He had spent 165 days of his life in examination halls. The servility to which even high officials were submitted aroused in

Zhang a feeling of repugnance (Zhang Xiaoruo, *Zhuanji*, 29-31, 68; *Diary*, GX18/IV/11, 20).

53. Zhang Jian, *Nianpu*, 40.

54. This citation follows the passage translated in note 48. It was used by Zhang's biographers to define his ideology in 1895 (S. Chu, *Reformer in Modern China*, 17; Zhang Xiaoruo, *Zhuanji*, 68, 90; Li Shiyue, *Zhang Jian he lixianpai*, 17; Chang Min, "More on Zhang Jian," 10-11; Jiang Min, "On the Reformism of Zhang Jian," *Jianghai xuekan* 9, no. 55 [September 1963]: 30-39; Liu Housheng, *Zhang Jian zhuanji* [Shanghai, 1959], 73; Song Xishang, *Zhang Jiande shengping* [Taibei, 1963], 137). Here also there are certain reservations. In the same way, when some writers cite the famous slogan for this period "the source of food and clothing has education for its father and industry for its mother," it should be noted that it only appeared in 1907 (Zhang Jian, *Jiaoyu*, II/27a).

55. Zhang Jian, *Diary*, GX21/X/10. The Society for the Study of Self-Strengthening was a political club founded in Beijing in September 1895 by reform supporters, in which Kang Youwei played a key role. At first patronized by some high officials, it was proscribed by the authorities and disappeared in April 1896 (Levenson, *Liang Ch'i-ch'ao*, 20-22; Hu Huaizhen, *Shanghaide xueyi tuanti* [Shanghai, 1936], 111).

56. Zhang Jian, *Diary*, GX21/VIII/4, 16, GX23/IV/7, 8, GX23/V/12, 17; Zhang Jian, *Shiye*, I/3b-7b; *Shiwu bao* 3, no. 28 (1 May 1898): 1928; 6, no. 47 (1 November 1898): 3238.

57. *Jiangsu sheng fangzhiye zhuangkuang* (Wuxi, 1919), *fubian*, 1-2; and also Zhang Jian, *Diary*, GX21/IV/6, GX23/III/10. On the difficulties concerning the supply of thread, see Peng Zeyi, *Zhongguo jindai shougongyeshi ziliao*, 4 vols. (Beijing, 1957), 2: 196, 198, 244.

58. Zhang Jian, *Shiye*, I/6a.

59. Ibid., I/7b, 11a.

60. On the influence of enlightened thinkers and on Zhang's thought at the time of the establishment of the Dasheng mill, see the letter of 11 April 1897 to Shen Zipei (Zhang Jian, *Diary*, GX23/III/10), and that of 8 May 1897 to Ding Lijun (ibid., IV/7), reproduced in Zhang Jian, *Wen*, XI/13b-14a and 11b-12b.

61. Zhang Kaiyuan, "On the Nature of the Contradictions of Zhang Jian," *Lishi yanjiu*, no. 3 (1963): 89.

62. Zhang Jian, *Shiye*, I/5a.

63. Zhang Jian, *Diary*, GX24/III, ibid., IV, V.

64. Unpublished letter kept in the archives of Nantong, cited by Zhang Kaiyuan, "On the Nature of the Contradictions of Zhang Jian," 91.
65. The complete text forms the second *juan* of the *Zhengwen lu*. The *Diary*, GX27/II/4-20 relates the circumstances of its composition. It had been preceded by numerous discussions and exchanges of letters with Shen Zipei, Tang Shouqian, He Sikun, Zheng Xiaoxu, Zhao Fengchang, and Liu Kunyi on the subject of the "new administration" (*xinzheng*); see *Diary*, GX27/I/12.
66. Zhang Jian, *Zhengwen*, II/2a.
67. Ibid., 12a.
68. Ibid.
69. Liang Qichao, "On Respect for the Emperor," *Qingyi bao*, no. 9, GX25/II/2 (22 March 1899): 519-22; Liang Qichao, "Proposal to Establish a Constitution," ibid., no. 81, GX27/IV/21 (7 June 1901): 5170-72.
70. One can refer to a pamphlet by Li Yingjue, written in the same year, entitled *Bianfa pingyi zhuo*, which was presented as complementing Zhang Jian's work.

Chapter II

1. Liu Housheng, *Zhang Jian zhuanji*, 250-51. The *China Times*, 26-28 September 1920, "A Survey of Nantong," gives a population of 1,090,000. In 1921, Zhang Jian mentioned a figure of 1,200,000 (*Jiaoyu* V/9b). The census of 1932 counted 1,358,461 inhabitants (Zhao Ruheng et al., *Jiangsu sheng jian* [Shanghai, 1935], 31-34).
2. A. Brou and G. Gibert, *Jésuites missionnaires, un siècle 1823-1923* (Paris, 1924), 49-63; *Ershinian lai zhi Nantong* (Nantong, 1930), 114.
3. A. McLean, *The History of the Foreign Christian Missionary Society* (London, 1919), 260-64.
4. *Jiangsu sheng fangzhiye zhuangkuang, fubian*, 4; *Ershinian lai zhi Nantong*, 3.
5. Zhang Xiaoruo, *Zhuanji*, 10; Wang Peitang, *Jiangsu sheng xiangtu zhi* (Shanghai, 1933), 478, reports that in 1937, 150,000 dollars annually were still spent in the town of Nantong on incense paper and sticks.

6. Liang Yuexin and Mo Xiangzhi, comp., *Tongzhou zhilizhou zhi*, ed. Gu Zenghuan and Gu Zengxuan (Nantong, 1875), V/70b.

7. Huang Yanpei, *Zhongguo jiaoyushi yao*, 82.

8. However, the *shexue* are sometimes difficult to distinguish from the *yixue:* see T. Grimm, *Erziehung und Politik im Konfuzianischen China der Ming-Zeit 1368-1644* (Hamburg, 1960), 139.

9. Zhang Jian, *Nianpu*, 3-9; Hu Shi, *Sishi zi shu* (Shanghai, 1933), 36-46; Chen Dongyuan, *Zhongguo jiaoyu shi* (Shanghai, 1937), 425; Chai Yu-heng, *Etude sur l'obligation scholaire et l'enseignement primaire en France et en Chine* (Paris, 1935), 75-76.

10. Zhang Jian, *Nianpu*, 1-7; S. W. Williams, *The Middle Kingdom*, 1: 519-40; W. Martin, *The Lore of Cathay*, 288-95.

11. Chen Dongyuan, *Zhongguo Jiaoyu shi*, 432-34; K. Tanaka, "The Life of Pupils in Private Schools in Traditional China," *Tōhō Gakuhō* 15, no. 2 (January 1945): 217-32.

12. Hu Shi, *Sishi zi shu*, 45-46.

13. S. W. Williams, *The Middle Kingdom*, 1: 544.

14. J. Arnold, "Educational Activity in Foochow China," *Reports of the Department of the Interior* (Washington D.C., 1908), 194. Hu Shi's teacher earned about 25 dollars a year, but he did not receive food rations. The responsibility for paying the salary was shared among the families.

15. On this problem, the quarrels Zhang's father had with his family are very revealing; he was obliged to terminate his studies (Zhang Xiaoruo, *Zhuanji*, 6-7). Hu Shi recounted a similar situation concerning his friends at the primary school (*Sishi zi shu*, 38-46).

16. Calculated according to the list of *shengyuan* in *Tongxiang timing lu, juan* 4.

17. See Chang Chung-li, *The Chinese Gentry*, 143. According to Chang's calculations, the prefectures with the more favorable quotas only had 39 places for the examinations. Canton was the only one to have more than 40 places.

18. The number of *juren* was determined by province. Proportionally, the number of *juren* had increased much less than the quotas for *shengyuan* (ibid., 124).

19. The total number of *juren* for Jiangsu has been calculated from the figures given by Chang Chung-li (ibid.), E. Zi (*Pratique des Examens*, 118), and the number of *juren* examinations recorded in the *Jingxiang timing lu* and the *Tongxiang timing lu*. The

latter work gives the exact number of *juren* from Nantong. The population figure for Jiangsu was estimated by contemporaries and official sources to be approximately twenty million; see I. Taeuber and Wang Nai-chi, "Population Reports in the Ch'ing Dynasty," JAS 29, no. 4 (August 1960): 415.

20. *Tongzhou zhilizhou shi,* 5/52b. According to E. Zi, *Pratique des examens,* 123, in Jiangsu about 10,000 candidates in all presented themselves for the first stage of the *juren* examinations at the end of the nineteenth century. The department of Tongzhou would have therefore presented 1,000 candidates, among whom several hundred would have been from the district of Nantong.

21. See the biographies in appendix 1.

22. These figures are calculated from statistics provided by the Ministry of Education and published in 1908 (*Jiaoyu tongji tubiao, gesheng,* 26-27). The figures are certainly incomplete since the organization of census returns for schools dated only from 1906. Nevertheless, the general picture corresponds with information from other sources.

23. M. Cameron, *The Reform Movement in China 1898-1912* (Stanford, 1931), 65.

24. E. Morrison, "The Modernization of the Confucian Bureaucracy: An Historical Study of Public Administration" (Ph.D. diss., Radcliffe, 1959), 688, 713.

25. Li Jiannong, *Zhongguo jin bainian zhengzhi shi,* 2 vols. (Shanghai, 1948), 1: 229; Ch'ien Tuan-sheng, *The Government and Politics of China 1912-1948* (Cambridge, Massachusetts, 1961), 52.

26. Zhang Jian, *Diary,* GX27/I/12, 22, 23, 26, II/23, V/28, VII/5, 10, 11, IX/4, 11, 13, 20, 21; GX28/I/17, 18, II/28, 29, III/3, 4, 5, 6, 14, 19, 22, 30.

27. In particular, see the memorial presented by Zhang and Liu on 12 July 1901, in which they requested the establishment of a school system based on the Japanese model, the abolition of the military examinations, and the sending of students abroad (*Donghua xulu,* 169/7-15): Zhang Jian had discussed all these questions with the two governors-general during the several months before the memorial was submitted (*Diary,* GX27/I/12, 26, II/23, V/28). As for the memorial on schools that Liu Kunyi addressed to the emperor on 15 May 1902 (*Liu Kunyi yiji,* 1341-43), it was drawn up by Zhang Jian (Zhang Jian, *Diary,* GX28/III/4).

28. Ding Zhipin, *Zhongguo jin qishinian lai jiaoyu jishi* (Shanghai, 1935), 9; NCH, 30 April 1902, 257; *Jiaoyu xiaoce huiji*, nos. 13, 24, 30 (1898-1911).
29. Zhang Jian, *Diary*, GX28/II/29 (7 April 1902).
30. Ibid.
31. These regulations were known as the *Qinding xuetang zhangcheng* [Imperial regulations on the schools]. The text was published in the form of a special booklet; large extracts from it are reproduced in Shu Xincheng, *Zhongguo jindai jiaoyushi ziliao*, (Beijing, 1961), vol. 2.
32. On those schools dating before 1894, see K. Biggerstaff, *The Earliest Modern Government Schools in China*. Among those established later, the Sino-Western school in Tianjin (Zhongxi xuetang) and the South Seas College (Nanyang gongxue) in Shanghai were the most famous.
33. W. Franke, *Reform and Abolition*, 58, gives some examples of this tendency, but he seems to have overlooked the existence of Zhang Baixi's regulations which preceded those of January 1904.
34. *Donghua lu*, GX2: 4780. This was a restoration of the system inaugurated during the 1898 reforms. There was no demarcation between educational establishments *per se* and educational administration: all the schools in the empire were under the control of the University of Beijing.
35. Zhuang Yu, ed., *Zuijin sanshiwunian zhi Zhongguo jiaoyu* (Shanghai, 1931), 77-79.
36. Despite the importance attached to moral training, the amount of time devoted to it was less than that laid down afterwards by Zhang Zhidong. Zhang Baixi's curriculum thus represented a considerable change in comparison to that of traditional education.
37. In November 1902 some pupils from Nanyang College in Shanghai had left to establish a separate college. In April 1903, students from the University of Beijing organized a strike in protest against the treaties signed with Russia; similar action took place in other schools.
38. For the content of education, we shall limit ourselves to the curricula for general education, which are the best indication of the authorities' aims. Besides, they were the only ones which were implemented in any way. For other branches of the education system, one can refer to the complete edition of these regulations: Zhang Baixi et al., *Zouding xuetang zhangcheng*

(Shanghai, 1904); to the abridged text reproduced in *Da Qing Guangxu xin faling* (Shanghai, 1901), vol. 9; and in Shu Xingcheng, *Zhongguo jindai jiaoyushi ziliao* (Beijing, 1961), vol. 2. Ho Yen-sun, *Chinese Education from the Western Viewpoint* (Chicago, 1913), 58-62, and H. E. King, *The Educational System of China as Recently Reconstructed* (Washington D.C., 1911), 68-78, give details on the curricula for higher education. In these two works there are good descriptions of the 1904 regulations, but the most complete account is in Chinese in Chen Qingzhi, *Zhongguo jiaoyu shi* (Shanghai, 1936), 586-610.

39. W. Franke, *Reform and Abolition*, 69-71. It must not be forgotten, however, that in certain regions the development of education had already begun. In Shanxi, which had eight million inhabitants, there were, in 1904, eighty-one official primary schools and eight official secondary schools, in addition to fifty small private establishments in Taiyuan alone, one college of agriculture, one college for Manchus, one military college, and one university (*East of Asia*, June 1904, 1-10; Duncan Moir, "The Imperial University of Shansi," *East of Asia* 3 [1904]: 102). In Hunan, Changsha had, in 1904, sixteen higher schools with 975 students and ninety-one teachers, seven middle schools with 425 pupils and forty teachers, eight elementary schools with 407 pupils and forty teachers, two military academies with 220 students and fourteen instructors, twenty-four half-day schools with 960 pupils, and numerous private schools (Archives du ministère des Affaires étrangères, *Correspondance de Chine*, new series, no. 582, folio 128: Report of 14 December 1905, according to the annual report of the customs commissioner at Changsha). In 1905, according to a foreign observer, there were "modern school buildings in all the prefectures" (T. Preston, "Progress and Reform in Hunan Province," *East of Asia* 4 [1905]: 215-17). At Chengdu, in November 1905, 2,000 young people and children, in striped uniforms, from schools in the city, that is to say "about two-thirds of the total number of school pupils," participated in a large public display of gymnastics and military exercises organized by the authorities (Archives du ministère des Affaires étrangères, *Correspondance de Chine*, new series, no. 582, folio 69: Report from Chengdu on 5 December 1905). In the summer of 1905, the director of studies of the higher school in Yunnanfu visited Japan with seven colleagues in order to study the administration of schools and to recruit teachers, who were to

arrive in China a few months later (ibid., folio 140, Report from Yunnanfu of 20 February 1906). In Zhili progress was even more advanced because of the initiatives taken by Yuan Shikai: the number of pupils increased from 1,000 in 1902-3 to 36,000 in 1904-5 (*East of Asia*, June 1904, 92-95; Ho Yen-sun, *Chinese Education*, 53). In Zhejiang, also, development had begun: in 1903 there were already 16 modern schools in Hangzhou alone (*Zhejiang hu*, no. 8, cited by Abe Hiroshi, "Modern Schools at the End of the Qing," in *Rekishi Hyōron*, no. 3 [1965]: 63). Certain districts in Guangdong had established an elaborate school system (*Jiaoyu xiaoce huiji*, nos. 4, 5, 28). In Jiangsu, Duan Fang had begun to implement measures in 1904; by 1905 considerable progress had already been made: Duan Fang, *Duan Chongmin gong zougao* (N.p., 1918), *juan* 4, 62b-65a; DFZZ 2, no. 6 (1905): *zazu*, 55.

40. Zhang Jian, *Diary*, GX32/II/26 (Yangzhou); *Nianpu*, 56-60; *Diary*, GX31/II/17, 24. In 1905 some of the students and Chinese teachers, irritated with the authority of foreign priests who refused to teach in English, organized a separate establishment, Aurore College (Fudan gongxue).

41. *Tongzhou xingban shiye zhangcheng* (Nantong, 1905), *Dasheng*, 63b, 67b, 72b. *Tongzhou xingban shiye zhi lishi*, 2 vols. (Nantong, 1910), *Dasheng*, 231, 243.

42. Sun Jia'nai (1828-1909) had been in charge of the University of Beijing during the Hundred Days Reform. Among high officials, Sun was one of those who lent their authority to the development of modern education.

43. In Zhili, the complex and specialized organization created by Yuan Shikai in August 1902 was known as the "office of schools" (*xuexiaosi*); it only had an administrative role (Yuan Shikai, *Yangshouyuan zouyi jiyao*, ed. Shen Zuxian [Xiangcheng, 1937], *juan* 18, 1a-1b; *Zhengyi congshu, neizheng tongji*, 5; the regulations are also reproduced in Shu Xincheng, *Jindai Zhongguo jiaoyu shiliao*, 4 vols. [Shanghai, 1928], 2: 122-26). In Hubei and Nanjing, offices of education had been established before July 1904 by Zhang Zhidong; Duan Fang opened the one in Suzhou (*Zhengyi congshu neizheng tongji*, 3); Shu Xincheng, *Shiliao*, 2: 122; Duan Fang, *Duan chongmin gong zougao*, 4: 5a-b). As in Zhili, they were under the control of the governor-general, but their consultative and legislative roles were more evident. The existence of these offices of education is overlooked by writers describing educational

administration (e.g., the copious work of Xue Renyang, *Zhongguo jiaoyu xingzheng zhidu shi lüe* [Shanghai, 1931], 70). They are important for understanding the role that education was able to play in the dialogue between the authorities and the governed, as will be seen later on.

44. Zhang Jian, *Diary*, GX30/XII/26, GX31/V/1. Establishments of this kind were already functioning in other districts, for example in Nanhai, Guangdong, from 1904 (*Jiaoyu xiaoce huiji*, nos. 4, 5).

45. The work of W. Franke, *Reform and Abolition*, gives all the details of the conditions surrounding the abolition of the examinations. Here, we shall limit ourselves to focusing on the results of this measure for education proper.

46. *Jiaoyu tongji tubiao*, 1907, *gesheng*, 27-28.

47. Xue Renyang, *Zhongguo jiaoyu xingzheng zhidu shi lüe*, 61-104, gives a detailed description of the administrative system inaugurated in 1905. Unfortunately he does not indicate his sources, although he has cited essential texts. The principal documents concerning the new administrative system are collected in *Da Qing Guangxu xin faling* (Shanghai, 1909), in the sections on "officials" and "education." The edict of 6 December 1905 establishing the Ministry of Education is in *Donghua xulu* 197/13. Among the memorials that precede the edict, the most important one was that of the Office for Political Affairs (Zhengwuchu). However, it must be noted that Wang Kangnian had proposed the establishment of such a ministry in 1896 in his "Zhongguo ziqiang ce" [On China's self-strengthening] (*Shiwu bao* 1, no. 4 [7 September 1896]: 206-9). For the creation of provincial administrative organs, the memorial addressed by Yuan Shikai on 26 February 1906 was decisive (*Yangshouyuan zouyi jiyao, juan* 36, 1a-3b).

48. The Japanese regulations are easily accessible in *Education in Japan* (1904), vol. 1, and *Notice sur l'organisation actuelle de l'instruction: publique au Japon:* they can be compared with the Chinese regulations of 1902 and 1904. See also text 1.

49. *Revue Indochinoise*, no. 271 (28 December 1903): 1131; NCH, 12 February 1902, 274.

50. J. Harada, "Japanese Educational Influence in China," *Chinese Recorder*, July 1905, 51-52.

51. Brownwell Gage, "Education in Hunan," *Chinese Recorder*, December 1907, 667-74.

52. Moir Duncan, "The Imperial University of Shansi," *East of Asia*

3 (1904): 102.
53. C. Tenney, "Government Schools of Chihli Province," *East of Asia*, June 1904, 90-95.
54. J. Arnold, "Educational Activity in Foochow China," 201-20.
55. The activities of the Tōa Dōbunkai also extended to Korea. Its founding indicated the growth of Japanese imperialism at the beginning of the twentieth century. The Shanghai school contained 180 pupils in 1902, and 320 in 1905 (M. Courant, "L'éducation européenne des Asiatiques," *Revue Indochinoise*, 23 November 1903, 1061; J. Harada, "Japanese Educational Influence in China"). The history of the society is described in M. Jansen, *The Japanese and Sun Yat-sen* (Cambridge, 1954).
56. "Le Japon et l'Extrême-Orient ," *Revue de Paris*, 15 March 1905, 225-44; A. Maybon, "La réforme scolaire en Chine," *La Revue*, 15 November 1907, 234-39.
57. At the higher school in Baoding, for example, where half of the teaching body was Japanese (M. Courant, "L'éducation européenne des Asiatiques"), at the normal school in Fuzhou (J. Arnold, "Educational Activity in Foochow"), and in Shanxi (*East of Asia*, June 1904, 23). The first "Chinese" school textbooks published by the Commercial Press in 1903 were simple translations (Zhang Jinglu, *Zhongguo chuban shiliao, bubian* [Shanghai, 1953-54], 140).
58. Zhang Jian, *Diary*, GX27/IX/20, GX30/VI/20.
59. This is the title of an article written by M. Pinon in the *Revue des deux mondes* of 15 August 1905, 806.
60. For example, Wang Feng-gang, *Japanese Influence on Educational Reform in China from 1895 to 1911* (Beijing, 1933).
61. J. Darroch recorded 1,100 works translated in 1904, among which 60 were on pedagogy; the figure is certainly incomplete (*Chinese Recorder*, November 1904, 559-60). In 1905, J. Harada referred to a catalogue of 608 Japanese titles published in Chinese by a Japanese firm in Shanghai (*Chinese Recorder*, July 1905, 356-61). There are some references on this subject in Saneto Keishū, *Nippon bunka no shina e no eikyō* (Keisetsu Shōin, 1940). Two contemporary catalogues, Xu Weize, *Dongxixue shulu* (1899), and Gu Xieguang, *Yi shujing yanlu* (Reprint, Hangzhou, 1934), give specific details on the origin of these translations, many of which were done by Luo Zhenyu's Jiaoyushe (Education Society). According to M. Jansen (FEQ 13, no. 3 [May 1954]: 324), from 1899 to 1919, 60.2 percent of translated books were from Japanese works.

62. In fact, the year when students started going to Japan in great
numbers was 1905-6. It was not these students who contributed to the "Japanization" among official and gentry circles in
the first years of the century. On their return, the first of them
certainly contributed to reinforcing the imitation of Japan, but
by the time the majority of them returned to China, the period
of servile imitation had already ended. Sources vary as to the
number of students in Japan. The figures with their sources are
indicated below.

1902	271	(Lewis, *The Educational Conquest of the Far East*, 184)
1903	591	(NCH [16 March 1906], 569-70)
	579	February
	1,058	October (DFZZ, I/2, 159-60)
1904	+100	Each month (NCH [16 March 1906], 569-70)
	1,400	(DFZZ, I/2, 159-60)
1905	2,406	January (NCH [16 March 1906], 569-70)
	8,620	End of November (ibid.)
	11,000	End of December (ibid. [12 January 1906], 68)
1906	8,000	January (ibid.)
	5,418	June (*"Jingwai xuewu baogao," Xuebu guanbao*, no. 8: 40)
	12,301	October (ibid.)
1907	15,000	Spring (H. E. King, *Educational System of China*, 92)
	17,000	Autumn (ibid.)
1909	3,000	(JYZZ, I/2, 11)
	5,000	(*Chinese Recorder* [October 1909], 570-79)
	4,744	(H. E. King, *Educational System of China*, 92)
1910	5,000	(Ibid.)
1911	7,000	September (JYZZ, III/12, *jishi*, 94)
	3,000	December (ibid.)
1912	500	January (ibid.)

63. On the establishment of the Nonghui, see *Shiwu bao* 2, no. 13 (5
December 1896): 891-92; 3, no. 22 (2 April 1897): 1519-20.
The list of members is in the first *ce* of *Nongxue bao* (n.p.).

Harvard-Yenching Library has two editions of this journal, which seems only to have appeared from April 1897 to December 1901 (twice, then three times monthly). On Luo Zhenyu's role in the Agricultural Society and journal: Duan Fang, *Duan chongmin gong zougao, juan* 4, 4.

64. *Nantong tushuguan diyici mulu* (Nantong, 1914), passim. Having contributed fifty dollars to the Nonghui, Zhang Jian received the journal free.

65. *Shiwu bao* 6, no. 50 (3 January 1898): 3440. The regulations and list of founding members are in *Nongxue bao*, 35/1a-2b. See also Dong Zuoblin, "A Short Account of the Life of Luo Xuetang," *Dalu zazhi* 24, no. 4 (1962); and also Wang Yi-t'ung, "Biographic Sketches of 29 Classical Scholars of the Late Manchu and Early Republican Era" (typed ms., Pittsburgh, 1963), 80.

66. Zhang Jian, *Diary*, GX28/I/22, GX29/II/3. See also the biography of Wang Guowei in appendix 1.

67. Duan Fang, *Duan chongmin gong zougao, juan* 4, 4; Xu Tongxin, *Zhang Wenxiang gong nianpu* (Shanghai, 1944), 153. Chen Yi was also a member of the expedition, in his capacity as professor at the Ziqiang xuetang (Self-strengthening school) established by Zhang Zhidong.

68. *Jiaoyu shijie*, no. 16 (December 1901): 1a; *Jiangsu xuewu wendu* (Suzhou, 1910), vol. 3, memorial of 9 October 1909 requesting honorific distinction for Fujita in reward for his services. The 1932 edition of his *Research on the History of the Relations Between East and West* [*Tōzai kōshō shi no kenkyū*] contains a bibliography of his works as well as a brief biography. There is also some information on Fujita in the biographies of Luo Zhenyu cited earlier (note 65).

69. Zhang Jian, *Diary*, GX27/IX/20. See also text 1, commentary.

70. Wang Guowei, "Postface to Regulations on the Department of Classics and Faculty of Letters," *Jiaoyu shijie*, nos. 118, 119 (January-February 1906), reproduced in Shu Xincheng, *Shiliao*, 2: 30.

71. DFZZ 3, no. 11 (1906): *jishi.*

72. Zhang Jian, *Diary*, GX28/IX/15, 16, 19. A biography of Wu Rulun (1840-1903) is given in A. Hummel, *Eminent Chinese of the Ch'ing Period 1644-1912*, 2 vols. (Washington D.C., 1943-44), 2: 870-72.

73. Zhang Jian, *Zhuan*, IV/1b.

74. Zhang Jian, *Diary*, GX30/III/28, IV/4, 27, 29, V/6, 9, X/13, 14; *Nianpu*, 56.
75. In the catalogue of Gu Xieguang, *Yi shujing yanlu*, out of 533 translations from 1902 to 1904, 57 were translated from English, 17 from French, and 321 from Japanese works. Western works were nearly all translated from a Japanese version. In the first three volumes of Luo Zhenyu's *Jiaoyu congshu*, out of 36 translated works 4 were Western but their translation in each case was from a Japanese version (*Jiaoyu congshu chuji, erji, sanji*, ed. Jiaoyushe [Shanghai, 1901]).
76. Zhang Jian, *Jiaoyu*, I/18b-20a.
77. This applies to even after 1912; the schools that trained people for the "new China" were not missionary schools, but rather Chinese establishments such as the universities of Beijing and Qinghua.
78. E. Williams, "The Progress of Educational Reform in China," *Annual Reports of the Department of the Interior* (Washington D.C., 1907), 265.
79. B. Schwartz, *In Search of Wealth and Power: Yen Fu and the West* (Cambridge, Massachusetts, 1964), introduction and 238.
80. "Le Japon et L'Extrême-orient," *Revue de Paris*, 15 March 1905, 225-44.
81. For foreign influences on modern Japanese education: H. Passin, *Society and Education in Japan* (New York, 1964), 70-103; Yoshida Kumaji, "European and American Influences in Japanese Education," in *Western Influences in Modern Japan*, ed. I. Nitobe (Chicago, 1931), 25-55.
82. For example, Wang Guowei. See his article on the aims of education in *Jiaoyu shijie*, no. 56 and that on philosophy (ibid., no. 55) in August 1903.
83. Edict of 14 September 1901 (*Donghua xulu*, 169/1a); memorial of Zhang Zhidong and Liu Kunyi of 12 July 1901 (ibid., 7b; Zhang Zhidong, *Zhang Wenxiang gong quanji* [Beijing, 1937], *juan* 52, 9b; Shu Xincheng, *Shiliao*, 1: 78); memorial of Yuan Shikai in 1901 reproduced in Shu Xincheng, *Shiliao*, 1: 94.
84. Memorial on the abolition of the examinations from the governors-general and governors on 31 August 1905 (*Donghua xulu*, 195/9a).
85. Edict of 2 September 1905 abolishing the examinations (*Donghua xulu*, 195/11b).
86. Zhang Baixi, *Zouding xuetang zhangcheng*, "Chudeng xiaoxuetang," 1a, "Gaodeng xiaoxuetang," 1a, "Zhongdeng

xiaoxuetang," 1a; the memorial and edict of 19 April 1906 on the aims of education (Shu Xincheng, *Ziliao*, 220).

87. *Zouding xuetang zhangcheng*, "Xuewu gangyao," 2a. The entire passage was drafted by Zhang Zhidong; it is reproduced in Shu Xincheng, *Ziliao*, 200.

88. Edict of 19 April 1906 (Shu Xincheng, *Ziliao*, 225).

89. Memorial from the Ministry of Education, sanctioned by the edict of 19 April (ibid., 221).

90. Speech on the opening of the normal school in 1903 (Zhang Jian, *Jiaoyu*, I/16b-17a).

91. End of year speech at the normal school in February 1904 (Zhang Jian, *Jiaoyu*, I/18a-19b). The reference to Filipino resistance (often associated with that of the Boers) was commonplace in reformist literature of the time: see *Qingyi bao*, no. 32: 2059-62, no. 67: 4293, no. 78: 4978, no. 85: 5405-8.

92. See J. Fass, "A Few Notes on the Birth of Nationalism in China," *Archiv Orientalni* 32, no. 3 (1964): 376-82. The author attempts to demonstrate that revolutionary leaders had anti-imperialist ideas, but in his description of the growth of their nationalism one is struck by the absence of references to the foreign danger. The revolutionaries' awareness of the nation was stimulated more in relation to the internal oppression represented by Manchu nationalism. At this time antiimperialism was a feature of reformist thought. A similar situation occurred during the early years of the Chinese Communist Party when the banner of antiimperialism was held by members of the Guomindang and not by the Communists.

93. Luo Zhenyu, "Personal Opinion on Education," *Jiaoyu shijie*, no. 1 (May 1901).

94. Liang Qichao, "Some Necessary Aims for Education," *Xinmin congbao*, no. 1 (8 February 1902).

95. There is no reference to these publications in Zhang's diary. Zhang was perhaps being cautious, avoiding any mention of compromising material; however, his biographers also do not mention that he had ever read them. Liang Qichao was 10 to 20 years younger than reformist leaders in China and it is not surprising that the latter hardly ever imagined being inspired by a younger person, especially one who was *persona non grata* at court. Those who did have contact with Liang between 1895 and 1898 (of whom Zhang was one) treated him as an equal and not as an intellectual leader; the *Shiwu bao* and the Qiangxuehui appeared to them the result of a collective effort.

After the failure of the Hundred Days Reform, they even tended to think that Liang's foolhardy enthusiasm had jeopardized the common enterprise and they were ready to begin again more or less judging that they would succeed better without him.

96. On 12 October 1901, *Qingyi bao* published an article on the role of education in the growth of the nation (no. 94: 5943-48); several articles on the same theme had appeared in *Jiaoyu shijie*, no. 1 (May 1901), no. 3 (June 1901), and no. 8 (August 1901). On 21 December 1901, *Qingyi bao* (no. 100: 6485-87) warned of the danger facing China of losing her "educational rights" (*jiaoyu zhi quan*) if she allowed foreigners to monopolize the control over schools; the same theme, with the same arguments, had already been developed by Luo Zhenyu in September 1901 (*Jiaoyu shijie*, no. 9: 1a-3a); see also the articles in nos. 1, 3, 4, 8, 9, 12, 13, 14, 15, 16, 17, 18 (1901) of *Jiaoyu shijie*, in comparison with *Xinmin congbao*, no. 1 (8 February 1902): 61-68, no. 2 (22 February 1902): 21-28, no. 3 (10 March 1902): 33-40.

97. Unfortunately, information on Liang Qichao during these few months is sparse and does not contain any reference to this question (see Ding Wenjiang, *Liang Rengong xiansheng nianpu* [Taibei, 1958]); neither is there any relevant information in Luo Zhenyu's writings describing his trip to Japan.

98. Chen Chi, *Yong shu*, preface, 2a, I/17a-19a; memorial of Kang Youwei on 29 January 1898 (*Wuxu bianfa*, 2: 201-2); Liang Qichao, "Proposal for the Chambers of Commerce," *Qingyi bao*, no. 10 (1 April 1899): 583-this article contains the earliest use of the term I have come across in a Chinese text.

99. Zhang Jian, *Diary*, GX29/XII/30.

100. Ibid., 8 (20 January 1904).

101. Ibid., GX32/II/26, IV/7.

102. This sudden change can be noticed in the first months of 1907 with the decrease in the number of reforms that followed the edict of 1 September 1906 announcing a constitution. One can also compare the tone of the articles in *Xinmin congbao* (1902-6), with that in *Zhenglun* [Political discussion], which Liang Qichao founded in 1907. The former preached enlightened despotism (e.g., the articles of Kang Youwei on local autonomy in nos. 5, 6, 7), while the latter preached the establishment of a parliamentary regime. It is the same for *Guomin xinbao* and DFZZ (e.g., Jue Min, "The Relationship Between the Constitution and Education," DFZZ 2, no. 12: *sheshuo*, 243-48), and an article in *Nanfang bao* [Southern

journal] reprinted in ibid.: *neiwu*, 216-18, in January 1906, compared with the article by Miao Zhao, "Explanation on the Level of the People," DFZZ, special supplement (February 1907).

103. See the professions of faith expressed by Zhang Jian during the revolutionary agitation that menaced the government in 1905: he wrote, "Constitutionalism is not dead; it seeks ways to prolong its life"; also, "I do not know if a constitution will work or not, but I cannot give up hope. Perhaps it shall be functioning by next year" (*Diary*, GX29/XI/21, 29).

104. Such fears and the reasons for them were expressed in 1901 in *Jiaoyu shijie*, nos. 9, 13, 14, 16, 17, 18. *Xinmin congbao* took up these ideas in 1902 and they were frequently discussed in other reformist journals.

105. Zhang Yuanqi, "Reply to a Friend on Educational Matters," *Jiaoyu shijie*, no. 20 (February 1902). See Zhang's biography in appendix 1.

106. On its consequences for China, see Y. C. Wang, *Chinese Intellectuals and the West, 1872-1949* (Durham, 1965), in particular 378-93, 502-3.

107. The terms *guoxue* and *guocui* seem to have been used for the first time in an article on the University of Beijing in *Xinmin congbao* (no. 34 [24 June 1903]: 61-62). The idea, however, had already been developed in several articles in *Jiaoyu shijie*, particularly those in no. 9 (September 1901) (Luo Zhenyu, "Five Imperatives for Education"), and no. 13 (November 1901) (Xia Xiefu, "Simple Talk about Schools"). The latter writer, in charge of overseas students, used the term "nationalism" (*guominzhuyi*) to designate what was later called *guoxue;* the expression was no doubt preferred because it avoided the problem of the Manchus. Zhang Jian spoke of the "national essence" (*guocui*) in a speech at the normal school in 1903 (Zhang Jian, *Jiaoyu*, I/17b-18a). The idea and the term came from Japan where it had appeared around 1884-85, first of all as a reaction against romanization of the Japanese written language (Fujiwara Kiyozo, *Meiji kyōiku shisō shi*, 174-76).

108. The vocabulary of the time tended to be ambiguous. During the years 1901-5 reformist scholars frequently wrote that Confucianism (*Kongjiao* or *Kongdao*) should be established as the *guojiao*, a term that is generally translated as "state religion" since this Confucianism was a reaction to the proselytism of missionaries and was always presented as the equivalent of

national religions in the West (which, along with the imperial cult in Japan, were referred to by Chinese as *guojiao*). In reality, this Confucianism had nothing religious about it; neither did it signify blind submission to the emperor, but rather the obedience to written laws, the respect for morality and national discipline. In sum it was a revived Confucianism, which reformers claimed represented the original teachings of the sage. Among the most important texts one can cite the articles by Luo Zhenyu, "Explanation of the *Analects* of Confucius," and "The Five Imperatives of Education," in *Jiaoyu shijie*, nos. 6, 7, 9 (1901); Zhang Yuanqi, in *Jiaoyu shijie*, no. 20 and articles in nos. 3, 24, 49 (1901-3); the letter of Tang Shouqian in *Xuebu guanbao* 1, no. 12 (24 January 1907), *fulu*; *Xinmin congbao*, no. 34 (24 June 1903): 61-62.

109. This difference is underlined in an article in *Xinmin congbao*, ibid.

110. Zhang Jian, *Diary*, GX30/II/11.

111. Zhang Jian, *Jiaoyu*, I/17b-18a. Actually, it was much more a question of the written style practiced at the beginning of the twentieth century than the classical Chinese in ancient works.

112. Such is the meaning of the text entitled "The School System Should Imitate that of the Zhou and Apply the Precepts of Confucius" (Zhang Jian, *Jiaoyu*, I/14b-16b). S. Chu, *Reformer in Modern China*, 109-10, gives a translation of the text.

Chapter III

1. Huang Yanpei, *Minguo yuannian gongshang tongji gaiyao* (Shanghai, 1915), 1-67.

2. The total reached 159,654,812 dollars in 1911, according to Yan Zhongping, *Tongji ziliao* (Beijing, 1955), 93. This figure does not take into account enterprises entirely owned by foreigners or enterprises having less than 10,000 dollars capital.

3. *Jiangsu sheng fangzhiye zhuangkuang*, I/1.

4. S. Chu gives a detailed account of most of these enterprises (*Reformer in Modern China*, 36-42). The Industrial Company of Nantong (Nantong shiye gongsi), was created at a meeting of Dasheng shareholders in 1907, on the suggestion of Zheng Xiaoxu.

5. Calculated from *Tongzhou xingban shiye zhi lishi*, passim, and *Jiangsu sheng shiye xingzheng baogaoshu* (Shanghai, 1914), V/39-65. Zhang's interests in the railway company of Jiangsu, the capital of which amounted to ten million *taels* (ibid., V/55) are not included. The growth since 1898, when the capital of Dasheng amounted to 500,000 *taels* (machinery included), can clearly be seen. Such a figure represented 7 percent of Chinese industrial capital.

6. On Tang Shouqian: *Nonggongshangbu tongjibiao* (Beijing, 1909), V/3, 8, VI/25b; DFZZ 2, no. 9 (1905): *zazu*, 68. On Shen Zipei: *Dalu zazhi*, 24, no. 6 (31 March 1962): 32. On Zheng Xiaoxu: *Biographical Dictionary of Republican China*, ed. H. Boorman, 4 vols. (New York, 1967-68), 1: 271-75. Some information is given in appendix 1.

7. On Ma Liang's economic interests: *Jiangsu sheng shiye xingzheng baogaoshu*, III/45; DFZZ 3, no. 12 (1907): *shiye*, 237. On those of Xiong Xiling: *Nonggongshangbu tongji biao*, V/27a. On those of Zhang Yuanji: DFZZ 4, no. 11 (1907): *zazu*, 28. On Lei Fen: ibid. On Chen Sanli: ibid., 27, and the biography in Wang Yi-t'ung, *Biographic Sketches*. See also appendix 1.

8. The first time was with the French, in 1905 (Zhang Jian, *Diary*, GX31/X/1). At this time he considered establishing a Chinese industrial national bank. The second time was with the Americans in 1910-11 (see text 7).

9. For an account of the boycott: Zhang Cunwu, *Guangxu sanshiyinian zhongmei gongyue fengchao* (Taibei, 1965). Akira Iriye, "Public Opinion in Late Ch'ing China," 10-16, gives a clear analysis of its role in the formation of a public opinion.

10. On the role of Zhang Jian in the boycott: Zhang Cunwu, *Zhongmei gongyue fengchao*, 102, 150, 155, 201.

11. Li Chien-nung, *The Political History of China, 1840-1928* (Stanford, 1967), 221-25.

12. The most famous were the attacks on the official envoys of the constitutional mission in the autumn of 1905 and on the regent in March 1910.

13. See the study by E-tu Zen-sun, "The Chinese Constitutional Missions of 1905-1906," *Journal of Modern History* 24, no. 3 (September 1952): 251-68.

14. *Donghua xulu*, 202/2b-3b. Translated in J. Rodes, *La Chine Nouvelle* (Paris, 1910), 122-24.

15. Zhang Jian, *Diary*, GX32/XI/1; NCH, 21 December 1906, 661, gives a list of members. Huang Yanpei ("Chinese Constitutional Movements in Which I Was Involved from Early to Recent Times," *Xianzheng*, January 1944, 10-11) gives a vivid description of the association's opening meeting, its membership, and its activities. He notes that members had to contribute 500 dollars a month, which appears to be a large sum; no doubt Huang was thinking in terms of the 1944 dollar.

16. Established on 22 December 1907 (DFZZ 4, no. 12 [1908]: *zazu*, 30). Several papers presented at the Wentworth Conference in 1965 describe the activities of these associations, especially those of W. Johnson on Guizhou and Yunnan, and C. Hedtke on Sichuan. There was no paper describing the situation in Jiangsu.

17. At the beginning of 1907 (DFZZ 3, no. 12 [1907]: *neiwu*, 232).

18. DFZZ 2, no. 9 (1905): *zazu*, 66; ibid., 3, no. 9 (1906): *zazu*, 41; see also the memorial of 23 August 1907 in which Yuan Shikai gave information on the first attempt at local autonomy in Tianjin (*Yangshouyuan zouyi, juan* 44, 10a-12b).

19. *Xinhai geming*, 8 vols. (Shanghai, 1957), 4: 65-66; Li Zonghuang, *Zhongguo difang zizhi gailun* (Taibei, 1952), 43-44.

20. The transfer of officials clearly increased from 1907 onwards. From then on it was no longer a question of governors-general remaining in the same post for eighteen years, as Zhang Zhidong had been able to do.

21. The provincial education association of Guangdong seems only to have existed from February 1911 (JYZZ 3, no. 2: *jishi*, 16).

22. *Jiaoyu tongji tubiao*, 1908, *gesheng*, 38-39; ibid., 1909, *gesheng*, 37-38; *Jiangsu sheng jiaoyu xingzheng baogaoshu*, II/144.

23. For example, those of Yangzhou, Dantu, Wuxian, and other districts in Jiangsu (DFZZ 3, no. 2 [1906]: *jiaoyu*, 329), as well as Shanghai.

24. These observations on the social composition of education associations are drawn from scattered information in Zhang Jian's diary, in DFZZ, JYZZ, NCH, as well as *Jiangsu sheng jiaoyu xingzheng baogaoshu*, II/144-58, which gives a list of the leadership of the Jiangsu associations; *Jiangsu sheng shiye xingzheng baogaoshu*, V/2-14; and *Nonggongshangbu tongjibiao* IV, which gives the names of the leadership of the chambers of commerce. On the people referred to, see appendix 1.

25. Subsidies normally amounted to several thousands of dollars for a whole province. Jiangsu, which was richer, contributed 28,656 dollars in 1908: *Jiaoyu tongji tubiao*, 1908, *gesheng*, 18-22, Jiangning, 1-2, Jiangsu, 1-2. Subscriptions varied from 0.5 to 1 Mexican dollar a month. In general, a larger sum had to be paid on joining and this necessarily prevented intellectuals of modest means from joining. The Jiangsu Education Association was especially wealthy since it had inherited property in Shanghai. In 1910 a merchant contributed 100,000 dollars (*Jiangsu sheng jian*, VII/198).

26. See other examples in Jingjiang and Liyang (*Jiangsu xuewu wendu* I, GX33/VIII/3, 11, GX33/XII/13), Suzhou (Zhang Jian, *Jiaoyu*, III/5b-6a). In this latter reference, Zhang Jian protested against the transfer of local tax receipts to the provincial treasury: "The officials are the mother of the people," he wrote, "how can they twist the arms of their children in order to deprive them of food!" For Sichuan: Archives du Ministère des Affaires étrangères, *China, new series*, no. 583, folio 165: Report from Chengdu of 1 December 1910.

27. In 1906 the Jiangsu Education Association created a society of legal studies and a school of law, which was managed by Lei Fen. Lei had graduated from Waseda University in Japan and was a well-known constitutionalist. He was chairman of the provincial assembly's secretariat in 1909. The law school produced 231 graduates in three years. Lectures and debates, more or less of a political nature, were also organized.

28. On the activities and numerous publications of the society: *Jiangsu sheng jian*, ed. Zhao Ruheng et al. (Shanghai, 1935), VII/183-98; *Ten Years of the Kiangsu Provincial Education Association*, 1-9. From 1910 to 1911 Huang Yanpei, on behalf of the society, undertook inspections throughout the province, beginning with Nantong. His reports were published in 1911-12. They would have constituted a valuable source for this study but unfortunately they seem to be no longer in existence.

29. JYZZ 2, no. 7: *jishi*, 35; 3, no. 1: *jishi*, 6; NCH, 6 May 1911, 369.

30. Liu Guiwu, "The Constitutional Party and Movement before and after the 1911 Revolution," *Lishi jiaoxue*, no. 8 (1962): 22; papers from the Wentworth Conference, cited earlier (note 16).

31. Yuan Shikai, *Yangshouyuan zouyi jiyao*, *juan* 44, 1a-12b. The others were chosen by the authorities and the chamber of commerce.

32. JYZZ 2, no. 3: *jishi*, 24; no. 4: *zhangcheng wendu*, 27-28.
33. JYZZ 3, no. 1; no. 5: *jishi*, 37; no. 6: *fulu*, 1-8, gives the names of the participants, the procedural details, and the resolutions of the Gesheng jiaoyu zonghui lianhehui.
34. Up until this time, elementary education was conducted in the local dialect. It was a question of increasing the use of *guoyu* (what foreigners called "Mandarin"), the pronunciation and grammar of which were close to those of the Beijing dialect.
35. The regulations followed those of the Japanese Council of Higher Education, which was itself patterned after the French institution of the same name. However, its role was purely consultative and it only dealt with primary and secondary education. Its establishment was met with mixed feelings although educators decided to make as much use of it as possible; in this they were successful. The provinces made efforts to send members to Beijing; out of 172 people summoned, 100 responded. They included members of education associations, school principals, and well-known scholars-they all actively encouraged others to side with them. The regulations are reproduced in JYZZ 3, no. 6: *faling*, 67-72; this issue also contains a translation of the regulations for the French Council of Higher Education and an anonymous commentary that reflects educators' opinions (*jishi*, 43-44). See also DFZZ 8, no. 5 (1911): *jishi*, 4-6; NCH, 22 July 1911, 227; 29 July 1911, 290.
36. Lu Feikui, "The Central Education Committee," JYZZ 3, no. 8: *yanlun*, 69. This account by one of the participants gives a good description of the atmosphere during the debates, the varying opinions and the problems that beset the participants. Lu Feikui was elected to the committee of the Chinese Society of Education.
37. Besides the article cited in note 36, see also JYZZ 3, no. 7: *jishi*, 52-54; no. 8: *jishi*, 60.
38. Zhongguo jiaoyuhui, Quanguo shifan lianhehui. They were created on 11 August 1911, before the dispersal of provincial delegates to the Central Education Committee. For their regulations, aims, and membership: JYZZ 3, no. 8: *jishi*, 59-60: *fulu* 13-17. Forty people took part in the inaugural meeting of the Federation of Normal Schools, an organization that had a more specific aim. However, 227 people were present at the opening meeting of the Chinese Society of Education, including members of political groups, parliamentary delegates, well-known people

in Beijing, and important liberal officials. Obviously, they were not all members of the Central Education Committee.

39. *Jiangsu sheng jiaoyu xingzheng baogaoshu* (Shanghai, 1914), I/151-58. The district of Shanghai had fourteen secondary and specialist schools with 2,700 pupils. Wuxi had nine with 488 pupils. The district of Wujin surpassed that of Nantong with regards to the number of pupils (387, as opposed to 332), but not with regards to the number of schools (five, as opposed to eight in Nantong).

40. Chang Chung-li estimates that in the 1880s the per capita income was equivalent to two times the amount of the necessary annual food rations to feed one adult (*The Income of the Chinese Gentry*, 296-325). At the beginning of the twentieth century the increase in population offset the potential benefits of early industrial growth; conditions were therefore not much better.

41. One is inclined to think that this may have been the case, judging by the renewed outbreaks of peasant riots in protest against school taxes in 1910 and 1911.

42. Besides the 50 percent of funds which are known to have come from industry and commerce, it is probable that among the 48 percent of funds whose origin is undetermined, a part of the sum was contributed by people who had interests in Zhang Jian's enterprises.

43. In 1907 Dasheng contributed 35,000 dollars to education, while net profits amounted to 76,000 dollars.

44. JYZZ 1, no. 6: *jishi*, 40-41; 2, no. 4: *jishi*, 32-33; no. 6: *jishi*, 47; no. 7: *jishi*, 59; no. 8: *jishi*, 67; 3, no. 1: *jishi*, 7; no. 5: *jishi*, 37. In Fujian and Zhejiang Japanese Buddhist missions aided Chinese monks in stirring up the crowds: NCH, 10 March 1905, 490; 24 August 1906, 457.

45. Zhang Jian, *Jiaoyu*, II/11a-b. DFZZ and JYZZ carefully omit any reference to the gentry's role in the riots directed against the schools. I have found only two cases where gentry acted on their own. In Wuxi, in 1904, rice merchants, supported by two scholars, burnt down the house and school of a *juren*. The latter, due to lack of funds, had arranged that his school receive an official subsidy, paid for by an increase on the tax paid by rice merchants. The merchants claimed that people in other occupations should also have been subject to increased taxes (DFZZ 2, no. 1 (1905): *zazu*, 5-6; see also the memorials of Duan Fang on this incident: *Duan chongmin gong zougao, juan*

4, 14b-15a, 56a-59b). In 1905, in Nanjing, some scholars solemnly protested against the conversion of academies into schools, but without violence (DFZZ 2, no. 3 (1905): *zazu*, 40).

46. On the famines: NCH, May, June, 28 September, November 1906, March 1907, April-June 1910. On the destruction of schools for purely economic reasons in 1906-7: NCH, 20 July 1906, 146; DFZZ 3, no. 6 (1906): *zazu*, 32; 4, no. 6 (1907): *zazu*, 16; 4, no. 9 (1907): *zazu*, 21; 5, no. 1 (1908): *zazu*, 1. Unfortunately, the periodicals consulted give much less detail on the other provinces. Nevertheless, one can detect the coincidence between famine and destruction of schools in Guangdong, in 1907, and in Henan, in 1905 and 1906.

47. This census was undertaken as part of the reform movement and was aimed at making tax distribution more equitable. However, alarmist rumors were frequently heard; for example, it was said that the population was being counted in order to sell people to foreigners, or in order to increase taxes, or in order to collect names for placing under railways sleepers-an action that would cause the immediate death of the person named (NCH, 13 May 1910, 379; JYZZ 2, no. 3: *jishi*, 21).

48. JYZZ 2, no. 6: *jishi*, 46. On the destruction of schools in 1910, the most complete account is found in the *jishi* of JYZZ: 2, no. 3: 21; no. 4: 32-33; no. 5: 38-39; no. 6: 46-49; no. 7: 59; no. 8: 67; no. 11: 92; and 3, no. 1: 1-7; no. 2: 15. They report on incidents in Jiangsu, Anhui, Zhejiang, Hunan, Zhili, and Guangdong. DFZZ 6, no. 8 (1909): *jishi*, 222-24 and no. 9 (1909): *jishi*, 274-76 report on the disturbances during the taking of the census in Jiangxi, emphasizing that no school was destroyed. This seems to be an exception. It should also be noted that popular anger was often directed at institutions of local autonomy which, in certain places, were used as a pretext for imposing a new tax, a part of which went towards the upkeep of schools.

49. At Nantong, for example (*Xinhai geming Jiangsu diqu shiliao* [Nanjing, 1961], 227).

50. The problem cannot be dwelt on here, but it is curious to compare the eyewitness reports of missionaries in the eighteenth century with those of the end of the nineteenth century: for example, P. Premare, *Lettre de Nantchang* of 1 October 1701 (Manuscript in the Bibliothèque Nationale) and S. Williams, *The Middle Kingdom*, 1: 544. In 1847, on the basis of accounts in the preceding century, E. Biot did not hesitate in

observing that primary education was much more widespread in China than in France (*Essai sur l'histoire de l'instruction publique en Chine et de la Corporation des Lettrés depuis les Anciens Temps jusqu'à nos Jours* [Paris, 1847], 494).

51. For primary education, which is the essential sector, it is very difficult to evaluate the decline since there were no statistics on traditional schools. On the other hand, one can compare the number of academies and their enrollment with those of modern establishments above the primary level. On the eve of modern educational reform, there were 2,000 to 3,000 academies with a minimum of 100,000 students (probably 150,000 to 200,000); in 1909 there were 702 schools above the primary level with 72,000 students. By this time academies had completely disappeared. The eyewitness report of a missionary in Gansu, in 1910, can also be cited; he mentioned the difficulty experienced by the schools in recruiting pupils: "Since the new system has come in vogue, there has been a great falling-off of scholars." (NCH, 17 June 1910, 679).

52. See p. 31.

53. However, the students had three dishes per meal and normally ate meat every day. During times of famine they still had two dishes per meal and meat twice a week (Zhang Jian, *Jiaoyu,* II/28b-29b).

54. H. Passin, *Society and Education in Japan,* 43-44. The critical period was between 1867 and 1872. School attendance was already very high before the Meiji Restoration; the national average was 40 percent and the average for Edo was 86 percent. It is thought that by 1900 nearly all children of school age were attending school.

55. S. Nurullah, *A History of Education in India during the British Period* (Bombay, 1943), xxii-xxiv, 5-43, 447-50. In the state of Madras, in 1822, one-third of school-age children were educated; in 1921-22, 7.2 percent of school-age children were literate.

56. Zhang Jian, *Jiaoyu,* II/27a. See also text 5, and *Jiaoyu,* III/8a.

57. See the biography of scholar Chang in Fei Hsiao-t'ung, *China's Gentry* (Chicago, 1955), 157-65. One can also cite the examples of Huang Yanpei and Chiang Monlin.

58. I hoped to gain information on this subject from a list of pupils of the Nantong Normal School, which is located in the Beijing National Library. Unfortunately, despite repeated efforts, it remains inaccessible.

59. *Tongxiang timing lu* (N.p., 1933), *juan* 4, 27a-b. Despite going through fifteen biographical dictionaries, I have been unable to find additional details on these individuals.
60. *Ershinian lai zhi Nantong*, 56-58.
61. NCH, 17 August 1906, 389.
62. *Xinhai geming Jiangsu diqu shiliao*, 226.
63. One has only to read the advice on hygiene that Zhang Jian attempted to give his students, whose ages ranged from fifteen to twenty, to realize the extent of the problem (Zhang Jian, *Jiaoyu*, I/19a). This text, dealing with events in February 1904, gives useful information on the students' behavior; they took holidays at will, caused disturbances, and demanded liberty and equality.
64. Lee Teng-hwee, *The Problem of New Education in China* (Bruges, 1910), 7; *China Mission Yearbook*, 1911, 104-11; NCH, 25 November 1910, 468-69; Huang Yanpei, *Kaocha jiaoyu riji*, 2 vols. (Shanghai, 1914-15), 1: 205-8, 2: 155-60.
65. On student strikes during the last three years of the monarchy: NCH, 5 June 1909; JYZZ 1, no. 13: *jishi*, 100-101; 3, no. 4: *jishi*, 5.
66. There are scattered references to this problem in Huang Yanpei, *Kaocha jiaoyu riji*.
67. Even in schools that were well thought of by the authorities, such as those in Nantong, students had access to all kinds of revolutionary journals and newspapers (*Xinhai geming Jiangsu diqu shiliao*, 217).
68. See the article by Lu Feikui already cited, DFZZ 3, no. 8 (1906): *yanlun*, 69.
69. "Personal Opinion on Compulsory Education," DFZZ 3, no. 5 (1906): *jiaoyu*, 59-68; Fang Yan, "That It Is Necessary to Make Education Compulsory in Order to Expand It," DFZZ 3, no. 6 (1906): *sheshuo*, 126-33.
70. The regulations are in JYZZ 1, no. 5: *faling*, 25. In 1908 it had first been proposed to offer "short courses" of four and three years, while still retaining the complete course of five years.
71. Shu Xincheng, *Ziliao*, 446-49.
72. These establishments are described by Gao Jiansi in *Zuijin sanshiwunian zhi Zhongguo jiaoyu* (Shanghai, 1931), 153-63.
73. DFZZ 2, no. 2 (1905): *jiaoyu*, 23-26; no. 11 (1905): *jiaoyu*, 290; NCH, 27 October 1905, 229. The regulations are also in Shu Xincheng, *Shiliao*, 2: 149-56. The Sishu gailianghui was active in Jiangsu, Zhejiang, and Anhui.

74. NCH, 13 February 1909, 374. *Xuebu guanbao* 3, nos. 91, 92, 93, 94, and 95 (28 June-6 August 1909) contains a detailed report on the reform of private schools in Beijing in 1909. In 1907 there were 12 private schools, with 300 pupils, which had attained the required standard. At the beginning of 1910 there were 172 such schools, with 4,300 pupils. Only 1,370 *taels* had been spent (Kuo Ping-wen, *The Chinese System of Public Education*, 103).

75. The word itself, *zhiye jiaoyu*, appeared in 1904 in a memorial written by the director of the Shanxi Agricultural School (*Zuijin sanshiwu nian zhi Zhongguo jiaoyu*, ed. Zhuang Yu [Shanghai, 1931], 137). Before this, educators had spoken of "industrial" education (*shiye jiaoyu*). In 1902 Luo Zhenyu emphasized the political and economic necessity for developing such an education (*Jiaoyu shijie*, no. 33).

76. Luo Zhenyu, "The Ten-Year Educational Plan for All the Provinces," *Jiaoyu shijie* (1906), no. 7 (summarized in DFZZ 3, no. 9 (1906): *jiaoyu*, 181-205); Zhang Jian, *Jiaoyu*, II/15a, III/18b-19b.

77. Luo Zhenyu, "Personal Opinion on Education," *Jiaoyushije*, no. 1 (18 May 1901).

78. M. Burton, *The Education of Women in China* (New York, 1911), 100, reproduces the regulations for this school and gives a detailed description of it. Female education is certainly the topic about which one can find the most complete studies and documents. I shall limit myself here to a brief description. Besides the work cited above, which clearly reveals the influence of Anglo-Saxon missionaries, see also Yu Qingtang, "Female Education," in *Zuijin sanshiwunian zhi Zhongguo jiaoyu*, 175-211, and specific chapters in the histories of education and documentary collections cited earlier. Missionary help was certainly used more in girls' schools than in any other type of school, but general development was brought about, as elsewhere, under Japanese influence.

79. *Da Qing Guangxu xin faling*, 13/35-47. Shu Xincheng, *Ziliao*, 800-18.

80. Such were the ideas that Zhang Jian developed in a memorial he wrote in the name of his wife to collect funds for the Nantong Girls' Normal School in February 1907 (Zhang Jian, *Jiaoyu*, II/20a-21b; *Diary*, GX32/XII/30).

81. The change in attitudes became apparent during 1906 (see the eyewitness account of A. Maybon, *La Revue*, 13 November

1907, 239; and Ministère des Affaires étrangères, *China new series*, no. 582, folio 182: Report from Canton on 1 September 1906). In 1908 there was even a boycott against Japan. In 1909 it was from Germany that Chinese borrowed the idea of dividing secondary schools into literary and technical sections.

82. Chinese complained of their pernicious influence in general education (Duan Fang, *Duan chongmin gong zougao, juan* 4, 62b; DFZZ 4, no. 9 [1907]: *jiaoyu*, 187-98; "On the Danger of the Foreign Conspiracy to Secure Power Over Our Education," *Waijiao bao*, no. 185 [23 August 1907], reproduced in *Xinhai geming qian shi nian jian shilun xuanji*, ed. Zhang Nan and Wang Renzhi, 2 vols. [Hong Kong, 1962-63], 2: 577-79). In 1908 regulations appeared limiting their employment.

83. J. Fryer, *The Educational Reform in China* (Washington D.C., 1910), 516-21.

84. Kuo Ping-wen, *The Chinese System of Public Education*, 154-55.

85. Its success is also explained by the fact that from 1905 onwards Zhang Taiyan incorporated it into revolutionary propaganda, although it contained a more anti-Manchu aspect than that advocated by the reformers; however, whichever group made use of the concept, "national knowledge" at this time was an element in the arsenal of progressive ideas (*Xinhai shilun*, II: 16-18; Yang Tianshi, "On the Concept of the National Essence Before the 1911 Revolution," *Xin jianshe* [1965], no. 2: 67-77).

86. N. Peri, "L'éducation nouvelle en Chine," *Revue de Paris*, 15 June 1907, 873-94, analyzes the textbooks on sale in Shanghai.

87. The revolutionaries extolled exactly the same virtues, without mentioning the struggle against the foreigners, in order to overthrow the Qing and gain power (Zhang Taiyan, "Revolutionary Virtue," *Minbao*, no. 8 [1907], reproduced in *Xinhai shilun*, II: 513; Zhang Taiyan, "On the State," *Minbao*, no. 7 [1907], reproduced in ibid., II: 777-85.

88. Liu Xianzhi, "On the Principles of Chinese Education," *Zhongguo xinbao*, no. 6 (1907), reproduced in *Xinhai shilun*, II: 892.

89. *Jiangsu sheng jiaoyu xingzheng*, I/222. At Shanghai, Wuxi, and Wujin the rate of school attendance reached between 8 and 10 percent. R. Cheng, *The Financing of Public Education in China. A Factual Analysis of Its Major Problems of Reconstruction* (Shanghai, 1935), 25, gives the national percentage and figures for the total population.

90. DFZZ 3, no. 1 (1906): *zazu*, 1; 2, no. 10 (1905): *zazu*, 73. There was no incident during the serious famines of 1906-7, nor

during the census compilations of 1910.

91. They were compelled to accept posts in the area instead of going elsewhere; this sometimes aroused protests on their part (DFZZ 4, no. 10 (1907): *jishi*, 71).

92. Those attending normal schools have been included in these figures. If one excludes these students, the rate falls to 15 percent for Nantong and 1 percent for the national average (calculated from: *Jiangsu sheng jiaoyu xingzheng; Jiaoyu tongji tubiao*, 1915; Huang Yanpei, "General Overview of Nationwide Educational Statistics in China for the Last Twenty-five Years," *Renwen* 4, no. 5 [15 June 1933]: 1-28).

93. In 1912 there were 562 girls in Nantong schools (*Jiangsu sheng jiaoyu xingzheng*, II/222), and 141,430 in schools throughout the country (T. E. Hsiao, *The History of Modern Education in China* [Shanghai, 1935], 48).

94. The only information on this is in *Xinhai geming Jiangsu diqu shiliao*, 217, where the author notes that "the pupils of the schools regularly read newspapers and journals, and were stimulated and influenced by the new theories, some of which inclined towards advocating the adoption of foreign constitutions while others advocated revolution by overthrowing the Manchus. In sum, their thought was stirred by passionate feelings."

95. Liu Guiwu, "The Constitutionalists and the Constitutional Movement before and after the 1911 Revolution," *Lishi jiaoxue* (1962), no. 8: 19-29.

96. This was particularly noticeable after the death of Guangxu in 1908. Zhang Jian had been sincerely devoted to Guangxu (Zhang Jian, *Diary*, GX32/V/17, GX34/X/22), whereas he had disliked the empress-dowager, Cixi. Xuantong and the regent aroused no feelings of devotion in him.

97. Cai Yuanpei (1868-1940), a member of the Tongmenghui, had been appointed minister of education in Sun Yat-sen's government at Nanjing. He kept the post in Yuan Shikai's government until 14 July 1912.

98. DFZZ 3, no. 12 (1907): *jishi*, 87-89; 4, no. 3 (1907): *jishi*, 17-18; NCH, 3 August 1912, 297. In Beijing, in April 1912, nine schools out of ten were empty!

99. On Cai Yuanpei's proposals: JYZZ 3, no. 12: *fulu*, 65-73; 4, no. 3: *jishi*, 17-18. On the temporary education conference: JYZZ 4, no. 4: *jishi*, 24; no. 6: *tebie jishi*, 1.

100. The schools were called *xuexiao* instead of *xuetang* and the ministry became the Jiaoyubu (Ministry of Education) instead

of the Xuebu (lit.: Ministry of Studies).
101. Cai Yuanpei, "Opinion on Educational Aims," JYZZ 3, no. 11 (April 1912). This fundamental text is reproduced in Shu Xincheng, *Ziliao*, 1031-38, and in *Shiliao*, 4: 26-32. It can also be found in collections of Cai's works: *Cai Jiemin xiansheng yanxing lu*, 2 vols. (Beijing, 1920), 1: 189; *Cai Yuanpei xuanji* (Beijing, 1959), 1: 8-15. The *China Mission Yearbook*, 1913, 253-57 gives an English translation of the text.
102. *Faling quanshu* (Beijing, 1912-16), XIII/1; Shu Xincheng, *Ziliao*, 226.
103. These laws are collected in *Faling quanshu*, XIII. They are also published, as they were promulgated, in JYZZ 4, nos. 8-12. The main items are reproduced in Shu Xincheng, *Ziliao*.
104. JYZZ 4, no. 7: *jishi*, 41.
105. Cai had just returned from a stay in Leipzig for three years, a fact which explains the influence of Kant and Schleiermacher on his thought. It was difficult for Cai's compatriots to understand him on these matters. Pan Maoyuan, "The Educational Thought of Cai Yuanpei," *Xiamen daxue xuebao* (1955), no. 4: 86-98, gives a clear analysis of the origins of Cai's thought.
106. Fan Yuanlian had been Liang Qichao's student at Changsha in 1896. He took part in Tang Caichang's 1900 uprising, after which he became active in the constitutional movement. Jiang Weiqiao, one of the editors of JYZZ, presided over the reorganization committee of the education ministry. Huang Yanpei was appointed education director for Jiangsu and Tang Eryong was appointed education director for Guizhou. By following the change of personnel through the accounts given in JYZZ, one can notice this control exercised by former constitutionalists over the educational bureaucracy.
107. It was Zhang Jian who drafted the imperial abdication proclamation (Liu Housheng, "Zhang Jian and the Revolution of 1911," in *Xinhai geming huiyi lu*, VI: 261-65. He immediately accepted Huang Xing's offer to become minister of industry in the Nanjing government. He resigned and withdrew his support of the government when Sun Yat-sen, without Zhang's knowledge, negotiated a Japanese loan, the terms of which would have allowed the Japanese to gain partial control of the Hanyeping. Zhang then shifted towards supporting Yuan Shikai (Zhang Jian, *Diary*, XT3/IX/27, 28, X/12, 13, XI/11, 13, 14, 23, XII/20-25, MG1/4, 19, 24, 27).
108. This cell was called Tongshi zhibu (Cao Congpo, "The Tragedy

of Zhang Jian," *Jianghai xuekan*, no. 41 [1962]: 34).

Conclusion

1. Lu Feikui, "The Central Committee of Education," JYZZ 3, no.
   8: *yanlun*, 69.
2. Some revolutionaries had personal views that conflicted with
   each other; generally, however, as far as education was concerned, the majority of revolutionaries adopted the ideas of the
   constitutionalists (see the texts reproduced in *Xinhai shilun*, I:
   400-10, 547-59, II: 52-60, 632-34). The texts in which Sun
   Yat-sen dealt with the topic, in 1912, are not noted for their
   originality (Shu Xincheng, *Ziliao*, 1015-18).
3. According to the expression used by Weng Tonghe, *Riji*
   (Shanghai, 1925), GX34/IV/18 (37/56b).

Text 1: Translation

1. This edict was not issued on the fourth day, but on the second
   day (14 September 1901). In addition to ordering the conversion of academies into schools of various categories, the edict
   laid down the school curriculum, the main part of which had to
   be devoted to the Four Books and the Five Classics, supple-
   mented by Chinese and foreign history and politics. The edict
   charged the governors-general with implementing concrete
   measures, in particular with the recruitment of teachers and
   pupils; it also requested them to propose school regulations
   (*Donghua xulu*, 169/1a-b; *Shilu*, 507/1b-2b).
2. The name of this institution (*shuyuan*) dates from the Tang
   dynasty. At that time it designated a library where books were
   kept or restored and where scholars could come to read. Under
   the Song dynasty the academies also became places of education, but with no links to the examination system. They underwent considerable development under the Ming; at the end of
   the dynasty they functioned as centers of vociferous opposition
   to the Manchus. Up until this time most academies had been
   private institutions. Under the Qing the majority of them were
   either fully or partly subsidized by the government, whereupon

they came under the control of the local magistrate. After this the academies increasingly became places where scholars prepared for the examinations: they in fact substituted for public schools. However, some academies remained centers of research and general culture; it was in these particular academies that the greatest scholars received their training and where many scholarly publications were compiled during the Qing. The conversion of academies into schools of various levels had been ordered by the edict of 10 July 1898, which adopted the proposal put forward by Li Duanfen in a memorial of 1896. The measure was abolished on 13 November 1898, during the reaction that followed the Hundred Days Reform (Sheng Langxi, *Zhongguo shuyuan zhidu* [Shanghai, 1934]; Chen Dongyuan, *Zhongguo keju shidai zhi jiaoyu shi* [Shanghai, 1934], 63-80; *Wuxu bianfa*, 2: 34, 3: 292-97).

3. The edict of 14 September 1901 provided for four levels of education, corresponding approximately to the country's administrative hierarchy. The system was proposed in a memorial drafted by Tao Mo, presented to the court at the beginning of 1901 (Shu Xincheng, *Shiliao*, 2: 99-101).

4. The edict of 25 November 1901 ordered that the country follow the school regulations proposed by Yuan Shikai for Shandong, and that efforts be concentrated on schools in the provincial capitals in order to hasten the training of teachers necessary for the spread of education. The edict of 15 December 1901 laid down guidelines for the promotion of pupils from the primary school level up until graduation from university, as well as giving school graduates the opportunity to present themselves as candidates for the traditional examinations. The edict of 12 March 1902 simply urged the governors-general to adopt measures quickly in order to implement the preceding edicts (*Donghua xulu*, 170/9b, 170/10b-11b, 172/2b).

5. "Jianghai" designates the peninsula situated between the sea and the north bank of the mouth of the Yangzi; the town of Nantong is located there. Zhang Jian resided there from 1892 onwards. However, the word is also used in a figurative sense, expressing seclusion with regard to public life.

6. This division was borrowed from Japanese school administration, with which Zhang was familiar through the work of Fujita Toyohachi and the translations published in *Jiaoyu shijie* (in particular nos. 2, 3, 4, 5 [1901]). Even in Japan this school organization had been based, from the beginning of educational

reform, on the American model. Up until this time China had only known official schools, receiving government funds, and private schools, called *sishu;* there had been no separate category for schools subsidized by local authorities (Zhang Jian, *Diary,* GX27/IX/20; Passin, *Society and Education in Japan,* 65-71).

7. The idea was borrowed from Japan. The very term that Zhang used, *wenbu,* was that used in Japan to designate the Ministry of Education. When an organization of this kind was created in China, in 1905, it was called the *xuebu;* then, in 1912, it became the *jiaoyubu* (*L'instruction Publique au Japon,* 5).

8. The idea was borrowed from Japan, but originally came from the West. In Japan this system had allowed the government to develop education by controlling private schools, the creation of which it encouraged due to a lack of financial resources for the establishment of local schools.

9. In fact, Zhang was especially thinking of Japan, whose example was already influencing official educational reform.

10. An independent department was under the direct control of the governor and other officials in the higher provincial administration. The magistrate of an independent department had the same rank as a prefect (Brunnert, *Political Organization of China,* 426).

11. Citation from *Xunzi,* ch. 5, "Against Physiognomy" (edition of Wang Xianqian [Shanghai, 1935], 54).

12. Zhang Jian had suggested this plan to the governor-general, Liu Kunyi. On the death of the latter, at the end of 1902, his successor, Zhang Zhidong, drafted a memorial along similar lines which was sanctioned by an imperial decree on 6 January 1903. The school, situated in Nanjing, was reserved for students from Jiangsu, Jiangxi, and Anhui; it adopted the name the Normal School of the Three Jiang (Sanjiang shifan xuetang). Based on the model of Japanese normal schools, from which the terminology was borrowed, the lower section was equivalent to a secondary school, aimed at training primary school teachers, while the higher section was equivalent to a university preparatory school and trained secondary school teachers (Zhang Jian, *Diary,* GX27/V/28, 28/III/5, X/13; *Zhang wenxiang gong quanji,* 58/15b-18a).

13. At the Nanyang College established by Sheng Xuanhuai in 1896, a primary school was attached to the normal school section. This practice was taken from Japan, from where Zhang

also borrowed the idea of dividing primary schools into two levels, lower and higher. This division was only officially adopted with the regulations drafted by Zhang Baixi on 15 August 1902. In order to gain support for his proposal, Zhang did not neglect to present it as the application of the *ti-yong* concept (theory and practice, or according to J. Levenson's translation, substance and function), which was very important in the Confucian educational ideal (Chen Yilin, *Zuijin sanshinian Zhongguo jiaoyu shi* [Shanghai, 1930], 53; Shu Xincheng, *Shiliao*, 1: 36; Levenson, *Confucian China and Its Modern Fate*, 59-78).

14. The term *juren* designated those candidates who had succeeded in the provincial examinations. The title of *gongsheng* was awarded as compensation to those *shengyuan* who had failed in the provincial examinations, but whose literary merits were worthy of recognition. Theoretically, they had the right to study in the Imperial College (Guozijian) following a special examination or selection by the provincial authorities. The title could also be purchased. *Shengyuan* referred to those candidates who had successfully passed the district and prefectural examinations. *Jiansheng* literally means "student of the Imperial College." This title was obtained by purchase or sometimes through imperial favor. It allowed the holder to take the provincial examinations without possessing the *shengyuan* degree. The recruitment of traditional degree-holders for the new schools had been suggested in 1896 by Li Duanfen with reference to Beijing University; it was, in fact, already the practice adopted by the Tongwenguan since 1866 (Shu Xincheng, *Shiliao*, 1: 2; Martin, *A Cycle of Cathay*, 311).

15. The idea of having courses of differing duration and difficulty was not new; it had already appeared in the organization of Beijing University and in Yuan Shikai's regulations in Zhili. However, this particular formula was unique; Zhang Zhidong adopted it the following year for the normal school in Nanjing.

16. This division was not Chinese. Traditionally, since the Zhou, and still today, Chinese educators have divided education into moral, intellectual, and physical aspects (*deyu, zhiyu, tiyu*). Even in the terminology, moral training had priority over physical training. As with other reformers of the time, Zhang attributed much importance to reestablishing the dignity and practice of physical exercise, which had disappeared from the schools since the Han, in order to improve the quality of the

Chinese army. The expression "education of mind and body" served better to express the idea than the traditional terminology, but Zhang only used it here as an example of modernity. Elsewhere he preferred to use the Chinese expression which, without overlooking the physical aspect, gave a clearer emphasis on the moral and social functions of education (Gao Jiansi, *Zuijin sanshiwunian zhi Zhongguo jiaoyu*, 225-30; Wang Fengjie, *Zhongguo jiaoyu shi dagang*, 303).

17. According to the local gazetteers consulted by Zhang Jian, the Temple of the One Thousand Buddhas had been built in 1599, and dedicated to the heavenly spirits and the dead; it was used simultaneously as a place for Confucian, Taoist, and Buddhist cults. The building was brought to Zhang's attention in February 1902, when the main section of the temple was destroyed by fire without anyone apparently showing concern. At this time, however, Zhang was thinking of locating the school in the collective building of Jingjiang. It was only when faced with the inconveniences the building presented that Zhang began to make inquiries about the Temple of the One Thousand Buddhas. He personally visited it on 21 June 1902 and devised plans for the construction work, which began in August after the resident monk and his father had been expelled (Zhang Jian, *Jiaoyu*, I/14a; *Diary*, GX28/I/13, III/23, 24).

18. Chinese buildings are measured in *jian*, that is to say, the space between two columns. All the *jian* of a given building are of the same size, which varies according to whether the construction is small or large. One room comprises an exact number of *jian*, generally one or two but rarely more than three.

19. Jingjiang is one of the names for the Yangzi. The building no doubt belonged collectively to people originating from towns along the river, who were residing in Nantong. It is not mentioned in the local gazetteer.

20. The edict of 10 July 1898 ordered local authorities to convert ancestral halls and temples not used for sacrificial rites into schools. Zhang Zhidong, in his *Quanxuepian*, and Kang Youwei, in a memorial presented in July 1898, had proposed this measure, the idea of which had first been conceived of by Huang Zongxi (1610-95) (*Wuxu bianfa*, 2: 34, 219-22; J. Tobar, trans., *Koang-siu et Ts'e Hi, Décrets impériaux 1898* [Shanghai, 1900], 12-13; id., trans., *K'iuen-hio P'ien*, 95-96; *Huang Lizhou yizhu huikan, Ming yi dai fang lu, Qu shi*, 6a-b; W. Franke, *Reform and Abolition*, 22).

21. Citation from *Mencius*, 14/19 (Couvreur, *Les quatre livres*, 638).
22. The district of Rugao was situated to the northwest of Nantong. The district of Taixing lay to the west of Rugao. The township of Jinghai was situated at the east of Nantong. Along with the area of Nantong, these places formed the department of Tongzhou. Haimen, to the southeast of Nantong, had been an independent subprefecture since 1768; however, since it comprised areas that had previously belonged to Tongzhou, it retained close links with the department.
23. This procedure was the same for those who registered for the traditional examinations: a guarantor was needed. However, the requirements for the normal school were less strict and the magistrate's approval was not necessary (Zi, *Pratique des Examens*, 33).
24. The normal school did not break with the traditional practice of subsidizing the upkeep of academies and schools from land endowment revenues.

Text 1: Commentary

1. Zhang Jian, *Diary*, GX28/IV/17.
2. Ibid., GX28/II/29, III/5.
3. Ibid., GX27/IX/4, 11, GX28/I/17, III/5, 14, 19, 22.
4. *Jiaoyu shijie*, nos. 5, 6, 7, 8 (1901).
5. Zhang Jian, *Diary*, GX27/XI/20, GX28/III/27.
6. The text translated here reveals in particular some striking similarities with an article published by Luo Zhenyu at the beginning of November 1901 (*Jiaoyu shijie*, no. 12) entitled "Proposal for Teachers Training Crash Programs." In this article one finds the ideas of using collective buildings to house the schools, of fixing the number of students between forty and one hundred, recruited from among virtuous degree-holders, of temporarily abridging and simplifying Japanese curricula, of purchasing modern school equipment, and of not charging tuition fees.
7. Zhang Jian, *Diary*, GX28/II/29. The sum of 20,000 dollars represented the salary owed to Zhang by the Dasheng mill during the last five years and which he had not yet drawn upon.

Text 2: Translation

1. The edict of 2 September 1905 approved of the memorial presented on 31 August by Yuan Shikai, Zhang Zhidong, Zhao Erxun, Zhou Fu, Cen Chunxuan, and Duan Fang; it ordered the abolition of the examinations at all levels from 1906 onwards in order to develop the schools as places which would train competent officials and spread education among the people. From this time on, there were numerous imperial decrees ordering the increase in the number of schools (*Donghua xulu*, 195/8b-11a, translated in *Chine, Ceylan, Madagascar* [March 1907]: 440; Ding Zhipin, *Jiaoyu jishi*, 15-18).

2. Zhang was following even in the same terms an idea expressed by the governors-general in their memorial requesting the abolition of the examination system on 31 August 1905 (Shu Xincheng, *Shiliao*, 4: 125).

3. The attached primary school was opened on 27 August 1903 (*Diary*, GX29/VII/1). The other primary school dated from April 1905 (*Xuebu guanbao* 3, no. 82 [1 April 1909], *Jingwai xuewu baogao*, 148a).

4. The surface area of Tongzhou district was 7,435 square *li*, approximately 1,860 square kilometers, of which two-thirds were occupied by the three aforesaid townships (Zhang Jian, *Zizhi*, I/19a-b; *Tongzhou zhilizhou zhi*, O/4, I/33a-34a).

5. The four-tenths share proposed by Zhang Jian was that enjoyed by Nantong in relation to Haimen, Rugao, Jinghai, and Taixing in the total quota of places offered these districts for the civilian and military district examinations. In 1876 the quota was 36 for civilian examinations and 25 for military examinations, that is to say 122 in three years; such a number is not much less than the number of students from Tongzhou that Zhang anticipated entering the normal school at the beginning (*Tongzhou zhilizhou zhi*, V/51).

6. On 7 January 1906 Zhang Jian inspected the Yuanmiaoguan, near the eastern gate of the town, with a view of establishing the secondary school there. Construction work began shortly afterwards (*Diary*, GX31/XII/13, GX32/V/11).

7. The rapid development of construction work and industry in Nantong had caused a relative increase in certain prices, which was accentuated in 1905-6 by the effects of the famine. At the same time militia forces were being raised to combat local

bandits and this also reduced the number of laborers available (*Tongzhou xingban shiye zhi lishi*, 238; NCH, January-February 1906).

8. This meeting took place on the arranged date, 13 April 1906. The gentry and officials who attended calculated that costs for the construction of the secondary school would amount to 160,000 dollars. They decided that Tongzhou, Taixing, and Rugao should each contribute 1,000 dollars, Haimen 500 dollars, and that Zhang Jian and his brother would add a further 5,000 dollars to Tongzhou's contribution, 1,000 dollars to Haimen's contribution, and 500 dollars to Rugao's contribution; these were areas with which they had close links. One of the richest gentry at the meeting promised to donate a further 500 dollars (Zhang Jian, *Diary*, GX32/III/20).

9. The normal school began its courses on 30 April 1903. The apprentice school was opened on 23 February 1905 and was reserved for the sons of Zhang Jian's workers. In 1905 a special class on sericulture was added to the normal school. The construction of a museum was decided upon in January 1906. The orphanage was opened in July 1904 by Zhang Jian's wife (Zhang Jian, *Nianpu*, 54, 56, 57; *Jianpu*, 4; *Diary*, GX31/XII/9, 12).

10. This was a type of *lijin* in Jiangsu, whereby a surtax was added to the fee for a brokerage license that was levied by the state on the *yahang*. The *yahang* were commercial enterprises which most often specialized in a particular trade. They served as intermediaries between the producer and wholesaler (Luo Yudong, *Zhongguo lijin shi*, 2 vols. [Shanghai, 1936], 1: 159, 234).

11. The *tiezhuan* was a stamp or registration fee collected on all deeds and documents that required official authentication.

12. I have found no information on this establishment.

13. Until 1672, the township of Jinghai, which mainly comprised villages situated to the east of Nantong, formed a district with the name of Haimen (under the jurisdiction of the district of Tongzhou). After this date, when the river had encroached upon a large part of its terrain, it became a township within the department of Tongzhou. In 1832 this township adopted the name of Jinghai in order to avoid confusion with the subprefecture of Haimen created in 1768. After 1672, therefore, Jinghai no longer had the right to have a special examination quota nor the right to have its own magistrate. However, the

memory of its former administrative independence enabled it to receive special consideration among the townships of Tongzhou. The gazetteer of 1875 mentions that the township of Jinghai had a quota of ten places for the district examinations but adds elsewhere that this quota was added to that of Tongzhou and that all the candidates took the examinations together (*Tongzhou zhilizhou zhi*, I/4a-5, V/50b-51b).

14. The granary was established in 1727, due to the contributions from salt merchants; its function was to lend grain before the harvests to those farmers whose provisions were low and to recuperate it after the harvest. The stocking of grain and management was the responsibility of private individuals (*Tongzhou zhilizhou zhi*, O/15b-16a, III/43-44; Hsiao Kung-chuan, *Rural China: Imperial Control in the Nineteenth Century* [Seattle, 1960], 145-48, 552).

15. In 1906, according to official statistics published by the Ministry of Education, there were 310 official schools, 600 public schools and 272 private schools in the province. The official schools had been generally established in the towns that were important administrative centers and in which resided influential gentry. They were also towns that received the province's financial receipts: Nanjing, Suzhou, and Shanghai. Tongzhou, relatively poor and remote, had no official school (*Jiaoyu tongji*, 1907, *gesheng*, 27).

16. Xianfeng: 1851-61. Tongzhi: 1862-74.

17. Zhang was referring to the increase in the examination quota awarded by the emperor in reward for the special contributions paid by the gentry in order to finance the suppression of the Taiping rebellion. During the reign of Tongzhi, the department of Tongzhou as a whole obtained twenty-four more permanent places for the district civil examinations and twenty-nine more permanent places for the district military examinations, without taking into account forty-four temporary places for each of the two examination categories that were granted for special sessions as reward for contributions offered (*Tongzhou zhilizhou zhi*, V/50b-52a; for a similar phenomenon in the rest of China, see Chang Chung-li, *Chinese Gentry*, 72).

18. This was a form of *lijin*, instituted in order to subsidize the expenses for the army charged with suppressing the Taipings. Tongzhou was one of the first regions in China where this tax was raised; the *lijin* was established in April 1854 and comprised a tax on goods in transit and another imposed on resident

merchants. After the capture of Nanjing by imperial forces in July 1864, the tax was retained, despite memorials and even edicts favorable to its repeal (E. Beal, *The Origin of Likin, 1853-1864* [Cambridge, 1958], 25-42, 58-67, 87).

19. The Taipings.

20. In 1864 an edict stipulated that reconstruction of the regions affected by the Taiping rebellion would be financed by *lijin* receipts. A special office, situated in Nanjing and known as the Shanhouju, was established to supervise reconstruction work. Since 1898, however, its expenditures were nil since the restoration of temples and administrative buildings, which had been practically the only task envisaged by the government in its reconstruction plan, was all completed (*Qing chao xu wenxian tongkao* [Shanghai, 1936], *zhengque*, 21/17a; Luo Yudong, *Lijin shi*, 212, 501, 502). The office was theoretically abolished on 30 August 1905 (DFZZ 2, no. 10 (1905): *zazu*, 69).

21. During the Sino-Japanese war of 1894-95, Zhang Zhidong endeavored to organize the defense of the Jiangsu coast. He had then asked Zhang Jian to organize a local militia at Nantong and Haimen. Zhang accepted and even sold books to defray some of the expenses; the remainder was obtained by the remittance of a part of the *lijin* that Haimen and Tongzhou had to pass on to the revenue-collecting centers of Nanjing, Yangzhou, and Qingjiang (Zhang Xiaoruo, *Zhuanji*, 52; Zhang Jian, *Zizhi*, I/1-8; *Zhang wenxiang gong zouyi*, 36/2a-6b, 30a-30b, 31a-34b).

22. For this slightly obscure phrase, I have followed one of the interpretations suggested to me in Beijing.

23. The *tongzhuan*, the combined tax, involved paying at one time all the *lijin* owed by one particular good (at the place of production, at the place of sale, and in transit). Thereupon, the particular good was able to circulate freely in the interior of the province without any additional tax being imposed upon it. The tax referred to here was imposed on commercial cloth. In 1905 Zhou Fu, the governor-general, laid aside a certain amount from the tax receipts to subsidize education. This subsidy was abolished in December of the same year by a reactionary provincial treasurer (Luo Yudong, *Lijin shi*, 238, 502; NCH, 2 February 1906, 227, 253).

24. The public treasury of Tongzhou passed on its receipts to the central office at Nanjing. The structure and functioning of the *lijin* offices under Nanjing's jurisdiction cannot be discussed in detail since the only documents available are those posterior to

1908, when the Nanjing office was amalgamated with the Jiangnan caizheng gongsuo (Luo Yudong, *Lijin shi*, 234).

25. This organ, created in 1905 on the request of Zhang Jian, was composed of gentry who were charged with administering education (*Ershinian lai zhi Nantong*, 104).

Text 2: Commentary

1. Zhang Jian, *Diary*, GX32/III/20.
2. Zhou Fu, *Zhou queshen gong quanji* (N.p., 1922), *zougao*, IV/24a.
3. Zhang Jian, *Jiaoyu*, II/20a; *Zizhi*, I/13a.
4. He took up his post in December 1905 (NCH, 2 February 1906, 227, 253); *Jiangsu xuewu wendu*, I/GX32/X/14, 29 November 1906 (Memorial from the education commissioner, Zhou, on the financial resources of the office of education).
5. Zhang Jian, *Zhuan*, IV/passim.
6. *Jiangsu sheng jiaoyu xingzheng baogaoshu*, I/222, gives a total of 90,000 children in 1912 aged between seven and thirteen years. If one refers to the first reliable census, which gave a total of 1,360,000 inhabitants in 1932, the figure seems probable.
7. Yun Wo, "General Theory of Education," *Jiangsu*, no. 3 (June 1903) (cited in *Xinhai shilun*, I: 551-59).
8. From 1901 to 1903 there was a whole series of articles on this theme: Xia Xiefu, "Proposals on Schools," *Jiaoyu shijie*, nos. 13-15 (November-December 1901); Zhang Yuanji, "Reply to a Friend on Educational Matters," ibid, no. 20 (February 1902); Luo Zhenyu, "Eight Principles for Education," ibid., no. 21 (March 1902); Luo Zhenyu, "Personal Opinion on the School System," ibid., no. 24 (April 1902); Liang Qichao, "Personal Opinion on Educational Policy," *Xinmin congbao*, no. 8 (22 May 1902): 51-61; Zheng Wenyi, "Survey of the National Expansion of Primary Education and Its Financial Means," ibid., no. 25 (29 January 1903): 143-60.
9. Zhang Jian, *Diary*, GX29/XII/3 (15 February 1904). See also chapter II, 54-5.
10. As examples of this second series of projects to spread education, one can cite the articles published in DFZZ 3, nos. 5, 6, 9 (1906); 4, no. 9 (1907); and *Xuebu guanbao* 1, nos. 23-26 (11 June-10 July 1907).

Text 3: Translation

1. The governor-general of Liangjiang was Duan Fang (1861-1911), a relatively liberal Manchu who had close links with Zhang Jian (A. Hummel, *Eminent Chinese of the Ch'ing Period, 1644-1912*, 2 vols. [Washington D.C., 1943-44], 2: 780-82). The governor of Jiangsu was Chen Kuilong, who afterwards became governor-general of Huguang. The Jiangsu education commissioner was Zhou Shumo, and the Jiangning education commissioner was Chen Botao (*Shilu*, 558/1b).

2. Established in 1884 at Jiangyin, principal town of the district dependent on the prefecture of Changzhou in Jiangsu, this academy quickly gained fame. It was well-endowed and offered reasonable scholarships and salaries. However, the academy only accepted as students those who had succeeded well in the district examinations. The scholars who taught there, like Miao Quansun and Zhang Wenhu, were among the most brilliant of their time. Instruction in literary and scientific studies was given (the academy possessed an observatory). It was due to the patronage of this academy that some of the most important collections of classical and scholarly works of the late Qing Period, like the *Nanqing congshu*, were published (Chen Dongyuan, *Zhongguo keju*, 79; Chen Dongyuan, *Zhongguo jiaoyu shi*, 455).

3. Huang Tifang (1832-99) was a native of Rui'an in Zhejiang, hence the surname given him in the text. He obtained the *jinshi* in 1863 and was appointed provincial examiner for Jiangsu in 1881, a post he occupied until 1885. In 1885 he was appointed second vice-president of the Board of War, the title that Zhang gives him in the text. An accomplished scholar, Huang made effective contributions to educational development while he was in Jiangsu. He established Nanqing in order to train scholars through an extensive study of the classics, but also through acquainting them with science by having them study astronomy, mathematics, and geology (*Qingshi gao*, ed. Zhao Erxun [reprint, Hong Kong, 1964], *liezhuan*, I/450/1a; Hummel, *Eminent Chinese*, 2: 348-49).

4. Zuo Zongtang (1813-85) was one of the principal commanders charged with suppressing the Taipings, Nian, and Hui. He was

governor-general of Liangjiang from October 1881 until his death. He was active in the *yangwu* group and attempted to reinforce Confucian tradition while introducing Western technology (Hummel, *Eminent Chinese*, 2: 762-67).

5. The provincial examiner (*xuezheng*, an abbreviation for *tidu-xuezheng*: superintendent for the control of studies) was an official of equal rank with that of the governor-general. He was independent of the governor-general, appointed by the emperor from among *jinshi*, and charged with the control of education and supervision of district examinations. There was one provincial examiner for each province; he resided in the provincial capital and toured the prefectures in his official capacity of examination supervisor. However, the provincial examiner for Jiangsu resided in Jiangyin instead of Nanjing. The post was abolished by a decree of 25 April 1906 (*Zhongguo jiaoyu cidian* [Shanghai, 1928], 721; *Shilu*, 558/1b).

6. Following the edict of 10 July 1898 on the conversion of academies into schools, Nanqing, due to the level of its instruction, was expected to become a higher school (*gaodeng xuetang*), although it was not situated in the provincial capital. The reorganization, after being interrupted by the edict of 14 September 1898 which restored the traditional system, was continued after the promulgation of the edict of 14 September 1901; due to the intervention of the provincial examiner, Nanqing became "the Nanqing higher school for all the province of Jiangsu" (Jiangsu quansheng Nanqing gaodeng xuetang) instead of being converted into a primary school as the other district-level academies (Sheng Langxi, *Shuyuan zhidu*, 238; *Zhengyi congshu*, Guangxu renyin, *zhengshu tongji*, I).

7. Instituted by the decree of 25 April 1906, the post of education commissioner replaced that of provincial examiner. Under the authority of the governor-general, the education commissioner was charged with administering education in each province, assisted by councils and special offices. In Jiangsu there were already two offices of education; each was headed by an education commissioner in order to facilitate administrative procedure. One commissioner supervised the northern region, dependent on Nanjing, and the other supervised the southern region, dependent on Suzhou (*Shilu*, 558/1b; Duan Fang, *Duan chongmin gong zougao, juan* 4, 5a-b).

8. See note 7 above. The education commissioners resided in Nanjing and Suzhou. This directly affected the students of Nanqing,

since the provincial examiner had traditionally supervised the students from Jiangyin itself. The local pride of Jiangyin inhabitants was also wounded.

9. *Dichao* designated the *Peking Gazette*, which was also known as the *Jingbao*. It consisted of copies of documents sent from the capital to high provincial officials for their information. This generic term referred to several publications, both official and nonofficial (J. Fairbank, *Ch'ing Administration: Three Studies* [Cambridge, 1960], 96). In accordance with the regulations of 13 January 1904, Beijing University was the sole university for all of China. The governor-general of Liangjiang, Duan Fang, and Zhang Jian had proposed establishing a university for the south of China (Zhang Jian, *Jiaoyu*, II/22b-25b).

10. This association was established in October 1905 by Zhang Jian and other gentry in the province (see commentary for text 4). The meeting to which Zhang referred took place from 6 to 8 November in Shanghai (Zhang Jian, *Diary*, GX32/IX/20-22).

11. Zhang was expanding on Zhang Zhidong's slogan "Chinese studies for the foundation, Western studies as the supplement" by illustrating the possible decay of Chinese culture with a quotation from the *Yijing; "shuoguo"* signifies the last and best fruit.

12. Quotation from the *Analects* of Confucius, IX/5 (Couvreur, *Les quatre livres*, 163).

13. It has not been possible to identify this person.

14. The inhabitants of the south were uneasy about all measures that tended to favor the north and which, according to them, thus harmed the south. They had been extremely hostile to the short-lived province of Jianghuai (January-May 1905) in the northern part of the province, Jiangning, created on the suggestion of Zhang Jian. After the province was abolished the authorities attempted to compensate Jiangning, especially by increasing the number of students it could send to the schools: hence the strikes and protests by those originating from the south (NCH, February-May 1905; Duan Fang, *Duan chongmin gong zougao, juan* 4, 50a-51b; DFZZ 3, no. 1 (1906): *zazu*, 7-8).

15. Miao Quansun (1844-1919), a native of Jiangyin in Jiangsu, obtained the *jinshi* in 1876; he was a Hanlin compiler of the second class. A celebrated scholar, bibliophile, and poet, he had taught at Nanqing before it became a school. He was the first librarian of the Beijing National Library, from 1909 to 1912. He was a close friend of Zhang Jian (Chen Dongyuan, *Zhongguo jiaoyu shi*, 455; *Zhongguo wenxuejia da cidian*, no. 6780, 1727;

Wang Yi-t'ung, *Biographic Sketches*, 54-58).

16. Ma Liang (Xiangbo) (1840-1939) was born in Jiangsu; his family had been Catholics since the time of Matteo Ricci. A student of the Jesuits at Zikawei and a doctor of theology, Ma had a knowledge of Latin, Greek, French, and English and was well versed in classical Chinese and mathematics. With Li Hongzhang's patronage, he became involved in modern industrial projects as well as with diplomatic negotiations and administration in Korea at the end of the nineteenth century. In 1903, at Zikawei, Ma established, with the aid of Cai Yuanpei, a school known as Zhendan xueyuan (Aurore Institute), where he taught Latin, French, English, and philosophy. In 1905 a number of students rebelled against the authority of the Jesuits; Ma had them move and he created a new school, Fudan gongxue (Aurore College) with the help of Jiangsu gentry, including Zhang Jian, and the local authorities. In 1906 Ma became principal of the college and also assumed some teaching duties. Zhang Jian was a member of the administrative committee for the college and thus frequently met with Ma on his trips to Shanghai (Zhang Ruogu, *Ma Xiangbo xiansheng nianpu* [Shanghai, 1939]; Zhang Jian, *Diary*, 31/II/17, 24, 25, GX32/VIII/11, IX/22).

17. Jin Shi was born in Taixing, in the department of Tongzhou. He obtained the *jinshi* in 1895 and was a Hanlin compiler of the second class (*Cilin jilue*, ed. Zhu Ruzhen, [Beijing, n.d.], "Guangxu yiwei," 37).

18. Quotation from the *Li ji*, II/1/18 (Couvreur, *Mémoires sur les bienséances et les cérémonies*, I: 126).

19. The school contained one hundred pupils, who therefore each paid about eight to ten dollars a month for board and lodging; at this time these fees varied from an average of four dollars a month at the good provincial secondary schools to about six dollars a month at Beijing University (*Zhengzhi guanbao* 34: 30, XT2/VI/1; *Caizheng shuoming shu*, 9 vols. [Beijing, 1915], 2: 44; *Revue Indochinoise*, 6 July 1903, 693-95).

20. Quotation from *Li ji*, 2/III/3 (Couvreur, *Mémoires sur les bienséances*, I: 164).

Text 3: Commentary

1. Zhang Jian, *Diary*, GX32/X, XI/1-4.

2. An accurate census of existing academies at the end of the Qing would require a systematic survey of all local gazetteers, which has not been possible for this study. For Guangdong, Liu Boyi estimates a total of 411 academies founded between 1662 and 1909, but some of them had certainly fallen into disuse well before the beginning of the twentieth century (*Guangdong shuyuan zhidu yange* [Shanghai, 1939], 79). For Jiangsu, there is the survey by Liu Yizheng, who unfortunately does not mention the dates when academies ceased to function. Liu lists several hundred academies for Jiangsu (*Jiangsu shengli tushuguan niankan*, no. 4 [1931]: 1-112: "Jiangsu shuyuan zhi chugao"). In any event, the figure given by W. Franke of 300 academies for all of China is well below the real total (*Reform and Abolition*, 14). Perhaps the figure is a misprint. Shang Yanliu reckons a total of 2,000 to 3,000 academies (*Qingdai keju kaoshi shulu* [Beijing, 1958], 225).

3. Sheng Langxi, *Zhongguo shuyuan zhidu*, 173, 185, 191-96; Chen Dongyuan, *Zhongguo jiaoyu shi*, 444-59; Shang Yanliu, *Qingdai keju kaoshi shulu*, 224, give information on science instruction given in the most famous academies. A deeper study of local gazetteers would no doubt reveal the existence of places other than the treaty ports where modern knowledge was propagated.

4. Sheng Langxi, *Zhongguo shuyuan zhidu*, 239-40.

5. Miao Quansun, *Jiangyin xian xuzhi* (N.p., 1921), 6/2a-4b; *Jiangsu sheng jiaoyu xingzheng*, II/49-50.

6. Miao Quansun, *Jiangyin xian xuzhi*, 6/10b-12b; NCH, 7 April 1905, 12, mentions that gentry had pocketed half of the revenues.

7. According to the eyewitness account of an Anglo-Saxon missionary, the teacher of English at Nanqing was incapable of speaking or understanding the language. When the students became aware of this they went on strike and the school had to close for several days (NCH, 24 July 1903).

8. Duan Fang, *Duan chongmin gong zougao, juan* 15, 40a-41b; *Jiangsu xuewu wendu* (Suzhou, 1910), ch. 1, memorial from the education commissioner Mao Qingfan of GX33/X/5. Zhang Jian deliberately feigned ignorance of the education ministry's proposal, which was not to the liking of his friends. Zhang's letter was, in fact, a counter-proposal.

9. Zhang Jian, *Diary*, GX27/IX/11.

10. See the articles in DFZZ 3, no. 5 (1906): *jiaoyu*, 59-68; 4, no. 2

(1907): *jiaoyu,* 13-20; 4, no. 9 (1907): *jiaoyu,* 187-98; and *Xuebu guanbao,* 1 no. 12 (14 January 1907): *fulu,* 1-3. A "Society for the Protection of National Knowledge" (Guoxue baocun hui) was founded in Shanghai in November 1906 (DFZZ 3, no. 13 (1906): *jiaoyu,* 410).

11. Chiang Monlin, *Tides from the West: a Chinese Autobiography* (New Haven, 1947), 48, 64; NCH, 30 June 1905, 698, 724, 28 April 1905, 183-84, 15 June 1906, 633; DFZZ 3, no. 1 (1906): *zazu,* 7-8; no. 7 (1906): *zazu,* 37; *Donghua lu,* GX10, 5658.

12. NCH, 24 March 1905, 550, 30 March 1906, 742; Jiang Weiqiao, "Memories of the Chinese Education Society," DFZZ 33, no. 1 (1 January 1936): 7-15.

13. The proposal concerning Nanqing was quickly accepted by the Ministry of Education in March 1907 (Duan Fang, *Duan chong-min gong zougao, juan* 15, 40a).

Text 4: Translation

1. The association was founded at the end of 1905 (see text 3, note 10). Zhang Jian was elected chairman on 7 October 1905 and was reelected on 8 November 1906 (Zhang Jian, *Diary,* GX31/IX/9, GX32/IX/22).

2. On 8 November 1906, at the annual general meeting of the association, he handed in his resignation, which was refused. He was reelected chairman by a unanimous vote and thus assumed the post for another year (Zhang Jian, *Diary,* GX32/IX/20-22).

3. See text 3, note 7. Following the decree and regulations of 13 May 1906, offices of education (*xuewu gongsuo*) had been instituted under the authority of the provincial educational commissioners. They consisted of an administrative section and a consultative council. There were offices of education in Nanjing and Suzhou. According to article four of the decree on education associations, the provincial education associations had to be established in the same places as the offices of education; Jiangsu was thus an exception (*Donghua lu,* GX10, 5496; Xue Renyang, *Zhongguo jiaoyu xingzheng zhidu shilue* [Shanghai, 1929], 99).

4. Zhang Jian was a native of the department of Tongzhou, which came under the jurisdiction of Nanjing.

5. From a linguistic point of view, Jiangsu was divided into two

regions, roughly separated by the Yangzi: to the north *putonghua* was spoken, while to the south a variety of different dialects was spoken. However, two towns in the southern region were an exception-Nanjing and Zhenjiang. Both of these towns had been strongly influenced by the north, Nanjing because it had long been the capital, and Zhenjiang because it was situated at the end of the Grand Canal (Li Zhangpu, *Jiangsu* [Shanghai, 1936], 103).

6. Nantong is situated 140 kilometers from Shanghai. Zhang made the journey by sedan-chair and then by boat. The time required for the journey was one day. Zhang noted in his diary at the end of the previous year: "this year, from the first to last days of the year, I have spent in total 39 days at my home" (Zhang Jian, *Diary*, GX32/XII/30).

7. See Introduction chapters I, II, III. After the appearance of his *Reasoned Discussion on Reform* in 1901, Zhang Jian became an influential individual among political circles. His moderate ideas were well received by provincial gentry and high officials. With his closest friends, Zhang formed a small active group. After the edict of 1 September 1906 concerning the granting of a constitution, Zhang became one of the founding members, in October, of the Public Association for the Preparation of a Constitution (Yubei lixian gonghui); he became vice-chairman of this association on 16 November 1906. The association, which was loosely organized, had nothing in common with a true political party. However, among the ideas discussed, those held by Zhang Jian were prominent-such ideas were based on the desire to see the court itself take the initiative, as had happened in Japan, in implementing reforms. The accusation levelled against Zhang that he was the leader of a party was serious because "parties" (*dang*) were forbidden; they were permitted only when the court accepted the principle of a responsible cabinet (Zhang Jian, *Diary*, GX32/IX/4, XI/1; *Xinhai geming*, IV, 67, 164).

8. Fan Pang lived in the middle of the second century. He was accused of having been involved in a conspiracy. Since the magistrate charged with arresting Fan did not dare to execute the order, Fan went to prison of his own accord. It was under these circumstances, having requested to see his son in order to say goodbye, that he spoke the words quoted in the text (*Houhanshu*, 97/5a-b).

9. Quotations from the *Shijing*, VII/16 (Couvreur, *Cheu King*, 98).

The poem from which the quote comes was written in praise of
a sage who came to restore order in the kingdom of Zheng; the
effect of his coming was compared to the cry of a cock in a
storm. This is why, in Chinese literature, the cock became a
symbol for the virtuous man.

Text 4: Commentary

1. Zhang Jian, *Diary*, GX31/IX/9, GX32/IX/20, 21, 22, XII/30,
   GX33/IX/9, 24, GX34/XI/1.
2. On the study societies in general: Wang Ermin, "A List of
   Study Societies at the End of the Qing," *Dalu zazhi* 24, no.
   2 (31 January 1962): 14-21; no. 3 (15 February 1962): 16-23. On
   those in Shanghai: Hu Huaizhen, *Shanghai de xueyi tuanti*
   (Shanghai, 1935). On the Chinese Education Society, see the
   account by one of its members: Jiang Weiqiao, "Memories of the
   Chinese Education Society," DFZZ 33, no. 1 (1 January 1936):
   7-15. It is interesting to note that a similar growth of "study
   societies" took place between 1895 and 1898 (see Luo Bingzhi,
   Zhongguo jindai jiaoyujia [Wuhan, 1958], 103); such a phenomenon was typical during periods of political change.
3. Hu Huaizhen, *Shanghai de xueyi tuanti*, 24; *Education in China:
   Ten Years of the Kiangsu Provincial Education Association*
   (Shanghai, 1915), 1-4.
4. DFZZ 2, no. 12 (19 January 1906): *jiaoyu*, 333-36: text of the
   regulations promulgated in October 1905.
5. *Difang zongtong:* this term referred to gentry who managed the
   charitable granaries and public works, as well as more modern
   public institutions such as the chambers of commerce.
6. See text 3, note 14. On the attempts at establishing unity in
   1907, besides the article by Wang Ermin already cited: Akira
   Irye, "Public Opinion in Late Ch'ing China," 7-21; DFZZ 2, no.
   8 (1905): *jiaoyu*, 201 (Guangdong); no. 9 (1905): *zazu*, 66; no.
   10 (1905): *zazu*, 69 (Beijing); 3, no. 2 (1906): *neiwu*, 27-33
   (nationwide); no. 9 (1906): *zazu*, 41 (Zhili); 5, no. 1 (1908): *zazu*,
   1 (Jiangxi and Hunan). On the chambers of commerce:
   Chūgoku kindaika no shakai kōzō (Tokyo, 1960); *Nonggong
   shangbu tongjibiao*, I/18 and IV, gives the chronology of their
   establishment. The first chamber of commerce was that of
   Shanghai; its regulations are in NCH, 26 November 1902,

1124-26.

7. In the series of articles entitled "The Theory of a New People," in *Xinmin congbao* from 1902 to 1904.

Text 5: Translation

1. Mao Qingfan (1846-1924), a native of Fengcheng in Jiangxi, obtained the *jinshi* in 1889 and was appointed education commissioner for the Suzhou area on 27 May 1907. He remained in the post until 20 August 1908, whereupon he became military commander of Gansu (*Donghua lu*, GX10, 5653; *Shilu*, 595/4a; Chen Naiqian, *Qingdai beizhuanwen tongjian* [Shanghai, 1959], 12; Qian Shifu, *Qingji zhongyao zhiguan nianbiao* [Shanghai, 1959], 229).

2. The letter was sent between 2 February and 2 March 1908, but there is no mention of it in Zhang's diary.

3. See text 3, notes 2 and 6. After 1902 the status of Nanqing was, in principle, between that of a secondary school and that of Beijing University. Since it was in financial difficulty, the Jiangsu Education Association proposed, at the end of 1906, that its curriculum be limited to purely literary studies. In August 1907 the proposal was transmitted to the emperor by the Ministry of Education. The emperor accepted the proposal and ordered the appropriate authorities to investigate the methods and concrete measures required to implement it (*Zhengzhi guanbao*, vol. XXII, 196-97; XVI/13, no. 629, 14; text of the memorial written by the governor-general Duan Fang, which gives a summary of the precedents for the proposal concerning Nanqing).

4. Zhang Jizhi (1855-1923), from Jiangyin in Jiangsu, received the *jinshi* in 1898. He was a compiler of the second class at the Hanlin Academy with special responsibilities for education. *Cilin jilue*, ed. Zhu Ruzhen (Beijing, n.d.), Guangxu wuxu, 41; Chen Naiqian, *Qingdai beizhuanwen tongjian* (Shanghai, 1959), 218.

5. At this time Zhang directed fifteen enterprises, situated mainly in the region of Nantong and Haimen: the Dasheng cotton mill, founded in 1895; the Tonghai land reclamation company, founded in 1900; the Guangsheng oil-works and Daxing flour mill, founded in 1902; the Lusi Tongrentai salt-works, Lusi

fisheries and Dalong soap factory, founded in 1903; the Dada wharf company at Shanghai, the port of Tiansheng company, the graphite company of Mount Luosi at Zhenjiang, the Hanmolin printing-works, Dasheng no. 2 mill, the Dada internal navigation company, and the Fusheng sericulture company, established in 1904; and the Zisheng steel-works and Yisheng distillery, founded in 1906.

6. See text 4, commentary. The regulations of 28 July 1906 had placed these associations under the official control of the provincial education commissioner. This is why Mao involved himself in the business of the Jiangsu Education Association, even though this association had received the right, because of its former existence, to retain the main body of rules that it had laid down itself (*Da Qing Guangxu xin faling*, VII/95-98; Xue Renyang, *Xingzheng zhidu*, 98).

7. See text 4, note 3. The consultative council of the education office comprised a chief adviser, appointed by the governor-general, and four advisers, appointed by the education commissioner. The regulations of 13 May 1906 gave details on the council's functions (to give advice to the education commissioner and to compile reports for the governor-general), but not on debate procedures since, in the view of the authorities, this council had only a purely administrative role (*Da Qing Guangxu xin faling*, IV/6b-9b; Xue Renyang, *Xingzheng zhidu*, 77, 80).

8. The supremacy of law and the supremacy of man were questions over which Confucianists and Legalists clashed in Chinese tradition. By referring to the same terms, at the beginning of the twentieth century, the supporters of a constitution, following the example of Liang Qichao, sought to give their political ideas the sanction of tradition in order to silence the opposition of those scholars horrified at the intrusion of foreign ideas. However, the content of their ideas was quite different from what it had been during the fourth and third centuries B.C. The law as defined by the constitutionalists had an abstract and general character. It comprised a collective agreement aimed at guaranteeing the interests of the majority of citizens, and not a system of rewards and punishments as advocated by Han Fei. In attacking the notion of the supremacy of man in government, Zhang Jian and his friends were thinking of the arbitrary power of an absolute monarchy and not the ineffectiveness of morality in establishing order in the state.

9. Xiao He, who died in 193 B.C., was a friend and adviser of Liu

Bang, the founder of the Han dynasty. Xiao assisted Liu in attaining power. He became prime minister and played an important role in the organization of the new empire. In tradition, Xiao is considered the model of a skillful, virtuous, and loyal minister (H. Giles, *A Chinese Biographical Dictionary* [London and Shanghai, 1898], no. 702, 279-80). Cao Can, who died in 190 B.C., was a faithful follower of Liu Bang. Liu promoted him to the highest offices of state. Cao succeeded Xiao as prime minister in 193 B.C. and carefully continued with Xiao's policies, refusing to modify any laws or regulations laid down by his predecessor (ibid., no. 2012, 761).

Text 5: Commentary

1. He dealt at this time with pending business (Zhang Jian, *Diary*, GX34/III/16).
2. The correspondence of the Jiangsu education commissioner gives an account of frequent clashes: *Jiangsu xuewu wendu* II, GX33/XII/13 (the authorities capitulate to gentry after attempting to dissolve an education association), I, GX33/VIII/3 (an association rebels against a local office of education). These conflicts could center on specific problems as well as on questions of principle, as shown in this text. In any event, it would be wrong to consider these semi-official associations as the docile tools of the authorities.

Text 6: Translation

1. The duke of Zhou was the younger brother of Wu Wang, whom he assisted in the founding of the Zhou dynasty. It was said that he compiled a legal code, improved morals, and worked for the public good (Giles, *A Chinese Biographical Dictionary*, 162).
2. Wei Yang, who died in 338 B.C., was a follower of Duke Xiao of Qin. He instilled in the duke the ambition of establishing an empire. In order to attain this objective, Wei reformed the civil and military administration of Qin and promulgated a strict legal code that was rigorously applied (ibid., 868-70). The contrast between the government of the duke of Zhou, which

made use of morality and persuasion, and that of the prince of Shang, which made use of self-interest and brute force, has been a common theme in philosophical and political literature since antiquity. Through this allusion, Zhang wanted to show that once the Qing monarchy had established a constitution, thereby renouncing itself as a tyranny which executed the laws under the threat of punishment, it had to provide for the education of the people so that the latter could be able to understand and apply the new laws and thus to obey the government.

3. The requirement of one school for every two hundred households was contained in the 1904 regulations on lower primary schools (*Da Qing Guangxu xin faling*, VII/2/1a). It was repeated at the end of March 1909 (JYZZ 1, no. 3: *jishi*, 13). This requirement was also referred to in the education ministry's program of 16 April 1909, as part of the nine-year preparation program for a constitutional regime (*Da Qing Xuantong xin faling* [Shanghai, 1910-10], III/50-52).

4. See chapter I. On 29 January 1901, an edict requested officials to submit reform proposals, especially those on education, to the court. On 14 September 1901, the government converted academies into schools and ordered that education be developed (*Shilu*, 507/1b-2b; *Donghua lu*, GX10, 4583-84).

5. The University of Beijing had been established by an edict of 11 June 1898 during the Hundred Days Reform. It was closed in the summer of 1900 and then reopened on 11 January 1902, completely reorganized by its director Zhang Baixi, before any plans for primary and secondary education had been drawn up (Shu Xincheng, *Shiliao*, 1: 117-57, 2: 1-4).

6. Reference to his *Reasoned Discussion on Reform*, which was submitted to Liu Kunyi in April 1901 and which proposed an educational program (Zhang Jian, *Zhengwen*, II/13a-b), and also to the steps he took to establish the normal school (see text 1).

7. These were the two normal schools founded by Zhang Zhidong-those of Nanjing (Sanjiang shifan xuetang, see text 1, note 12) and Wuchang created in October 1902 under the name of Liangchu shifan xuetang, the normal school of Liangchu (Chu is the literary name for Hunan and Hubei) (Zhang Zhidong, *Zhang wenxiang gong quanji*, 57/1a-22b).

8. See above, note 3. The estimates for the surface area and number of households were taken from the tax rolls. The survey that Zhang had done a little later gives a higher population figure (Zhang Jian, *Zizhi*, I/19a).

9. Jiang Qian, Zhang Jian's former pupil at the Wenzheng academy in Nanjing, was one of Zhang's closest collaborators in all
matters concerning politics and education. During the first
years of the Republic, Jiang was director of education for
Jiangsu, and then director of the Nanjing Higher Normal
School. Afterwards, he withdrew to a Buddhist monastery
(Zhang Xiaoruo, *Zhuanji*, 99, 473; Ding Zhipin, *Jiaoyu jishi*,
52).

Text 6: Commentary

1. *Shilu*, 595/1a-2b.
2. JYZZ 1, no. 3: *jishi*, 13.
3. *Da Qing Xuantong xin faling*, III/49-52; JYZZ 1, no. 4: *jishi*, 24.
   JYZZ 1, no. 5: *zhangcheng wendu*, 15 (text of the memorial
   from the Jiangsu Education Association), *jiaoyu faling*, 25 (text
   of the new regulations).
4. The sources are numerous: for foreign opinion, see in particular:
   J. Fryer, *The Educational Reform in China* (Washington D.C.,
   1910); H. E. King, *Educational System of China*, 52-53, 61; E.
   T. Williams, *The Progress of Educational Reform in China;*
   NCH, 7 September 1906, 553-54, 6 February 1909, 329, 356-
   57, 29 May 1909, 486; A. Maybon, "La réforme scolaire en
   Chine," *La Revue,* 15 November 1907, 228-42; N. Peri,
   "L'éducation nouvelle en Chine," *Revue de Paris*, 1 June 1907.
   For Chinese opinion, in addition to the inspection reports
   published in *Xuebu guanbao*: Zhili: 1, nos. 13, 29 (5 March, 9
   August 1907); Henan: 1, nos. 28-31 (GX33/21 June-21 July),
   2, no. 53 (10 May 1908); Beijing: 1, no. 32 (8 September 1907),
   2, no. 33 (18 September 1907), 3, nos. 91-95 (28 June-6
   August 1909); Shanxi: 2, nos. 44-51 (4 January-21 April
   1908); Shandong: 2, nos. 54-56 (20 May-9 June 1908);
   Guangxi: 2, nos. 64-65 (27 August-6 September 1908); Jiangxi:
   2, nos. 34-36 (28 September-17 October 1907), the following
   can be cited: Lee Teng-hwee, *The Problem of New Education in
   China; China Mission Yearbook* 1911, 104-11; NCH, 25
   November 1910, 468-69; DFZZ 3, no. 5 (1906): *jiaoyu*, 59-68;
   4, no. 2 (1907): *jiaoyu*, 13-20; *Zhongguo xinbao*, no. 6 (July
   1907) (cited in *Xinhai shilun*, II/884-94).
5. *Jiaoyu tongji tubiao*, 1907, 1908, *gesheng*. Guangdong was the

only province where there was a reduction in the total number of schools.

6. H. E. King, *Educational System of China*, 52-53.

7. Other examples are: in June 1908, at the head of a group of Overseas Chinese, Kang Youwei presented a memorial; in July a telegram was sent to the court by Liang Qichao's Society for Political Information. In August, Zhang Jian sent a delegation, representing ten provinces, to Beijing with a memorial, while the governors of eight provinces sent a telegram. The court acquiesced by promulgating the edict granting a constitution on 27 August 1908 (Li Shiyue, *Zhang Jian he lixianpai*, 49-53).

8. Liang Qichao, "A Discussion of the Direction Education Should Take," *Xinmin congbao*, no. 1 (8 February 1902): 61-68, and the series of articles entitled "The Theory of a New People," ibid., 1902-3; Luo Zhenyu, *Jiaoyu shijie*, nos. 3, 13, 14, 20, 24, 32, 33 (1901-3).

9. Duan Fang and Zai Hongzi wrote this in their report of January 1907 on their journey abroad, which proposed the adoption of the German model (Shu Xincheng, *Shiliao*, 4: 17).

10. Memorial from the Ministry of Education on the aims of education, March 1906 (ibid., 2: 97-99).

11. Section II, article 7 of the plan of 27 August 1908, translated in J. Rodes, *La Chine et le Mouvement Constitutionnel*, 18.

Text 7: Translation

1. On 20 June 1911 Zhang Jian was invited to give a speech at the Beijing Commercial School, a new private establishment comprising several hundred students (Zhang Jian, *Diary*, XT3/V/24; King, *Educational System of China*, 80).

2. Zhang left Shanghai at the end of May and arrived in Beijing on 8 June, after having stopped on the way at Hankou and Changde, where he stayed with Yuan Shikai. Then, from 29 June to 14 July he made a tour of Manchuria. He returned afterwards to preside over the meetings of the Central Committee of Education in Beijing. He left Beijing on 4 August in order to reach Shanghai by 12 August. On the way he stopped over in Tianjin, where Yuan Shikai invited him to visit some factories and schools. Zhang's trip had three aims. The delegates from several provincial assemblies had sent two

representatives to Nantong to beseech Zhang to go to Beijing personally in order to express dissatisfaction over the composition of the cabinet to the regent. At the same time, Zhang was commissioned by the Shanghai, Hankou, Tianjin, and Canton chambers of commerce to negotiate in Beijing the implementation of a plan of economic cooperation with the United States, primarily concerning Manchuria. Finally, Zhang had to participate in the first session of the Central Committee of Education, held in Beijing from 15 July to 3 August 1911 (Zhang Jian, *Diary*, XT3/V/11-VI/ibid./18; Liu Housheng, *Zhuanji*, 180; NCH, 1 July 1911).

3. In 1894 and 1898, while in the quarters of Weng Tonghe in Beijing, Zhang had been in a position to reflect upon the limited viewpoints of conservative high officials (Zhang Jian, *Nianpu*, 36-37, 44-47).

4. The expression *"shi wen zhi yi"* referred to the "eight-legged essay" (*bagu*), which had to comply with very strict rules. From the sixteenth century onwards the eight-legged essay comprised one of the most important tests in the traditional examinations. By this criticism Zhang Jian was not only opposing the extreme conservatives, but also the supporters of *yangwu*, who only wanted to adopt Western technology (Quan Hansheng, "Ideas Hostile to Westernization at the End of the Qing," *Lingnan xuebao* 5, nos. 3-4 [December 1936]: 122-66; Quan Hansheng, "The Theory of the Chinese Origins of Western Science at the End of the Qing," ibid., 4, no. 2 [June 1935]: 57-102; G. H. C. Wong, "Wang Jen-tsün: A Late Nineteenth Century Obstructor of the Introduction of Western Thought" [unpublished paper, 1967]).

5. Mathematics, astronomy, chemistry, medicine, and mechanics were the sciences in which the Chinese thought they had themselves attained a high level (Quan Hansheng, "Chinese Origins of Western Sciences," 76-83).

6. See text 6, note 5. This was in reference to the establishment of the University of Beijing in 1898.

7. Quotation from *Mencius*, V/2 (Couvreur, *Les quatre livres*, 347).

8. Tongzhou cotton was very much in demand by neighboring areas because of the length of its fibers and superior texture. In fact, the amount of rainfall and quality of soil was very beneficial to cotton-growing in this region (R. Odell, *Cotton Goods in China* [Washington D.C., 1916], 199; T. H. Shen, *Agricultural Resources of China* [Ithaca, 1951], 310; *Ershinian lai zhi*

Nantong, 6).

9. At the end of 1896 and beginning of 1897, out of the four Chinese-owned Shanghai textile mills in existence, the three most important (Huasheng, Dachun, and Yujin), affected by the economic depression which was to last until 1899, were on the point of closing down or selling out (*Jiangsu sheng fangzhiye zhuankuang, fubian* 1, 2; *China Imperial Maritime Customs, Decennial Reports 1892-1901*, 1/472-73, 516; Odell, *Cotton Goods in China*, 157).

10. In February 1896 the initial capital had been fixed at 600,000 *taels*. In October, following the withdrawal of two shareholders and a reorganization of the association, the anticipated amount of capital was reduced to 500,000 *taels*. The government was to supply the machinery, at a cost estimate of 500,000 *taels*. In March 1897 the Nantong investors contributed 59,000 *taels*. In July the Shanghai investors withdrew from the scheme. In August 1897 Zhang concluded an agreement with Sheng Xuanhuai to share the equipment between two mills, one in Nantong and the other in Shanghai, each mill to have a capital of 250,000 *taels*. Sheng was to assume full responsibility for the Shanghai mill and share the duty of amassing the capital for the Nantong mill (i.e., he was to be responsible for collecting 150,000 *taels*).

However, he did not fulfill his commitments. The construction of the Nantong mill began in January 1898; by June of the same year 180,000 *taels* had been collected and spent. In November the governor-general, Liu Kunyi, contributed 38,000 *taels* from the funds of the customs office and salt bureau. He also obtained a loan of 46,000 *taels* from the receipts of the magistrates of Haimen and Tongzhou. The mill was completed in April 1899, by which time 10,000 *taels* remained as working capital. In order to begin production Zhang had to sell some of the raw cotton supplies and borrow from a magistrate and foreign banks. The financial situation only stabilized in October 1899 when Zhang, taking advantage of an increase in the price of cotton thread, accelerated production, even at the risk of prematurely exhausting all supplies of raw cotton.

The operation was ultimately successful. Deducting the amount used for repayment of loans and the purchase of machinery, capital investment rose to 195,100 *taels*. It had thus taken forty-four months (from February 1896 to October 1899) to get the mill working effectively (Zhang Jian, *Nianpu*,

43, 45, 47, 48; Zhang Jian, *Shiye*, I/11b-12a, 14b, 16-18a; *Dasheng ziben jituan shi*, passim, cited by Zhang Kaiyuan, "The Contradictions of Zhang Jian," 87-104; *Jiangsu sheng fangzhiye zhuangkuang, fubian* 1, 1-5).

11. See note 10 above. As early as August two investors had withdrawn, and in July 1897 two others withdrew. Sheng Xuanhuai, also, did not keep to his word. The magistrates to whom Liu Kunyi made several appeals showed little enthusiasm. Since Zhang Jian had only had a literary training, few had confidence in his ability to manage an economic enterprise. On the other hand, the support that Zhang enjoyed among official circles worried the merchants, who had no desire to let the government make use of all their capital without offering any interest. Such a state of affairs had come about in a jointly managed mill and other enterprises in Wuchang. Finally, even if Zhang received the support of high officials, he still had to overcome the opposition of their subordinates (Zhang Jian, *Shiye* I/17a; Zhang Xiaoruo, *Zhuanji*, 72; *Jiangsu sheng fangzhiye zhuangkuang, fubian* 1, 2-3).

12. In October 1900 Zhang drafted a memorial for Liu Kunyi, requesting the emperor's permission to develop the coastal land in the region of Tongzhou and Haimen. The request was granted. In May 1901 Zhang himself drew up the regulations of the company. In January 1902, with most of the land bought, work began on organizing cultivation; by the end of the year the first cultivator was settled on the land. The land area totalled 123,279 *mu*, and the initial capital of 220,000 *taels* was increased to 300,000 in 1906 and then to 400,000 in 1911. Cotton, corn, and soybeans were grown. During the Republic Zhang participated in the creation of fifteen other land-clearing companies, all operating in the area north of Tongzhou and Haimen (*Donghua lu*, GX10, 4762-63; Zhang Jian, *Nianpu*, 50-52; Zhang Jian, *Shiye*, II/2a, VII/10b; Song Xishang, *Shengping*, 171-74; *Ershinian lai zhi Nantong*, II/39ss).

13. In February 1902 Zhang decided on the area north of the port of Tangzha, next to the Dasheng mill, as the site for the oilworks. In April he reached an agreement with Sha Yuanbing, who became director of the enterprise (which was given the name of Guangsheng). The oil-works began operating in 1903. By 1909 the initial capital of 50,000 *taels* had increased to 213,000; the oil-works also no longer had to depend on the Dasheng mill's machine-power since it now had its own

machinery. The shareholders decided to increase the capital yet
again by 107,000 *taels* (Zhang Jian, *Nianpu*, 53; Zhang Jian,
Diary, GX28/II/21; Zhang Chaohán, "A Survey of Industry in
Nantong," *Shiye zazhi*, no. 52 [February 1922]; *Ershinian lai
zhi Nantong*, II/10-13).

14. Zhang created two navigation companies. One of them, the
Dasheng Steamship Navigation Company (Dasheng lunchuan
gongsi), plied between the Dasheng cotton mill and Shanghai.
This transport service had been controlled by a Shanghai
merchant. In 1900 Zhang reorganized the company, increasing
the capital to 32,000 dollars, of which 12,000 came from the
Dasheng mill (which therefore gave its name to the company).
From this time on the service also catered for passengers.
Finally, in October 1902, in the name of the cotton mill, Zhang
bought up the shares still held by the Shanghai group. The
other company, the Dada Internal Steamship Navigation
Company (Dada neihe lunchuan gongsi), was created in 1903
with a capital of 20,000 dollars. In the beginning the company
only had one small steamship which transported raw cotton,
from the district of Nantong, to the mill. In 1906 the capital
was increased by 10,000 dollars and two more small
steamships were purchased in order to maintain links with the
neighboring districts of Tongtai, Yancheng, and Xinghua
(*Tongzhou xingban shiye zhi lishi*, "Dada neihe lunchuan
gongsi," 17, "Dasheng lunchuan gongsi," 1-2; *Ershinian lai zhi
Nantong*, II/72).

15. See text 1, note 12 and text 6, note 7. In 1905 the Sanjiang
Normal School adopted the name of the Liangjiang Normal
School (*Zhengzhi guanbao*, vol. 3, 148-49, GX33/XII/9, no. 79,
4).

16. The boys' normal school was opened in 1903 (text 1). The girls'
normal school was opened in 1906. Zhang added banking
courses to the normal school curriculum in order to train personnel acquainted with the modern methods which were increasingly necessary. In May 1910 the teaching of these
courses became the responsibility of a newly-established commercial school (Zhang Xiaoruo, *Zhuanji*, 98; Zhang Jian, *Diary*
XT2/IV/22; Zhang Jian, *Nianpu*, 64). In 1906 Zhang added
special agricultural courses to the normal school with an experi-
mental plot of land for the use of both students and peasants. In
February 1910 these courses became independent of the normal
school and by 1911 they virtually constituted an agricultural

school in itself (Zhang Jian, *Nianpu*, 59, 64; Zhang Jian, *Jianpu*, 4, 6; Zhang Jian, *Diary*, XT/I/19; Song Xishang, *Shengping*, 220; *Ershinian lai zhi Nantong*, 26-27; *Jiangsu sheng jiaoyu xingzheng*, II/65). On Zhang Jian's suggestion, the Nantong Education Association had just adopted a plan to establish a school for every 16 square *li* of arable land by the end of 1915. The plan did not take into account population density. It was partially implemented: by 1915 there were 227 primary schools. This was, in effect, the first systematic and positive attempt to implement universal education. (On Zhang Jian's plan, see Zhang Jian, *Jiaoyu*, II/18a-19b; JYZZ 3, no. 4: *jishi*, 31. On the plan adopted by the education association, see JYZZ 3, no. 5: *jishi*, 40. On the results, see Chuang Chaihsuan, *Tendencies Toward a Democratic System of Education in China* [Shanghai, 1922], 71-73).

17. Wu Xun (1838-96), a native of Tangyi district in Shandong, was a model for Zhang Jian and he had his portrait hung in the normal school's ceremonial hall, alongside those of Confucius, Pestalozzi, Yan Yuan, and Wang Yangming. Wu, the illiterate son of a poor peasant relying on begging for a livelihood, succeeded in amassing enough money to establish three schools designed for poor children (and hence, in principle, free). This gesture was enough for Wu to receive numerous praises from the emperor. Thus even before his death Wu was officially honored as a paragon of virtue and unselfish benevolence. In its policy of creating a moral order, the Guomindang revived the praises of Wu Xun's merits. In 1951 Wu became the subject of a lively controversy. The detailed examination of Wu's activities carried out during the controversy concluded that Wu's schools were the achievement of a social parasite protected by gentry and officials. The conditions of admission into the schools were such that they hardly benefitted anyone except the sons of gentry and merchants (*Ershinian lai zhi Nantong*, I/48; *T'ien Hsia Monthly*, 1938, 235ff; *Wu Xun xianshengde zhuanji; Pipan "Wu Xun zhuan"; Wu Xun yu Wu Xun zhuan pipan; Wu Xun lishi diaocha ji*).

18. These thoughts were inspired from the *Analects* of Confucius IV/26 (Couvreur, *Les quatre livres*, 106) and from a saying attributed to Liu Xiu, the founder of the Eastern Han dynasty: "Where there's a will, there's a way."

19. The three northeastern provinces were Qilin, Fengtian, and Heilongjiang. Ever since his stay in Korea in 1882-83 Zhang

had been interested in the northeast, which he considered essential to China's security and sovereignty. While he had regarded the strengthening of military organization as the primary guarantee against Japanese and Russian ambitions in his "Six Points on the Improvement of Policy in Korea" (see chapter I), after 1900 he advocated a policy of settling and cultivating this large area (which was one of the principal outlets for Zhang's cotton industry in Tongzhou) by Chinese emigrants.

During the course of the nineteenth century, especially in the later years and in the beginning of the twentieth century, after the lifting of the ban on emigration, emigrants (mainly from Shandong) began to settle the area. In Fengtian more than 4,250,000 hectares were being cultivated by 1908, in contrast to 180,000 in 1661. In Heilongjiang the population increased from 250,000 in 1887 to 1,850,000 in 1911. In April 1907 the administration of the northeastern provinces was integrated with that of China proper: the governor-general of Fengtian became governor-general of all three provinces and a governor was appointed for each of them. After 1905, when China agreed to the ceding of Russian rights in Liaodong and the South Manchurian railway to Japan, Japanese influence in the northeast had greatly increased at the expense of Chinese sovereignty and American commercial interests.

The agreement signed between Russia and Japan on 4 July 1910 to maintain the *status quo* in Manchuria was a further threat to China's integrity. On 29 August 1910 Japan annexed Korea. In order to block Japanese penetration of the area, the Chinese government thought of developing industry in Manchuria by relying on an American loan. The United States, alarmed at Japan's increasing influence in the Far East, willingly took on the role of China's defender but pressure from England, Germany, and France finally obliged them to participate in a loan extended by an international banking consortium. The loan was concluded on 15 April 1911; it was designed only for the financing of the Huguang railway and monetary reform. Coinciding with these official negotiations, a group of forty American capitalists, who had come to China in the autumn of 1910 on the occasion of the Nanjing trade fair, began discussions with Zhang Jian and other Jiangsu businessmen. They reached an agreement on developing commercial exchanges, on establishing a commercial bank whose capital would be put up jointly by the Americans and Chinese, and which would finance development in Manchuria, and on the creation of a Pacific navigation company.

When the American delegation visited the Jiangnan provincial assembly Zhang made a speech on the subject. Attracted by the apparent spirit of equality that the Americans had introduced in the sphere of international relations, Zhang saw a link with the United States as the means to hold Japanese power at bay. He in fact expressed this idea to the regent during the interview of 13 June 1911. During the course of his journey to Beijing and Manchuria Zhang prepared the groundwork for his plan; on his return to the south he created a special office to deal with the project. The 1911 Revolution put an end to his plans, but when he became a minister in 1913 Zhang again took up the question of collaboration with the United States (Zhang Jian, *Zhengwen*, III/35b-36b; Zhang Jian, *Diary*, XT2/VII-XII, passim, XT3/V/17, VI/8-20; *Qilin daxue shehui kexue xuebao*, no. 1 [1962]: 52ss; *Zhongguo jindai nongyeshi ziliao*, 10-17; E. H. Zabriskie, *American-Russian Rivalry in the Far East: a Study in Diplomacy and Power Politics, 1895-1914* [Philadelphia, 1946], 170-79; R. Dollar, *Diary*, 27, 66-73; DFZZ 7, no. 11 [1910]: *jizai*, 367-68).

20. Tianqi (1621-28) and Chongzhen (1628-44) were the last two emperors of the Ming dynasty.
21. Quotation from the *Analects* of Confucius, 14/29 (Couvreur, *Les quatre livres*, 231).
22. This is a reference to the official titles (*bagong, juren*, etc.) given to school graduates (see table 2).
23. Zhang was appointed principal of the secondary and higher commercial school of Nanjing on 10 November 1909 (Zhang Jian, *Diary*, XT1/IX/28). The speech to which he refers was doubtless made between this date and the beginning of 1911. The text does not appear in the existing editions of Zhang Jian's works.

Text 7: Commentary

1. Zhang Jian, *Diary*, XT3/V/24. On his journey to the north, see note 2 of the text.
2. See chapter I, 23-24.

3. Song Xishang, *Shengping*, 137-38; Zhang Xiaoruo, *Zhuanji*, 13, 46, 68-69, 82, 319-20, 347, 357; Liu Housheng, *Zhuanji*, 249-51. The most revealing text showing the influence of enlightened seventeenth-century thinkers on Zhang Jian is a letter that he wrote to Shen Zipei in 1897, at a time when the situation concerning Dasheng had reached a critical stage. Zhang wrote that he had read and reread the works of Huang Zongxi and Gu Yanwu in order to "bolster his will" and "steady his courage" (Zhang Jian, *Wenlu*, XI/13b). By their opposition to neo-Confucian idealism, the seventeenth-century thinkers developed a philosophy of practical rationalism which was bound to find an echo in Zhang's personality and interests (Zhang Jian, *Diary*, GX30/II/11; Zhang Jian, *Zhengwen*, II/4a).

Text 8: Translation

1. The *Treatise on Schools* is chapter 16 of the *Li ji* [Classic of Rites] (Couvreur, *Mémoires sur les bienséances et les cérémonies*, II: 39).
2. *Emile* was translated in 1901 under the name of *Aimeier chao* by Nakajima; it was based on a Japanese translation by Yamaguchi Shōtarō and published in the third volume of *Jiaoyu congshu* which was edited by Luo Zhenyu. Zhang Jian, who followed closely the publications of his friend, may very well have been acquainted with the work. He would also have been informed by numerous books and articles on the history and doctrines of education which appeared after 1901 (in 1901, the *Short History of Education in China and Abroad* [Neiwai jiaoyu xiaoshi] translated by Shen Hong in *Jiaoyu congshu*, vol. 1, contained details of Rousseau's life, 14a-15b). Nevertheless, it was above all through his political ideas that Rousseau exerted a large influence at this time: the theory of the social contract had been explained in *Qingyi bao*, nos. 98, 99, 100 (21 November, 1 and 11 December 1901) and in *Xinmin congbao*, nos. 11 and 12, 5 and 19 July 1902; some extracts were translated in the journals *Kai zhi lu* (1900), *Yishu huibian* (from 1900), *Jiangsu* (1903); two complete translations were published by Yang Yandong and Yan Fu (Zhang Jinglu, *Zhongguo jindai chuban shiliao*, 1: 173).
3. Reference to the 1911 Revolution.

4. Quotation from the *Zuo zhuan*, "Zhao Gong ninth year" (Couvreur, *Tch'ouen Ts'iou et Tso Tchouan*, III: 164).
5. Proverb drawn from the *Zhan guo ce* [History of the Three Kingdoms].
6. Zhuge Liang (181-234) was a famous tactician, state minister, and scholar during the period of the Three Kingdoms. Writings under the title *Zhuge Zhonjwu hou wenji* have been attributed to his authorship. The passage cited here is from I/22b (in the Chaling tanfuchou tang cangban edition).
7. Quotation from the *Zuo zhuan*, Xiang gong thirty-first year (Couvreur, *Tch'ouen Ts'iou et Tso Tchouan*, II: 581).

Text 8: Commentary

1. Shu Xingcheng, *Shiliao*, 60-61. This text employed the same terms used by Zhang Jian.
2. Information on the strikes and disturbances of 1912 can be found in JYZZ 4: *jishi*, no. 1: 6 (Suzhou); no. 3: 21 (Anhui, Wuxian); no. 4: 28 (Wuxian); no. 6: 38 (Nanchang); no. 7: 45-46 (Hangzhou); no. 8: 50, 58 (Beijing, Baoding); no. 11: 77 (Beijing, Nanjing, Jinan, Chongqing, Fujian).
3. J. S. Burgess, "What Chinese Students Are Reading," *China Mission Yearbook*, 1911, 117-26.
4. Zhu Yuanshan, "On the Disturbances in the Schools," JYZZ 5, no. 14: *yanlun*, 47-57. The author gives these figures while adding that there are no complete statistics. However, he noted that strikes were numerous everywhere.
5. He did not encourage them either, but he did admit that they had a certain political usefulness (Zhang Jian, *Diary*, GX31/II/17, 24, VII/28, XI/15, 20 and also text 3).
6. Zhang Xiaoruo, *Zhuanji*, 121.
7. The expressions and quotations used by Zhang Jian were followed by several other texts on the same subject during the following months: Zhu Yuanshan, "On the Disturbances in the Schools"; telegram from the education ministry (JYZZ 4, no. 6: *jishi*, 34); resolution of Jiangsu provincial authorities (JYZZ 5, no. 8: *jishi*, 65); decree of Yuan Shikai (JYZZ 5, no. 4: *jishi*, 25). Zhang's text is included in a 1915 collection of writings by famous contemporaries (*Xiandai shi dajia wenchao* [Shanghai, 1915]) and in all the anthologies of Zhang's works.

8. Shu Xincheng, *Jiaoyu sixiang shi*, 113-33; Ren Shixian, *Jiaoyu sixiang shi*, 329-39.
9. Cai Yuanpei, "New Educational Ideals," *China Mission Yearbook*, 1913, 253-54; Cai Yuanpei, *Cai Jiemin xiansheng yanxinglu*, 189.
10. Chen Qingzhi, *Zhongguo jiaoyushi*, 656-57. This outlook is clearly evident in the directives issued by the education ministry implementing *junguomin jiaoyu* (national military education), on 18 December 1912 (JYZZ 4, no. 11: *jishi*, 73).
11. See chapter II, 56-7, chapter III, 81, commentary for text 3, note 9.
12. See note 7. All these writings and publications were produced by conservatives. On the criticisms that the text aroused, see Hou Hongjian, "Notes on a Visit to the Attached Primary School of the Nantong Substitute Normal School," *Zhonghua jiaoyujie*, no. 19 (July 1914): 5.

Text 9: Translation

1. Renzhi was the *zi* (style name) of Huang Yanpei (1878-1965), who was then director of education for Jiangsu. He was one of the most important educators of the twentieth century in China. A native of Chuansha in Jiangsu, Huang obtained the *juren* degree in 1902. He continued his studies at Nanyang College in Shanghai where he established relationships with the revolutionary intellectuals gathered around Cai Yuanpei. He seems to have been a member of the Tongmenghui, but this did not prevent him from being active in the Jiangsu Education Association. After the 1911 Revolution his career advanced by leaps and bounds. He was given important duties in the sphere of education and was an enthusiastic promoter of practical and vocational education. He played an active role in the resistance against Japan. As the head of the Chinese Association for National and Democratic Reconstruction, which he had founded in December 1945, Huang presided over the first session of the Consultative Political Conference. He afterwards became its vice-chairman, as well as vice-chairman of the permanent committee of the People's National Assembly (DFZZ 33, no. 1 [1 January 1936]: 14; *Guangming ribao*, 25 December 1965).
2. The expression *tongsu jiaoyu* (general education), which first appeared in 1906, had a wider meaning than *putong jiaoyu* (lit.:

ordinary education), which simply referred to educational content. *Tongsu jiaoyu* not only meant that subjects taught were general but also that the teaching of these subjects had to be universal. Zhang's use of the expression reveals the transition to the Republic.

3. See text 1, note 8. In December 1912 the Nantong Normal School was recognized as a substitute school (JYZZ 4, no. 10: *jishi*, 71). Under this arrangement the province had to finance half of the expenditures, but on the other hand it also had controlling power.

4. See text 1, note 23.

5. This was the school attached to the normal school, opened on 27 August 1903 (see text 1, note 13).

6. These were agricultural schools maintained by the province. There was one in Wuxian, one in Nanjing, and one to the north of the Yangzi in Qingjiang. On the school in Nantong, see text 7, note 16. In 1912 Zhang expanded the curriculum by including secondary-level training and then, in 1920, higher-level training. The latter was to form one of the departments of Nantong University (*Jiangsu sheng jiaoyu xingzheng*, I/145; *Ershinian lai zhi Nantong*, I/24-27).

7. Yangzhou was a prefecture situated to the west of Nantong and north of the Yangzi; Huai'an was a prefecture in north Jiangsu on the Grand Canal.

8. The school was opened in April 1906 (Zhang Jian, *Jiaoyu*, VI/16b).

9. The local assemblies, established by the Qing in 1910, remained in existence until 1914. The district assemblies (*yishi hui*) had deliberative powers. As far as education was concerned they had, in theory, quite a considerable leeway although in practice they could do little since they had no financial resources (Li Zonghuang, *Gailun*, 43-45).

10. The district council (*canshi hui*) was the executive organ at the local level from 1910 to 1914. It was presided over by the magistrate, it in fact held the real power and controlled the finances (Chen Zhimai, *Zhongguo zhengfu*, 3 vols. [Shanghai, 1944-45], 3: 67ss; Li Zonghuang, *Gailun*, 43-45). Nevertheless, the girls' normal school received 6,000 dollars from the district in 1912-13 (*Jiangsu sheng jiaoyu xingzheng*, I/235).

11. This school was established in May 1910 (see text 7, note 16).

12. The Lodge of the Kui Stars, the patron constellation of literature, was situated on an island in the water-channel

southwest of Nantong. The Guandi Temple (Guan Yu, a hero of the Three Kingdoms period, had been elevated to the rank of divinity in 1594 and was worshipped as the god of war) was situated at the eastern gate of the town. Zhang Jian had considered converting it into a primary school (*Tongzhou zhilizhou zhi*, O/15b-16a; Zhang Jian, *Diary*, GX31/XII/13). Local products, as well as other items purchased from Shanghai, were displayed in the commercial exhibition hall. Few other towns possessed an establishment of this kind (DFZZ 3, no. 13 [1907]: *shangwu*, 215).

Text 9: Commentary

1. DFZZ 9, no. 8 (1913): *shiji*. He remained in the post until the end of January 1914 (JYZZ 5, no. 11: *jishi*, 96).
2. JYZZ 4, no. 10: *jishi*, 71.
3. Ibid., 71-72. During the Republic the *dudu* was the highest provincial authority, holding military power and controlling the civil powers.
4. These figures are only meant to give a general picture and no claim is made for their complete accuracy. For Nantong, the figures are calculated from the information in the following texts: Zhang Jian, *Jiaoyu*, II/29a; the Jiangning education inspector's report of 1907 in *Xuebu guanbao* 3, no. 82 (20 March 1909), *Jingwai xuewu baogao*, 147-61; DFZZ 3, no. 12 (1907): *jishi*, 92; *Jiaoyu tongji tubiao, gesheng*, 1907, 39-46, 1908, 23-29; *Jiangsu sheng jiaoyu xingzheng*, I/6, 235, 251-66, 270, II/57-58, 65-75. These last two works also permit one to calculate figures for the other districts in the province and the rest of the country.
5. In 1912 the district provided a subsidy of one thousand dollars for the students of the normal school (JYZZ 3, no. 12: *jishi*, 92).
6. The original plan exempted students from tuition fees (text 1), but budgetary difficulties forced a quick renunciation of the plan. Besides tuition fees, each pupil paid forty dollars boarding fees per year: Zhang Jian, *Jiaoyu*, 1/12a.
7. In order to avoid abuses, a ruling of 29 September 1912 had stipulated that no more than three dollars a year were to be charged as fees by lower primary schools, ten dollars by higher primary schools, and twenty dollars by secondary schools

(JYZZ 4, no. 9, "Ruling on Tuition Fees Charged by the Schools").

8. Odell, *Cotton Goods in China*, 168, 179.

9. These figures are calculated from the detailed information given by Qiao Qiming in *Jiangsu Kunshan Nantong Anhui Suxian nongtian zhidu zhi bijiao*, 9, 14, 23-33.

10. On this group, the tables given in the appendix of the survey carried out by the South Manchurian administration (*Kōsoshō Nantsūken Nōson Jittai Chōsa Hōkokusho* [Shanghai, 1941]) are very useful.

11. Chang Chung-li, *The Income of the Chinese Gentry*, 326-30.

12. Besides the text itself, see *Jiangsu sheng jian*, VII/211; *Jiangsu sheng jiaoyu xingzheng*, I/130, 133.

13. J. Chesneaux, "Le Mouvement federaliste en Chine," *Revue Historique*, no. 480 (October-December 1966).

BIBLIOGRAPHY

Because of limits imposed by publication, the bibliography does not include well-known general works or the occasional references which have little connection with education. The most important works concerning education from 1900 to 1912 are marked with an asterisk.

Bibliography of Chinese and Japanese Works

Primary Sources and Documents

Works of Zhang Jian

Seweng ziding nianpu 啬翁自订年谱 [Zhang Jian's autobiography]. Nantong, 1925. 2 *juan* 卷.

Diary entries were written by Zhang Jian himself until 1922. The work was then completed by his son. It is included in the "special topics" of the *Nine Collections* (*juan* 6 and 7), as well as in the various editions of Zhang Jian's biography by Zhang Xiaoruo.

Zhang Jian riji 张謇日记 [Zhang Jian's diary]. Jiangsu renmin chubanshe, 1962. 江苏人民出版社 15 *ce* 册.

This photolithographic edition contains one *ce* for 1883-84 and 14 *ce* for 1892-1926. It was reprinted in Hong Kong by the Eastern Bookstore in 1967. The manuscript covering the years 1873-82 and 1885-92 was taken to Taiwan by Zhang Jian's descendants. An edition of 4 *ce* (2 *ce* for 1873-82 and 2 *ce* for 1885-92) was published by Wenhai chubanshe 文海出版社 in Taibei in 1967, under the title *Liu xi caotang riji* 柳西草堂

269

日记 [Diary of the thatched cottage to the west of the willow grove], with a preface by Shen Yunlong 沈云龙 .

Zhang Jizi jiu lu 张季子九录 [The nine collections of writings by Zhang Jian], ed. Zhang Xiaoruo 张孝若 . Shanghai, 1931. Reprint, 6 vols. Taibei, 1965. 80 *juan.*

Zhang Se'an xiansheng shiye wenchao 张啬菴先生实业文钞 [Zhang Jian's writings on industry]. Nantong, 1948. 4 *juan.*

Zhang Se'an xiansheng wen gai zhu 张啬菴先生文既注 [Zhang Jian's writings with general annotations]. Nantong, 1947.

Other Sources

*Bianfa zouyi congchao 变法奏议丛钞 [Collection of memorials on reform]. N.p., 1904?, 4 *ce.*

Contains thirteen memorials of high officials.

*Cai Yuanpei 蔡元培 . *Cai Jiemin xiansheng yanxing lu* 蔡孑民先生言行录 [The life and works of Cai Yuanpei]. 2 vols. Beijing, 1920.

*Cai Yuanpei xiansheng yanxing lu 蔡元培先生言行录 [The life and works of Cai Yuanpei]. Shanghai, 1932.

Cai Yuanpei xuanji 蔡元培选集 [Selected works of Cai Yuanpei]. Beijing: Zhonghua shuju, 1959. 中华书局

Caizheng shuoming shu 财政说明书 [Statement of finances], ed. Caizhengbu 财政部 (Ministry of Finance). 19 vols. Beijing, 1915.

Chen Chi 陈炽 . *Yong shu* 庸书 [Book of practical words]. 1896 ed., preface by Song Yuren 宋育仁 . 4 *ce.*

*Chen Ronggun 陈荣衮 . *Chen Zibao xiansheng jiaoyu yiyi* 陈子襃先生教育遗议 [Posthumous proposals on education by Chen Ronggun]. Canton, 1952. 1 *ce.*

The writings of a modern educator from Guangdong who lived from 1862 to 1922.

Chen Sanli 陈三立 . *Xu Dinglin muzhi* 许鼎霖墓志 [Epitaph for Xu Dinglin]. Shanghai, 1949. 1 *ce.*

Cilin jilüe 词林辑略 [Annual record of *jinshi* during the Qing], ed. Zhu Ruzhen 朱汝珍 . Beijing, n.d. 5 *ce.*

Da Qing Guangxu xin faling 大清光绪新法令 [New laws during the reign of Guangxu]. Shanghai, 1909. 20 *ce.*

Da Qing Xuantong xin faling 大清宣统新法令 [New laws during the reign of Xuantong]. Shanghai, 1909-10. 35 *ce.*

Difang zizhi jiangyi 地方自治讲议 [Lecture notes on local autonomy], ed. Shen Zesheng 沈泽生 . Hubei difang zizhi yanjiuhui 湖北地方自治研究会 (Hubei Local Autonomy Study Society). Tokyo, 1908. 4 *ce.*

Diyici Zhongguo jiaoyu nianjian 第一次中国教育年鉴 [First Chinese education yearbook], ed. Jiaoyubu 教育部 (Ministry of Education). 2 vols. Shanghai, 1934.

Donghua xulu 东华续表 [Continuation of the Donghua records for the reign of Guangxu 光绪朝], ed. Zhu Shoupeng 朱寿朋 . Shanghai, 1909. 220 *juan.*

*Duan Fang 端方 . *Duan chongmin gong zougao* 端忠敏公奏稿 [Memorials of Duan Fang]. N.p., 1918. 16 *juan.*

Ershinian lai zhi Nantong 二十年来之南通 [Nantong in the last twenty years], ed. *Nantong ribao* guan bianjibu 南通日报馆 编辑部 (Editorial office of *Nantong Daily*). Nantong, 1930. Reprint, Nantong, 1938.

Faling quanshu 法令全书 [Complete collection of the laws]. Beijing, 1912-16. 64 *ce.*

*Fang Zhaoying 房兆楹 . *Qingmo minchu yangxue xuesheng timinglu chuji* 清末民初洋学学生题名录初辑 [First collection of lists of students studying abroad at the end of the Qing and beginning of the Republic]. Taibei, 1962.

Feng Guifen 冯桂芬 . *Jiao bin lu kangyi* 校邠庐抗议 [Protests from the Jiaobin studio]. Wuxian, 1898.

Gesheng suichu yusuan biao 各省岁出预算表 [Table of estimated provincial expenditures], ed. Zizhengyuan 谘政院 (National Assembly). N.p., 1911. 36 *ce.*

*Gu Xieguang 顾燮光 . *Yi shujing yanlu* 译书经眼录 [List of translated books]. Reprint, Hangzhou, 1934.

Guangxu zhengyao 光绪政要 [Important political documents during the reign of Guangxu], ed. Shen Tongsheng 沈桐生 . Shanghai, 1909. 30 *ce.*

Haimen ting tuzhi 海门厅图志 [Illustrated gazetteer of the subprefecture of Haimen], comp. Liu Wenche 刘文澈 and ed. Zhou Jialu 周家录 . Haimen, 1900.

Hu Shi 胡适 . *Sishi zi shu* 四十自述 [Autobiography written at the age of forty]. Shanghai, 1933.

*Huang Yanpei 黄炎培 . *Huang Yanpei kaocha jiaoyu riji* 黄炎培 考察教育日记   [Diary of educational inspections]. 2 vols. Shanghai, 1914-15.

————. *Minguo yuannian gongshang tongji gaiyao* 民国元年工商 统计概要   [Summary of statistics concerning industry and commerce during the first year of the Republic]. Shanghai, 1915.

Jiangsu fazheng xuetang jiangyi 江苏法政学堂讲议   [Lecture manual for Jiangsu law schools]. N.p., n.d.(but before1911). 50 *ce.*

Jiangsu quansheng yutu 江苏全省与图 [Map of Jiangsu]. N.p., 1875. 3 *ce.*

Jiangsu sheng fangzhiye zhuangkuang 江苏省纺织业状况 [Situation of the textile industry in Jiangsu], ed. Jiangsu shiye ting 江苏实业厅 (Jiangsu Industrial Bureau). Wuxi, 1919.

The appendix *(fubian)* (附编) reproduces several texts by Zhang Jian not included in the *Nine Collections* concerning Dasheng.

Jiangsu sheng nongcun diaocha 江苏省农村调查 [Investigation of Jiangsu villages], ed. Xingzhengyuan nongcun fuxing weiyuanhui 行政院农村复兴委员会 (Committee for the Revival of Rural Areas, Executive Council). Shanghai, 1934.

Jiangsu sheng shiye xingzheng baogaoshu 江苏省实业行政报告书 [Report on administration of enterprises in Jiangsu], ed. Jiangsu shiyesi 江苏实业司 [Jiangsu Industry Department]. Shanghai, 1914.

Contains much information on gentry activities in Jiangsu.

*Jiangsu sheng xingzheng gongshu jiaoyusi 江苏省行政公署教育司 (Education Department of the Jiangsu Public Administration Office). *Jiangsu sheng jiaoyu xingzheng baogaoshu* 江苏省教育行政报告书 [Report on educational administration in Jiangsu from August 1912 to July 1913]. Shanghai, 1914.

Jiangsu xuewu wendu 江苏学务文牍 [Documents on educational affairs in Jiangsu], ed. Jiangsu xuewu gongsuo 江苏学务公所 (Education Bureau of Jiangsu). Suzhou, 1910. 10 *ce.*

Jiaoyu congshu chuji, erji, sanji 教育丛书初集 , 二集 , 三集 [Collection of writings on education, first, second, and third series], ed. Jiaoyu shijie she 教育世界社 (Society of the World of Education). Shanghai, 1901. 30 *ce.*

Jiaoyu fagui huibian 教育法规汇编 [Collection of laws and regulations concerning education], ed. Jiaoyubu 教育部 (Ministry of Education). Beijing, 1919.

Only produces texts of laws and regulations still in force in 1918.

Jiaoyu tongji tubiao 教育统计图表 [Education statistics], ed. Xuebu 学部 (Board of Education); *diyici* 第一次 (first series), Beijing, 1907; *di'erci* 第二次 (second series), Beijing, 1908; *disanci* 第三次 (third series), 1909. *Disici* 第四次 (fourth series), ed. Jiaoyubu 教育部 . Beijing, 1915-16.

Jiaoyu xiaoce huiji 教育小册汇辑 [Collection of pamphlets on education]. 1898-1911. Assembled at Columbia University East Asia Library. 34 *ce.*

Jiaoyubu xingzheng jiyao 教育部行政纪要 [Record of administration of the Education Ministry], ed. Jiaoyubu 教育部 (Education Ministry). Beijing, 1916.

Especially useful for the first years of the Republic.

Jingxiang timing lu 静庠题名录 [List of *shengyuan* from Haimen]. N.p., 1933. 2 *ce*.

Kaneko Baji 金子马治 . *Jiaoyuxue shi* 教育学史 [History of pedagogy]. Translated from the Japanese by Chen Zongmeng 陈宗孟 . Shanghai, 1903.

Kōsoshō Nantsūken nōson jittai chōsa hōkokusho 江苏省南通县 农村实态调查报告书 [Report of an investigation on the rural situation in the district of Nantong, Jiangsu], ed. Minami Manshū Tetsudō kabushiki kaisha, Shanhai jimusho chōsashisu 南满州株式会社调查部，编上海事务所调查室 (South Manchurian Railway Society, Research Bureau of the Shanghai Office). Shanghai, 1941.

Useful and very informative.

Kyō Ain Kachu renra kubu 兴亚院华中连络部 (China Bureau of the Institute for the Awakening of Asia). *Sohoku kyōsantō jiku jitsujō chōsa* 苏北共产党地区实情调查 [Investigation of the situation in the Communist-held areas of Subei]. N.p., 1941.

Li Baojia 李宝嘉 . *Guanchang xianxing ji* 官场现形记 [The true face of officialdom]. Reprint, Beijing, 1963.

Li Yingjue 李应珏 . *Bianfa pingyi zhuo* 变法平议酌 [A consideration of the *Reasoned discussion on reform*]. N.p., 1901. 1 *ce*.

Li Zhangpu 李长溥 . *Jiangsu* 江苏 [Jiangsu]. Shanghai, 1936.

Liang Qichao 梁启超 . *Yin bing shi wenji* 饮冰室文集 [Collection of writings from the ice-drinker's studio]. Shanghai: Zhonghua shuju, 1936. 中华书局 16 *ce*.

Liu E 刘鹗 . *Lao Can youji* 老残遊记 [The travels of Lao Can]. Reprint, Hong Kong, 1965.

Liu Housheng 刘厚生 . *Zhang Jian zhuanji* 张謇传记 [Biography of Zhang Jian]. Shanghai, 1958.

*Liu Kunyi 刘坤一 . *Liu Kunyi yiji* 刘坤一遗集 [Works of Liu Kunyi]. 6 vols. Beijing, 1959.

Ma Jianzhong 马建忠 . *Shike zhai jiyan* 适可斋记言 [Proposals from the Shike studio]. Reprint, Beijing, 1960.

Miao Quansun 缪荃孙 . *Jiangyin xian xuzhi* 江阴县续志 [Continuation of the Jiangyin gazetteer]. N.p., 1921. 28 *juan*.

Nantong nongxiao mianzuo zhanlanhui baogaoshu 南通农校棉作展览会报告书 [Report on the cotton exhibition of the Nantong Agricultural School]. Nantong, 1915.

Useful for details on agriculture in Nantong.

Nantong shiye jiaoyu cishan fengjing 南通实业教育慈善风景 [Industry, education, charity works, and beauty spots of Nantong], ed. Nantong youyi julebu 南通友谊俱乐部 (Nantong Friendship Club). Shanghai, 1920.

Photo album with commentary.

Nantong tushuguan diyici mulu 南通图书馆第一次目录 [First catalogue of the Nantong library]. Nantong, 1914. 7 *ce*.

Nonggongshangbu tongjibiao 农工商部统计表 [Statistical tables issued by the Ministry of Agriculture, Industry, and Commerce]. ed. Ministry of Agriculture, Industry and Commerce 农工商部 . Beijing, 1909. 6 *ce*.

Qiao Qiming 乔启明 . *Jiangsu Kunshan Nantong Anhui Suxian nongtian zhidu zhi bijiao yiji gailiang nongtian wenti zhi jianyi* 江苏昆山南通安徽宿县农佃制度之比较以及改良农佃问题之建议 [Comparison of tenancy systems of Nantong and Kunshan in Jiangsu, and Suxian in Anhui, with suggestions on the problem of tenancy reform]. Nanjing, 1926.

A very informative source.

Qing (Huang) chao xu wenxian tongkao 清(皇朝)续文献通考 [Continuation of the encyclopedia of historical documents during the Qing], ed. Liu Jinzao 刘锦藻 . Shanghai, 1936. 400 *juan*.

Qingji xuexiao zhangcheng huicun 清季学校章程汇存 [Collection of school regulations during the late Qing]. Texts dating from 1903-6 and assembled at the University of Columbia library, New York. 12 *ce*.

Qingshi gao 清史稿 [Draft history of the Qing], ed. Zhao Erxun 赵尔巽 . 2 vols. Beijing, 1927. Reprint, Hong Kong, n.d. (1964?).

Qingshi liezhuan 清史列传 [Qing dynasty biographies]. Shanghai, 1928. 80 *juan*.

*Shang Yanliu 商衍鎏 . *Qingdai keju kaoshi shulun* 清代科举考试述录 [Description of the examination system during the Qing]. Beijing, 1958.

Shi'er chao Donghua lu 十二朝东华录 [Donghua records]. Reprint, Taibei: Wenhai chubanshe, 1963. 文海出版社 10 vols. for the reign of Guangxu.

Shilu (Da Qing lichao shilu) 大清 (大清历朝实录) [Records of the successive reigns of the Qing dynasty]. Tokyo, 1937. Reprint, Taibei, 1964; *Da Qing Dezong jinghuangdi* 大清德宗景皇帝 [Reign of Guangxu]. 597 *juan*.

*Shu Xincheng 舒新城 . *Jindai Zhongguo jiaoyu shiliao* 近代中国教育史料 [Historical materials on education in modern China]. 4 vols. Shanghai, 1928.

*Shu Xincheng 舒新城 . *Zhongguo jindai jiaoyushi ziliao* 中国近代教育史资料 [Materials on the history of modern education in China]. 3 vols. Beijing, 1961. A largely revised version of the preceding.

Song Xishang 宋希尚 . *Zhang Jiande shengping* 张謇的生平 [Life of Zhang Jian]. Taibei, 1963.

Sun Yat-sen 孙逸仙 . *Sun Zhongshan xuanji* 孙中山选集 [Selected works of Sun Yat-sen]. Beijing, 1956.

Tang Zhen (Shouqian) 汤震(寿潜) *Weiyan* 危言 [Words of warning]. Shanghai, 1890.

Tōa Dōbunkai 东亚同文馆 . *Shina keizai zensho* 支那经济全书 [The economy of China]. 12 vols. Tokyo, 1907-8.

*Tongxiang timing lu 通庠题名录 [List of *shengyuan* from Nantong]. N.p., 1933. 6 *juan.*

Tongzhou xingban shiye zhangcheng 通州兴办实业章程 [Regulations on the establishment and management of enterprises in Tongzhou]. Nantong, 1905. 4 *ce.*

Tongzhou xingban shiye zhi lishi 通州兴办实业之历史 [History of the establishment and management of enterprises in Tongzhou]. 2 vols. 3d ed., Nantong, 1910.

Tongzhou zhilizhou zhi 通州直隶州志 [Gazetteer of the independent department of Tongzhou], comp. Liang Yuexin 梁悦馨 and Mo Xiangzhi 莫祥芝 ; ed. Gu Zenghuan 顾曾焕 and Gu Zengxuan 顾曾烜 . Nantong, 1875. 16 *juan.*

Wan Guoding et al. 万国鼎 . *Jiangsu sheng Wujin Nantong tianfu diaocha baogao* 江苏省武进南通田赋调查报告 [Report of an investigation into land taxes at Wujin and Nantong in Jiangsu province]. Shanghai, 1934.

Wang Tao 王韬 . *Tao yuan wenlu waibian* 韬园文录外编 [Supplement to writings of Wang Tao]. Reprint, Beijing, 1959.

Weng Tonghe 翁同龢 . *Weng Wenkong riji* 翁文恭日记 [Diary of Weng Tonghe]. Shanghai, 1925. 40 *ce.*

Wuxu bianfa 戊戌变法 [The 1898 reforms], ed. Zhongguo shixuehui 中国史学会 (Chinese Historical Society). 4 vols. Shanghai, 1953. Rev. ed., Shanghai, 1957.

Xiandai shi dajia wenchao 现代十大家文钞 [Writings of ten important contemporaries]. Shanghai, 1915. 20 *ce.*

Xinhai geming 辛亥革命 [The 1911 Revolution], ed. Zhongguo shixuehui 中国史学会 (Chinese Historical Society). 8 vols. Shanghai, 1957.

Xinhai geming huiyi lu 辛亥革命回忆录 [Recollections of the 1911

Revolution]. 6 vols. Beijing, 1961-63.

Xinhai geming Jiangsu diqu shiliao 辛亥革命江苏地区史料
[Local historical materials on the 1911 Revolution in Jiangsu],
ed. Yangzhou shifan xueyuan lishixi 杨州师范学院历史系
(History Department of the Yangzhou Normal School). Nanjing,
1961.

**Xinhai geming qian shi nian jian shilun xuanji* 辛亥革命前
十年间时论选集 [Selection of essays from the ten years before
the 1911 Revolution], ed. Zhang Nan 张枏 and Wang Renzhi
王忍之 . 2 vols. Hong Kong, 1962-63.

Xu Tongxin 许同莘 . *Zhang Wenxiang gong nianpu* 张文襄公年谱
[Chronology of Zhang Zhidong's life]. Chongqing: Commercial
Press, 1944.

*Xu Weize 徐维则 . *Dongxixue shulu* 东西学书录 [Catalogue of
Japanese and Western books on science]. 1st ed., n.p., 1899. 2d
ed., n.p., 1902. 4 *juan.*

Xuantong zhengji 宣统政纪 [Collection of political documents during
the reign of Xuantong], comp. Liu Jiaye 刘嘉业 . Dalian, 1934.
Reprint, Taibei, 1964. 43 *juan.*

Xue Fucheng 薛福成 . *Yong'an quanji* 庸盫全集 [Complete works
of Xue Fucheng]. Shanghai, 1897.

Yan Zhongping 严中平 . *Zhongguo jindai jingjishi tongji shiliao*
xuanji 中国近代经济史统计资料选辑 [Selected statistical
materials on the modern Chinese economy]. Beijing, 1955.

Yihetuan 义和团 [The Boxers], ed. Jian Bozan 翦伯赞 . 4 vols.
Shanghai, 1951.

*Yuan Shikai 袁世凯 . *Yangshouyuan zouyi jiyao* 养寿园奏议辑要
[Selected memorials of Yuan Shikai]. Edited by Shen Zuxian
N.p., 1937. 44 *juan.*

*Zhang Baixi 张百熙 , Zhang Zhidong 张之洞 , and Rong Qing 荣庆 .
Zouding xuetang zhangcheng 奏定学堂章程 [Memorials and
edicts on school regulations]. Shanghai, 1904. 5 *ce.*

Zhang Jizi rong'ai lu 张季子荣哀录   [Collection of funeral eulogies to Zhang Jian], ed. Xu Pengnian 许彭年 and Kong Rongzhao 孔容照 . Reprint, Taibei, 1964.

Zhang Jusheng xiansheng qishi shengri jinian lunwen ji 张菊生先生七十生日纪念论文集   [Collection of articles to commemorate the seventieth anniversary of the birth of Zhang Jusheng], ed. Hu Shi 胡适 , Cai Yuanpei 蔡元培 , and Wang Yunwu 王云五 . Shanghai, 1937.

Zhang Ruogu 张若谷 . *Ma Xiangbo xiansheng nianpu* 马相伯先生年谱 [Chronology of the life of Ma Liang]. Shanghai, 1939.

*Zhang Xiaoruo 张孝若 . *Nantong Zhang Jizi xiansheng zhuanji fu nianpu nianbiao* 南通张季直先生传记　附年谱　附年表 [Life of Zhang Jian of Nantong with an appendix of his autobiography and chronology of his life]. Shanghai, 1930. Reprint, Taibei, 1965.

*Zhang Zhidong 张之洞 . *Zhang Wenxiang gong quanji* 张文襄公全集 [Complete works of Zhang Zhidong]. Beijing, 1937. Reprint, Taibei, 1963.

*Zhang Zhongru 章中如 . *Qingdai kaoshi zhidu* 清代考试制度 [The examination system under the Qing]. Shanghai, 1931.

A detailed description.

Zheng Guanying 郑观应 . *Shengshi weiyan* 盛世危言 [Warnings to a prosperous age]. 2 vols. Reprint, Taibei, 1965.

————. *Yiyan* 易言 [Words on change]. ed. Zhonghua yinwu zongju [China Central Publishing Bureau], 1880. 中华印务总局 .

Zhongguo chuban shiliao bubian 中国出版史料补编 [Supplement to materials on the history of publishing in China], ed. Zhang Jinglu 张静庐 . Shanghai, 1957.

Zhongguo jindai chuban shiliao 中国近代出版史料 [Materials on the history of modern publishing in China], ed. Zhang Jinglu 张静庐 . 2 vols. Shanghai, 1953-54.

Zhongguo jindai gongyeshi ziliao 中国近代工业史资料 [Materials on

the history of modern industry in China], ed. Wang Jingyu 汪敬虞, vol. 2 (1895-1914). Shanghai, 1957.

Zhongguo jindai shi nongye ziliao   中国近代农业史资料   [Materials on the history of modern agriculture in China], ed. Li Wenzhi 李文治, vol. 1 (1840-1911). Beijing, 1957.

Zhongguo jindai shi ziliao xuanji   中国近代史资料选辑   [Selected materials on the modern history of China], ed. Rong Mengyuan 荣孟源. Beijing, 1954.

Zhongguo jindai shougongyeshi ziliao 中国近代手工业史资料 [Materials on modern handicraft history in China], ed. Peng Zeyi 彭泽益. 4 vols. Beijing, 1957.

Zhongguo jindai sixiangshi cankao ziliao jianbian   中国近代思想史参考资料简编 [Concise collection of reference materials on the history of modern Chinese thought], ed. Shi Jun 石峻. Beijing, 1957.

*Zhongguo xiandai chuban shiliao   中国现代出版史料   [Materials on the history of contemporary publishing in China], ed. Zhang Jinglu 张静庐. 5 vols. Shanghai, 1954-59.

*Zhonghua minguo xin jiaoyu faling   中华民国新教育法令   [New laws on education of the Chinese Republic], ed. Jiaoyubu 教育部 (Ministry of Education). Beijing, 1912. 3 *cc*.

Also includes circulars.

Zhou Fu 周馥. *Zhou queshen gong quanji*   周悫慎公全集   [Complete works of Zhou Fu]. Edited by Zhou Xuexi 周学熙. N.p., 1922. 42 *juan*.

Contemporary Periodicals

*Dongfang zazhi 东方杂志 [DFZZ] [Eastern miscellany], monthly. Shanghai, 1904- .

*Jiaoyu shijie   教育世界   [JYZZ] [The world of education], fortnightly. Shanghai, 1901-3.

The periodical was issued after 1903, but I have been unable to find any issues in the libraries I have visited.

*_Jiaoyu zazhi_ 教育杂志 [Educational review], monthly. Shanghai, 1909- .

*_Nongxue bao_ 农学报 [Journal of agronomy], twice monthly, then three times monthly after no. 25. Shanghai, 1897-1901.

*_Qingyi bao_ 清议报 [The China discussion], three times monthly. 12 vols. Yokohama, 1898-1901. Reprint, Taibei: Chengwen chubanshe, 1967. 成文出版社 .

*_Shiwu bao_ 时务报 [The times], three times monthly. 6 vols. Shanghai, 1896-98. Reprint, Taibei: Huawen shuju, 1967. 华文书局 .

*_Xinmin congbao_ 新民丛报 [New people's miscellany], fortnightly. Yokohama, 1902-5. Reprint, 17 vols. Taibei: Yiwen yinshuguan, 1966. 益文印书馆 .

*_Xuebu guanbao_ 学部官报 [Official journal of the Board of Education], three times monthly. Beijing, 1906-11.

*_Zhengyi tongbao_ 政艺通报 [Bulletin of politics and the arts], fortnightly. Shanghai, 1902-4. Became _Zhengyi congshu_ 政艺丛书 [Series on politics and the arts]. Shanghai, 1905-6.

*_Zhengzhi guanbao_ 政治官报 [Official government gazette], daily. Beijing, 1908-11. Reprint, Taibei: Wenhai, 1965. 53 vols.

Articles

*Hou Hongjian 侯鸿鉴 . "Canguan Jiangsu Nantong daiyong shifan xuexiao fushu xiaoxuexiao biji" 参观江苏代用师范学校附属小学校笔记 [Notes on a visit to the attached primary school of the Nantong Substitute Normal School]. _Zhonghua jiaoyujie_ 中华教育界 [Chinese educational world], no. 19 (July 1914): 5.

A concise eyewitness account.

Huang Yanpei 黄炎培 . "Wo suo shenqin zhi Zhongguo zui chuqi ji

zui jinqi xianzheng yundong" 我身亲之中国最初期及最近期
宪政运动   [The Chinese constitutional movements in
which I have personally participated, from the earliest times to
more recent times]. *Xianzheng* 宪政 [Constitution], January
1944, 10-11.

*Jiang Weiqiao 蒋维乔 . "Zhongguo jiaoyuhui huiyi" 中国教育
会回忆   [Memories of the Chinese Education Association].
DFZZ 33, no. 1 (1 January 1936): 7-15. 东方杂志 .

*Li Yuanheng 李元蘅 . "Nantong daiyong shifan fushu xiaoxue
gailan"   南通代用师范附属小学概览   [General description of
the attached primary school of the Nantong Substitute Normal
School]. JYZZ 6, no. 2 (May 1914): *chengji*, 1-6. 教育杂志 .

A useful and informative description.

Qi Zhi 启之 . "Nantong pingmin shenghuo zhuangkuang" 南通平民
生活状况   [The living conditions of the people of Nantong].
Jiaoyu yu zhiye 教育与职业 [Education and vocation], no. 72 (1
February 1926): 117-22.

*Qian Gongpu 钱公溥 . "Nantong xian xuewu canguan ji" 南通
县学务参观记 [Record of a visit of Nantong educational institu-
tions]. JYZZ 8, no. 11 (15 November 1916): *fulu*, 25-30. 教育杂志.

*Shen Shouzhi 沈寿之 . "Jiechao biji" 借巢笔记 [Notes by Shen
Shouzhi]. *Renwen* 人文 [Humanities], *juan* 7, nos. 3, 4, 5, 6, 8,
9, 10 (15 April-15 December 1936).

On traditional examinations.

Yang Huan et al. 杨焕 . "Tong Ning Xi Su jiaoyu canguan ji"
通宁锡苏教育参观记   [Account of a visit concerning
education at Nantong, Nanjing, Wuxi, and Suzhou]. *Zhonghua
jiaoyujie* 中华教育界 [Chinese educational world] 12, no. 12;
13, nos. 1-5 (June-November 1923).

Yuan Xishou 袁希寿 . "Ji Nantong yuyingtang youweiyuan"
记南通育婴堂幼稚园 [An account of the kindergarten and orphanage at Nantong]. *Zhonghua jiaoyujie* 中华教育界 [Chinese
educational world], no. 24 (December 1914).

A somewhat flattering, although concise, article.

Zhang Chaohan 张朝汉 and He Siqing 何思清 . "Nantong gongye zhi diaocha" 南通工业之调查 [Investigation of industry in Nantong]. *Shiye zazhi* 实业杂志 [Journal of industry], no. 52 (February 1922): 54-66; no. 55 (May 1922): 49-56.

*Zhuang Yu 庄俞 . "Zhang Jizhi xiansheng jiaoyu tan" 张季直 先生教育谈 [Interview with Zhang Jian on education]. JYZZ 9, no. 1 (15 January 1917): *yanlun*, 33-36. 教育杂志 .

Interesting on the myth of Nantong.

Secondary Sources and References

Books

A Ying 阿英 . *Wanqing xiaoshuo shi* 晚清小说史 [History of the novel at the end of the Qing]. Shanghai, 1937.

Bao Cun 包村 . *Zhang Jian* 张謇 [Zhang Jian]. Beijing, 1965.

A simple sketch.

Beijing lishi xuehui diyi di'erceng nianhui lunwen xuanji 北京历史学会第一二届年会论文选集 [Collection of essays from the first and second annual meetings of the Beijing historical society]. Beijing, 1964.

Especially the essay by Shao Xunzheng 邵循正 , 258-80.

Chang Min 厂民 . *Dangdai Zhongguo renwu zhi* 当代中国人物志 [Personalities of present-day China]. Shanghai, 1945.

Chen Baoquan 陈宝泉 . *Zhongguo jindai xuezhi bianqian shi* 中国近代学制变迁史 [A history of changes in the modern educational system of China]. Beijing, 1927.

A useful summary, although it contains no references.

*Chen Dongyuan 陈东原 . *Zhongguo jiaoyu shi* 中国教育史 [A history of Chinese education]. Shanghai, 1937.

Interesting for the references.

*————. *Jiaoyu zazhi suoyin* 教育杂志索引   [Index to the *Educational review*]. Shanghai, 1935.

*————. *Zhongguo keju shidai zhi jiaoyu shi* 中国科举时代之教育史 [A history of Chinese education during the time of the examination system]. Shanghai, 1934.

Useful for the description of the evolution of institutions.

Chen Naiqian 陈乃乾 . *Qingdai beizhuanwen tongjian* 清代碑传文通检 [Catalogue of stone tablet biographical inscriptions during the Qing]. Shanghai, 1959.

*Chen Qingzhi 陈青之 . *Zhongguo jiaoyu shi* 中国教育史 [History of education in China]. Shanghai, 1936. Reprint, Taibei, 1963.

A detailed study of institutions.

Chen Ruxuan 陈如玄 . *Zhongguo xianfa shi* 中国宪法史 [Chinese constitutional history]. Shanghai, 1933.

*Chen Yilin 陈翊林 . *Zuijin sanshinian Zhongguo jiaoyu shi* 最近三十年中国教育史 [History of Chinese education in the last thirty years]. Shanghai, 1930.

A good study of institutions.

Chen Zhimai 陈之迈 . *Zhongguo zhengfu* 中国政府 [The Chinese government]. 2 vols. Shanghai, 1944-45.

Cheng Fang 程方 . *Zhongguo xianzheng gailun* 中国县政概论 [Treatise on district government in China]. Shanghai, 1939.

Chūgoku kindaika no shakai kōzō 中国近代化の社会构造 ["Social phase in Chinese modernization"]. Tokyo: Tokyo Education University, 1960.

*Ding Zhipin 丁致聘 . *Zhongguo jin qishinian lai jiaoyu jishi* 中国近七十年来教育记事   [Chronology of education in China during the last seventy years]. Shanghai, 1935. Reprint, Taibei, 1966.

Contains a wealth of information.

Fan Shoukang 范寿康 . *Jiaoyu shi* 教育史 [A history of education].

Shanghai, 1923.

A summary.

Fan Yinnan 樊荫南 . *Dangdai Zhongguo mingren lu* 当代中国名人录 [Famous people of present-day China]. Shanghai, 1931.

Fang Xianting 方显廷 . *Zhongguo zhi mianfangzhiye* 中国之 棉纺织业 [The cotton spinning industry in China]. Shanghai, 1934.

*Fujiwara Kiyozo 藤原喜代藏 . *Meiji kyōiku shisō shi* 明治教育 思想史 [A history of Meiji educational thought]. Tokyo, 1909.

*————. *Meiji Taishō Shōwa kyōiku shisō gakusetsu jimbutsu shi* 明治大政昭和教育思想学说人物史 [A history of personalities and theories in the realm of education during the Meiji, Taisho, and Showa periods]. 4 vols. Tokyo, 1942-44.

Ge Gongzhen 戈公振 . *Zhongguo baoxue shi* 中国报学史 [A history of Chinese journalism]. Hong Kong, 1964.

Gendai Chūka minkoku Manshū teikoku jinmeikan 现代中华 民国满洲帝国人名鉴 [Contemporary biographical dictionary of the Chinese Republic and Manchukuo], ed. Gaimushō seihōbu hensō 外务省情报部编 (Foreign Ministry). Tokyo, 1937.

Gendai Shina jinmeikan 现代支那人民鉴 [Biographical dictionary of contemporary China], ed. Gaimushō seihōbu hensō 外务省 情报部编纂 (Foreign Ministry). Tokyo, 1928.

Gendai Shina Manshū kyōiku shiryō 现代支那满洲教育资料 [Materials on education in contemporary China and Manchukuo], ed. Tōkyō Kōtō shihan gakkō 东京高等师范学校 (Tokyo Higher Normal School). Tokyo, 1940.

Useful for the bibliography.

Gengwu lunwenji 庚午论文集 [Collection of articles from 1930], ed. Yanjing daxue zhengzhixue xi 燕京大学政治学系 (Yanjing University Political Science Department). Beijing, 1930.

Contains some information on the constitutional movement.

Gu Dunrou 顾敦鍒 . *Zhongguo yihui shi* 中国议会史   [Chinese parliamentary history]. Suzhou, 1931.

Gu Zhongxiu 谷钟秀 . *Zhonghua minguo kaiguo shi* 中华民国开国史 [History of the establishment of the Chinese Republic]. Shanghai, 1914. Reprint, Taibei, 1962.

*Guo Zhanbo 郭湛波 . *Jin wushinian Zhongguo sixiang shi* 近五十年中国思想史 [History of Chinese thought in the last fifty years]. Beijing, 1935. Reprint, Hong Kong, 1965.

Hu Bin 胡滨 . *Zhongguo jindai gailiangzhuyi sixiang* 中国近代改良主义思想   [Modern reformist thought in China]. Beijing, 1964.

*Hu Huaizhen 胡怀琛 . *Shanghaide xueyi tuanti* 上海的学艺团体 [Literary and artistic groups of Shanghai]. Shanghai, 1935.

Lists 273 associations and gives historical background of the most important.

*Huang Yanpei 黄炎培 . *Zhongguo jiaoyushi yao* 中国教育史要   [A concise history of Chinese education]. Shanghai, 1931.

Contains a number of interesting details.

Jiang Shuge 姜书阁 . *Zhongguo jindai jiaoyu zhidu* 中国近代教育制度 [The modern educational system in China]. Shanghai, 1934.

A general survey.

Jiangsu sheng jian 江苏省鉴 [Jiangsu yearbook], ed. Zhao Ruheng 赵如珩 , Huang Yanpei et al. 黄炎培 . 2 vols. Shanghai, 1935.

A mine of information.

**Jiaoyu da cishu* 教育大辞书   [Dictionary of education], ed. Zhu Jingnong 朱经农 , Tang Yue 唐钺 , and Gao Juefu 高觉敷 . Shanghai, 1930.

Jiaoyu lunwen suoyin 教育论文索引   [Index of articles on education], ed. Taiwan shengli shifan daxue tushuguan 台湾省立师范大学图书馆 (Taiwan Province Normal University Library). Taibei, 1962. Concerns recent articles.

Jin bainian lai zhongyi xishu mulu 近百年来中译西书目录 [Catalogue of Chinese translations of Western books during the last one hundred years], ed. Guoli zhongyang tushuguan 国立中央图书馆 (National Central Library). Taibei, 1958.

A useful list, but does not give the date of the translations.

Jin wunian jiaoyu lunwen suoyin 近五年教育论文索引 [Index of articles on education in the last five years], ed. Taiwan shengli shifan daxue tushuguan 台湾省立师范大学图书馆 (Taiwan Province Normal University Library). Taibei, 1963.

*Le Sibing 乐嗣炳 and Cheng Boqun 程伯群 . *Jindai Zhongguo jiaoyu shikuang* 近代中国教育实状 [The situation of education in modern China]. Shanghai, 1935.

Especially focuses on laws and regulations.

Li Jiannong 李剑农 . *Zhongguo jin bainian zhengzhi shi* 中国近百年政治史 [Political history of China during the last one hundred years]. 2 vols. Shanghai, 1948. English translation by Teng Ssu-yu and J. Ingalls, *The Political History of China, 1840-1928.* Stanford: Stanford University Press, 1967.

Li Shiyue 李时岳 . *Zhang Jian he lixianpai* 张謇和立宪派 [Zhang Jian and the constitutionalists]. Beijing, 1962.

A short, but penetrating, study, especially with regard to the political aspects.

Li Zonghuang 李宗黄 . *Zhongguo difang zizhi gailun* 中国地方自治概论 [Treatise on local autonomy in China]. Taibei, 1952.

————. *Zhongguo difang zizhi zonglun* 中国地方自治总论 [A general discussion of local autonomy in China]. Taibei, 1954.

*Liu Boyi 刘伯骥 . *Guangdong shuyuan zhidu yange* 广东书院制度沿革 [Evolution of the system of academies in Guangdong]. Shanghai, 1939.

*Luo Bingzhi 罗炳之 . *Zhongguo jindai jiaoyujia* 中国近代教育家 [Modern Chinese educators]. Wuhan, 1958.

Contains good summaries of the ideas of Kang Youwei, Liang Qichao, and Cai Yuanpei on education.

Luo Menghao 罗孟浩 . *Difang zizhi yuanli* 地方自治原理 [Principles of local autonomy]. Taibei, 1954.

Luo Yudong 罗玉东 . *Zhongguo lijin shi* 中国厘金史   [History of the *lijin* in China]. 2 vols. Shanghai, 1936.

*Mao Bangwei 毛邦伟 . *Zhongguo jiaoyu shi* 中国教育史   [A history of education in China]. Beijing, 1932.

Useful for traditional education.

Meng Xiancheng 孟先成 . *Xin Zhonghua jiaoyu shi* 新中华教育史 [History of education in the new China]. Shanghai, 1930.

A summary.

Minobe Tatsukichi 美濃部達吉 . *Nihonkoku kempō genron* 日本国 憲法原論   [Principles of the Japanese constitution]. Tokyo, 1948.

*Miyazaki Ichisada 宮崎市定 . *Kakyo* 科举 [The Chinese civil service examination system]. Osaka, 1946. Reprint, Tokyo, 1963.

A description of the system and its decay.

Nantong Zhang Jizhi xiansheng shishi sishi zhounian jinian ji 南通张季直先生逝世四十周年纪念集   [Collection of articles to mark the fortieth anniversary of the death of Zhang Jian], ed. Nantong Zhang Jizhi xiansheng shishi zhounian jinianhui 南通张季直先生逝世四十周年纪念会 (Commemorative Society for the Fortieth Anniversary of the Death of Zhang Jian). Taibei, 1966.

Contains some recollections of former students of the normal school.

Nichi-ro sensō shi no kenkyū   日露戦争史の研究   [Historical studies on the Russo-Japanese War], ed. Shinobu Seizaburo 信夫清三郎 and Nakayama Jiichi 中山治一 . Tokyo, 1959.

Especially "Nichi-ro sensō to Chūgoku no minzoku undō"

日露戦争と中国の民族運動　　[The Russo-Japanese War and the nationalist movement in China].

*Pan Dakui　潘大逵　. *Jiaoyu lunwen suoyin*　教育论文索引　[Index of articles on education]. Beijing, 1924.

Pipan "Wu Xun zhuan"　批判「武训传」　[Criticism of the "Life of Wu Xun"]. 2 vols. Beijing, 1951.

Qian Shifu　钱实甫　. *Qingji zhongyao zhiguan nianbiao*　清季重要职官年表　[Chronological tables of important officials during the Qing]. Shanghai, 1959.

*Ren Shixian　任时先　. *Zhongguo jiaoyu sixiang shi*　中国教育思想史　[A history of educational thought in China]. Shanghai, 1937. Reprint, Taibei, 1964.

Describes the main currents and cites numerous texts.

Saikin Shina kanshinroku　最近支那官绅录　[Record of recent Chinese officials], ed. Beijing Shina kenkyūkai　北京支那研究会　(Beijing China Study Society). Beijing, 1919.

*Saito Akio　斎藤秋男　and Niijima Atsuyoshi　新岛淳良　. *Chūgoku gendai kyōiku shi*　中国现代教育史　[A history of modern education in China]. Tokyo, 1962.

A study of institutions and ideas.

Shanghai gongshang renmin lu　上海工商人名录　[Biographical record of people involved in industry and commerce in Shanghai]. Shanghai, 1936.

Shao Xunzheng　邵循正　. "Lun Zheng Guanying"　论郑观应　[On Zheng Guanying]. Unpublished article, mimeographed by the Beijing University History Department, 1964.　北京大学历史系

The best study on the subject.

*Sheng Langxi　盛朗西　. *Zhongguo shuyuan zhidu*　中国书院制度　[The system of academies in China]. Shanghai, 1934.

Contains much information.

Shu Xincheng　舒新城　. *Jiaoyu tonglun*　教育通论　[A general

discussion on education]. Shanghai, 1927.

General problems in education as seen by a Chinese educator.

*————. *Jindai Zhongguo jiaoyu sixiang shi* 近代中国教育思想史 [A history of modern Chinese educational thought]. Shanghai, 1928.

Classifies educational ideas under eighteen headings and cites numerous texts.

*————. *Jindai Zhongguo liuxue shi* 近代中国留学史 [History of overseas students in modern China]. Shanghai, 1927.

————. *Zhongguo xin jiaoyu gaikuang* 中国新教育概况 [The general situation of new education in modern China]. Shanghai, 1928.

A useful overview, especially with regard to the years 1920-25.

Sonoda Hitokame 园田一龟 . *Xin Zhongguo fensheng renwu zhi* 新中国分省人物志 [Biographical dictionary of new China by province]. Chinese translation by Huang Huiquan 黄惠泉 and Diao Yinghua 刁英华 . Shanghai, 1930.

*Tai Shuangqiu 邰爽秋 . *Zengding jiaoyu lunwen suoyin* 增订教育论文索引 [Enlarged and revised index of articles on education]. Shanghai, 1932.

Lists articles from 22 important journals up to 1929.

Wang Fengjie 王凤喈 . *Zhongguo jiaoyu shi dagang* 中国教育史大纲 [An outline of Chinese educational history]. Shanghai, 1930.

A convenient summary.

Wang Peitang 王培棠 . *Jiangsu sheng xiangtu zhi* 江苏省乡土志 [Geographical gazetteer of Jiangsu province]. 2 vols. Shanghai, 1938.

**Wushinian laide Zhongguo* 五十年来的中国 [China in the last fifty years], ed. Pan Gongzhan 潘公展 . Chongqing, 1945.

Especially Cheng Lifu 陈立夫 , "Wushinian laide jiaoyu fangzhen" 五十年来的教育方针 [Directions in education in the last fifty years], 137-44.

Wu Xiangxiang 吴湘相 . *Zhongguo xiandaishi congkan* 中国现代史丛刊 [Series on contemporary Chinese history]. 4 vols. Taibei, 1960-62.

Wu Xun lishi diaocha ji 武训历史调查记 [Investigation of the history of Wu Xun]. Beijing, 1951.

Wu Xun xianshengde zhuanji 武训先生的传记 [The biography of Wu Xun], ed. Li Shizhao. Shanghai, 1948.

Wu Xun yu Wu Xun zhuan pipan 武训与「武训传」批判 [A critique of Wu Xun and of *The Life of Wu Xun*]. Canton: Huanan renmin chubanshe, 1951. 华南人民出版社

Contains a useful bibliography on the subject.

*Xie Guozhen 谢国桢 . "Qingdai shuyuan xuexiao zhidu bianqiankao" 清代书院学校制度变迁考 [An examination of the changes in the system of academies and schools during the Qing]. In *Zhang Jusheng xiansheng qishi shengri jinian lunji*, Shanghai, 1937. 281-322. 张菊生先生七十生日纪念论集

*Xu Daling 许大龄 . *Qingdai juanna zhidu* 清代捐纳制度 [The system of purchasing offices by contribution during the Qing]. Beijing, 1950.

*Xu Shigui 徐式圭 . *Zhongguo jiaoyu shi lüe* 中国教育史略 [A short history of Chinese education]. Shanghai, 1931.

A convenient survey.

*Xue Renyang 薛人仰 . *Zhongguo jiaoyu xingzheng zhidu shi lüe* 中国教育行政制度史略 [A short history of Chinese educational administration]. Shanghai, 1929.

A detailed and precise study.

Yan Zhongping 严中平 . *Zhongguo mianye zhi fazhan* 中国棉业之发展 [The development of the Chinese cotton industry]. Shanghai, 1943. Revised as *Zhongguo mianfangzhi shi gao* 中国棉纺织史稿 [Draft history of the Chinese cotton textile industry]. Shanghai, 1955.

Yang Jialuo 杨家骆 . *Minguo mingren tujian* 中国名人图监

[Illustrated dictionary of famous people of the Republic]. 2 vols. Nanjing, 1937.

Yang Youjiong 杨幼烱 . *Jindai Zhongguo lifa shi* 近代中国立法史 [A history of legislation in modern China]. Shanghai, 1936.

————. *Zhongguo zhengdang shi* 中国政党史 [A history of political parties in China]. N.p.: Commercial Press, n.d.

Yao Neng 姚能 . "Zhang Jian jiawu wuxu riji zhu" 张謇甲午戊戌日记注 [Annotations to Zhang Jian's diary of 1894 and 1898]. Unpublished manuscript, 1965.

Ye Can 叶参 . *Zheng Xiaoxu zhuan* 郑孝胥传 [The life of Zheng Xiaoxu]. Mukden, 1938.

Yin Weihe 殷惟龢 . *Jiangsu liushiyi xian zhi* 江苏六十一县志 [Gazetteer of the 61 districts of Jiangsu]. 1st ed., Shanghai, 1936; 2d ed., Shanghai, 1937.

Yu Jiaju 余家菊 . *Zhongguo jiaoyu shi yao* 中国教育史要 [A concise history of Chinese education]. Shanghai, 1934.
A summary.

Yu Shulin 余书麟 . *Zhongguo jiaoyu shi* 中国教育史 [History of education in China]. Taibei, 1961.
Especially focuses on regulations.

Zeng Lubai 曾卢白 and Xu Fuxiao 徐蒲梢 . *Hanyi dongxiyang wenxue zuopin bianmu* 汉译东西洋文学作品编目 [Catalogue of Chinese translations of Japanese and Western literary works]. N.p.: Zhenmeishan shudian, 1929. 真美善书店
Does not give the date of the translations.

Zhang Cunwu 张存武 . *Guangxu sanshiyinian Zhong-Mei gongyue fengchao* 光绪三十一年中美工约风潮 [The riots concerning the Sino-American agreement on Chinese workers in 1905]. Taibei, 1965.

Zhang Qinpan et al. 张晋藩 . *Jiu Zhongguo fandong zhengfu zhixian choushi* 旧中国反动政府制宪丑史 [An account of the shameful history of the drafting of constitutions by reactionary governments of the old China]. Beijing, 1955.

Zhao Quandeng 赵泉澄 . *Qingdai dili yange biao* 清代地理沿革表 [Tables of the changes in administrative geography during the Qing]. Shanghai, 1941.

Zhongguo jiaoyu cidian 中国教育辞典   [Dictionary of Chinese education]. Shanghai, 1928.

Zhongguo shi gangyao 中国史纲要   [Outline of Chinese history] (1840-1919), ed. Jian Bozan 翦伯赞 , vol. 4. Beijing, 1964.

Zhou Gucheng 周谷城 . *Zhongguo jiaoyu xiao shi* 中国教育小史 [A short history of Chinese education]. Shanghai, 1929.

A brief summary.

*————. *Zhongguo shehui zhi jiegou*   中国社会之结构   [Structures of Chinese society]. Shanghai, 1930.

Contains an interesting analysis of the intelligentsia.

Zhou Sizhen 周思真 . *Zhongguo jiaoyu ji jiaoyu sixiang shi jianghua* 中国教育及教育思想史讲话   [Lectures on education and educational thought in China]. Shanghai, 1943.

A summary.

Zhou Yibin 周异斌 and Luo Zhiyuan 罗志渊 . *Zhongguo xianzheng fazhan shi* 中国宪政发展史 [History of constitutional development in China]. Chongqing, 1944.

Zuijin sanshiwunian zhi Zhongguo jiaoyu 最近三十五年之中国教育 [Chinese education in the last 35 years], ed. Zhuang Yu 庄俞 . Shanghai, 1931.

A collection of interesting and informative articles.

Zuijin zhi wushinian: Shen Bao guan wushi zhounian jinian 最近之五十年 ： 申报馆五十周年纪念 [The last fifty years: a commemoration of the fiftieth anniversary of *Shen bao*]. Shanghai, 1923. Especially articles nos. 14, 15, 17, 18 in part 2. Contains five important articles on education.

Articles

*Abe Hiroshi 阿部洋 . "Shinmatsu no kindai gakkō Kōsaishō o chūshin ni" 清末の近代学校江西省を中心に历史评论 [Modern schools at the end of the Qing: the example of Jiangxi]. *Rekishi hyōron* 历史评论 [Historical criticism], no. 173 (1965): 47-60; no. 175 (1965): 56-65.

*Cai Shangsi 蔡尚思 and Jin Chongji 金冲及 . "Lun Song Shude sixiang" 论宋恕的思想 [On the thought of Song Shu]. *Fudan daxue xuebao* 复旦大学学报 [Bulletin of Fudan University], no. 1 (1964): 33-41.

Cao Congpo 曹从坡 . "Zhang Jiande beiju" 张謇的悲剧 [The tragedy of Zhang Jian]. *Jianghai xuekan* 江海学刊 [Bulletin of Jianghai], no. 41 (July 1962): 28-34.

Refers to some unpublished material on Zhang Jian's agricultural enterprises and modern schools.

Chang Min 畅民 . "Ye lun Zhang Jian" 也论张謇 [More on Zhang Jian]. *Jianghai xuekan* 江海学刊 [Bulletin of Jianghai], no. 36 (February 1962): 10-16.

Brings out well the originality of Zhang Jian.

Chen Qiao 陈鍪 . "Wuxu zhengbian shi fanbianfa renwu zhi zhengzhi sixiang" 戊戌政变时反变法人物之政治思想 [The political thought of reform opponents at the time of the 1898 reforms]. *Yanjing xuebao* 燕京学报 [Bulletin of the University of Yanjing], no. 25 (1939): 59-106.

Chen Xulu 陈旭麓 . "Xinhai geming shide fenqi he yanjiu zhongde ruogan wenti" 辛亥革命史的分期和研究中的若干问题 [Some problems of chronology and research concerning the history of the 1911 Revolution]. *Xueshu yuekan* 学术月刊 [Scholarship monthly], no. 58 (October 1961): 10-15.

Deng Siyu 邓嗣禹 . "Zhongguo keju zhidu qiyuan kao" 中国科举制度起源考 [An examination of the origins of the Chinese civil service examination system]. *Shixue nianbao* 史学年报 [Yearly journal of historiography] 2, no. 1 (September 1934): 275-84.

*Ding Fenglin 丁风麟 . "Zhang Zhidongde *Quan xue pian* tixian shenmo jingshen?" 张之洞的「劝学篇」体现什么精神 [What attitudes are reflected in Zhang Zhidong's *Exhortation to Study*?]. *Xueshu yuekan* 学术月刊 [Scholarship monthly] (1964) no. 12: 20-26.

An unremitting condemnation.

Dong Zuobin 董作宾 . "Luo Xuetang xiansheng zhuan lüe" 罗雪堂先生传略 [Brief biography of Luo Xuetang]. *Dalu zazhi* 大陆杂志 [Mainland magazine] 24, no. 4 (28 February 1962): 34.

Gao Liangzuo 高良佐 . "Kaiguo qian geming yu jun lixian zhi lunzhan" 开国前革命与君立宪之论战 [The debate over revolution and constitutional monarchy before 1911]. *Jianguo yuekan* 建国月刊 [Construction monthly] 7, nos. 3, 4, 5, 6 (1932); 8, nos. 5, 6 (1933).

*Gao Shukang 高叔康 . "Zhishifenzi yu shengchan wenti" 知识分子与生产问题 [Intellectuals and the problems of production]. *Xin jingji* 新经济 [New economy] 2, no. 8 (1939): 180-84.

Some interesting views on attitudes.

Han Sheng 汉声 . "Zenyang renshi yangwu yundongde xingzhi yu zuoyong" 怎样认识洋务运动的性质与作用 [How to understand the nature and role of the foreign affairs movement]. *Jianghai xuekan* 江海学刊 [Bulletin of Jianghai] (1964) no. 4: 34-38.

Negative approach.

Hu Bin 胡滨 . "Zhang Zhidong yu yangwu yundong" 张之洞与洋务运动 [Zhang Zhidong and the foreign affairs movement]. *Wen shi zhe* 文史哲 [Literature, history, and philosophy], May 1963, 22-29.

Shows that Zhang obstructed the development of a national bourgeoisie.

Huang Yanpei 黄炎培 . "Qingdai gesheng renwen tongji zhi yi ban"

清代各省人文统计之一斑   [On provincial statistics for men of letters during the Qing]. *Renwen* 人文 [Humanities] 2, no. 6 (15 August 1931): 1-10.

Geographical and social origins of the top three *jinshi* from 1644 to 1904.

————. "Zhongguo ershiwunian quanguo jiaoyu tongjide zong jiancha" 中国二十五年间全国教育统计的总检查   [General overview of nationwide educational statistics in China for the last twenty-five years]. *Renwen* 人文 [Humanities] 4, no. 5 (15 June 1933): 1-28.

Huang Yifeng 黄逸峰 . "Lun Zhang Jiande qiye huodong" 论张謇之起业活动   [On Zhang Jian's economic activities]. *Xueshu yuekan* 学术月刊 [Scholarship monthly] (1962) no. 3: 1-8.

A precise chronological analysis, placing economic motives before everything else.

Jiang Min 江民 . "Lun Zhang Jiande gailiangzhuyi" 论张謇的改良主义 [On Zhang Jian's reformism]. *Jianghai xuekan* 江海学刊 [Bulletin of Jianghai], no. 55 (September 1963): 30-39.

Jiang Shunxing 蒋顺兴 . "1900-1911 nian Jiangsu nongminde zifa douzheng" 1900—1911江苏农民的自发斗争   [Spontaneous peasant struggles in Jiangsu 1900-11]. *Jianghai xuekan* 江海学刊 [Bulletin of Jianghai], no. 38 (April 1962): 18-24.

A useful listing of peasant riots.

Jiang Yixue 蒋逸雪 . "Zhang Jian ni zhuan" 张謇拟传 [Draft biography of Zhang Jian]. *Shuowen* 说文 [Doctrines] 3, no. 8 (September 1942): 101-2.

A traditional eulogy.

Li Puguo 李普国 . "Qingdai Dongbeide fengjin yu kaifa" 清代东北的封禁与开发   [The closing and opening of the Northeast during the Qing]. *Jilin daxue shehui kexue xuebao* 吉林大学社会科学学报   [Social science bulletin of Jilin University] (1962) no. 1: 39-52.

Liu Hehui 刘和惠 and Du Wenhuan 杜文焕 . "Guanyu dui Zhang Jian pingjiade jige wenti" 关于张謇评价的几个问题

[Some problems concerning the evaluation of Zhang Jian]. *Jianghai xuekan* 江海学刊 [Bulletin of Jianghai], no. 42 (August 1962): 23-29.

A differing interpretation.

Liu Guiwu 刘桂五 . "Lun xinhai geming shiqide xianzheng yundong" 论辛亥革命时期的宪政运动 [On the constitutional movement at the time of the 1911 Revolution]. *Xin jianshe* 新建设 [New construction], no. 1 (1954): 38-41.

A general view.

―――――. "Xinhai geming qianhoude lixianpai yu lixian yundong" 辛亥革命前后的立宪派与立宪运动 [The constitutionalists and the constitutional movement before and after the 1911 Revolution]. *Lishi jiaoxue* 历史教学 [Pedagogy of history] (1962) no. 8: 19-29.

Contains some interesting details on the movement.

Liu Shihai 刘世海 . "Xue Fuchengde shehui jingji sixiang ji qi shehui jingji beijing" 薛福成的社会经济思想及其社会经济背景 [The economic and social thought of Xue Fucheng and his economic and social background]. *Xin jianshe* 新建设 [New construction] (1955) no. 3: 52-59.

*Liu Yizheng 刘治徵 . "Jiangsu shuyuan zhi chugao" 江苏书院志初稿 [Initial draft of an account of academies in Jiangsu]. *Jiangsu shengli tushuguan niankan* 江苏省立图书馆年刊 [Jiangsu provincial library yearbook], no. 4 (October 1931): 1-112.

*Nozawa Yutaka 野沢豊 . "Chūgoku no hanshokuminjika to kigyō no unmai-Chō Ken no kigyō keiei to seiji kōdō o megutte" 中国の半殖民地化と企業の運命―張謇の企業経営と政治行動 をめぐつて [The semicolonialization of China and the fate of enterprises-as seen through Zhang Jian's management of enterprises and his political activities]. *Tōyō shigaku ronshū* 東洋史学論集 [Asian history miscellany], no. 4 (1955): 481-546.

A detailed study, although more descriptive than analytical.

*Pan Maoyuan 潘懋元 . "Cai Yuanpeide jiaoyu sixiang" 蔡元培的

教育思想   [The educational thought of Cai Yuanpei]. *Xiamen daxue xuebao* 厦门大学学报   [Bulletin of the University of Amoy] (1955) no. 4: 86-98.

Analyzes Cai's ideas and refers to their sources.

Peng Zeyi 彭泽益 . "Zhang Jiande sixiang ji qi shiye" 张謇的思想及其事业 [The thought and activity of Zhang Jian]. DFZZ 40, no. 14 (31 July 1944): 55-60. 东方杂志

Written to encourage youth to enter industry rather than government service.

Qi Longwei 祁龙威 . "Didang yu wuxu bianfa" 帝党与戊戌变法 [The party of the emperor and the Hundred Days Reform]. *Xin jianshe* 新建设 [New construction] (1963) no. 9: 35-42.

An important analysis, using numerous unpublished documents.

Qi Longwei 祁龙威 and Yao Neng 姚能 . "Guanyu Zhang Jian riji" 关于张謇日记   [On Zhang Jian's diary]. *Jianghai xuekan* 江海学刊 [Bulletin of Jianghai], no. 39 (May 1962): 32-35.

A brief bibliographical discussion of the publishing of the *Diary*.

Qian Shifu 钱实甫 . "Lun Zhang Jian" 论张謇 [On Zhang Jian]. *Wenhui bao* 文汇报 [Journal of culture] (24 November 1961).

A condemnation.

*Quan Hansheng 全汉昇 . "Qingmode xixue yuanchu Zhongguo shuo"   清末的西学源出中国说   [The theory of the Chinese origins of Western science at the end of the Qing]. *Lingnan xuebao* 岭南学报 [Bulletin of Lingnan University] 4, no. 2 (June 1935): 57-102.

Shen Naizheng 沈乃正 . "Qingmo zhi dufu jiquan zhongyang jiquan yu tongshu ban gong" 清末之督抚集权中央集权与同署办公 [The concentration of power in the hands of the governors-general and the central government and the joint management of administration at the end of the Qing]. *Shehui kexue* 社会科学 [Social sciences] 2, no. 2 (January 1937): 311-42.

Shi Bei 史北 . "Guanyu yangwu yundong ruogan wenti taolun zongshu" 关于洋务运动若干问题讨论综述   [A summing up of the discussion on problems of the foreign affairs movement].

Lishi jiaoxue 历史教学 [Pedagogy of history], no. 153 (March 1964): 50-53.

Outlines the main problems and gives a useful bibliography.

*Shi Jin 石锦 . "Jiawu zhan hou riben zai huade huodong" 甲午战后日本在华的活动 [Japanese activities in China after the war of 1894]. *Dalu zazhi* 大陆杂志 [Mainland magazine] 31, no. 8 (31 October 1965): 21-26.

A useful article concerning cultural aspects.

*Tanaka Kenji 田中謙二 . "Kyū Shina ni okeru jīdō no gakujuku sei katsu" 旧支那に於ける児童の学塾生活 [The life of traditional school pupils in old China]. *Tōhō gakuhō* 東方学報 ["Journal of Oriental Studies"] 15, no. 2 (January 1945): 217-32.

Uses literary works to give a concrete view of schools.

*Wang Ermin 王尔敏 . "Qingji xuehui biao" 清季学会表 [Table of study societies at the end of the Qing]. *Dalu zazhi* 大陆杂志 [Mainland magazine] 24, no. 2 (31 January 1962): 14-21; no. 3 (15 February 1962): 16-23.

An accurate and useful record.

Wen Yu 问渔 . "Du Zhang Jizi jiulu" 读张季子九录 [On reading the *Nine Collections* of Zhang Jian]. *Renwen* 人文 [Humanities] 7, no. 4 (15 May 1936): 1-24; no. 5 (15 June 1936): 25-61.

A general introduction to the publishing of Zhang Jian's works.

Xie Benshu 谢本书 . "Lun Zhang Jian shiye huodongde mudi" 论张謇实业活动的目的 [On the aims of Zhang Jian's economic activities]. *Jingji yanjiu* 经济研究 [Economic research] (1966) no. 1: 44-48.

Harsh and superficial.

"Xinhai geming shiqi Jiangsu guangfu qingkuang jianjie" 辛亥革命时期江苏光复情况简介 [Brief introduction concerning the liberation of Jiangsu at the time of the 1911 Revolution]. *Jianghai xuekan* 江海学刊 [Bulletin of Jianghai], no. 30 (August 1961): 44-49; no. 31 (September 1961): 47-49.

Uses many interesting documents.

*Xu Lingxiao 许凌霄　and Xu Yishi 许一士 . "Lingxiao Yishi suibi" 凌霄一士随笔　[Notes of Lingxiao and Yishi]. *Guowen zhoubao* 国闻周报 [National news weekly] 9, no. 28 (18 July 1932): 1-4.

Describes the difficulties Zhang Jian experienced in taking the civil service examinations.

Xu Lun 徐仑 . "Zhang Jian zai xinhai geming zhongde zhengzhi huodong"　张謇在辛亥革命中的政治活动　[The political activities of Zhang Jian during the 1911 Revolution]. *Wenhui bao* 文汇报 [Journal of culture] (26 December 1961).

*Yang Chao 杨超　and Zhang Qizhi 张岂之 . "Lun shijiu shiji liushi zhi jiushi niandaide 'xixue'" 论十九世纪六十至九十年代的'西学' [On 'Western knowledge' during the years 1860-90] *Xin jianshe* 新建设 [New construction], no. 9 (1962): 14-25.

Traces the evolution of the concept.

*Yang Tianshi 杨天石 . "Lun xinhai geming qiande guocuizhuyi sixiang"　论辛亥革命前的国粹主义思想　[On the concept of the national essence before the 1911 Revolution]. *Xin jianshe* 新建设　[New construction], no. 2 (1965): 67-77.

An analysis of the role of the concept and of its meaning as described by various thinkers of the time.

Zhang Kaiyuan 章开沅 . "Lun Zhang Jiande maodun xingge" 论张謇的矛盾性格　[On the nature of the contradictions of Zhang Jian]. *Lishi yanjiu* 历史研究 [Historical research] (1963) no. 3: 87-104.

An excellent study, relying on numerous unpublished documents.

*Zhang Qiguang 张其光 . "Yong Hong jiaoyu jihuade shizhi ji qi yingxiang"　容闳教育计划的实质及其影响　[The real nature and influence of Yong Hong's educational plans]. *Xueshu yanjiu* 学术研究　[Scholarship research] (1963) no. 2: 86-91.

A convenient summary.

*Zhang Zhiben 张知本 . "Wuchang shouyi chenggong zhi yinsucong jiaoyu shang zhui shu wang shi" 武昌首义成功之因素—从教育上追述往事　[The factors in the success of the Wuchang uprising-from the point of view of education]. *Zhonghua zazhi* 中华杂志 [China review] 1, no. 3 (16 December 1963): 6-7.

Interesting reminiscences concerning student opinion at the time.

*Zheng Yunshan 郑云山 . "Tan wuxu gailiangpai zhengzhi taidude maodun" 谈戌戌改良派政治态度的矛盾 [On the contradictions in the political attitudes of the 1898 reformers]. *Jianghai xuekan* 江海学刊 [Bulletin of Jianghai], no. 66 (August 1964): 47-51.

The reformers were not radically opposed to imperialism or feudalism.

*Zhuang Zexuan 庄泽宣 . "Sanshinian lai Zhongguo zhi xin jiaoyu" 三十年来中国之新教育 [New education in China during the last thirty years]. *Jiaoyu yanjiu* 教育研究 [Educational research], no. 2 (March 1928): 1-7.

A general summary, with some useful details on the Japanese influence.

Bibliography of Western-Language Works

Primary Sources and Documents

Archives

Ministry of Foreign Affairs, Paris, *Correspondance de Chine*, New Series. Vols. 298, 299, 300, 301, 302 (Tchentou Medical School, 1897-1911). Vols. 303, 304 (French School of Canton, 1898-1910). Vols. 305, 306, 307, 308 (various French schools, 1898-1911). Vols. 581, 582, 583 (education, 1897-1911).

Sources and Documents

*Arnold, J. H. "Educational Activity in Foochow, China." In *Reports of the Department of the Interior, Report of the Commissioner of Education for 1907*. Washington, 1908. Ch. 6, 191-220.

Brou, A., and G. Gibert. *Jésuites Missionnaires, Un Siècle 1823-*

1923. Paris, 1924.

Chang Chien. *La Situation Économique Actuelle de la Chine*. Comité national d'études sociales et politiques (National Committee for Social and Political Studies), no. 235 (19 November 1923), Paris. This talk is, in fact, that of Zhang Jian's son, Zhang Xiaoruo.

Chang Polin. *Le Problème d'Éducation Nationale en Chine*. Comité national d'études sociales et politiques (National Committee for Social and Political Studies), no. 404b (12 July 1929).

*Chiang Monlin. *A Study in Chinese Principles of Education*. Shanghai, 1918.

*————. *Tides from the West, a Chinese Autobiography*. New Haven: Yale University Press, 1947.

China Imperial Maritime Customs, Statistical Series, no. 6, Decennial Reports, 2d issue (1892-1901); 3d issue (1902-11), Shanghai, 1904 and 1913.

China Mission Yearbook, ed. D. MacGillivray. Shanghai, 1910, 1911, 1912, 1913.

Dollar, R. *Private Diary of Robert Dollar on His Recent Visits to China*. San Francisco, 1912.

*Edmunds, C. K. *Modern Education in China*. Department of Interior, Bureau of Education Bulletin (1919) no. 44. Washington, 1919.

Education in China (collection of pamphlets at Harvard University Library), especially no. 5: *National Education in China* (before 1898); no. 6: *Progress of Western Education in China and Siam* (1880), no. 10: *Ten Years of the Kiangsu Provincial Education Association* (see below).

Education in Japan. 4 vols. Department of Education, Japan. Prepared for the Louisiana purchase exposition at St. Louis, 1904.

*Fryer, J. *The Educational Reform in China*. Report of the

Commissioner of Education for 1909. Washington, 1910. Vol. 1, ch. 12, 513-21.

*Graybill, H. B. *The Educational Reform in China.* Hong Kong, 1911.

*Lee Teng-hwee. *The Problem of New Education in China.* Bruges, 1910.

The Life of the Honourable Chang Chien with an Account of Industrial Enterprises Inaugurated by Him. Shanghai, 1915.

*Martin, W. A. P. *Awakening of China.* New York, 1907.

*————. *A Cycle of Cathay.* New York, 1896.

*————. *The Lore of Cathay.* New York, 1901.

*————. *Report on the System of Public Instruction in China.* U.S. Bureau of Education (1877) no. 1.

*Maybon, A. *La Politique Chinoise. Étude sur les Doctrines des Partis en Chine 1898-1908* [Chinese politics. A study of the doctrines of factions in China 1898-1908]. Paris, 1908.

Notice sur l'Organisation Actuelle de l'Instruction Publique au Japon [An account of the present day organization of public education in Japan], ed. Japanese Ministry of Public Education. Japanese Imperial Commission for the Universal Exhibition of 1900.

Odell, R. M. *Cotton Goods in China.* Department of Commerce, Bureau of Foreign and Domestic Commerce, Special Agent Series no. 107. Washington, 1916.

A Revolution in Education. Beijing, 1908.

Rheinsch, P. S. *Intellectual and Political Currents in the Far East.* New York, 1911.

Rodes, J. *La Chine et le Mouvement Constitutionnel, 1910-1911.* Paris, 1913.

*————. *La Chine Nouvelle.* Paris, 1910.

*Soothill, W. E. *China and Education, with Special Reference to the University for China.* Proceedings of the Central Asian Society. London, 1912.

Ten Years of the Jiangsu Provincial Education Association. Shanghai, 1915.

Thwing, C. F. *Education in the Far East.* New York, 1909.

*Tobar, J., trans. *K'iuen-hio p'ien. Exhortation à l'étude par son excellence Tchang Tche-tong* [Quanxue pian. Exhortation to study by the honourable Zhang Zhidong]. Shanghai, 1909.

————, trans. *Koang-Siu et Ts'e Hi, Décrets Impériaux 1898* [Imperial edicts of Guangxu and Cixi 1898]. Shanghai, 1900.

*Williams, E. T. "The Progress of Education Reform in China." *Annual Reports of the Department of the Interior,* Commissioner of Education, 1905, vol. 1: 256-66. Washington, 1907.

*Williams, S. W. *The Middle Kingdom.* 2 vols. New York, 1883. Reprint, Taibei, 1965.

*Wylie, A. *Chinese Researches.* Shanghai, 1897.

Contemporary Periodicals

L'Asie Française, monthly from 1901. Paris.

Chinese Recorder and Missionary Journal, monthly. Shanghai.

Life and Light for Woman, quarterly. New York, 1907-9.

North China Herald and Supreme Court and Consular Gazette, weekly. Shanghai.

Articles

*Bazin, M. "Traduction d'un règlement d'étude et de discipline à l'usage des écoles primaires composé par un lettré de la province de Nankin vers 1700. Comprenant 100 articles, contenu dans la 'Collection Complète des Joyaux de famille'" [Translation of regulations on study and discipline used by primary schools and drawn up by a scholar of Nanjing about 1700, comprising 100 articles and included in the "Complete Collection of Family Treasures"]. *Journal Asiatique*, 3d series, 7 (1839): 32-81.

*Clinton, J. M. "Chinese Students in Japan." *Chinese Recorder* (October 1909): 570-79.

*"Competitive Examinations in China." *Blackwood's Edinburgh Magazine* (October 1885): 479-85.

"Cost of Higher Education." *Chinese Recorder*, October 1906, 565-70.

*Courant, M. "L'Éducation Européenne des Asiatiques." *Revue Indo-chinoise*, 23 November 1903, 1056-62.

Duncan, Moir. "The Imperial University of Shansi." *East of Asia* 3 (1904): 102-15.

East of Asia Magazine, Special Educational Number. Shanghai, June 1904. Articles on Shanxi, Shandong, Zhejiang, Guangdong, Zhili, and Jiangsu.

*"Education in Chihli." *Chinese Recorder*, September 1906, 506-8.

*Ewer, F. H. "The Triennial Examination." *Chinese Recorder* 3, no. 11 (1871): 330-32.

*Harada, J. "Japanese Educational Influence in China." *Chinese Recorder*, July 1905, 356-61.

*"History of China." *The Chinese Repository* (April 1833): 483-85. On the civil service examinations.

*"Le Japon et l'Extrême-Orient" [Japan and the Far East]. *Revue de Paris*, 15 March 1905, 225-44.

*Lacey Sites, C. M. "The Educational Edicts of 1901 in China." *Educational Review*, no. 25 (January 1903): 67-75. Also published in NCH, 23 April 1902, 809-10, 856-57.

————. "Educational Psychology of the Chinese: a Study in Pedagogy." *Chinese Recorder*, May 1904, 245-56.

Martin, W. A. P. "On the Competitive Examination System in China." *American Oriental Society Journal*, Proceedings at Boston, 9 (19 May 1869): 54-55.

*Maybon, A. "La Réforme Scolaire en Chine et l'Influence Intellectuelle des Nations Savantes" [Educational reform in China and the intellectual influence of the learned nations]. *La Revue*, 15 November 1907, 228-42.

Pelliot, P. "La Réforme des Éxamens Littéraires en Chine" [The reform of the civil service examinations in China]. *L'Asie Française* (April 1903): 160-65.

*Peri, N. "L'Éducation Nouvelle en Chine." *Revue de Paris*, 1 June 1907, 473-94; 15 June 1907, 873-94.

*Pilcher, L. W. "The New Education in China." *Chinese Recorder*, July 1889, 305-10; August 1889, 343-48; September 1889, 403-10.

*Preston, T. J. "Progress and Reform in Hunan Province." *East of Asia*, no. 4 (1905): 215-17.

*Richard, T. "The New Education in China." *Contemporary Review*, no. 445 (January 1903): 11-16.

Sites, F. R. "Chang Chien, a Man who Would Reform a Nation by Precept and Practice in a Model City." *Asia* (Journal of the American Asiatic Association), no. 18 (July 1918): 587-92.

*Tobar, J. "La Réforme des Études en Chine" [Educational reform in China]. *Études* 97 (5 December 1903): 703-17.

*Wisner, O. F. "Western Education in South China." *East of Asia Magazine* (June 1904): 73-89.

Secondary Works and References

Books

Anderson, M. R. *Protestant Mission Schools for Girls in South China.* Mobile, Ala., 1943.

*Ayers, T. W. "Chang Chih-tung and Chinese Educational Change." Ph.D. diss., Harvard University, 1959.

Beal, E. G. *The Origin of Likin, 1853-1864.* Cambridge, Mass., 1958.

Beckmann, G. M. *The Modernization of China and Japan.* New York, 1965.

Belov, E. A. *Revolutsia 1911-1913 gadov v Kitaïe* [The 1911-13 revolution in China]. Moscow, 1958.

Bergère, M. C. *Une Crise Financière à Shanghai à la fin de l'Ancien Régime* [A financial crisis in Shanghai at the end of the ancien regime]. Paris, 1964.

Bianco, L. *Les Origines de la Révolution Chinoise* [Origins of the Chinese revolution]. Paris, 1967.

*Biggerstaff, K. *The Earliest Modern Government Schools in China.* Ithaca, 1961.

Biographical Dictionary of Republican China, ed. H. L. Boorman. Vol. 1, New York and London, 1967; vol. 2, New York and London, 1968.

Biot, E. *Essai sur l'Histoire de l'Instruction Publique en Chine et de la Corporation des Lettrés depuis les Anciens Temps jusq'à Nos Jours* [An account of the history of public education in China and of the guild of scholars from ancient times to the present day]. Paris, 1847.

Britton, R. S. *The Chinese Periodical Press 1800-1912*. Shanghai, 1933.

Brunnert, H. S. and V. V. Hagelstrom. *Present Day Political Organization of China*. Shanghai, 1912.

*Burton, M. E. *The Education of Women in China*. New York and Chicago, 1911.

Cameron, M. E. *The Reform Movement in China 1898-1912*. Stanford, 1931.

Chai Yu-heng. *Étude sur l'obligation scholaire et l'enseignement primaire en France et en Chine (historique, comparaison, avenir)* [A study of compulsory education and primary instruction in France and China]. Paris, 1935.

*Chang Chung-li. *The Chinese Gentry, Studies on Their Role in Nineteenth Century Chinese Society*. Seattle, 1955.

————. *The Income of the Chinese Gentry*. Seattle, 1962.

Chang Yu-hsing. "L'Autonomie locale en Chine" [Local autonomy in China]. Ph.D. diss., University of Nancy, 1933.

*Chen Chi-yun. *Liang Ch'i-ch'ao's "Missionary Education," a Case Study of Missionary Influence on the Reformers*. Harvard Papers on China, vol. 16: 66-125. Cambridge, Mass., 1962.

*Cheng, Ronald Yu-song. *The Financing of Public Education in China. A Factual Analysis of Its Major Problems of Reconstruction*. Shanghai, 1935.

Cheng Yen-cheng. *Les Principaux Mouvements constitutionnels en Chine de 1897 à 1935* [The principal constitutional movements in China from 1897 to 1935]. Lyon, 1936.

Ch'ien Tuan-sheng. *The Government and Politics of China 1912-1948*. Cambridge, Mass., 1961.

Chow Tse-tsung. *The May Fourth Movement: Intellectual Revolution in Modern China*. Cambridge, Mass., 1960.

*————. *Research Guide to the May Fourth Movement.* Cambridge, Mass., 1963.

**Christian Education in China.* Committee of Reference and Counsel of the Foreign Missions Conference of North America. New York, 1922.

Chu, S. C. *Reformer in Modern China: Chang Chien 1853-1926.* New York and London, 1965.

Ch'u T'ung-tsu. *Local Government in China under the Ch'ing.* Cambridge, Mass., 1962.

Chu You-kuang. *Some Problems of a National System of Education in China.* Shanghai, 1933.

*Chuang Chai-hsuan. *Tendencies toward a Democratic System of Education in China.* Shanghai, 1922.

Chudadeev, Y. V. *Nakanounie revoliutsii 1911 goda v Kitaïe.* Moscow, 1966.

*Chyne, W. Y. *Handbook of Cultural Institutions in China.* Shanghai, 1936.

Confucianism in Action, ed. D. S. Nivison and A. F. Wright. Stanford, 1959.

Confucian Personalities, ed. A. F. Wright and D. Twitchett. Stanford, 1962.

The Confucian Persuasion, ed. A. F. Wright. Stanford, 1960.

Djung Lu-dzai. *A History of Democratic Education in Modern China.* Shanghai, 1938.

Eastman, L. "The Early Institutional Reformers 1890-1895." Paper presented at the Meeting of the Association for Asian Studies in New York, 4 April 1966. Published under the title "Political Reformism in China before the Sino-Japanese War." *Journal of Asian Studies* 27, no. 4 (August 1968): 695-710.

————. *Throne and Mandarins: China's Search for a Policy during the Sino-French Controversy 1880-1885.* Cambridge, Mass., 1967.

Education and Political Development, ed. J. S. Coleman. Princeton, 1965.

Fairbank, J. K. and Ssu-yu Teng. *Ch'ing Administration, Three Studies.* Cambridge, Mass., 1960.

Fei Hsiao-t'ung. *China's Gentry.* Chicago, 1955.

Fincher, J. H. "Perspectives on Chinese Experiments with Representative Institutions, 1907-1916." Paper for a Research Conference on Contemporary China sponsored by the Joint Committee on Contemporary China of the ACLS and SSRC, August 1965.

*Franke, Otto. "Das Konfuzianische System und sein Ende" [The Confucian system and its end]. In O. Franke, *Aus Kultur und Geschichte China's* [Chinese culture and history]. Beijing, 1945, 331-48.

————. "Die wichtigsten chinesischen Reformschriften vom Ende des neunzehnten Jahrhunderts" [Important reform movements in China at the end of the nineteenth century]. In O. Franke, *Aus Kultur,* 1-12.

Franke, Wolfgang. *Die Staatspolitischen Reformversuche K'ang Yu-wei und seiner Schule* [The reformer K'ang Yu-wei and his school]. Hamburg, 1935.

*————. *The Reform and Abolition of the Traditional Chinese Examination System.* Cambridge, Mass., 1963.

Gasster, M. "Revolutionary Intellectuals and the Political Modernization of China." Paper presented at the Conference of Wentworth-on-sea, August 1965.

*Gee, N. G. *The Educational Directory of China: An Account of the Various Schools and Colleges Connected with Protestant Missions and also Government and Private Schools under Foreign*

Supervision, 2d ed. Suzhou, 1905.

Grigorief, A. M. *Antiimperialistceskaia programma kitaiskich bour-joiznich revoliutsionerov, 1895-1905* [The anti-imperialist program of the revolutionary Chinese bourgeoisie, 1895-1905]. Moscow, 1966.

Grimm, Tilemann. *Erziehung und Politik im konfuzianischen China der Ming-Zeit 1368-1644* [Education and politics in Confucian China during the Ming 1368-1644]. Hamburg, 1960.

Hao Yan-p'ing. *A Study of the Ch'ing-liu Tang: The Disinterested Scholar Official Group 1875-1884*. Harvard Papers on China, vol. 16, 40-65. Cambridge, Mass., 1962.

Hart, S. L. *Education in China*. London, 1923.

Hedtke, C. H. "The Genesis of the Revolution in Szechwan." Paper Presented at the Conference of Wentworth-on-the-sea, August 1965.

History of Industrial Education in Japan, 1868-1900. Japanese National Commission for UNESCO. Tokyo, 1959.

*Ho Ping-ti. *The Ladder of Success in Imperial China, Aspects of Social Mobility 1368-1911*. New York and London, 1962.

*Ho Yen-sun. *Chinese Education from the Western Viewpoint*. Chicago, 1913.

*Hoh Gunsun. *Physical Education in China*. Shanghai, 1926.

*Holcombe, C. *The Real Chinaman*, 2d ed. New York, 1909.

Hsiao Kung-ch'uan. *Rural China: Imperial Control in the Nineteenth Century*. Seattle, 1960.

*Hsiao, Theodore E. *The History of Modern Education in China*. Shanghai, 1935.

Hsieh Pao-chao. *The Government of China*. Baltimore, 1925.

Hu Nan. *Étude comparée des programmes et des méthodes d'enseignement pour les enfants de 6 à 12 ans en Chine et en France* [Comparative study of curricula and teaching methods for six- to twelve-year-olds in China and France]. Paris, 1935.

Hummel, A. *Eminent Chinese of the Ch'ing Period 1644-1912,* 2 vols. Washington, 1943-44.

Hyatt, I. T. *Protestant Missions in China (1877-1890), the Institutionalization of Good Works.* Harvard Papers on China, vol. 17: 67-100. Cambridge, Mass., 1963.

Iriye Akira. "Public Opinion in Late Ch'ing China." Paper presented at the Conference of Wentworth-on-sea, August 1965.

Ishii Ryosuke. *Japanese Legislation in the Meiji Era.* Trans. W. J. Chambliss. Tokyo, 1958.

Jansen, M. B. *The Japanese and Sun Yat-sen.* Cambridge, Mass., 1954.

Japan's Growth and Education. Japanese Ministry of Public Education, ed. Tokyo, 1963.

*Johnson, W. R. "Revolution and Reconstruction in Kweichow and Yunnan." Paper presented at the Conference of Wentworth-on-sea, August 1965.

Kikuchi Daikoku. *Japanese Education.* London, 1909.

*King, H. E. *The Educational System of China as Recently Reconstructed.* U.S. Bureau of Education Bulletin, 1911, no. 15. Washington.

*Kuo Heng-shih. "The Early Development of the Modern Chinese Business Class." In *The Rise of the Modern Chinese Business Class,* ed. International Secretariat Institute of Pacific Relations. New York, 1949.

*Kuo Ping-wen. *The Chinese System of Public Education.* New York, 1915.

Lasswell, H. D., D. Lerner, and C. F. Rothwell. *The Comparative Study of Elites*. Stanford, 1952.

Leong Sow-theng. *Wang T'ao and the Movement for Self-strengthening and Reform in the Late Ch'ing Period*. Harvard Papers on China, vol. 17: 101-30. Cambridge, Mass., 1963.

Levenson, J. R. *Confucian China and Its Modern Fate*. 3 vols. Berkeley and Los Angeles, 1958-65.

————. *Liang Ch'i-ch'ao and the Mind of Modern China*. Berkeley and Los Angeles, 1967.

Lewis, R. E. *The Educational Conquest of the Far East*. New York, 1903.

Li Chow, Chung-cheng. *L'Examen provincial en Chine sous la dynastie des Tsing de 1644 à 1911* [Provincial examinations in China during the Qing 1644-1911]. Paris, 1935.

*Liang Ch'i-ch'ao. *Intellectual Trends in the Ch'ing Period*. Translated and with introduction and notes by Immanuel C. Y. Hsu. Cambridge, Mass., 1959.

Lin Paotchin. *L'Instruction féminine en Chine (après la révolution de 1911)* [Women's education in China (after the 1911 Revolution)]. Paris, 1926.

Liu Han. *Étude sur la réforme de l'éducation contemporaine en Chine* [A study of educational reform in contemporary China]. Paris, 1933.

MacCall, D. H. *Chang Chien-Mandarin Turned Manufacturer*. Harvard Papers on China, vol. 2: 93-102. Cambridge, Mass., 1948.

MacCully, B. T. *English Education and the Origins of Indian Nationalism*. New York, 1940.

MacLean, A. *The History of the Foreign Christian Missionary Society*. London, 1919.

*Marsh, R. M. *The Mandarins: The Circulation of Elites in China, 1600-1900.* New York, 1961.

Men and Politics in Modern China (preliminary), ed. H. L. Boorman. New York, 1960.

Morrison, E. "The Modernization of the Confucian Bureaucracy: An Historical Study of Public Administration." Ph.D. diss., Radcliffe College, 1959.

Morse, H. B. *The Trade and Administration of the Chinese Empire.* London and New York, 1921.

Nurullah, Syed and J. P. Naik. *A History of Education in India during the British Period.* Bombay, 1943.

Passin, H. *Society and Education in Japan.* New York, 1964.

*Peake, C. *Nationalism and Education in Modern China.* New York, 1932.

Purcell, V. *The Boxer Uprising.* Cambridge, Mass., 1963.

————. *Problems of Chinese Education.* London, 1936.

Rotours, Robert des. *Le Traité des Éxamens traduit de la nouvelle histoire des T'ang* [The treatise on the examinations, translated from the *New History of the Tang*]. Paris, 1932.

*Sakai, R. K. "Politics and Education in Modern China." Ph.D. diss., Harvard University, 1953.

Schram, S. R. *Mao Ze-dong, Une Étude de l'éducation physique* [Mao Zedong, a study of physical education]. Paris, 1962.

*Schwartz, B. *In Search of Wealth and Power: Yen Fu and the West: Western Thought in Chinese Perspective.* Cambridge, Mass., 1964.

Shen, T. H. *Agricultural Resources of China.* Ithaca, 1951.

*Tang Chung-hsuan. "Modern Education in China." M.A. thesis,

University of Chicago, 1911.

Tchang Lam. *Étude sur l'organisation et le fonctionnement du service de l'instruction publique dans la Chine moderne* [A study of the organization and functioning of public education in modern China]. Lyon, 1939.

Tchou, Ngaosiang Louis. *Le Régime des capitulations et la réforme constitutionnelle en Chine* [The treaty system and constitutional reform in China]. Londres, 1915.

Tchou Pao-tien. *Les Principes généraux de l'autonomie locale dans la Chine actuelle* [General principles of local autonomy in present-day China]. Lyon, 1933.

*Teng, Ssu-yu and J. K. Fairbank. *China's Response to the West: A Documentary Survey*. Cambridge, Mass., 1954.

*————. *Research Guide to China's Response to the West*. Cambridge, Mass., 1954.

Tikhvinski, S. L. *Dvijenie za reforme v Kitaïe v kantse XIX veka u Kang Yuwei* [Kang Youwei and reform in nineteenth-century China]. Moscow, 1959. Chinese translation by Zhang Shiyu. Beijing, 1962.

*Tsang Chiu-sam. *Nationalism in School Education in China since the Opening of the Twentieth Century*. Hong Kong, 1933.

Twiss, G. R. *Science and Education in China*. Shanghai, 1925.

*Wang Feng-gang. *Japanese Influence on Educational Reform in China from 1895-1911*. Beijing, 1933.

*Wang, Y. C. *Chinese Intellectuals and the West, 1872-1949*. Durham N.C., 1966.

*Wang Yi-t'ung. "Biographic Sketches of 29 Classical Scholars of the Late Manchu and Early Republican Era." Typed manuscript, University of Pittsburgh, Department of East Asian Languages and Literature, 1963.

Webster, J. B. *Christian Education and National Consciousness in China.* New York, 1923.

Western Influences in Modern Japan, ed. Nitobe Inazo. Chicago, 1931.

*Wong, George H. C. "Wang Jen-tsün: A Late Nineteenth Century Obstructor of the Introduction of Modern Thought." Article presented to the Twenty-seventh Congress of Orientalists, 1967.

*Wong Yin-kon. *L'Instruction publique de la Chine moderne* [Public education in modern China]. Paris, 1932.

Wright, M. C. *The Last Stand of Chinese Conservatism: The T'ung-chih Restoration, 1862-1874.* Stanford, 1957.

Yuan T'ung-li. *A Guide to Doctoral Dissertations by Chinese Students in America, 1905-1960.* Washington, 1961.

Zabriskie, E. H. *American-Russian Rivalry in the Far East: A Study in Diplomacy and Power Politics, 1895-1914.* Philadelphia, 1946.

Zen Sun, E-tu. *Ch'ing Administrative Terms.* Cambridge, Mass., 1961.

*Zi (Siu), Etienne. *Pratique des examens littéraires en Chine* [The practice of literary examinations in China]. Shanghai, 1894.

Articles

Bergère, M. C. "La révolution de 1911 jugée par les historiens de la République Populaire de Chine: thèmes et controverses" [The 1911 Revolution as viewed by historians of the People's Republic: themes and controversies]. *Revue Historique,* no. 468 (October-December 1963).

*Cheng Ch'i-pao. "Twenty-five Years of Modern Education in China." *Chinese Social and Political Science Review* 12, no. 3 (1928): 451-70.

Chesneaux, J. "Le Mouvement fédéraliste en Chine, 1920-1923" [The federalist movement in China, 1920-1923]. *Revue Historique*, no. 480 (October-December 1966): 347-84.

Eto, Shinkichi. "On the Role of the Yang-wu p'ai." *Acta Asiatica*, no. 12 (1967): 1-12.

Fass, J. "A Few Notes on the Birth of Nationalism in China." *Archiv Orientalni* 33, no. 3 (1964): 376-82.

*Galt, H. "Oriental and Occidental Elements in China's Modern Education System." *Chinese Social and Political Science Review* 12, no. 3 (July 1928): 405-25; 12, no. 4 (October 1928): 627-47; 13, no. 1 (January 1929): 12-29.

Hsiao Kung-ch'uan. "Rural Control in 19th Century China." *Far Eastern Quarterly* 12, no. 2 (1953): 173-81.

————. "Weng T'ung-ho and the Reform Movement of 1898." *Ts'ing hua hsueh pao*, new series 1, no. 2 (April 1957): 111-245.

Hsu Ti-shan. "Wuu Shiunn: The Great Beggar and Promoter of Free Education." *T'ien Hsia*, no. 7 (1938): 235-55.

*Jansen, M. and Tsuen-hsuin Tsien. "Western Impact on China through Translation." *Far Eastern Quarterly* 13, no. 3 (May 1954): 305-27.

King, P. C. "Modern Education in China." *Chinese Students' Monthly* 17, no. 4 (February 1922): 302-4.

Miller, R. A. "Some Japanese Influence on Chinese Classical Scholarship of the Ch'ing Period." *Journal of the American Oriental Society* 72, no. 2 (April-June 1952): 56-67.

*Pokora, Timoteus. "Komensky and Wang Kuo-wei." *Archiv Orientalni* 26, no. 4 (1958): 626-30.

"Political Parties in China under the Empire." *People's Tribune* 5, no. 5 (1 October 1933): 229-36.

"Political Parties in China: The Political Reformists." *People's*

Tribune 5, no. 7 (1 November 1933): 346-55.

Taeuber, I. and Nai-chi Wang. "Population Reports in the Ch'ing Dynasty." *Journal of Asian Studies* 19, no. 4 (August 1960): 403-17.

Zen Sun, E-tu. "The Chinese Constitutional Missions of 1905-1906." *Journal of Modern History* 24, no. 3 (September 1952): 251-68.

INDEX

A

academies [*shuyuan*], 12, 22, 30, 75, 99, 120–21, 166, 230 (text 1, n. 2), 242 (text 3, n. 6), 245 (commentary to text 3, n. 2); Nanqing, 117–18, 120, 241 (text 3, n. 2); Shishan, 20; Wenzhang, 30; Xiyin, 20

attitudes: of modern gentry, 64–65, 90, 128, 132, 137–38, 139–40, 146–47, 149–53; of youth, 78–79, 149–51; traditional, 25, 27–28, 30, 139–40, 143–44

B

bagu [eight-legged essay], 9–10, 22, 139, 255 (text 7, n. 4)

bianfa [change of methods], 7, 9, 12, 26

bianshi [change of things], 7, 9, 25, 26

bourgeoisie, 17, 59, 61, 85–86, 91–92

Boxers, 4, 5, 6, 13, 15, 26, 53, 134, 138

boycott, 60, 121, 226–27 (ch. 3, n. 81)

bureaucracy: economic activity, 17; attitude during the Boxer uprising, 4–6; establishment of schools after 1901, 34; opinion, 7–8, 14–15, 55–56, 139–40; relations with gentry, 15–16, 18, 25, 42–43, 57–58, 62–63, 64, 67, 72, 90, 131–32

C

S

Z